A SHORT HISTORY OF THE PARISH CHURCH OF ST JOHN THE EVANGELIST, MOULSHAM, CHELMSFORD

AND ITS CLERGY

PART 1: 1834–1937

D.R. Broad

**Grosvenor House
Publishing Limited**

The right of D.R. Broad to be identified as the author of this
work has been asserted in accordance with Section 78
of the Copyright, Designs and Patents Act 1988

The book cover is copyright to D.R. Broad
Front cover photograph ©Steve Docherty

This book is published by
Grosvenor House Publishing Ltd
Link House
140 The Broadway, Tolworth, Surrey, KT6 7HT.
www.grosvenorhousepublishing.co.uk

A CIP record for this book
is available from the British Library

ISBN 978-1-78623-518-3

*This book is respectfully dedicated to all those
who have come to know Jesus Christ in the parish church
of St John the Evangelist, Moulsham, Chelmsford.*

FOREWORD

Rex is a churchman through and through, erudite about all matters Anglican and much beyond. This excellent volume is much more than a homage to the parish church he serves. It is essentially about the people, clergy and laity, who have made it what it is. From its inception it was a tough parish at the working-class end of town, burdened by a significant degree of poverty. Dedicated clergy worked themselves to death or ill-health in their evangelising mission. But this is not a sombre catalogue. Meticulously researched, it displays charm and wit in describing the main participants and has enough controversies over pew rents, ritualism, inter-denominational rivalry and the vicars' personalities to keep the more sensationally minded reader interested. The pastoral work of the clergy is always confidential and unseen. We can never go behind that curtain, but the public approval of St John's clergy demonstrates the public affection in which they were held. It is fitting that Rex has cast a light on their good works.

Tony Tuckwell

PREFACE

The parish church of St John the Evangelist has been prominent in Moulsham since the late 1830s, and after the building of its tower in 1883, a prominent landmark as well. Both the building and the parish have had an intriguing history, mirroring much of the enthusiastic expansion of the Anglican revival in the first few decades of its existence. It has, since the decision was taken to build it in 1834, always struggled financially; the Victorians' generous enthusiasm for the construction of new churches rarely extended to the provision of a sufficient endowment. Indeed, had it not been for the private means of many of the early incumbents, the parish, populous as it was, may not have lasted to the present day. It is hoped that the following pages gives some idea of the development of the building, its style of worship over the years, its clergy, and, to a lesser extent, its impact on the parish of Moulsham in the period of this book.

My indebtedness for assistance in compiling this book must extend to many. To the staff at the Essex Record Office, who have always responded to my obscure queries with a smiling face (and, inevitably, the correct answer). To Tony Tuckwell and the late Professor John Roach, of Sheffield, whose encouraging comments on the initial chapters suggested that it might be worthwhile to complete the whole exercise, and thereby gave me the confidence that I otherwise would have lacked. To Dr Joanna Hornsby, who produced coherence (and sometimes sense) from what I had initially written. To Celia Kemp, whose incomparable knowledge of 'Old Moulsham' (that slightly vague entity) corrected many careless errors on my part. To all those who helped me to search through the junk in the churchwardens' cupboard at St John's, enabling me to find some real gems to illuminate this story. To all those whose steadfast Christian faith have enabled the parish church of St John the Evangelist to survive to this day, as a witness to Christ in this part of the country. And last, but by no means least, to Amanda, whose tolerance of my spells of intense concentration, writer's block and frustration was exceeded only by the care with which she added an extra layer of proof-reading.

CONTENTS

FIGURES

The Figure of Rev James Hutchinson (Figure 7, *page 22*) and the accompanying description are reproduced by kind permission of the Headmaster, King Edward VI Grammar School, Chelmsford. The majority of the other illustrations are from the Archive of St John the Evangelist, Moulsham, reproduced by permission of the (then) churchwarden and incumbent. The photograph of Rev Henry Hawkins (Figure 9, *page 44*) is reproduced by kind permission of the Charity 'Together: working for Wellbeing'.

"The blackish art of the historian involves much searching, very occasional finding and reading between blurred lines that are often very far apart, and out of all that swirling fog, to fashion something that might in the end be a coherent whole"

1. A CHAPEL IS BORN

(1834-39)

"On Sunday last, the worthy Rector of Chelmsford, in an interval of divine service, gave notice of a meeting to be held at the National School Room, for the purpose of considering the propriety of erecting a new Chapel in the hamlet of Moulsham. In the Rev Gentleman's subsequent sermon he again entered into the subject, and in most eloquent language impressed on his auditory the advantage that must arise from according additional accommodation for persons to attend Divine Service, according to the forms of the Established Church"[1]

'To provide the means of establishing a Chapel of Ease in the said Hamlet'

So the Rector of St Mary the Virgin, Chelmsford, the Rev Carew Anthony St John Mildmay, announced the start of the process that was to result in the building and the consecration of the "New Episcopal Chapel of Moulsham", now the parish church of St John the Evangelist. The meeting was held in the National School Room at twelve o'clock on the following day (Monday, 12 April 1834). The Rector was unanimously called to the chair. He immediately pointed out that if he had listened to the numerous suggestions that had been put to him he would have called this meeting a long time ago, but that various circumstances had prevented him from doing so. However, he went on, the need for a meeting had now become imperative. The reasons for this urgency were not hard to find. The population of Chelmsford in 1834 was about 5,600 and this figure was increasing at about one per cent per year. The Church of St Mary the Virgin could squeeze in about 1,600 when every space was occupied, but because of the system of rented pews, only about half that number were ever able to obtain seats at any given service. Yet the demand was there – the

1

churchwardens complained that they received applications faster than they could ever provide seats – and this alone, the Rector said, led him to justify the meeting that he had called. Speaking very much in the style of the era, he said that he felt sure that the meeting: *"would produce a result consistent with the wisdom, benevolence and charity which had always marked the inhabitants of this parish"*.

George Asser Gepp, a prominent local solicitor, then introduced the first resolution to be put to the meeting, that: *"the large and increasing population of this parish, the numerous attendance at the public services of the Church, and the well-known and generally acknowledged insufficiency of the accommodation afforded by that building (St Mary's) for many of those who desire to attend, imperiously* (sic) *call for the erection of a Chapel of Ease in that part of the town which is furthest from the existing Church"*. The resolution was then seconded by Mr James Butler, a local wine merchant, but before any vote was taken, Mr Gepp was on his feet again to apologise for the absence on Mr John Crabb, a *'grand Old English Gentleman'* who was one of the main benefactors of the Parish, and who was indisposed. He will appear later in the story. Mr Gepp's resolution was put to the vote and carried unanimously.

Mr Bartlett, the Clerk to the Magistrates, then rose. The meeting must have groaned inwardly. He was well-known for making long-winded, intricate speeches and on this occasion he did not disappoint his hearers. After a prolonged introduction, punctuated by periodic applause, he eventually got around to the resolution: *"that it is incumbent on all those that are well-wishers of the Established Church, and to the town of Chelmsford, and to the Hamlet of Moulsham, to unite in an energetic effort to provide the means of establishing a Chapel of Ease in the said Hamlet"*. Mr Arthur Chalk, the co-proprietor of the *Chelmsford Chronicle*, then seconded the motion, drawing attention to the handsome manner in which Lady Mildmay (the worthy Rector's mother) *"proposed to assist them with their object"*. This statement was followed by prolonged applause, after which the resolution was passed unanimously.

Mr Thomas Morgan Gepp, of Maynetrees, New Street, then proposed that a subscription should be raised for the purpose of building and endowing the Chapel of Ease. Mr Thomas Gilson seconded, alluding to the great advantages that would arise from this Chapel of Ease, and again the resolution was passed with much cheering and applause. This resolution, though, was no sinecure. Looked at in the hard light of day, away from the obvious enthusiasm that was sweeping through the meeting, there would need to be a large number of subscriptions. To build anything more than a simple box would need between four and five thousand pounds, and to have sufficient, when invested in, say, three per cent Consols, to provide for an incumbent, would need another two or three thousand pounds at least unless a wealthy individual could be persuaded to accept the post. The enthusiastic meeting might well have their hands full.

The worthy Rector then took the floor again. He pointed out that the erection of the Chapel would be the means of securing the ministry of a gentleman who had formerly officiated in the town and who was willing to enter upon terms *"for again giving them his valuable services"*. When he mentioned the name of that gentleman, the much-loved Rev James Hutchinson, the resultant cheering almost brought the meeting to a premature conclusion. James Hutchinson, who had been connected with Chelmsford and particularly with St Mary's, the Gaol and the Grammar School for many years, was held in almost as high esteem as the worthy Rector himself, and to associate him with this new undertaking markedly improved the chances of it being a success. Nevertheless, it was realised that if someone needed to be paid to take services at the New Chapel, it had to be remembered that James Hutchinson already had other sources of income. It could not have escaped the worthy Rector that the Rev James Hutchinson would not require the full income of an incumbent. A subscription was immediately commenced in the room. The Rector gave £200, and John Crabb matched his donation by proxy. The Rector's wife (the Hon Mrs Mildmay) gave £50, and the great and good of the county added their names. A committee was appointed to oversee the whole process, and by the end of the meeting £1,062 9s had been subscribed to the project and Lady Mildmay had promised a piece of ground. The New Chapel was up and running.

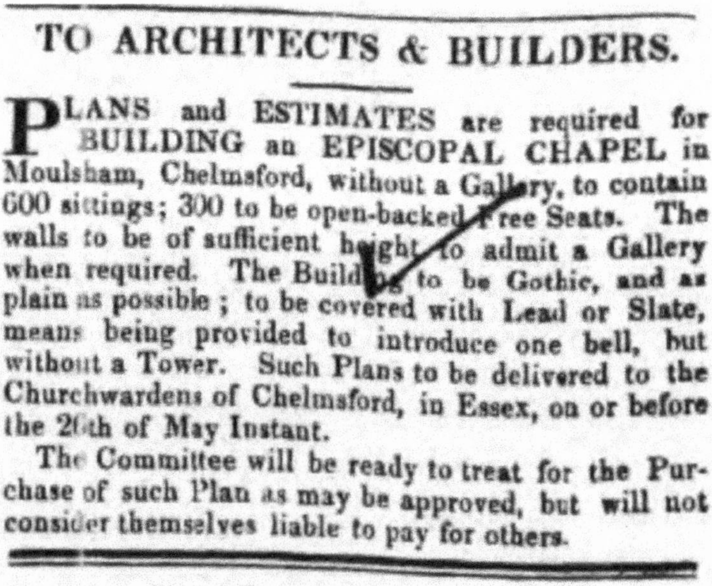

TO ARCHITECTS & BUILDERS.

PLANS and ESTIMATES are required for BUILDING an EPISCOPAL CHAPEL in Moulsham, Chelmsford, without a Gallery, to contain 600 sittings; 300 to be open-backed Free Seats. The walls to be of sufficient height to admit a Gallery when required. The Building to be Gothic, and as plain as possible ; to be covered with Lead or Slate, means being provided to introduce one bell, but without a Tower. Such Plans to be delivered to the Churchwardens of Chelmsford, in Essex, on or before the 20th of May Instant.

The Committee will be ready to treat for the Purchase of such Plan as may be approved, but will not consider themselves liable to pay for others.

Figure 1 – The newspaper advertisement seeking plans and tenders for erecting a new Episcopal Chapel in Moulsham

A flurry of other, minor resolutions (mostly mutual back-slapping) followed, and no doubt as a result of the influence of Mr Chalk (the co-editor of the *Chelmsford Chronicle* and a prominent member of St Mary's) the following issue of the paper contained a full report of the meeting and a paid-for advertisement listing the first 165 subscribers and full details of all the resolutions. By the following Friday, 11 April 1834, the total raised stood at £1,435 11s 6d, reaching £1,911 4s 9d by the Friday after that.[2] By Friday, 2 May, the total was up to more than £2,221, and in the issue of the newspaper that day appeared an advertisement (*Figure 1*) inserted by members of the committee, seeking: *"Plans and Estimates... ...for BUILDING an EPISCOPAL CHAPEL in Moulsham..."* These details are of interest, as they explain why the present building is quite unusually tall – the specifications called for a Chapel with *"...the walls of sufficient height to admit a Gallery when required".*[3]

'With a request that they would reduce the expense of the building'

The money continued to flow in, but at an ever-diminishing rate. By 29 May, when the committee met at the Shire Hall, it was to consider the plans that had been submitted in response to the earlier advertisement. There were twelve in all, and the estimates ranged from £1,500 to £5,600. The Committee expressed its admiration for the *"elegance and simplicity of the designs"* but in view of the sum that had so far been raised (about £2,500) of which at least £1,500 would need to be invested to provide income for any priest (and even that would barely produce £60 a year) the committee resolved that they return the plans to the architects: *"with a request that they would reduce the expense of the buildings, and the number of sittings (if the stipulated sum required it) in order that the estimate for the Chapel, with the same provision for a gallery, if hereafter found necessary, shall not exceed £1,450".* They then adjourned for fourteen days to allow new plans to be submitted.[4]

The committee next met again on 12 June but could not arrive at any firm conclusion,[5] only agreeing to inspect the amended plans again on 18 June, when they were able to select five. A sub-committee was appointed to investigate these five designs.[6] Meanwhile the lack of sufficient money to push the project along continued to hang around the committee's neck like an albatross, so it was no surprise that at this same meeting they were pleased to record that an early scheme for a Bazaar, to be held in Race Week (Galleywood Races were a notable event in the Essex social calendar) was to go ahead. It was hoped that Lady Mildmay would be present.[7] The Bazaar was held in the Shire Hall, a little later than intended, on Wednesday, 23 July, and was so successful that it was extended from the single day initially planned to the following Thursday and Friday.[8] By charging an entrance fee (1s on the first day) for the ordinary mortals to come and gawp at the quality, as well as selling some seriously valuable items (the worthy Rector's wife sold drawings by Queen Adelaide) a substantial sum of money was raised over the three days (almost £480). In the centre of the room was a model of the proposed building, enclosed in a glass case, and among the articles for sale was a lithographed view of the proposed west front of the Chapel to be erected under the direction of Mr Wild, Architect, of Albermarle Street, London. It stirred up the hidden poet in the *Chelmsford Chronicle's* reporter to produce some patronising doggerel (although some may have felt it better if it had stayed hidden):

> *"Link'd for one purpose – for one general end*
> *Here view the various arts subservient blend,*
> *Here beauty's smiles illume the grovelling mind,*
> *And pleasure learns to benefit mankind".*

So, aided by the pence of the 'grovelling minds', the total sum for the project now stood in excess of £3,100. The New Chapel for Moulsham was on its way.[9]

'Those obstacles which had presented themselves had been removed'

The 1830s were a time when the Church of England, and particularly the Bishop of London, Charles James Blomfield, was starting to express concern about the poor and religious provision for them. Bishop Blomfield, who was eventually to consecrate the New Chapel at Moulsham, was a great supporter of building new places of worship where there were large numbers of the poorer classes for whom no such provision had been made,[10] and Moulsham, with its growing industry and the Eastern Counties Railway on the horizon, must have encouraged him to lend his support to the worthy Rector's proposal (although no relevant correspondence seems to have survived).

Early in 1835 (8 February) John Crabb died. He had reached the grand old age of 83 and had been a widower since 1807. He was a very wealthy man and had become very prominent in Chelmsford and Essex society where he had been a local magistrate, a Deputy Lieutenant of the county and a distinguished supporter of both the Established and Dissenting churches. He had lived in Shelley Hall for 35 years before buying Mr Oxley Parker's magnificent house at 73, High Street, Chelmsford (which sadly burnt down in 1947). He was buried in Shelley churchyard on Saturday, 11 February, and on the following day the worthy Rector in his morning sermon attributed to Mr Crabb the successful provision of the New Chapel in Moulsham, saying that had it not been for the: *"munificence of the deceased, he (the Rector) would not have been induced to commence the undertaking"*. John Crabb has no memorial in the Chapel for which he was such an inspiration.[11]

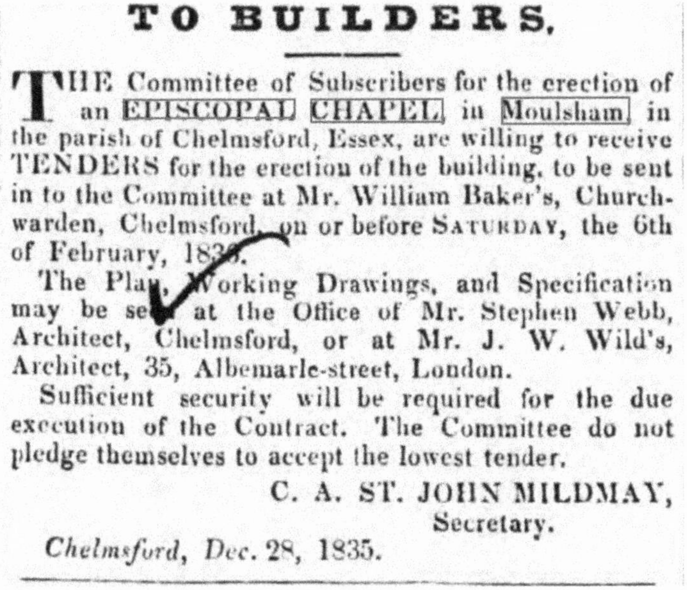

TO BUILDERS.

THE Committee of Subscribers for the erection of an EPISCOPAL CHAPEL in Moulsham, in the parish of Chelmsford, Essex, are willing to receive TENDERS for the erection of the building, to be sent in to the Committee at Mr. William Baker's, Church-warden, Chelmsford, on or before SATURDAY, the 6th of February, 1836.

The Plan, Working Drawings, and Specification may be seen at the Office of Mr. Stephen Webb, Architect, Chelmsford, or at Mr. J. W. Wild's, Architect, 35, Albemarle-street, London.

Sufficient security will be required for the due execution of the Contract. The Committee do not pledge themselves to accept the lowest tender.

C. A. ST. JOHN MILDMAY,
Secretary.

Chelmsford, Dec. 28, 1835.

Figure 2 – The newspaper advertisement seeking tenders for the erection of the new Episcopal Chapel in Moulsham

7

In spite of what the Rector described as the successful provision for the New Chapel in Moulsham, no mention is made of the project in the local press in 1835, and clearly either enthusiasm dwindled or unforeseen obstacles arose in the course of acquiring the site. It was certainly true that Lady Mildmay had promised the ground for the building, but it was only after building work had begun, in April 1836, that the Rector was able to state publicly at St Mary's Parish Dinner that: *"although Lady Mildmay was prevented by the technicalities of the law from giving the ground for the site, and had been compelled nominally to sell it for that purpose, her Ladyship has presented to the fund the sum of £200, the amount of the purchase money, and had thus in effect fulfilled her promise"*.[12] It is probable that difficulties with the Mildmay entailment, which were to be resolved in a few years' time, and which had such a profound effect on the development of the parish in the late 1830s and early 1840s, were a contrary factor in the construction of the building. Indeed, it was not until the last Sunday in 1835 that Rector Mildmay felt that he could at last announce to his congregation at St Mary's that: *"those obstacles that had presented themselves to the erection of this Chapel, had at last been removed, and that work would be commenced forthwith"*.[13]

'To raise a Church to God, and not to fame'

Possession of the site for the Chapel was achieved at the end of 1835. The site was that shown in the 1591 Map of Moulsham as the 'Upper Hop Ground' (it is a curiosity of the churchyard to this day that hops still grow from time to time, particularly along the northern boundary). The nurseryman Joseph Saltmarsh was paid £50 to surrender his lease on the ground.[14] In the *Chelmsford Chronicle* for Friday, 1 January 1836 the committee advertised for tenders for the building (*Figure 2*). The only tender was from James Moss, and was for £2,085, and the Committee speedily accepted this.[15] By the beginning of March it was reported that the site was fully in possession of those to whom the contract had been awarded (James Moss of Chelmsford, builder; Samuel Hart of Moulsham, carpenter; William Stock of Springfield Lane, painter, and George Wray, also of Springfield Lane, stonemason). The top spit of soil (having been nurtured by the Saltmarsh family for many years) had been sold to a Mr Hammond of Widford Hall. The contractors expressed their intention of completing the building by November 1836. Two weeks later the announcement was made that the first stone of the New Moulsham Chapel would be laid on 26 March 1836 (the original date of 21 March having been unavoidably postponed).

The appointed day was, according to the *Chelmsford Chronicle*, bitterly cold, with strong winds (although the same report also stated that the weather was *"unseasonably mild"*) yet none of this hampered the festivities. At an early hour flags were raised and the tolling of bells announced to the inhabitants of Chelmsford that the day was to be a holiday to celebrate: *"not a transient triumph or a rejoicing over realms undone"* but to honour, *"the pious hands that assisted to raise a Church to God, not to fame"*. The proceedings of the day commenced with Divine Service at nine o'clock in St Mary's, with prayers being read by the Rector, Rev C.A. St John Mildmay. Shortly after this, the committee and other select contributors partook of breakfast at the Rectory, and thus fortified against the cold, formed up in procession. Accompanied by a band, and augmented when they reached the Shire Hall by children from both the Old Charity and National schools, the procession wound its way through the town towards Moulsham. Prominent in the cavalcade were many local gentry, in a group headed by the Rector, his curate (Rev Grant) and the Master of the Grammar School (Rev Hatch). Many thronged to watch or marvel, although the *Chelmsford Chronicle's* reporter, as po-faced as ever was keen to note: *"several respectable Dissenters overstepping the petty bounds of doctrinal distinction and endeavouring with the honoured feelings of men to who true charity and integrity are dear, to give effect and regularity to the proceedings of the day"*.

It had been arranged that Lady Mildmay, who had provided the site for the Chapel, should lay the first stone, but regrettably she was indisposed (a very rare event for her). The wife of the Rector, the Hon Mrs Mildmay, stepped (literally) into the breach, and climbed down into the trench where the stone was to be laid and in which *"the Masonic duty was to be performed"*. The ceremony proper then began with an appropriate prayer read by the Rector, and then an ornamental trowel and mallet were passed to Mrs Mildmay, who spread mortar over the part prepared, a 'current coin of the realm' was deposited in the mortar by a bystander and the foundation stone itself, a block of Portland stone weighing 584lb bearing the date 'March 1836' was released from a platform and lowered to its final resting place (it is, sadly, no longer visible, being several feet below the present level of the churchyard). The laying of the stone again stirred the muse in the *Chelmsford Chronicle's* reporter. He wrote: *"May it settle there for ages, a barrier against the assaults of modern infidelity, a rallying cry for the broken spirit – and as an anchor, firm and sure, the Christian vessel that defied the blast"*. The Rector read another appropriate prayer, a hymn was sung, followed by the National Anthem, and with much mutual back-slapping and cheering, the procession returned to the Shire Hall, where all the children were regaled with a glass of wine and a bun (lessons must have been fun that afternoon) and *"the company finally separated amidst loud cheering"*. The building had formally been commenced, and the *Chelmsford Chronicle* was able to report that the New Chapel was to be seventy-two feet six inches long and thirty-seven feet wide, with a recessed Communion (a chancel) fourteen feet six inches by seven feet at the east end. The whole works would be under the supervision of Mr Webb.[16]

'To be annexed to the Rectory of the said parish (St Mary's)'

By September 1836 preparation was well in hand for the provision of a priest to officiate at the New Chapel, or, perhaps more correctly, the provision of an endowment for any such priest. On 1 September 1836 the Trust Deed was completed and signed.

It stated that the New Chapel for Divine Service which was in the process of erection in the hamlet of Moulsham was to be called 'St John's Chapel of Ease, Moulsham' (this is the first traceable dedication of the building to St John, and it is interesting that the St John in question is at this stage not further defined). It also stated that this building was: *"to be annexed to the Rectory of the said parish (St Mary's, Chelmsford) and used in aid of the parish church therefore"*. The Trust Deed went on to state that one thousand six hundred and forty-one pounds eleven shillings and six pence worth of stock in the Consolidated Three pounds per centrum annuities had been purchased in the name of the three Trustees of the Fund, namely the Reverend Carew Anthony St John Mildmay, Rector of St Mary's, Robert Bartlett, esquire, and Thomas Chalk, printer.[17] This would have produced just over £49 per annum (a very modest stipend even for a curate) but could well be attractive to an individual who already possessed other income.

The building was now in the course of erection and provision for a priest had been made. There were, also, at this time, other developments in Chelmsford which perhaps some of the more far-sighted citizens had realised would have an impact on the hamlet of Moulsham and the new Chapel of Ease. In August 1834 the Poor Law Amendment Act was passed, intending to abolish outdoor relief for the able-bodied poor and restricting them (both individuals and families) to relief in the workhouse. It was hoped that conditions in the workhouse (by being made deliberately harsher than outside) would encourage the destitute to use the institution only as a very last resort.[18] A year later the re-organisation of the Essex Boards was complete and the Chelmsford Union Guardians held their first meeting under the new act. The most urgent matter was to review the resources for which the new board was responsible, particularly the question of whether or not to bring all the Parish destitute into one workhouse, and, if so, whether that should be a completely rebuilt existing (New Street) institution or a brand new construction, elsewhere in the Parish. The Board commissioned an up and coming young architect, James Fenton, to look at both options (he was later

11

to design what is now the Ebenezer Strict Baptist Chapel on the corner of Parkway and New London Road, and lay out the nonconformist cemetery, also on New London Road). Fenton recommended a complete, new, purpose-built workhouse. The Chelmsford Board by 1836 was already investigating the possibility of purchasing the Old Barracks in Moulsham (Old Barrack Lane is now Wood Street). It cannot have escaped the Guardians, many of whom were intimately connected with St Mary's, that if the workhouse were to be moved near to the New Chapel of Ease in Moulsham, that baptisms, and, more importantly, burials of the inmates and their families would then become the responsibility of the Chapel. There was already much pressure on St Mary's burial ground.

In 1833 the Whig government passed the 'Act for the Abolition of Fines and Recoveries', in effect removing the constraints imposed on estates by Acts of Entailment. The Mildmay estates (much of whose land was in the hamlet of Moulsham) were thus freed from the legal straitjacket which had held them in its tight grip since the early seventeenth century. Dame Jane Mildmay would now be able to sell land and realise its capital.[19] One of the first beneficiaries of this was the Eastern Counties Railway (ECR), which, after its Bill had received the Royal Assent in 1836 concluded an agreement with the Mildmay family to purchase land on the company's projected route through the hamlet of Moulsham. The imminent construction of the railway would also involve the appearance locally of a substantial workforce with all their families. Most of these would settle in relatively temporary accommodation as close as possible to the line itself, and in Moulsham there would need to be significant construction work to carry the line over the flood plain of the river Cam. This workforce would need provision for the cure of their souls. So the hamlet prepared itself for the late 1830s, with the sense that it was an exciting and challenging time. The new Chapel of Ease was taking shape at just the right time.

On 18 April 1836 a meeting of the Incorporated Society for Promoting the Enlargement, Building and Repairing of Churches and Chapels was held in the society's chambers at St Martin's place in London with the Archbishop of York in the chair. Amongst other business transacted, it was recorded in the minutes that *"a grant was voted towards building a Chapel at Moulsham, in the parish of Chelmsford, in the County of Essex".*[20]

Throughout the remainder of 1836, work proceeded apace on the New Chapel, and by March 1837 the committee was able to announce in the *Chelmsford Chronicle* that: *"the Lord Bishop of London has fixed Tuesday, 11 April next for the Consecration of the Chapel, on which occasion a sermon will be preached. Admission to the Chapel will be by ticket only."*[21] Clearly the local population of Moulsham (except those who had good connections with St Mary's, or who had been particularly generous in subscribing to the Chapel fund) would be most unlikely to acquire a ticket for the consecration of what was, after all, their own new parish church. With only just over four hundred seats available after the gentry of Essex and the great and good of St Mary's had been accommodated, there would be precious little room left for anyone else.

The Lord Bishop of London, Charles James Blomfield, (*Figure 3*) wanted to make the most of the occasion. He was a great enthusiast for the building of new places of worship, and as there had already been considerable discussion about the formation of an Essex Church Building Society, this consecration would be a good opportunity to show what such a society might achieve. The building was now complete, and although lack of money had caused the original design for the western front to be markedly simplified (*compare figures 4 and 5*) it was still an imposing building in its own right.

Figure 3 – Charles James Blomfield, Lord Bishop of London (engraved at about the time he consecrated St John's, Moulsham)

'The exertions that have been made to supply the wants of the spiritually destitute'

Tuesday, 11 April 1837 was seen as a red-letter day for Chelmsford. The Committee had done their homework most meticulously, and the whole proceedings for the day were conducted smoothly and in accordance with the plan. Admission to the Chapel was, as described, by ticket only, and shortly after eleven o'clock the solitary bell was tolled to announce the arrival of the Bishop. Lady Mildmay and the Hon Mrs Mildmay held the principal places of honour at the front of the chapel, surrounded by the local clergy who on this occasion numbered no less than twenty-eight. The Lord Chief Justice, Lord Tindall, who had indicated his intention to be present, was at the last moment prevented from doing so by the extended trial of Greenacre, a notorious murderer, at the Central Criminal Court.

The Bishop was received at the gate of the new building by the Rector, Rev Mildmay. A procession then formed up which then filed up the path into the building in the following order – Beadles, Committee (two by two, with wands), churchwardens (with staves), Apparitor (the diocesan individual charged with ensuring that the legal procedures of the day were followed correctly), the Lord Bishop, the Chancellor of the Diocese, the Bishop's chaplain and minister and finally the registrar. The Bishop went straight to the small vestry, where he robed, then moved to the communion table on which stood the plate. This was an imposing collection. It comprised an ewer together with two chalices and patens, and was purchased from the High street jeweller, John Cremer, who was selling up, by Henry Guy. It was said that Henry Guy had obtained the plate at one third of the normal price. Even so, it was the first of many generous donations that the Chelmsford bookseller and insurance agent made to the new Chapel.

The petition for the consecration was delivered to his Lordship and read by the registrar, after which the procession moved down the middle aisle and back in the same order as they had entered the Chapel. On returning to the altar the Deed of Conveyance was delivered to the Bishop, who proceeded to recite, concluding: *"Let us humbly hope that our Heavenly Father will favourably approve our present purpose, of setting apart this place in solemn manner for the performance of the several offices of religious worship, and let us faithfully and devoutly pray for His blessing on this our undertaking"*. The usual prayer of communion was then followed, after which the sentence of consecration was read by the Chancellor. The Bishop signed it, and directed that it, together with the petition and the deeds, should be registered. The Rev James Hutchinson, who had been appointed curate at St Mary's, read the morning service, and psalm 64 was sung by a group of soloists assisted by the children of the National and Charity schools. Mr Chalk accompanied the whole proceedings on his seraphim (a small, early version of an American harmonium) there being no organ in the Chapel.

The West front of the Chapel to be built at Moulsham.

Figure 4 – The original proposed design for the West End of the new Episcopal Chapel of St John's, Moulsham

The Bishop read the communion service, psalm 100 was sung by the same group as before and the Bishop preached the Consecration sermon, taking as his text the 25th verse of the tenth chapter of the Epistle to the Hebrews, *"Not forsaking the assembling of ourselves together, as the manner of some is; but by exhorting one another, and so much the more as ye see the day approaching"*. He stressed the great benefit of providing many places of worship, for such was human nature: *"that unless the great truths of*

Figure 5 – The simplified design for the West End of the new Episcopal Chapel of St John's, Moulsham (saving a significant sum of money)

Christianity were constantly before mankind, and forced upon their notice, they would be forgotten". At the conclusion of the sermon, the Consecration hymn was sung during which a collection was taken that raised more than £150. Bishop Blomfield then performed the service of consecration for the burial ground in a marquee at the east end of the building, after which he returned to the vestry to unrobe. The ceremony was at an end. The crowds departed, the *Chelmsford Chronicle* reporting in its own inimitable way that they were: *"gratified, and we should hope, improved, by the exertions that have been made to supply the wants of the spiritually destitute – to bind the broken reed – to council* (sic), *instruct, encourage, sooth, assist; and to make tears of joy down grief-worn furrows flow".*

'To the prolonged plaudits of the assembly'

For the great and the good the day had only just begun. The nobility, clergy, ladies, gentlemen and the prominent tradesmen of the town all repaired to the Shire Hall where a 'cold collation' had been provided for 340 guests. It had been announced that T.W. Branston, MP, would take the chair but unfortunately the adjourned debate on the Irish Corporation Bill and the certainty of a division on the question that evening meant that in those pre-railway days he was unable to be present. Thomas Morgan Gepp, one of the churchwardens of St Mary's, was hastily summoned to the chair, and he somewhat diffidently proposed the first toast – 'Church and King' – followed by the health of the Bishop. Both toasts were greeted with prolonged, loud cheering and clapping. The Bishop then rose and replied at great length to the toast 'Church and King', using the most florid language. The toast, he said, *"has been such as to excite a feeling in my mind which almost deprives me of the spirit of utterance".* He spoke for just under an hour, stressing repeatably the promotion of the welfare of the National Church and how that welfare could be ensured through the Incorporated Society for the Building of

Churches. He ended eventually by proposing the health of Lady Mildmay *"for her liberality"*. Lady Mildmay's son, the rector, then rose and responded on her behalf *"as it not usual for ladies to do so"*. He stressed how much the New Chapel owed to the Bishop, who had promoted its cause tirelessly. The Bishop then rose again and proposed the health of Rev Mildmay (stumbling over his title and calling him the vicar of St Mary's, rather than the rector) who rose again and briefly replied. There then followed much more mutual back-slapping, and copious toasts, all *"drunk with much applause"*. Eventually the Bishop and Lady Mildmay had had enough and left the company *"to the prolonged plaudits of the assembly"*. The great and the good were driven (or perhaps staggered, according to their status) home. The New Chapel had been gratefully dedicated to God.[22]

Sunday, 9 April 1837 saw the first service in the New Chapel. The *Chelmsford Chronicle* reported that the building was open for divine service, and that the Rev James Hutchinson would officiate in the morning. In the afternoon an appropriate sermon was preached by Rev Mildmay, based on psalm 122, *"I was glad when they said unto me, let us go into the house of the Lord"*. The New Chapel, according to the report, was extremely well-filled.[23] On 30 April James Hutchinson carried out the first baptism service in the Chapel. Three children, John Bundock, David Clark and George Clark, all of them from old Barrack Lane (now Wood Street) became the first of many entries in the Registers.[24] The burial ground was first used on 31 May, when Ann Aldridge, aged 11 months, of Widford Street, became the first of many hundreds to be interred there.[25] James Hutchinson took the service. He signed, as always, as 'Officiating Minister', never as curate. He was probably only ever formally a curate at St Mary's. As there was as yet no district assigned to the New Chapel, it seems very unlikely that he could ever have been offered the post of curate there. The New Chapel was indeed an imposing addition to the hamlet of Moulsham (*Figure 6*).

NORTH EAST VIEW OF
S! John's Church, Moulsham,
CHELMSFORD.

Figure 6 – The new Episcopal Chapel of St John's, Moulsham,
from the north-east (as built in 1837)

'A man of strong understanding and a warm heart'

The Rev James Hutchinson was born early in 1780 and christened on 27 March of that year in Kingston upon Hull, Yorkshire. He was admitted to St John's College, Oxford, as a sizar (a student receiving an allowance from the college towards his expenses) on 3 July 1799, matriculating in Michaelmas that year. He graduated BA in 1803, obtaining his MA in 1823. He was ordained deacon in York Minster on 14 July 1805 and priest a year later on 13 July 1806. His first post was as curate at St Andrew-in-the-Grove, Briensor and clerk in holy orders at Halifax.[26] He was appointed curate at St Mary's, Chelmsford, in 1808 by the then rector, Rev John Morgan, having briefly held a similar appointment in Rochford. His eldest son was baptised in 1810 at St Mary's, and here he laboured diligently for some years. In 1827 he resigned his curacy and was elected the first chaplain of the new County Gaol which had been built in Springfield, a post he filled with great integrity and compassion. In December 1827, a hardened criminal, Reuben Martin (*alias* James Winter) who had been convicted of murder two days previously, was executed on the newly erected drop in front of the prison. He behaved with much swagger and bravado on his way from the Court house to the gaol, throwing his hat into the air with a smile, exclaiming: *"You may go, I shan't want you again"*. Immediately on his arrival at the prison he was visited by James Hutchinson, who repeatedly tried to offer him some spiritual consolation, and procure from him an admission of the justice of his sentence. Eventually Martin appeared to acknowledge his manifold sins to God, who, he said, he hoped would forgive him – but more than that he would not say. James Hutchinson persevered, and just before the drop, Martin was seen to pray inwardly. It was said that the chaplain to the gaol was much affected by the whole proceedings.[27]

In 1830 he resigned from the chaplaincy[28] in order to succeed Rev Thomas Roberts, as the headmaster of the Grammar School. James Hutchinson's excellent academic credentials clearly marked him out as a fit successor, and he was unanimously elected on a memorial of the inhabitants to the Trustees. However, he was still much missed at St Mary's, and in 1835 the rector felt that the parish church still needed his services, and offered him the position of second curate, an offer which he gratefully accepted. His licensing followed almost immediately. With the exception of the time that he spent at St John's he continued with his duties as headmaster and curate at St Mary's until his death in 1853, working tirelessly with the parishioners who were his cure. This dutiful and loving service was measured by the many substantial and heartfelt testimonies he received from his flock, including a silver tea service and a purse of 100 guineas. Subsequent to this, the ladies at St Mary's, led by Dame Jane Mildmay, purchased for him, by subscription, a silk gown and cassock, and in about 1840 his portrait was executed by a Mr Henderson. Such was the popularity of this portrait, when exhibited, that: *"it was afterwards engraved by the desire of the inhabitants, there being few of their houses in which a copy of it is not found adorning the wall"*. An illustration of this engraving shows a gentle looking man with a somewhat unworldly air (*Figure 7*) who was described by Rev A.J.

Figure 7 – The Rev James Hutchinson, curate of St Mary's,
who took the first normal service at St John's, Moulsham.
Taken from an engraving of Mr Henderson's portrait of him

Bartlett in the *Chelmsfordian* of 1900 as: *"a Yorkshireman with a strong will and a somewhat imperious manner, a quick but well-controlled temper and a keen sense of humour. As a preacher he was scarcely audible, but after a sentence or two, warmed to his work. In the memory of all those who knew him he lives on as the parish priest rather than the schoolmaster".*[29] This is borne out by the description in the *Chelmsford Chronicle* of his death, clearly showing the devotion of this elderly man, by now quite infirm, to his parishioners: *"The Rev. gentleman pursued his labours as curate of the parish... ...nearly up to his last hour. On the Thursday morning he performed the early service at the Church, attended the funeral of his old and valued friend, Miss Morgan, was in the evening administering religious consolation at the bedside of one of his sick parishioners,. and on Friday morning was preparing for the duties of the school, when his active career was arrested by the hand of death"*.[30] With all his duties at the Grammar School and St Mary's, and his officiating at the New Chapel, there must have been little time left to care for the people who lived in the hamlet of Moulsham, yet it was recorded on his death: *"a feeling of great sorrow was visible throughout the temple in which the Rev deceased had ministered"*. The Rev Muston, in the course of his sermon on the Sunday after James Hutchinson's death, described him as: *"a man of strong understanding and warm heart, his mental powers improved by diligent study and the advantages of general literature – an open and warm-hearted friend, and intelligent and agreeable companion, and above all, a faithful minister of Christ"*. Such was the man to whom the initial cure of souls for the New Chapel was entrusted. His funeral took place a few days later, and such was the esteem in which he was held, that all shops and businesses in the town closed as a mark of respect. The town and the hamlet had lost a good servant.

'A man deeply and visibly moved'

In 1837 work started on the erection of the new Chelmsford Union Workhouse on the site of the Old Barracks, later the site of St John's Hospital, to the west of Wood Street. The buildings were designed by William Thorold who was the architect of a number of workhouses in Essex and East Anglia. His design for Chelmsford was based on the model 'square' plan devised by Sampson Kempthorne for the Poor Law Commissionaires in 1835. He made provision for about 400 inmates, and the total cost of the building was £5,650, more than three times the cost of the New Chapel.[31] This new workhouse, responsible for the poor in a substantial part of central Essex, required a chaplain, and on 19 August 1838 Rev Hamilton was appointed to the post.

George Burton Hamilton was born in 1804, the third son on Ralph Hamilton, of Swanpool, Liverpool. He entered Corpus Christi College, Oxford, where he matriculated on 7 June 1823 and where he was subsequently awarded an exhibition. He took his BA in 1827 and his MA in 1830.[32] He was ordained deacon by Bishop Howley (then Bishop of London) in 1828 and priest by Bishop Howley's successor, Bishop Blomfield, in 1829. After serving as curate at Clothall, near Baldock, Hertfordshire,[33] he took up his appointment at the workhouse, where he stayed for four years. Although living with his wife Sarah and family at Sandon Lodge, Sandon, he was frequently to be found at the New Chapel, where he took his first baptism (a workhouse infant) in October 1838. Thereafter he took a substantial but supporting role at the Chapel, baptising infants from the workhouse (there were many) and almost certainly taking some of the services as well (sadly there are no registers of service extant prior to 1880 – it is thought that the family of one of the early Chapel clerks destroyed all papers relating to the Chapel (except the statutory registers) after his death).[34] In 1842 George Hamilton succeeded Rev J. Hinckley Lewis as Chaplain of Chelmsford Gaol, a position he held for thirty-five years, until his appointment as Chaplain to the Essex Militia, a post he held until his death in 1886.[35]

His funeral was held at Holy Trinity church, Springfield, on Monday 11 January 1886, the coffin being borne on a hand bier by warders from the County Gaol (at the express wish of the deceased). He is buried in the churchyard at Holy Trinity, and is commemorated by a memorial plaque in the church.[36]

He, too, clearly impressed everyone with his care and compassion during his period of office at the Gaol. It is reported in a long and detailed article that, at the execution of Richard Coates (he was convicted of murdering a nine-year-old girl under particularly horrific circumstances) the prisoner was comforted throughout the entire night prior to the hanging by the Rev Hamilton, and, that: *"as the procession made its way to the scaffold, the prison chaplain was seen to be deeply and very visibly moved by the demeanour of the prisoner".*[37]

'A particular district should be assigned to the said Chapel'

By 1838 the New Chapel was thriving and the need for the formalising of its legal status was pressing. Accordingly, in September of that year the Queen's Commissioners for building new churches and chapels met and in their submission sought to: *"beg leave further to represent to your Majesty that, having taken into consideration all the circumstances surrounding this parish, it appears to them expedient that a particular district should be assigned to the said Chapel, under the provisions of the 16th section of an Act passed in the 59th year of the reign of his Majesty King George the Third, entitled 'An Act to amend and render more effectual an Act passed in the last section of Parliament, for building and promoting the building, of additional churches in populous parishes' and that such a district should be named St John's district, Moulsham; such district to consist of the Hamlet of Moulsham, which hamlet is bounded on or towards the west by the respective parishes of Margaretting, Widford and Writtle; on the north by the River Cam, as far as that river forms the boundary line that divides the said hamlet from the township of Chelmsford; on or towards the east by the parishes of Springfield and Great Baddow; and on the south by the hamlet and parish of Orsett, as the same is delineated on the map hereunto annexed, and therein coloured yellow".*

The Queen was advised by the Privy Council to approve the petition and ordered *"that the proposed assignment be accordingly made"*. It was published in the *London Gazette* on 11 September, on the authority of Charles Greville.[38]

The Parish Church of St John, Moulsham, was now ready for its first incumbent.

2. CHRISTOPHER RALPH MUSTON

(1839–59)

"He was a faithful Minister among his flock, active in the discharge of his sacred duties to within the last year or two, when decaying health compelled him to withdraw from his labours".[1]

'An enthusiastic desire to expand his religious and philosophical ideas'

Christopher Ralph Muston was born on 17 November 1796 in the little village of Aston Tirrold, Berkshire (it is near Didcot, and is now in Oxfordshire), the son of Christopher Muston and Elizabeth Ralph. His parents were married on 10 April 1792 in the church of All Saints, Maidstone, Kent. They had six children in all (one of whom died in infancy) but Christopher Ralph was the only boy, and great things were expected of him.[2] Christopher Muston, his father, had already established something of a reputation as an independent preacher, being trained at Homerton College. Shortly after his marriage to Elizabeth, when he was pastor to the Meeting Chapel in Milton, Kent, he gave a sermon at the funeral of the daughter of the local squire, Thomas March of Borden (himself, unusually, a dissenter) which was sufficiently much appreciated for the grieving parents to commission its publication.[3] Christopher Ralph must have had a childhood surrounded by intellectual stimulation and a religious philosophy maintained by the tenets of dissenting belief. His father also had some minor reputation as a schoolmaster. By the early 1800s, after spells at Aston Tirrold (1798–1801) and Devizes (1801–03)[4] the family had moved to Epping[5] in Essex where Christopher Muston had been appointed Master of the Board School. Already, at the age of fifteen, Christopher Ralph had an enthusiastic desire to expand his religious and philosophical ideas. His name is listed as a subscriber in his own right to *"An Essay in Unbelief"* published by James Churchill of Henley in 1811. Unbelief was clearly a subject close to the Muston family's heart, as seven other copies were purchased by Christopher Muston so that all the family could have one each.[6] The book itself is a turgid tome and must have been meaty bedtime reading for nine-year-old Ann, the youngest sister. The family's financial position, was, though, far from secure. On 1 June 1816 Christopher Muston was declared bankrupt[7] although he continued in his post as Master of the school, and on 6 July all his house and property in Lindsey Street, Epping was sold. At this sale he was described as a *"Schoolmaster, Maker and Vendor of Medicines, Trader, Dealer and Chapman"* (a Chapman is a common pedlar). His property stretched to three acres in the centre of Epping, so he had clearly made some money in the past, but his bankruptcy may have been the result of an unwise speculation in shares (particularly canal shares, to which he seems to have been easily attracted)[8] or possibly from his attempts to publish. A book that he wrote in 1813 entitled: *"Grammatical Questions on the English Grammar,* (sic) *being an easy method to interrogate Young Persons in classes and useful to Teachers and Others to examine the progress of Education on that subject"* was scathingly reviewed, one critic writing *"...we have here a Multitude of Questions, without answers, which may certainly serve to assist the process of* **interrogation**; *but what other purpose can they possibly serve?"*[9]

'For exemplary propriety, diligence and ability'

By 1820 it was clear that if Christopher Ralph wanted at least to follow in his father's footsteps (or perhaps even better his father) either as a Dissenting Minister or as a schoolmaster it would be almost obligatory for him to have a university education. Yet the options open to dissenters were limited. An inability to subscribe to the Thirty-Nine Articles meant that Oxford and Cambridge were proscribed to them.[10] In the early nineteenth century that left only Scottish universities as a realistic possibility. Christopher Ralph chose (or was advised to choose) Glasgow, where he matriculated in 1820.[11] He was described as *"Filius nato Maximus Chrsitophori v.d.m. apud Cantabrigiani"* indicating that by 1820 his father had moved to Cambridge and was styling himself "VDM." (*verbi die minister* or *verbi divini magister*), an epithet often used by dissenting preachers who felt that 'Reverend' was too pretentious or too self-proclaiming a title. It also often indicated a responsibility to the Bible and Bible-based preaching and was frequently used by those who had no university degree.

At Glasgow, Christopher Ralph distinguished himself, being awarded a prize in the ethics class: *"for the best specimen of Composition on the various subjects connected with the business of the Class, and either prescribed weekly by the Professor or chosen by the students themselves"* in the session 1820–21 (where he was described as a *"Senior"*).[12] He kept up the standard in the following year (1821–22) with a prize in the Mathematics class *"for exemplary propriety, diligence and ability"*.[13] Perhaps at this stage he was still keeping his options (dissenting minister or schoolmaster) open. He graduated BA in 1821 and MA in 1822[14] although the latter year must have been a difficult one for all the family as in August his father died in Cambridge, aged only 52.[15] Christopher Ralph may have then had to provide for his family (perhaps as a schoolmaster) although he was able to attend Wymondley Academy to prepare for the ministry.

In 1824 the *London Christian Instructor* reported that: *"... the successful candidates (for Ministry) at the last election in April, and who are to enter at Midsummer, are – Griffiths – Muston – Hitchin..."* adding that *"... the Committee regret to state that on account of the limited state of their funds, they were enabled to select only three out of the eleven proposed for admission"*.[16] Christopher Ralph's first appointment came shortly after his successful candidature for ministry, when he was offered (and accepted) the post of pastor at the New Meeting in Bedford.[17] The Chapel itself was described as *"... plain and unassuming structure ...*" located near the more celebrated Old Meeting in Mill Lane. This latter was the Chapel of John Bunyan and was a substantial building with 120 pews, capable of seating over 800 persons. The pastor here was the redoubtable Samuel Hillyard. Christopher Ralph's Chapel was a simple rectangular building with the four sides of the roof converging to a point which was surmounted by a ball. This simple Chapel, with its own burial ground, had been established 1771 by Rev Joshua Symonds as a result of a difference of opinion over infant baptism.[18] It was very much the little brother of the Old Meeting, and in this period Christopher Ralph is often encountered taking a subordinate role, assisting Samuel Hillyard at important services.[19] During his time at Bedford, Christopher Ralph's outstanding intellect began to show its potential, and it was here in 1830 he produced his most celebrated work, *"Recognition in the World to Come, or, Christian Friendship on Earth perpetuated in Heaven"* which he finished in April of that year.[20] It is a substantial work (430 pages) and even today is a difficult and stodgy read. It is also not easy to see for whom the work was intended (the majority of the population, even if they could read, would have understood little of the author's arguments); it may have been that in early nineteenth century England, with its ever present and sometimes indiscriminate mortality, the title alone may have been enough to attract purchasers. And attract them it did. It sold well, and by the time Christopher Muston was the incumbent at St John's, it was into a fourth (and revised) edition. *"Recognition in the World to Come"* was well received. A critique in the *Eclectic Review* was fulsome in its praise. It also gives us a brief but fascinating glimpse into the mind of the man who was later to become the first incumbent of St John the Evangelist. The anonymous reviewer began by pointing out that: *"On first taking up this volume, an emotion of surprise may be excited, that it should have been deemed needful, or even possible, to occupy a volume with the discussion of the simple point of enquiry to which it professedly relates"* but concludes that an examination of the chapter headings demonstrates how well the author has treated the subject. The reviewer waxes eloquent in describing Christopher Muston's approach to writing the book, thus: *"He has conversed with his theme, till he has caught a glow from its celestial brightness. He has wrestled with it, till he has extracted a blessing for his reward; for how is it possible, indeed, to put forth one's mind in the energetic encounter with such subjects, without receiving their influence into our bosoms?"*[21] Wrestle with it Christopher Muston certainly did, and wrestle very successfully. In spite of selling at the then substantial price of 6s. 6d. a copy, it sold well enough to merit further editions, and the fourth edition mentioned above did not appear until 1840. It is, curiously, still today (2018) in print. Its encouraging reception and sales must have meant much to Christopher Muston in financial terms. During his incumbency at St John's he was able to give generous financial aid to the parish, both enlarging the church itself and building a fine parsonage house for himself, his family and any future incumbents.

'Conformity with the Church of England was expected of him'

In spite of the success of his first book, Christopher Muston was neither settled or particularly happy in his ministry at Bedford. Although he had received a strong dissenting education, at Glasgow and at Wymondley, he found himself experiencing: *"so much pain from the oppression and tyranny of the Voluntary system*[22] *that he was induced to consider the lawfulness and expediency of the Establishments"*.[23] The outcome of this dissatisfaction was an invitation from the Scottish Presbyterian church in Rotterdam for Christopher Muston to become their minister, and he accepted their offer in 1832.[24] Within this secure Establishment environment, after careful examination of the earliest ecclesiastical records, he became not only fully convinced that the Establishments afforded the most effective way of spreading the gospel, but also that episcopacy was the primitive form of church government. He realised that the advantages that he had gained from a position of union from the Dutch church were considerable, and he became increasingly persuaded that the history of the early church showed that there had been bishops, priests and deacons. He moved to a position where conformity with the Church of England was expected of him, and all obstacles that existed to his admission were skilfully removed by the Bishop of London (clearly keen to have such a powerful intellect in his diocese), Charles James Blomfield. Christopher Muston deeply appreciated all that Bishop Blomfield had done to ease his transition into the Church of England, and he showed this appreciation by dedicating his next publication *"Sermons preached in the British Episcopal church, Rotterdam"* which he completed in 1837, to the bishop,[25] who had ordained him deacon at St James', Westminster on 20 December 1835.[26]

After his ordination as deacon he was offered the post of Assistant Chaplain in the British Episcopal church in Rotterdam, an offer which he speedily accepted in 1836. Here he acted as assistant to the formidable Rev Joseph Bosworth (another individual who had achieved a position within the established church although he was not a graduate of Oxford or Cambridge). Joseph Bosworth had accepted a British consular chaplaincy in Amsterdam in 1829, moving to Rotterdam in 1832. During the following six years he dedicated his time and his energies to producing *"A Dictionary of the Anglo-Saxon language"*, a work of meticulous craftsmanship written against the background of the intense (and sometimes nasty) nineteenth century philological debate on the Anglo-Saxon controversy.[27] Although his dictionary nearly ended up as a messy compromise, it was a lexicographical *tour-de-force* and it stood for over 150 years as the seminal resource for scholars translating Anglo-Saxon texts.[28] Such an intellectual atmosphere must have suited Christopher Muston, although a great many duties of the day-to-day running of the church must have been his responsibility. It was also a time when Christopher Muston was still unsure of the direction that his life should take. Should it be in Academia or in the Church? When late in 1835 the chair of logic became vacant at the university of Edinburgh, he set out his qualifications for the position.[29] When the Lord Provost chaired the special meeting of the Council to appoint a Professor to this chair in July 1836, he summarised the strength of the candidates, and said

"*Of Mr Muston of Rotterdam, he hăd a high opinion, from his work on* Recognition in the Next World, *which he had been reading with delight*" but in spite of this heartfelt endorsement, Christopher Muston was not offered the chair.[30] He continued his work in Rotterdam, but the urge to publish was still strong, and in 1837 he produced the volume of sermons dedicated to Bishop Blomfield mentioned previously. They were well received. The review in the *Church of England Magazine* felt that: "*the congregation of the British Church in Rotterdam were highly privileged in having brought emphatically and energetically before them such a display of divine truth*" although that approbation was tempered with a note that, "*the sermons are only fourteen in number and are consequently longer than those normally preached*". In fact, the fourteen average thirty-five pages of close print each, and reading a typical one through at a gentle pace suggests each one would have taken at least three hours to deliver. The congregation of the British Church was clearly made of stern stuff.[31]

'Here was a man whose sound doctrinal approach fitted him for the position'

Christopher Muston was now in his early forties, and a clergyman within the Established Church. His thoughts now turned to marriage. The daughter of George Gibson,[32] a former deacon at the Scottish Church to which he had first been appointed (and here a deacon means a prominent lay official) had clearly caught his eye, but there was a hint of impermanence relating to his position as Assistant Chaplain and marriage was not to be undertaken without a secure incumbency. So Christopher Muston started his quest for a curacy in England. Bishop Blomfield had recently consecrated the Episcopal Chapel of St John, Moulsham and felt that here was a man whose enthusiasm, need and above all sound doctrinal approach (Bishop Blomfield was a stickler for sound doctrine) fitted him for the position in Chelmsford. Furthermore, here was an individual whose income from royalties could very well augment what was regrettably a relatively meagre stipend. Wheels started to turn, and in January 1839 he was installed as the curate of St John's, Moulsham. He found himself accommodation in Moulsham street, not far from the Anchor public house and conveniently close by his new responsibility. He took his first baptism in Chelmsford on 13 January 1839 at St Mary's, no doubt under the strict gaze of Rector Mildmay.[33] He signed St Mary's register as *'Curate of Moulsham'*, the Chapel having been formally constituted a district in 1838 *(see chapter 1)*. The new Chapel had its first incumbent.

'How, then, is this moral pestilence to be checked?'

Christopher Ralph Muston came to a Chapel still full of enthusiasm from its consecration some two and a half years previously, but nevertheless a Chapel beset with the typical problems facing a new parish at the end of the first third of the nineteenth century. For St John's, the problem could simply be summed up in one word – money. The income for the incumbent that was derived from the endowment set up in 1836 was small (probably no more than £60) and as such would have been a meagre stipend, even for a curate. The Church of England's traditional solution to this problem (particularly in rural parishes) was pew rents. So, in the late 1840s, even in the poor parish of St Luke's, Berwick street, in Soho, where rents were low, the pew rents still brought in enough to fund an incumbent. Indeed, the patron of the parish, the vicar of St James, Piccadilly pointed out that he would not have been able to finance the stipend in any other way.[34] This arrangement created a problem in many parishes, bearing in mind that at this time few, if any, parishes would have had an offertory. The offertory smelt of Rome. A seating plan of St John's which dates from 1838 shows only a limited number of free seats, and a limited number of free seats meant only limited room for the poor.[35] To many people in early Victorian England the Established Church was felt only to be for the well-to-do and the refined. Indeed, there were rich and influential parishes where the wealthy complained bitterly that they found it difficult to worship because of the stink of the ill-clad poor.

The presence of the poor in church was, however, a subject close to the heart of Christopher Muston and also to Bishop Blomfield. In part of the forward to the fourth edition of *"Recognition in the World to Come"* Christopher Muston wrote that: *"... no adequate efforts have yet been made to remedy the great evils attending the spiritual destitution which is known extensively to exist in our populous towns and districts...   ...how, then, is this moral pestilence to be checked without which some counteraction must prey on the vitals of our society?"* He goes on to rue the inefficacy of all appeals for a Parliamentary grant and ends by suggesting that two per cent, if raised on the whole income of the Church, could bring in up to £70,000. If this were done, he felt, a popular appeal would at least triple that amount and that such a fund: *"... thus annually created and dealt judiciously out... ...would in a few years suffice for the required number of churches."*[36] It is probable that Christopher Muston wrote this to catch the eye of the Bishop, who thought along similar lines, but they had all fallen into the same trap: it was relatively easy to raise money to build a new church, but it was devilish hard to create an adequate endowment to provide a sufficient stipend. Time and again in the early Victorian era drawings of an elegant building had the great and good willingly dipping into their pockets to fund a tangible project, whereas endowments and stipends were nebulous objectives that they rarely thought about.

Clearly extension of the building at St John's, access to worship for the poor of Moulsham (which was particularly relevant with the large, itinerant body of labour building the Eastern Counties Railway, and now living in the parish) and a better financial basis for the running of the parish would be the main challenges of Christopher Muston's incumbency. These all raised significant problems for Moulsham, and it is noteworthy that the parish was being looked at by others to see how it attempted to resolve these issues. The *Church of England Magazine* reported in 1847 that: *"...they had watched the efforts made to meet the wants of St John's, Moulsham, with considerable interest, not merely because of the local importance of the object in view, but*

34

particularly in reference to the bearing of such movements upon the general interests of the church. It is well-known that, for want of more adequate means, a large proportion of the new churches are put upon a footing as ill-adapted as they could well be to the necessities of the dark and impoverished masses of human beings for whose spiritual welfare they have been reared by the hand of Christian benevolence. In their appliances and internal arrangements they stand frequently forth in striking contrast with the time-honoured edifices which surround them, the machinery for working out the spiritual regeneration of the inhabitants imperfect and utterly inadequate to the purpose, the incumbents left single-handed to do the work of sometimes two or three active ministers of the church, the remuneration awarded for their services often barely sufficient to meet the demands on their private charity, and the mass of the swarming poor (sic) *around them (with much indifference to religion) virtually excluded from their public ministrations through want of suitable or inadequate accommodation."*[37] Strong stuff, this, but it was exactly the situation that Christopher Muston was facing at St John's.

Christopher Muston was now an incumbent, settled firmly in his parish. This meant that he was now in a position to marry. September 1840 saw him making the long journey to Dover, crossing by sail to Ostend and finally making his way to Rotterdam (in all, he was away for nearly two months). He married Katharine Mason Gibson at the Scottish Presbyterian church in Rotterdam, after banns, on 4 November 1840.[38] Katharine was a British subject, but had been born in Rotterdam on 10 October 1810. At the end of November the newly-wed couple made their tedious way back to Chelmsford where the continuing challenges of the new Chapel of St John the Evangelist awaited its incumbent.

'The privilege of attending divine service was now to be had without money or price'

The first challenge in getting the poor into church was to get rid of pew rents. In addition to the income from the endowment, pew rents raised about £55 a year, making the incumbent's total income about £115. This was barely adequate, but Christopher Muston had other income. Henry Guy felt as strongly as his incumbent about the abolition of pew rents, and in 1846 he promised £500 towards an endowment to enable all pews to be free. The worthy rector, Carew Anthony St John Mildmay agreed to give property worth £127 if they managed to raise £2,000 and with generous contributions from Christopher Muston himself as well as *"strenuous efforts by the ladies of the church"* the sum was raised. The incumbent himself reported at the 1849 Vestry meeting the: *"successful termination of the recent undertaking, which had for its object the doing away with the pew rents at St John's."* He also pointed out that, *"the privilege of attending divine service was now to be had without money or price."*[39] This advance was important at St John's, as it now put them on the footing of a parochial church. This also had a major bonus for the churchwardens (at that time Henry Guy and Joseph Saltmarsh) as they no longer had the onerous and sometimes rather awkward task of collecting pew rents and also trying to persuade those who had rented pews to allow anyone into 'their' pew if there was space at the start of the service. However, at that Vestry meeting Christopher Muston also warned the churchwardens that they now had a much more challenging task *"that of adjusting the accommodation to the altered state of things."* Not only would they now have a situation where no-one had an exclusive right to any pew, but they had to start thinking about the provision of the additional accommodation that would be necessary now that anyone could come and sit anywhere.

Again, St John's was being followed at a national level. A *Church of England Magazine* article in 1847 had also gone on to emphasise again (and critically) the inadequate provision in churches for the poor but concluded by pointing out that: *"the exertions made in* (sic) *behalf of St John's Church are likely to be crowned with complete success; but, as there still exists a deficiency in the funds required to secure a grant from Queen Anne's bounty, we trust that the friends of the*

Figure 8 – Sketch by the Diocesan Architect (Joseph Clarke) showing the proposed enlargement of 1851 to St John's Church, Moulsham, from the north-east. The tower and the spire were never built

undertaking will not have to labour under the disadvantage of an outstanding debt."[40]

'The work is being carried out with a vigorous hand'

The pew issue had now been resolved and efforts were concentrated on expanding the building. The plain, rectangular building did not lend itself easily to simple modifications which would add a substantial number of extra seats. With thick, load-bearing north and south walls, any classic additions such as full-length aisles alongside these would be very difficult and very expensive.

The simplest solution (although it would give the church a very piecemeal appearance) would be to deepen the chancel and add north and south transepts. These would provide plenty of extra seats, although some of these would have a significantly restricted view. A relatively ambitious plan was drawn up in 1850 by Joseph Clarke, the London Diocesan architect, which showed large north and south transepts, a chancel more than doubled in depth, north and south porches, and a tower. Vestries were also included on the north-east and south-east corners of the building. The north-east vestry is clearly visible on Joseph Clarke's sketch of the building as it was intended to appear (*Figure 8*). The drawing was approved by the Incorporated Society for Promoting the Enlargement, Building and Repairing of Churches and Chapels on 22 July 1850 and by the Diocese of London on 13 August.[41] It shows the pre-1851 Chapel as having accommodation for 547 individuals, with the proposed alterations seating an additional 476 (214 adults and 262 children). Clearly, for over a thousand to be squeezed into a building whose ground plan (apart from the 1996 modifications to the west end) was not so very different from that of today speaks volumes about Victorian worship. The cynics might say that by packing people that closely together the church would have been able to save on heating. Shortly afterwards Joseph Clarke produced a more detailed plan (it may even have been drawn post enlargement, as although it is dated 1851, it appears to have been 'signed off' by the churchwardens, Joseph Saltmarsh and Henry Guy, as well as Christopher Muston). It states that: "*This church was enlarged in the year 1851 by which means additional accommodation for 427 persons were obtained. A grant of £175 was made by the Incorporated Society for the Enlargement, Building and Repair of Churches and Chapels on condition the 365 of the extra seats described in the annexed should be set apart and declared to be free for the use of the poor for ever. The provision of Church room previously* (sic) *to the alteration being to the extent of 547, free for the use of the poor, and also shown upon this plan.*"[42] Both of these drawings, and the 1838 seating plan, are intriguing in that they show two aisles, diving the seating into three blocks. So what happened at a wedding? Did the bride process down one aisle and the groom down the other? And what about funerals? There are no reports in the press that offer any hints as to how this situation was dealt with.

It is also not clear how the money (£1,882) was raised for the enlargement (probably by subscription – there is a reference to the contribution of £20 made by Queen Adelaide) but it is recorded that: *"The first stone in the erection of the new aisles of Moulsham Church was laid towards the end of April by Mr H. Guy, one of the main contributors to the improvement"*[43] and by 23 April the work was well under way. It was further reported that, *"The work of widening the walls* (sic) *and extending the accommodation of the building, so that the areas majority of the inhabitants of the hamlet may enjoy the full means of public worship, has commenced, and is being carried out with a vigorous hand. The architect has found it necessary in extending his line for the new foundations for the new aisles to disturb a few of the graves, but where this has been the case, the coffins, which, from none of them having been deposited in the earth more than a few years, were in a good state of preservation, were removed with every care and decency and lowered to* (sic) *new graves provided for them. The extensions which we have described, will now be rapidly proceeded with, and ere many months we shall see an important addition to the church room of the district."*[44] The work proceeded rapidly through the summer and by September the *Chelmsford Chronicle* was able report that: *"the alterations in this church... ...are rapidly approaching completion; it is hoped by the first or second week in the ensuing month the doors of the sacred edifice will again open for divine service. It is now a spacious and most commodious building: and the only feeling of regret connected with it is that the funds are now inadequate to meet the charge of the work. We learn, however, that Lady Mildmay has subscribed £50, and this example, we hope, will stimulate the liberality of others, so that those who have taken so warm an interest in the matter may have the satisfaction of re-opening the church free from encumbrance."*[45] In spite of the traditional St John's albatross re-appearing (in other words, the church was short of money to pay for these improvements) the work was completed by the end of October and was re-opened for divine worship on Thursday the twenty-third. At this service the sermon was preached by the Archdeacon of St Albans based on verse eight of the first chapter of the Acts of the Apostles. The reverends Christopher Muston, Carew Anthony St John Mildmay and Henry Hawkins (the recently appointed first curate of St John's) assisted in the service which was very well attended. A Miss Brown presided at the organ (although according to the records, no organ was installed in the church until 1858, so she may have played something like a harmonium). The re-opening was followed by the inevitable cold collation (for those that mattered – but then St John's has always been very good at food and drink) at which it was reported that a sum of nearly £300 was still required to clear the expenses still outstanding. The *Chelmsford Chronicle* went on to state how the committee had been very keen to ensure the additions to the earlier building had kept the appropriate form and character of the original and stressed this point in all their dealings with the Diocesan Architect. It had been Mr Clarke's idea simply to have additional transepts and an enlarged chancel, and this had duly been the basis of his modifications. The new arrangements included a chancel with proper choir (or chancel seats) and arches open on each side of the aisles. The altar was now placed on steps in front of a triplet window, formed internally under one arch. The new stained glass, including the vesica window, was executed by Mr Hudson of Pentonville and paid for jointly by the ladies of St John's and Mr Henry Guy. At the time of the re-opening for divine service, the Creed, the Lord's Prayer and the Ten Commandments had still not been painted, but this work was completed shortly afterwards. All the new stonework was of Coombedown or Somerset stone and the opportunity was taken during the additions to lay the floor with tiles. It was regretted that the funds had not extended to the planned new tower and spire (St John's would have to wait another thirty years for a tower, and never got a spire) but all connected with the project were full of praise for the contractor (Mr George Myers of London) who had shown great skill and attention to detail in carrying out the alterations.[46]

'His own dear little church'

Henry Guy was born in the High Street, Chelmsford, on 18 September 1783 and christened in the parish church of St Mary the Virgin by the then rector, John Morgan, on 12 October of that same year.[47] His father, Boaz Guy junior, a miller (and a widower) had married Mary Holmes of Chelmsford on 28 January 1783 and Henry was their eldest child. He was followed by three brothers and two sisters, one brother (Edmund) dying in infancy in 1788. The Guy family were well-established in Chelmsford. Henry's grandfather, Boaz Guy senior, had been the miller at Bishop's Hall Mill and Boaz junior had started his commercial career selling sweetmeats at the Old Flour shop near the Spotted Dog in Back Street.[48] Henry grew up in Chelmsford, and with his family's widespread business contacts, was soon able to set himself up as a bookseller with premises in the High Street. In 1808, disaster struck near Henry's shop when fire broke out in the early hours of 18 March at Bretons on Poultry Hill (now the site of 77 High Street). A number of individuals were trapped on the upper floors of the house, and Henry Guy distinguished himself by climbing up a ladder and rescuing a child from certain death in the flames, an action which said much about the character of this young man.[49]

This episode must have brought his name to the attention of some of the prominent people in the town as he was elected High Sherriff of the Hundred later in the year. His business as a bookseller grew, and he expanded into publishing, his *"Circumstantial Account of the proceedings which took place in Chelmsford, on Tuesday 19 July 1821"* (celebrations for the Coronation of King George IV) proving a local bestseller. In 1834 he was appointed by the Corporation of the Royal Exchange Company to the prestigious and well-remunerated post of Agent for Chelmsford and Central Essex.[50] This position, together with his other business interests, set him well on the way to becoming a wealthy man. He was one of the first to subscribe to the New Chapel in Moulsham in 1836, and for its consecration he generously donated the communion plate as part of its furnishings. He acquired additional property in the High Street but with the

41

increasing noise and bustle of the thriving town decided that he and his wife Jane would move somewhere quieter. In 1845 he had built an imposing residence, Hamlet House (now Dovedale House, part of Chelmsford college) in what was then very quiet countryside south-west of St John's church. He played a prominent role in the first major expansion of St John's, and in his will provided munificently for the future of what he called; *"his own dear little church"*, leaving £3,000 *"to be invested, and the income to be paid to the incumbent of St John's Church, Moulsham, on condition that evening service is performed there every Sunday ... ... and on condition that no pew rents are to be raised for the purposes of augmenting the income of the incumbent"*.

His will also included benefaction to provide fuel for the local poor and substantial sums for local schools, among them St John's school and the Charity school. In all, he left more than £11,000, a substantial sum for the period.[51] He died on 15 October 1859, not long after his great friend Christopher Muston, having not only given generous donations to the church but also having served as people's warden for many years. Christopher Muston's successor as incumbent, Alfred Mason, speaking on the Sunday after Henry Guy's funeral (which took place on 22 October) said that he had seen *"tears on the faces of many at his graveside"*. His widow Jane continued to live at Hamlet House until her death in July 1861. They are buried together in St John's churchyard in a grave with a coffin-shaped coped stone top surmounted with a carved ornamental cross, next to the grave of Christopher Muston and his family, near the vestry door on the south-east corner of the church. Henry Guy is also commemorated by the large tablet of white Sicilian marble inlaid with black and coloured marble on the south wall of the nave.

'To meet him in the street was a privilege and a delight'

By the late 1840s the growing congregation, together with the plans for the expansion of the building, meant a significantly increased workload for the incumbent. Christopher Muston, whose health was always slightly precarious, felt the need for assistance. By then, James Hutchinson was in his late sixties and was finding his duties at the Grammar school and St Mary's left him little time to come to St John's and assist with the services. The need for an additional priest was pressing. In early 1844 Christopher Muston was preferred to the perpetual curacy of St John's[52] and with his income from his writing now significant, he started to look for an assistant. The search was not easy. To many, St John's must have fallen ''twixt heaven and hell' – neither a wealthy, well-appointed parish (for those clergy who wanted a comfortable and cultured start to their ministry) nor truly vocational, as were many of the difficult, poor parishes of East London (for those clergy who felt that was where their true calling lay). However, after diligent enquiry Henry Hawkins was duly licensed to assist Christopher Muston in the parish.

Henry Hawkins was born on 25 September 1825 at St Pancras, London, the son of Francis James Hawkins, a prominent surgeon, and Mary Hancock. He was baptised on 26 January 1826 at St Stephen's, Walbrook in the City of London.[53] He grew up in the family home in the little village of Gosmore in Hertfordshire, now almost swallowed up in the conurbation of Hitchin. From an early age he was tutored by Rev John May, a man who exercised great influence on the young Henry. Henry Hawkins was educated at Exeter College, Oxford, where he matriculated 15 February 1844, aged eighteen. He graduated BA in 1848 and MA in 1859. After his spell at Oxford he attended Wells theological college from 1848 to 1849 and was ordained deacon by the Bishop of Rochester in June of the latter year.[54] He took his first baptism at St John's in July 1849 and conscientiously carried out his duties assisting Christopher Muston until April 1852 when he left St John's to be licensed as a curate in Barking. His tutor, John May, had instilled in him a deep love for the most down-trodden individuals in Victorian society – the poor and mentally ill – (John May went on to be one of the first chaplains to an asylum) and he clearly showed his love and concern for the many individuals in his first parish who fell in these categories, making his feelings for the poor

Figure 9 – The Rev Henry Hawkins, the first curate of St John's,
Moulsham. A photograph taken in middle age (from the website of
'Together', the mental health charity he helped to found)

known in his sermons and strongly emphasising what the attitude
of the true Christian should be. While curate at St John's, he lived in
New London Road, near Christopher Muston, lodging in the house
of a widow, Mary Ann Arthy, whose unmarried son Charles
worked for Henry Guy. Henry Hawkins' days in Chelmsford were
not unclouded by pain; his beloved younger sister Matilda died
aged ten, in 1850, when Henry was twenty-five.

In May 1853, while he was a curate in Barking. he married his
cousin Mary Hawkins. It was a happy marriage that produced

four sons and four daughters, although two of the sons died young. Following their marriage, Henry and Mary moved to Sussex, where Henry had obtained a post as a curate at Cuckfield. The post of chaplain to the nearby Sussex County Asylum in Hayward's Heath became vacant in 1859 and Henry Hawkins realised where his true vocation in life lay. He was appointed to this position the same year and held it until 1867. He revealed himself as a caring, loving priest and by making a number of small alterations in procedures, brought about marked improvements in the lives of the inmates. He brought in, for example, a number of outside speakers to give talks to the inmates, some of whom for the first time began to perceive that their lives, too, had value.

In 1867 Henry Hawkins moved to the chaplain's post at the Middlesex County Pauper Asylum at Colney Hatch, and here he stayed for the rest of his working life. It was the largest asylum in Europe when built, holding over 2,000 patients. Here, whilst being a compassionate chaplain and champion of the poor and the underdog, Henry wrote many books for SPCK on the subject of the mentally ill, perhaps taking Christopher Muston's example very much to heart. However, Henry's most lasting legacy began in 1879 when, after writing a seminal paper for the *Journal of Medical Science* on the subject of 'after care' (for those individuals leaving the asylum) he organised a meeting of a group of some of the most important names in the psychiatric field as a result of which the charity 'Together' was founded. The charity 'Together' is still as functional and as necessary today as it was in 1879, and is now the country's oldest community health charity.[55]

Henry Hawkins had indeed left a legacy of which he could be proud. He died on 16 December 1904, aged 79, after a short illness, and was buried at St James the Great in Friern Barnet. In a photograph taken in middle age (*Figure 9*) he appears as a firm, committed individual with just a hint that beneath this slightly waspish exterior lurked a warm and generous christian heart. Perhaps the words of the obituary in his parish magazine give the best clue to understanding the first of many curates to share the cure of souls at St John's Moulsham: *"To meet him in the street was a privilege and a delight, and one hears on every side how his pleasant little greetings, his humorous sayings or his tender words of sympathy have been welcomed and treasured by all who receive them."* The first curate of St John's, Moulsham, was going to be a hard act to follow.

'All clergymen of the Church of England'

Henry Hawkins' replacement as curate of St John's was ordained deacon by the Bishop of Rochester in January 1853 and was licensed almost immediately. Peter Rivers de Jersey was born early in 1829 in Claremont Place, St Peter Port, Guernsey. His father, Peter de Jersey senior was a fellow of the Royal College of Surgeons who married Harriet Maingay, the daughter of Nicholas Maingay, of Court Street, Guernsey, in 1821. Peter de Jersey had two brothers, Frederick and Charles Carey, and all three sons became clergymen of the Church of England. Moreover, all three made the long journey from Guernsey to be educated at Shrewsbury school and subsequently to Oxford.[55] Peter de Jersey matriculated at Trinity College on 8 March 1849, aged 20. He took his BA in 1852 and his MA in 1855. He was ordained deacon in 1853 by the Bishop of Rochester and priest in December the same year, at Archbishop Tennison's Chapel in London. He was licensed at St John's at the beginning of 1853 where he took his first baptism on 30 January, signing the register in a small, neat hand. He stayed as curate at St John's for two whole years before moving as curate to Doddington near St Neot's. Here he met and married Octavia Rebecca Wilkinson of Eaton Socon, Bedfordshire early in 1860. He moved to the tiny Norfolk village of Aslacton in 1865 as vicar for four years. His final move was to the much more prestigious incumbency of Empshott near Petersfield in Hampshire. He died in Empshott early in 1890, at the relatively young age of 61, leaving two daughters (Isabella and Nora) and a son (Octavius) as well as his widow. He seems to have had but slight impact on St John's (there being no press reports of presentations on his departure) and there are no details of his final service.

'A calf walked into Moulsham Church'

Peter de Jersey was followed as curate of St John's by the wonderfully-named William Osborne Pocock Wilson. He was born in 1831, the eldest son of William Gittens Wilson, gentleman, of St George's, Bristol. He went up to Balliol College, Oxford, where he matriculated on 13 June 1849, aged 18, and graduated BA in 1853 and MA in 1857. He was ordained deacon by the Bishop of Rochester on 24 December 1854 and priest by the same bishop, in Archbishop Tennison's Chapel , on 21 December 1855. He was licensed at St John's in March 1855, taking his first baptism almost straight away. He stayed at St John's until January 1857, moving as curate to Sonning (1857–63) and then Wokingham (1863–68) where he also officiated as workhouse chaplain. He then returned to Essex in 1868 as Rector of Holy Trinity, Colchester and was then clearly in a position to marry, being the incumbent of an important church in what was another thriving Essex town. He (as many young clergy at that time) sought to make a good marriage, choosing as his bride the youngest daughter of Frederick Thomas Veley, who had been a small girl aged eight when he first met her at St John's. They were married in Chelmsford in September 1869. William Wilson has the distinction of being the only clergyman of St John's to have graced the pages of 'Punch'. In September 1855, under the heading 'A Prodigy in the Pulpit', the following short lampoon appeared (and it is worth quoting in full):

"Some times in ancient Rome the ox used to speak but till lately the bovine species has not been known to utter articulate language in this country. Rustics, of all people, have the greatest experience of horned cattle; yet no rural person, worthy of credit has asserted himself to have heard any animal of that kind from time immemorial up to Sunday 26th ult., when according to a statement made to the 'Times' by 'A Militiaman' of the West Essex Regiment, a calf walked into Moulsham Church, ascended the pulpit, and pronounced the following words:-

"Now the people of the City of Corinth were exceedingly wicked people, for they were idolators and indulged in evil and idle sports; and the people of Chelmsford would be equally as wicked as the people of the City of Corinth if they (the people of Chelmsford) were all like the Militia"

The calf, then says the MILITIAMAN 'Proceeded with his sermon wherein he expressed himself as follows upon his own responsibility:-

*"That the people of Chelmsford were tired and
disgusted with the Militia, and that they
(the Militia) were a perfect nuisance to the town,
that the people of Chelmsford wished them away;
that the Militia were going headlong to
Hell – nay – everyday deeper and deeper".*

Sensible, no doubt, that these assertions would encounter general incredulity, the MILITIAMAN does not call the calf a calf, but names it the Reverend Mr Wilson. But surely, it is more easy to believe that the language above quoted proceeded from a calf than a clergyman. Yes – beyond doubt, it the words were uttered at all, the tongue that spoke them might be an ingredient of mock-turtle, and the possessor of that organ must be one of the Essex calves."[57]

Strong stuff. But it is certainly true that at that time there was much ill-feeling and discontent with the presence and the behaviour of the West Essex Militia in the town and it seems that William Wilson was only voicing the thoughts of many of his congregation with his comments from the pulpit. After his spell in Colchester he moved to Little Laver as Rector from 1876 to 1878, before taking up his final incumbency as Rector of the little parish of Huntspill in the Somerset levels in 1878. Here he saw out his time as a priest, dying in Newton Abbott in late 1897, aged 67.

'He served God and his fellow parishioners with love and dedication'

Walter James Sowerby was the son of Thomas Benn Sowerby, a pawnbroker of Long Acre, and his wife Eleanor. He was born 6 May 1832 in the parish of St Martin-in-the-Fields where he was baptised the following 5 June. He attended Blackheath school, from whence (in spite of his less than auspicious origins) he was admitted as a pensioner to St John's College, Cambridge, where he matriculated at Michaelmas 1851. He graduated BA in 1855 and MA in 1858. He was ordained deacon in 1856 and priest by the Bishop of Rochester in Mercer's Chapel, London on 20 December 1857. He took his first baptism at St John's on 2 February 1857 and his last before he moved on 24 December 1858. He made the not uncommon move from Chelmsford to Romford, serving as curate at St Edward's from 1859 to 1863. He followed this with a curacy at Lewisham for no less than six years (to 1869) and was then appointed as vicar of Eltham, Kent, a post he held until he retired in 1895. He had married Eliza Jane McRae in 1869 (as soon as he knew he had a firm offer from Eltham). He and Eliza retired to Shanklin in the Isle of Wight where he died at the grand old age of 91. He never sought the limelight quite like his predecessor, but served God and his fellow parishioners quietly with love and dedication.

'The friends of Mr Pennington contemplated the erection of a place of worship in which he might officiate'

Lewis Theodore Pennington was, in contrast to his predecessor, something of an enigma. He was only at St John's for just one year, served with great devotion, and received heartfelt tributes from the poor when he left, yet his time at St John's raises many questions which remain unanswered to this day. His subsequent existence, too, seems riddled with inconsistencies. Lewis Pennington was born, probably sometime in 1828, in Alford, Lincolnshire. He was the son of Rowland Pennington and Georgina Wells, who had in turn been married in the church of St Mary Woolnoth and

Woolchurch Haw, London, on 16 April 1818. Lewis Pennington trained at St Bees, graduating in 1851, and was ordained deacon by the Bishop of Bath and Wells in 1853 and priest by him in 1854. It was not until 1858 that he came to St John's, taking his first baptism in October, but it is not clear what his actual position was in the church. When Lewis Pennington arrived, Christopher Muston was still the incumbent, but increasing ill-health was rendering his participation in the running of the church less and less. Perhaps something of this was communicated to Lewis Pennington before (or when) he arrived, because from the outset he signed himself 'Officiating Minister', never curate, and it appears that he always took precedence over Walter Sowerby, who had already been there as curate for over a year. It is not apparent whether or not any understanding existed as to his taking over from Christopher Muston, but until the end of his period at St John's he seems to have thought so, as clearly did a substantial proportion of the congregation. By the beginning of September 1859 Alfred Mason had been installed as the new incumbent and the writing was on the wall for any dreams Lewis Pennington may have had at St John's.

However, his departure from the parish did not go unnoticed. On the evening of 20 September 1859... *"a deputation waited upon the Rev L.T. Pennington, the late Assistant Minister (sic) of St John's Church, Moulsham, to present a testimonial, which had been subscribed by the members of the congregation of the above-named church. This consisted of a handsome silver salver, and a purse containing £50, the following inscription engraved on the salver: 'Presented, with a purse of £50, to the Rev Lewis T. Pennington, by the congregation of St John's Church, Moulsham as an evidence of their appreciation of his Christian worth, as evinced in his unwearied labours in the church, the schools and the district generally; with heartfelt prayers for his future and eternal welfare.– 23 September 1859.' There was also a demonstration of the same feeling on the part of the teachers and children of the Sunday School, in which Mr Pennington has always taken a warm interest. The girls, their teachers and friends presented a massive gold pencil case and an exquisitely designed paper knife. The boys and their teachers came forward with an elegant silver cream jug, with the inscription. – 'Presented to the Reverend L.T. Pennington, as a mark of esteem, by the teachers and children of St John's Sunday School, Moulsham, on his leaving them – A.D. 1859'. We understand that each child in the school was presented with a Bible, a prayer-book or a hymn-book. We think these testimonials of regard and esteem need no comment – suffice it to say that the reverend gentleman had only been twelve months in the parish.*"[58] However, this was not quite the end of his connection with the parish, as in December of that year it was also reported that: "*...it has been generally understood in the neighbourhood that the friends of Mr Pennington, the late curate of Moulsham, contemplated the erection of a place of worship in which he might officiate. Application on this subject was made to the Bishop of Rochester but his Lordship has declined to sanction the erection of a new church for the purpose in the parish, alleging as a reason that it would lead to the introduction of schism where harmony had so long prevailed.*"[59] Obviously the parish came very close to splitting in 1859, although there are no details of how large a group the *"friends of Mr Pennington"* were. It seems likely that he was given some hint or hints during his time at St John's that he might be offered the incumbency in place of the ailing Christopher Muston, but nothing ever came of it. Perhaps Lewis Pennington's non-Oxbridge background (St Bees) and the marked way in which he endeared himself to the poor and working class of the parish got up the nose of the established clergy, and that Rector Mildmay (the patron of the living) ended up having cold feet. He proceeded to appoint Alfred William Mason (already a curate at St Mary's in 1858) as a much safer pair of hands to whom the parish could be entrusted.

Lewis Pennington's entry in *Crockford's* (1883) continued the pattern of inconsistencies. He was listed as Assistant Minister of St John's, Moulsham, 1859–69 (*sic*). He followed his year at St John's with curacies at Workington (1865–71), Tongue with Alkrington (1871–74) and Husband's Bosworth (1874–78) before becoming vicar of Grimston with Wartnaby from 1876 to 1877 (*sic*), Rector of Gretworth (1877–80) (*sic*) and finally vicar of Englishcombe, Somerset, from 1881 to 1882. There is a Lewis Theodore Pennington living in Hove, Sussex together with his wife Beatrice Ernestine Florence, whom he married in 1893, in a subsequent census, but both their ages are markedly different from this that would be expected – Lewis' age is given as 53 (when it should be 73) and Beatrice's as 48 (instead of 70). Lewis Theodore Pennington died at Steyning, Sussex in 1909 and his age was given as 77, not 81. Beatrice appears to have died in Paris in 1928, aged 58, but again this age is completely at variance with the other figures.

'An energetic white-bearded man who rode about the village of a tricycle'

Newman Tibbits was the son of William Bullock Tibbits and his wife Mary. He was born at Smeaton Westerby on 4 December 1833 and baptised at Our Langton, Leicestershire, on 5 January 1834. He attended Mr West's school in Northampton, followed by Mr Barratt's school in Dawlish before ending up in Dr Brereton's Academy in Bedford. He matriculated at Michaelmas 1852 and graduated BA from Sidney Sussex College, Cambridge in 1856. He was ordained deacon in 1858 and priest in 1859 by the Bishop of Rochester. He was licensed at the end of 1858 to St John's, just a few months after Lewis Pennington arrived as curate; this gives some indication of how ailing Christopher Muston was by this time. In the absence of an incumbent, as least two clergy would be required to cover the duties of the parish. After his spell in Moulsham, Newman Tibbits moved to Connington (Huntingdonshire) as curate (1860–63), Warboys as curate (1863–66), St John the Evangelist, Clifton, again as curate (1867) moving on (still as curate) to Redland, Gloucestershire (1867–70) and then Stoke Gifford (1870–73). When Newman Tibbits came to this latter parish the living had already been vacant for some seven years. It was said that the previous vicar (George Salt) and the other applicants for the post left because they could not stand the noise of the trains on the nearby main line to Bristol, which ran right past the vicarage. After his appointment as vicar, Newman Tibbits lodged at Court Farm until the vicarage had been decorated to his satisfaction. Here he stayed for forty-five years, marrying a local woman, Alice Julia Mortimer in 1893 (she was a year older than him). It was said that older people in Stoke Gifford remember the vicar as a caring and white-bearded man who rode around the village on a tricycle made by the local postman, George Taylor. Alice predeceased her husband, dying in 1912, aged 79, and Newman himself died in Clifton, Bristol (where he had retired) in June 1918, aged eighty-four. They are both buried in the churchyard at Stoke Gifford.[60]

Christopher Muston was still living in Moulsham Street when his first child, Isabella Elizabeth Muston was born in 1842. With the possibility of an expanding family and the necessity of having domestic staff appropriate to an incumbent, the simple house where he had lodged, initially on his own, would no longer suffice, and as early as 1845 he had written to Bishop Blomfield about his ideas to provide a parsonage house for St John's. The Bishop replied: *"Of course I can have no objection to your endeavouring to provide a house annexed to St John's, Moulsham; this being, in my opinion, as I believe I stated to you on a former occasion, the most eligible mode of augmentation. Whether or not this should be attempted by means of a subscription is a question I am not able to determine without more information as to the probability of your succeeding in your application. You will of course consult with Mr Mildmay on the subject."*[61] By 1845 Christopher Muston had decided that he would be happy to spend the foreseeable future in Moulsham – perhaps encouraged by the *Chelmsford Chronicle's* slightly patronising report in 1843 that: *"We have this week to note another of those pleasing instances that prove the respect and affectionate feeling that exists between the clergy and the humbler portion of their flocks. The poor of the hamlet of Moulsham, feeling deeply grateful to the Rev C.R. Muston, for the diligent care he has evinced for their welfare, particularly for the useful and edifying weekly lectures which he has delivered, resolved on presenting to him, by a subscription raised among themselves, a silver cream jug. Accordingly a handsome cream jug was procured ... ...and was last month forwarded to the rev. gentleman, with a letter in which the humble but grateful subscribers by his acceptance of the token as a proof of their attachment to him as their pastor and minister; and while regretting the smallness of the gift, they express a hope that they may long continue to enjoy the advantage of his spiritual superintendence. This letter, subscribed by the poor of Moulsham and this gift purchased by their well-earned mites of honest industry* (sic) *must prove as gratifying and encouraging to the rev. gentleman in his path of duty, as the costly and more formal tribute which wealth could offer him.*"[62] Also in late 1843 the official notice had been published preferring Christopher Muston (described as the 'Officiating Minister') to the perpetual curacy of St John's, Moulsham. More children continued to fill the small house in Moulsham Street; Caroline Amelia, baptised 6 August 1843; Christopher Pearson, baptised 2 November 1845 and Evelina, baptised 3 March 1847. Although there is no record of their births being registered in England, it is possible that they were born in Rotterdam, where Katharine's parents still lived. Sadly, as happened in many Victorian families, tragedy did not wait too long to visit the Muston household. Christopher Pearson, their only son, died less than a year old in 1846, just after Christopher Muston's unmarried sister Elizabeth. Caroline Amelia died in February 1854, aged eleven, and their eldest daughter Isabella died aged fourteen on Holy Innocents' day 1854. Christopher and Katharine must indeed have had their faith tested to the limit.

Christopher Muston had not entirely lost his academic inclinations. He was a prominent member of the Essex Church Schoolmasters' Association and in 1848 he delivered a comprehensive lecture on: *"The Pictorial Method of Instruction"* to the Association at a meeting in Witham.[63] A parsonage still remained high on Christopher Muston's wish list and in 1856 Baedel and Sons prepared a handsome design (*Figure 11*) for a large parsonage

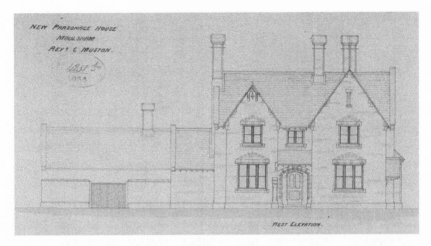

Figure 10 – Baedel and Sons' design for the parsonage house in Vicarage Road, which Rev Christopher Muston had built for himself (and his successors). This is the view from Vicarage Road

house, complete with stables and accommodation for a coach, to be built in what were then empty fields just to the east of Long Stumps Lane (now Vicarage Road). The substantial costs of this building were met by subscriptions, grants and a hefty slice of Christopher Muston's own money. Christopher Muston was never really able to make much use of it. For the last two or so years of his service in the parish the dreaded (but not uncommon) spectre of consumption had hung over his head, and towards the end of his incumbency he was forced to make periodic trips to the seaside where the air was thought to be much healthier, if not a cure. There it was that he died on 6 August at a Boarding house, 5, Eastcliffe, Dover, where his landlady, Sarah Mabb registered his death.[64] He left a widow, Katharine, and one surviving daughter, Evelina. Neither survived him very long. Evelina died at her college in Bromley, Kent on Boxing day, 1864, aged only eighteen, and her mother died in 1879 after living for many years with her widowed sister in Twickenham. In his will (probate was granted late in 1859) he left the very modest sum of just under £600.

The *Chelmsford Chronicle* reported that: "*The remains of the reverend gentleman having been brought to the parsonage (on Wednesday, 10 August 1859) the funeral took place under the superintendence of Messrs. J. and S. Wackrill, about forty of the inhabitants of the town and hamlet assembling in the sad procession, to testify their respect for the deceased. These were followed by the schoolchildren, two and two, then came the Reverend C.A. St John Mildmay and the Rev L.T. Pennington. The following gentlemen, the present and former curates of the district were the pall bearers – the Revs N. Tibbits, J. Sowerby, Hawkins and W.J. Wilson (sic). The mourners included the Revs W. Buswell, G.B. Hamilton, W.C. Arnold, A.W. Bullen, C. Dalton, J.C. Bingley and A. Pearson: T.M. Gepp, F.T. Veley, Esq, J.T. Gilson, Esq, Mr J. Saltmarsh and Mr F. Veley, jun. Large numbers of tradesmen and humbler classes gathered on the occasion, filling the church and thronging the churchyard, and while the service was read by the Rev C.A. St John Mildmay, their demeanour showed how fully the deceased had won the regard of those amongst whom he had ministered as pastor for nearly 20 years. The gift of the living is in the hands of the rector of Chelmsford, who has presented the Rev A.W. Mason, one of the curates of St Mary's parish."*[1]

So ends Christopher Muston's incumbency of St John's. He is commemorated by the fine stone wall memorial in the shape of a church window located on the north wall of the chancel carved by the local stonemason Hardy. However, it is incorrect. Christopher Muston was in his sixty-fourth year when he died, not aged sixty-four (although his death certificate also gives his age incorrectly, as sixty-five). But it is a fine monument to a man who devoted almost a third of his life to St John's. He was responsible for building up St John's on the rock of Christian love and service and he left it an attractive and forward looking church which could easily be of interest to a dynamic and devoted priest. Somehow, though, he never quite fitted in. This is best illustrated by a Public Meeting held in Chelmsford in August 1848 to consider some fitting testimonial to the late Lord Chief Justice Tindall. The great and the good of the town rushed to propose their effusive motions – yet all Christopher Muston was able to contribute was to second a vote of thanks to the chair, the worthy Rector.[65] Compared with those who counted in Chelmsford, Christopher Muston was still on the fringe; yet all Chelmsford was the poorer for his passing. He is also, sadly, the only incumbent of St John's for whom it has not been possible so far to trace a portrait.

3. ALFRED WILLIAM MASON

(1859–77)

*"We fully believe that your faithful and devoted ministry,
and truly consistent life and example over a residence of more
than seventeen years have had its beneficial effect, and we trust
that you will derive comfort in that belief"*[1]

So read one of the multitude of tributes, in this case from ordinary parishioners, to Alfred William Mason, when he left St John's in 1877, to move back to his beloved Dedham, as vicar. Worn out by his unstinting efforts to improve the lot of everyone in the parish, he reluctantly felt that he needed a physically less demanding post, and Dedham offered just that. He was to live another thirteen years, but of all his ministries, St John's is probably the one for which he is best remembered and where he made the most impact in his life.

'Not altogether with the assent of the Parish generally'

Alfred William Mason was born on 13 December 1818 at Berner Street, just off Commercial Road, Stepney, in the troublesome parish of St George-in-the-East. His parents were Alfred William Mason and his wife, Harriet. His father was a respected surveyor.[2] Berner Street in the early nineteenth century was a leafy, rural area of some note, and the dutiful parents had Alfred William junior christened at St George-in-the-East on 22 January 1819. In due time Alfred William was packed off to the well-known Endowed School at Dedham where he developed his great fondness for the place, being taught by the Rev George Taylor.[3] He was admitted as a pensioner to Trinity College, Cambridge on 28 March 1839, matriculating at Michaelmas of that year. He graduated BA in 1843 and MA in 1847 and was ordained deacon in 1843 and priest in 1844 in Canterbury Cathedral by Archbishop Howley. His first appointment in 1843 was as curate at Bocking, from whence he moved to Stamford Hill in 1848 and Loughton in 1852.[4] In 1858, perhaps with an eye to filling the imminent vacancy at St John's (Christopher Muston was, by then, already a very sick man) Alfred Mason was appointed a curate at St Mary's, Chelmsford, by the rector, Rev Carew Anthony St John Mildmay. On 8 June he took his first baptism at St Mary's, signing himself 'Officiating Minister'. At his next baptism, on 13 June, he signed as 'curate', suggesting that he was licensed at St Mary's in the second week of June 1858.[5] The announcement of his appointment to St John's was made with almost indecent haste almost immediately after Christopher Muston's funeral.[6] He took up his duties at once, but still helped out at St Mary's, where he took a marriage in October 1859, signing the register as 'incumbent of Moulsham'.[7] He had married Harriet Glaister Harris in West Ham in 1857[8] they were to have no children.

So Alfred Mason came to Moulsham. He came quite diffidently, as he himself said: *"As a stranger, and perhaps not altogether with the assent of the parish generally"*. There were clearly still some parishioners that felt that Lewis Pennington should have been offered the incumbency and who felt that their wishes had been ignored. However, he received a very warm welcome from Frederick Veley and also from Thomas Wackrill. Alfred Mason was deeply impressed by the warmth of that welcome, and Frederick Veley in particular was an enormous help to the forty year-year-old taking charge of his first parish, guiding him in the legal niceties as only a lawyer with long ecclesiastical experience could. Joseph Saltmarsh, the first Chapel warden, who served until 1864 (he died in 1872) was also a tower of strength in the early days. Alfred Mason was a priest who believed in giving his all to his duty of the cure of people's souls. He himself related the story of how, when he was a young man, working very hard in his first curacy at Bocking, Archdeacon Jones (the archdeacon of Essex) had told Alfred Mason's father a little fable: *"Tell your son that several years ago there were two coach horses. One was a very high-mettled fellow, and would do all the work. The other was several years older, and took it all very quietly, letting the young one do all the work for him. The consequence was that the young and high-mettled horse wore himself out in a little time and that the old stager is running, still"*. Alfred Mason admitted that he had worked very hard for the first two-and-half years in Bocking, perhaps too hard, and it had taken the rest of his spell in that parish to recover.[9]

'To promote the education of poor children'

One of the first tasks to which Alfred Mason turned his attention on taking up his incumbency was the provision of more efficient Church School accommodation. In her 1836 donation of land used for the building of St John's, Lady Mildmay had given the plot (larger than the present churchyard of St John's) in trust to the rector and churchwardens of St Mary's for the purpose (as stated in the trust deed) of erecting school buildings: *"in order to promote the education of poor children in the principles of true religion and useful knowledge"*. In 1840, not long after the consecration of St John's, an infants' schoolroom had been erected on the site, under the superintendence of Christopher Muston, and although adequate in its early days, by the late 1850s it was clear that more accommodation was needed. The building was then pulled down, and in 1860 Frederick Chancellor prepared new plans for St John's National School.[10] The site having been cleared, and with Alfred Mason's enthusiastic backing (and his deep purse) new buildings were constructed. The Bishop of Rochester (Chelmsford was now, however impractical the idea was, in the Diocese of Rochester) himself laying the foundation stone in July 1861. At the appropriate time Alfred Mason and his churchwardens applied for grant-in-aid to the building fund, to the committee of the Privy Council for Education. That committee raised the question of the admission into the trust deed of the Conscience Clause (the clause that permitted parents to withdraw children from Church of England worship or activities if that worship or activity violated the parents' religious principles) but on receiving a decidedly negative response, the committee had waived the question. Alfred Mason was then faced with the hurdle that as the site was part of a charity estate, the Committee of Council required the sanction of the Charity Commissioners to a new deed of trust, and this the Commissioners resolutely refused unless the Conscience Clause was inserted, basing their argument on the vagueness of the original deed and refusing to admit any evidence as to the original intentions of the donor. The Commissioners stated that for them it was an invariable principle that: *"according to a cardinal rule of legal construction, the objects of a trust must be collected solely from the terms of the instrument itself"*. Feeling that according to this requirement, they would be acting plainly contrary to the wishes and intentions of the donor of the site, as well as the purposes to which the building funds were subscribed, Alfred Mason and his churchwardens, ably advised by Frederick Veley, appealed to the Court of Chancery, where, fortunately, Vice-Chancellor Kindersley decided, in August 1862, that: *"the religious opinion of the founder could be given in evidence in order to explain the object of the trust"*. The new school could go ahead, and the Conscience Clause could be rejected.[11]

Building went on apace, and the new school was duly opened for business with a formal ceremony on Wednesday, 24 July 1861. The cost of the whole project was about £1,500, of which Alfred Mason personally contributed about two-thirds. The buildings, on a site adjacent to the church on its north-east side, are still in existence today (2018), although rapidly increasing numbers of children in the parish meant that by 1938 the move to new, purpose-built schools (now Moulsham Junior and Infants' schools) had become essential. Frederick Chancellor's design for St John's school sympathetically used yellow brick (with some red and black brick banding) and is still impressive in its present day guise as St John's Court. The structure, erected by Mr J. Brown, builder, of Braintree, included large boys' and girls' rooms and a smaller infants' room. The boys had their own hat room and the girls were provided with a bonnet room. One of the striking features of the buildings was the bell tower which not only housed the means of summoning the scholars each morning but also provided the school rooms with much needed ventilation during the summer.

Archdeacon Mildmay preached the sermon at the dedication service, which was then followed by a typical St John's jollification. The children all tumbled out of the church and into their new school rooms, where tea, bread-and-butter and cake awaited them along with the inevitable social cup for the adults. The band of the West Essex Militia, in attendance through the kind permission of Colonel Brise, contributed greatly to the proceedings. At the end of the feasting, everyone adjourned to Mr Darby's field in Long Stomps (probably the area bounded by Princes Road and Vicarage Road today) where the older children spent the evening playing popular games such as cricket, foot-ball (*sic*) and trap-bat (where the individual throws the ball into the air and endeavours to hit it between two posts some distance away) and the younger ones enjoyed their sweet hunts, races and the swings that had been erected for them. All, old and young, joined in, and the *Chelmsford Chronicle's* part-time poet was again moved, although this time the verse was in slightly more dubious taste:

> *"For it stirs the blood in an old man's heart,*
> *And makes his pulses fly,*
> *catch the gleam of a happy face,*
> *the light of a laughing eye"*[12]

Dancing continued in Mr Darby's field (the band of the West Essex Militia having decamped there) and as dusk fell, after a brief word from Alfred Mason congratulating everyone present on the success of the day, and proposing: *"… three hearty cheers for Mr Darby for his kindness"*, the evening closed with more cheers for Mr and Mrs Mason and the two curates, George Mallory and William Johnston. The children concluded the proceedings by singing the doxology.

The schools were up and running. From day one St John's church and the church's prominent individuals took a significant role in the management of the schools and the education of the children. Alfred Mason acted a secretary to the school managers and the managers themselves included Jabez Church, Joseph Saltmarsh, Frederick Veley (who also seems to have assumed responsibility for the financial affairs of the schools) and Thomas Tidboald. The school logbook[13] shows how closely involved with the children's education Alfred Mason and his curates were. Alfred Mason visited the school at least once a week (often more frequently) and we find him (and the curates) frequently *"taking first class for scripture"* or *"taking first class on the Duty towards God"*. The visits were not always to a full and enthusiastic school. There are also entries such as that on 2 June 1863 where: *"Attendance was poor owing to an afternoon performance of Sawyer's Circus – children being admitted on a small payment of 2d."* which shows that, in spite of the rejection of the Conscience Clause, power other than the Almighty's was at work in the hearts and minds of the young who attended the school. The schools were, however, to be one of Alfred Mason's great legacies to the parish of St John the Evangelist, Moulsham.

Life continued in its own quiet way in Moulsham. In 1863 it improved a little for the poor of the parish, as the first distribution of fuel to them from Henry Guy's charity took place in January. In his will he had directed (among many other generous charitable requests) that: *"£800 be invested and the income distributed in coals or fuel every new year's day amongst the necessitous inhabitants of Chelmsford but so that half should be distributed in Moulsham."*[14] In 1863 too, Alfred Mason had instituted a programme of lectures of a quasi-religious nature (mainly aimed at the working man) to raise money to better equip the schools. A typical lecture was that given by Frederick Veley who talked on the subject of 'Our Talents'. They were well-attended (except when they clashed with volunteers' dinners at the Shire hall) and must have done much to raise the education of the working classes and to engender a sense of community in Moulsham.[15] Moulsham now had another substantial Chapel in the district. Although James Fenton's Ebenezer Strict Baptist Chapel had been built just after St John's in 1842, and the Catholic church of Our Lady Immaculate had been consecrated early in 1843, it was not until 1863 when the Primitive Methodists erected their building in Hall Street that another substantial, competing religious building had been constructed in the parish.[16]

In 1864, after long and dedicated service, Joseph Saltmarsh stood down from his position of parish warden (in other words, the warden elected by the parishioners themselves – at this time, the other warden was nominated by the incumbent). He had acted as 'Chapel warden' from the consecration of the building in 1837 and had carried out the duties single-handedly until joined by Henry Guy in the late 1840s. The 1864 Vestry meeting elected Samuel Wackrill to replace him, Frederick Veley being re-appointed as Vicar's warden. The same meeting reluctantly accepted the resignation of Mr James Dace from the position of St John's organist.[17] He had been appointed organist when the first proper instrument was installed in 1858. In 1863 the organ had been removed[18] (it is not clear why) and James Dace felt that his increasing solo and business commitments meant he could no longer give adequate service to St John's.

'He must be a sound churchman'

When Alfred Mason had arrived at St John's, he had effectively taken the place of Lewis Pennington, who had departed very promptly once he had learned that the incumbency of St John's was not to be his. That left Newman Tibbits as the sole curate. He had already served as curate for more than a year by August 1859 and it would not have been unusual if he had wanted to move on. Alfred Mason was under no illusions that he would need more assistance. He was a firm believer in the parish having an effective house-to-house visiting scheme for all the sick and needy (irrespective of their Christian affiliation) and to do this he felt that he needed two full-time curates to assist him. So it was no surprise to see, not long after his arrival in the parish, advertisements such as those that appeared together in an issue of the *Ecclesiastical Gazette*:

"Wanted, at Michaelmas, as CURATE in a
Town Parish, a graduate who will take a zealous and
active part in the duties. He must be a sound
Churchman, and a good reader and
preacher. Stipend, £120

Apply to the Rev A.W. Mason,
Moulsham Parsonage, Chelmsford."

"A TITLE will be given at the December
Ordination of the Bishop of
Rochester, to a sound Churchman, a graduate of Oxford or
Cambridge, willing to devote himself heartily to
the duties of the sacred Ministry. Stipend, £100.

Apply to the Rev A.W. Mason,
Moulsham Parsonage, Chelmsford."[19]

These are generous stipends, and are similar to those offered to curates at St John's towards the end of the nineteenth century. They would also have been sufficient to possibly tempt even an incumbent from a very poor parish. Alfred Mason wanted dedicated clergy with good qualifications to share his work, and by using his own money, he would be able to get exactly the right kind of individual.

Alfred Mason was also keen to encourage the Sunday School, believing it to be a great force for good in the life of the community. In August 1859, not long after his arrival in the parish, he was given a taste of what the Sunday School had become. It was reported that: *"... on Thursday afternoon, the children of the* Sunday *School held high festival in the Park, near the Rising Sun, the materials for furnishing forth the feast* (sic) *being abundantly supplied by different members of the congregation – Mr Hemblen* (sic) *for instance contributing all the bread and butter for the tea party. Shortly after two o'clock, the children, numbering about one hundred and eighty, whose neat and orderly appearance reflected the highest credit on their parents and teachers, marched in procession through the principal streets with flags, banners &etc., headed by the band of the West Essex Militia, and arrived in due time at the park at the entrance of which had been erected an elegant floral arch, with the motto 'Welcome'. The weather was delightfully fine and the park presented a charming spot for the amusements of the children who entered with much zest into the sports provided for them by their benefactors. About half-past four the youngsters were regaled with a bountiful tea an the greensward, and were supplied with bread-and-butter, cake, &etc., ad libitum. A large party of the parents afterwards partook of the social cup, the sports were resumed and a pleasant evening spent, enlivened by the strains of the band."* [20]

In the 1830s in Chelmsford there had been vigorous opposition from Dissenters to the paying of church rates at St Mary's. One of those challenging the validity of the rate, John Thorogood, had become a *cause célèbre*, being imprisoned for his stand. [21] A truce had been called in the dispute in 1855, and all had been quiet for a number of years. However, in 1860, an argument had arisen as to which lands in the parish of St Mary's were to be rateable (and whose owners or tenants were therefore liable to contribute to the Chelmsford Local Board of Health). The latter sought to make a rate on all the properties in the parish, which included the hamlet of Moulsham. After prolonged legal argument in the Court of Queen's Bench, many of the properties in Moulsham were declared to be exempt, mostly on the grounds that they were too far away from the parish church (St Mary's). Had the decision gone the other way, many of the congregation of St John's would have faced hefty increases in bills for their rate. [22]

'No invidious or unchristian distinction between rich and poor'

Throughout the 1860s seating problems continued to affect St John's. Christopher Muston and Henry Guy had worked hard to raise sufficient money from donations and subscriptions in order to remove the bugbear of pew rents and their effects in excluding the poor from the church and their efforts had borne fruit. The church was accessible to all. Accessible, but not, in practice, available to all. The general right of any parishioner (bearing in mind that only those who were settled residents in the parish would be regarded as parishioners) to be accommodated with a seat for themselves and their families in the parish church was indisputable, but in practice this right meant only that an individual was able to apply to the officers of the church (in effect, the churchwardens) to allot him or her adequate accommodation if it was in the churchwardens' power to do so.[23]

The question then arose as to whether or not a pew could be reserved ('appropriated') for a particular family. In nearly all churches such appropriations had become simply a matter of custom; there was no legal basis for this custom. Members of any congregation had been allowed from time immemorial to erect their own box-pew at their own expense but there existed no basis in law that allowed them to exclude others from that pew. It simply became tradition. And with the passage of time it meant that the more important and influential families in the parish sat nearer the chancel (where the action was). The seating of the church was at the discretion (or the whim) of the churchwardens and this continued to cause anger and friction at St John's. At the 1867 Vestry meeting[24] Alfred Mason made a determined effort to solve the problem once and for all. He wrote a formal letter to the churchwardens: *"I am willing at my own expense to carry out the alterations described in the drawings that accompany this letter. These alterations will provide as many appropriated sittings as there are under the present arrangement – and these sittings are placed to cause as little disturbance to the present occupants – and these alterations will also provide the same number of sittings as those that are unappropriated. The benches for these alterations are considerable* (sic) *wider than those which I propose to move out of the Nave, and being uniform throughout the church will suggest no invidious or unchristian distinction between rich and poor ... ... the conditions under which I make*

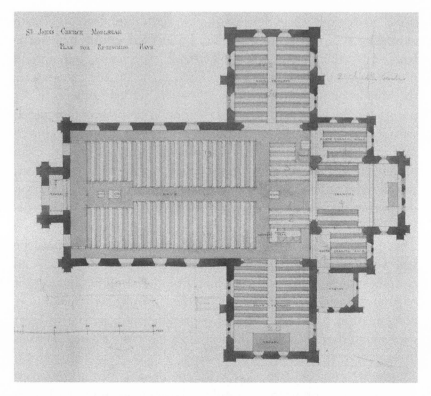

Figure 11 – Proposed 1867 alterations to St John's Church, Moulsham, based on Frederick Chancellor's Drawings

my proposals are that no doors be attached to the sittings; and that the whole of the central benches be entirely unappropriated, and that a notice be affixed to some conspicuous place inside or outside the Church, and also the same publicity to a rule which has long existed, that after the commencement of divine service, all the sittings in every part of the Church which remain unoccupied are free for the use of parishioners". The meeting resolved unanimously that Alfred Mason's proposals be accepted. His proposal also included plans to remove: *"the unsightly and unnecessary Western Gallery"*, which is of interest as it is the only reference so far located to the Gallery, which was provided for in the original specification of 1834 but does not appear in any of the surviving drawings.

Frederick Chancellor's drawing of 1867[25] shows the proposed re-benching scheme in some detail. The two aisles that had been present in the church since its consecration were to be swept away, and a much more conventional arrangement with a central aisle separating the two rows of pews substituted. The central aisle was widened at the west end to accommodate the font and one of the stoves for warming the church (the other was at the front of the pews, conveniently close to the pulpit). The same drawing (*Figure 11*) shows the organ against the south wall of the south transept. The whole arrangement met Alfred Mason's conditions for new, unappropriated sittings, yet it seems that (for whatever reason) it was never implemented. The drawings for the modifications carried out later in Alfred Mason's incumbency (1873–75) show the earlier, two-aisled version of the seating, and it seems that Frederick Chancellor's 1867 re-benching proposals were never implemented.

So Alfred Mason made a serious attempt to confront and remove the ill-feeling which could arise when someone sat in 'someone else's' pew. That such incidents could easily turn violent is illustrated by an example from the north Essex parish of Foxearth, where in 1862, arguments led to an assault, and the assault in turn led to an expensive and divisive court case.[26] Possibly because of the efforts of Alfred Mason, the problem of appropriated pews was swept under the carpet for the rest of his incumbency at St John's, but by 1878 it had resurfaced, and this time it came to a head with very bitter feelings (see chapter 4).

'A most impressive sermon was preached by the incumbent on Christ's forgiveness'

Alfred Mason was also revealing himself to be a very compassionate Christian minister. In 1864, a German who had lived in England for some time, working sporadically as a butcher and as a sugar baker, Karl Kohl, befriended a well-off fellow German named Theodore Furhop, taking him back to live with himself and his wife in Hoy Street, Plaistow. Theodore's headless body was discovered on 2 November by the river Thames near Barking, The head, later discovered nearby, and body had been dreadfully mutilated. Kohl was arrested and convicted of murder, He was executed at Chelmsford gaol, Springfield, on the drop outside the prison walls, facing Springfield Road. Such was the notoriety of the crime and the Victorian passion for lurid voyeurism that no less than 1,500 people (including many children), the vast majority of whom had travelled from east London on the three 'Excursion' trains that the Eastern Counties Railway had run that morning were outside the prison in time for the execution at nine o'clock.[27] Such were Alfred Mason's feelings that a special service was held at the exact time of the execution, *"when a sombre litany was read, and an eloquent and most impressive sermon was preached by the incumbent"* on the subject of Christ's forgiveness. It was a very compassionate gesture and was much appreciated by the parishioners of St John's.[28]

In spite of all the efforts by Alfred Mason and his curates, things could sometimes go very wrong, even though the clergy of St John's, in the final analysis might be shown to be blameless. In 1865, John Edwards, a pauper in the Chelmsford Union workhouse died at the workhouse. His son called on the governor and informed him that, as his father belonged to Springfield parish, he wished to be buried there. The son then proceeded to make the relevant arrangements with Rev Dr Manning, the rector of Springfield. However, when he arrived at the workhouse to collect his father's body for burial, he was astonished (and not a little annoyed) to discover *"that his father had already been buried"* by Alfred Mason in the churchyard of St John's (the churchyard of the parish in which he had died) two days previously. Alfred Mason was in no way at fault, but his compassionate nature felt very much for the young man in his grief, as nothing could be done to rectify the error, which had arisen from serious misunderstandings between the son and the governor of the workhouse.[29]

'His reputation as a horticulturalist had spread far outside Essex'

On 14 June 1872 Joseph Saltmarsh died. As mentioned above, he had been the very first Chapel warden of St John's after its consecration (he had previously served as churchwarden of the mother church, St Mary's). It was perhaps fitting that he was chosen for St John's, as the Chapel had of course been built on land he had leased from Lady Mildmay, and for which he had had to surrender the lease. The nursery, of which the Chapel plot had been part, had been started in a relatively small way by Joseph's father, John Saltmarsh, who had left the business to Joseph when he had died in about 1820. Joseph Saltmarsh, ably assisted by his son in later years, had, by a combination of hard work, sound business practices and an innovative knowledge of plants, built up the business so that by 1870 the nursery extended almost to twenty acres, mostly to the south and west of the church. Joseph's reputation as a horticulturalist had spread far outside Essex and he was a leading competitor at many of the local shows. He was a noted expert on geraniums including a fine zonal pelargonium, 'Mrs Pollock', that not only won many prizes but is still in cultivation today (2018). Although nominated for membership of the local Board of Health in Chelmsford, he steadfastly refused to undertake that office, feeling that he was not adequately qualified for such an important job. He was predeceased by his wife Susan (who died in 1866, aged 68) and survived by his unmarried daughter Susan who lived until 1891. All three are buried in St John's churchyard in a plain mantel top tomb raised on a plinth and located to the south west of the church, near the path from Moulsham Street. It is fitting that Joseph Saltmarsh is buried in the grounds of the nursery that he once made so celebrated (and which is still commemorated in the name of Nursery Road).[30]

'The church of St John has been utilised to the utmost'

By 1873 the church, in spite of the additions made in 1851 by Christopher Muston and any alterations carried out in 1867 by Alfred Mason, still only afforded accommodation for 700 worshippers. The population of Moulsham in 1871 (according to the census of that year) was about 4,775, and even allowing for the creation of the new ecclesiastical district of Galleywood[31] (which siphoned off some of the more southerly residents) it still exceeded 4,500. It was felt that the accommodation available in St John's was seriously inadequate for the needs of the population of the parish, even though the church was being used to the utmost. By 1873 there were three full services (with two celebrations of Holy Communion) every Sunday, together with daily morning and evening prayer. An additional Sunday service at half-past nine had been tried but was discontinued: *"on account of it not harmonising with the habits of the people"*.

In August 1873 Alfred Mason called the parishioners together to explain to them what he intended to do about it. He proposed: *"1. To add a new north transept to the present cruciform building, in order to accommodate the organ and the school children. The estimated expense was at least £600. This will afford additional accommodation to the extent of nearly 100 Sittings. 2. To lengthen the nave by 36 feet; covering the whole with a new roof, which is imperatively required for ventilation; to add a south porch and a western tower, conforming the entire building in architectural design to the existing chancel and transept* (sic). *The expense of this portion of the works, with a new warming apparatus, cannot be calculated under £2,600, and the extra accommodation afforded will be about 288 sittings"*. Alfred Mason then made the munificent gesture of opening the subscription list with no less than £1,000. Of this, £400 was toward the first section of the work (the new transept), £500 towards the lengthening and re-roofing of the nave and £100 towards the tower, the only condition being that the work should be carried out *"within a reasonable period of time"*. The gesture profoundly impressed the parishioners and hands were dug deeply into pockets to try and match the incumbent's generosity. Jabez Church (the vicar's churchwarden) and Thomas Tidboald (the parish churchwarden) each promised to contribute £100, splitting their individual contributions in half, one part for each section of the work.

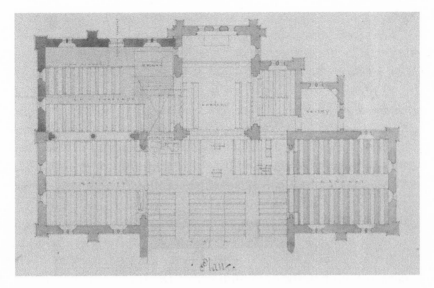

Figure 12 – Frederick Chancellor's plans for the 1873 enlargement of
St John's Church, Moulsham

Frederick Veley also contributed £50, and together with promises from other parishioners, a goodly sum was raised. St John's decided straight away to initiate the first section of these works (the new north transept) and accordingly Frederick Chancellor prepared plans (*Figure 12)* in October 1873 for the alterations.[32] The new north transept (the present robing vestry) was to be separated from the existing north transept (where the font is presently (2018) located) by two open arches and a single column; these arches were subsequently walled in. The opportunity was taken while works were being carried out on the building to install a new heating apparatus based on a hot water system, in place of the inadequate stoves, and to update the gas lighting. Frederick Chancellor supervised the work (as architect). Mr Brown of Braintree acted as contractor for the fabric and Mr Dennis of Chelmsford for the heating and lighting; work was begun early in 1874

There was still concern about sufficient funds for the completion of the project. In February 1874, "*a very pleasing entertainment*

*was given in the Boys' National schoolroom on Wednesday
11 February under the Presidency of the vicar, the Rev A.W.
Mason. The vocalists included the Misses Church, Miss Albyn,
Miss Wilsher, Miss Wackrill, Mr W.P. Gepp, Mr Charles Gepp and
the Rev W.E. Gray, together with the church choir and a choir of
girls from the school. The programme, we need hardly say, was
admirably carried out, and gave great satisfaction to the large and
respectable audience present. All the proceeds from the evening
are to be donated to the fund for the enlargement of the church"*.
As the works progressed, it became impossible to hold some
services in the church, and helpfully St Mary's offered their
building for Holy Communion in a joint service with St John's on
a number of occasions.[33] The work was progressing well and the
congregation of St John's looked forward to reopening their
enlarged church in the early summer of 1874.

'Armageddon'

On the afternoon of Friday, 22 May 1874, the work of alteration
and enlargement that had started some months previously
was moving to its completion. A small number of men in the
employment of Mr Dennis were still working in the church,
putting the finishing touches to the gas lighting and laying the
additional gas supply to the north transept. A further small group
of workmen were in the west end, finishing a trench that was part
of the new heating system. In all, about a dozen individuals were
in the church. The gas meter for the church was contained in a
closed box near the west door, and one of the workmen (according
to his later statement) turned on the gas during the afternoon to
see if all of the fixtures that had been installed were functioning
satisfactorily. He tested the burners with a light, then extinguished
the lights and turned off the gas, claiming that it had not been
turned on for more than five minutes at the most. Two other
workmen thought that just after that there had been a slight smell
of gas, enough for one of them to open a window in the nave.
A few moments later, one of these workmen, who was in the
chancel, saw the whole of the benching in the middle of the nave

suddenly rise up bodily towards the roof. Simultaneously with this there appeared a blinding flash, accompanied by the noise of an enormous explosion, and the western portion of the benching shot up to the height of the roof (some forty feet above ground level) descending in splintered fragments. Nearly every window in the church was shattered. The noise was heard as far away as St Mary's, although many of those in the town thought it was simply the West Essex Militia firing blank cartridges. It was astonishing that none of the workmen in the church at the time of the explosion was injured. Indeed, one young boy who was sitting on a bench at the east end was carried by the receding woodwork a considerable distance, yet the shock wave in the air only blew his cap off. One of the men in the trench at the west end suffered nothing worse than his collar being stripped off his neck yet the door right next to where he had been standing was split from top to bottom. Alfred Mason and his wife, who were out walking in the town at the time, were summoned immediately and they and one of the churchwardens (Thomas Tidboald) arrived at the church almost simultaneously. They must all have been heartbroken, particularly Alfred Mason, who had given so much of his time and his money to the project, and who was looking forward with an almost boyish enthusiasm to the reopening of the enlarged and beautified church. The destruction was truly astonishing. The middle part of the benching in the nave had been destroyed, with those benches nearest to the west end reduced to matchwood. Joists, sleepers and tiles from the nave had been reduced to fragments, and gas pipes had been transformed into eerie, unearthly twisted shapes. The centre of the church was simply a huge pile of broken timber, bricks, mortar, glass from the windows and other debris. The beautiful, original three-light stained glass window from the west end was completely destroyed, every light having been blown out and the wire guarding crumpled up like gauze. The elegant stained glass lower portion of the central window in the east end was damaged beyond repair and the small oval window, with the figure of a dove representing the descent of the Holy Ghost, at the top of the chancel wall (roughly where the present vesica is) was reduced to fragments the size of penny pieces. The news that St John's had 'blown up' attracted onlookers in droves, so much so that by seven o'clock in the evening the gates of the churchyard had to be locked and guarded by the parish constable. People were allowed to visit the scene in small groups on the following day (Saturday). The churchwardens, mindful of the fact that now even more expenditure might be required, were sharp enough to charge them sixpence a time to view the ruins. Worship had to continue, and arrangements were speedily made for the following Sundays. Regular Sunday worship would take place in the schoolrooms, and for all those who wanted a service of Holy Communion, St Mary's continued to offer joint services as they had throughout the whole of the reconstruction phase.[34]

There was, however, a faint silver lining to this very black cloud. The fine organ was totally unharmed, and Thomas Tidboald (who for many years had been an astute businessman) had taken the precaution of insuring the fabric of the church (including during the period of the work) with the Alliance office for £1,300 and the fittings with the Imperial for £500, thus covering almost all of the cost of the remedial work. Friday, 22 May 1874 was indeed a day to remember for the parish, for the parishioners and for the town.

'Resurgat'

Nobody was able to offer a clear and unambiguous explanation for the cause of the explosion. Ignition must have taken place under the benching, yet it is difficult to understand how such a large quantity of gas could have accumulated in that space without anyone being aware of it. In addition, there seems to have been no obvious, direct source of ignition, although it was always possible that there was a discharge of static electricity. With the need to repair the church came the opportunity to replace much of the church furniture and fittings. The east end window was to be completely new, and a handsome design (a *Te Deum*) was commissioned from Messrs Clayton and Bell, through the generosity of a parishioner. New painted glass was to be installed in the west end. All the important furniture of the church, with the exception of the lectern, was to be new. A new pulpit was provided, in Caen stone, having ten panels in the form of small arches, with shafts of vari-coloured marble (this is the existing pulpit). The several panels were to be elaborately carved and the top of the pulpit was to bear the text 'The Son of Man is come to save that which was lost'. Mrs Mason herself personally took charge of the subscription list for this new item. The choir stalls and the chancel fittings were also new, while the altar was re-positioned on a step and the chancel floor, both within and outside the communion rails, was laid with bright encaustic tiles of contrasting colours. A completely new lighting system, comprising a corona of sixteen lights, was installed to illuminate the chancel. A new altar desk, of brass, was provided together with a new set of altar linen. Mrs Mason had also provided a new altar frontal with a cross and orphreys, the super frontal bearing a crown. A completely new heating system was eventually installed by Mr Dennis and this was extended to include hot water for church purposes. The new system was said to be much cheaper to operate. The organ, which thankfully had remained undamaged, was to be the subject of some needful repairs and the addition of some new pipes. The work had been entrusted to Mr James Taylor of Islington Street, London; the total cost being about £120. The overall sum spent on the alterations and improvements was in excess of £1,600 and the total raised by subscription and from insurance payments was short of this sum by about £200. The whole of the money subscribed was raised by the vicar and the parishioners, no grants of any kind being sought or received.

Services to celebrate the re-opening of the church took place on Wednesday, 23 September and it was felt that as the annual harvest festival services were usually held at about that time, it would be sensible to combine the two. The first service, a celebration of holy communion, took place at eleven o'clock and since the weather was remarkably unfavourable, a relatively small number of people attended. Great care had been taken over the decorations. Before the central light of the east window was a beautiful floral cross in white asters and lilies. The front of the lectern carried a cross of dark red dahlias against a traditional background of harvest produce. The font, however, was the centrepiece of all the decorations. It was covered in fruits, flowers, cereals and ferns, which all served to set off a floating, upright cross of roses in the water filling the bowl. In the nave, on the window sills of both sides was the text 'Honour the Lord with thy first fruits, so that thy barns shall be filled with plenty' worked in ears of wheat against a green cloth background. Prayers at the eleven o'clock service were said by the curate, Rev William Lumley; and the litany and the gospel by the archdeacon of Ely, the Ven W. Emery. Alfred Mason read the communion service; and the new assistant curate of the parish, Rev Edward Clive, read the epistle. Alfred Mason preached on Acts xlv, 17 and the *Chelmsford Chronicle* noted that the preacher: *"proceeded to contrast the Biblical account of the creation of the world with the account recently suggested by various professors"*. Darwinism was starting to make an appearance in Moulsham.

In the evening the weather was much more pleasant, and the labouring people having finished their work for the day, the church was crowded in every single part, suggesting that there were more than 800 present at the service. A full choral service took place, ably sung by the church choir. Rev Hearn, the vicar of Roxwell and Alfred Mason sang the prayers between them, and Rev James Tanner (the Master of the Grammar school) and Edward Clive read the lessons. The Archdeacon of Ely preached on this occasion, his sermon being based on Psalm cxlv, 1, ending with a pep talk for the fundraisers and the vicar: *"Now ask you, brethren, to encourage him* (the vicar, who had given £2 for every £1 contributed by the parishioners) *in his self-denying labours by determining to bear some portion of the pecuniary burden. I fear that he may be angry with me for speaking to you in this way, but I cannot help it. What is a great burden for one becomes a light burden when borne by many"*.[35] At the end of the service, in spite of all the ecclesiastical exhortation, the collection amounted only to £15 5s. – less than 6d. per head of the assembled congregation.

The first phase of Alfred Mason's plans for the enlargement of the building were now complete, but even this modest scheme had given the parish a £200 debt. Alfred Mason had realised that he could easily pay off the debt from his own pocket, but saw that the parish and parishioners needed to take responsibility for the building and its running expenses themselves. His earlier offers, though, were not withdrawn, His agreed contribution towards lengthening the nave and erecting a western tower would still be available as long as the work was started: *"within a reasonable period of time"*. It would be 1882, under the Rev George St Alban Godson, before this phase was completed, but Alfred Mason kept his promise and made further donations for a building over which he no longer had any responsibility. His was, indeed, a true, devoted Christian generosity.

'His death was marked with great respect in the parish'

Not long after the re-opening of St John's church, Jabez Church died. He had not been well for some time, and at the 1875 Vestry meeting, although he was re-appointed vicar's warden, Alfred Mason expressly asked that it be recorded that: *"a fervent wish was expressed by the meeting that he (Jabez Church) be returned to health"*.[36] A photograph taken of him at about that time shows a prematurely-aged man, with a face worn by the cares of life.[37]

Jabez Church was born in London in 1824 and moved to Colchester as a young man when his father, who was an engineer, found employment there. He was apprenticed at a young age to his father, and early on showed great interest (and promise) in developing the fledgling gas lighting industry. He discovered a greatly superior method of converting coal to coke and recovering the coal gas (he designed a new type of oven) and in 1845 was able to patent it; this eventually made him a wealthy man.[38] He married Mary Ann Clubb in 1844 in Colchester. The partnership he had forged with John Hudson Theobald when they took over the lease of the Chelmsford Gas and Coke company[39] was beginning to bear fruit and shortly after his marriage he was appointed engineer to the company. His eldest son (Jabez junior) was born in Colchester and another son and four daughters followed. In the late 1850s the family moved to Springfield to be nearer the gas works. They continued to prosper. By 1860 Jabez junior had been apprenticed to his father. He too was to make his mark in the engineering world, later on in life being elected President of the Incorporated Gas Institute.[40] The family home in Springfield, over the coach builders' works, eventually became too small for them all, and with the death of Jane Guy in 1862 Hamlet House became available. The family were now able to move into accommodation that befitted their status. Jabez senior was not however to enjoy the fruits of his labours into a peaceful old age as he died on 20 May 1875, aged only 51, much to the sorrow of the parishioners and especially Alfred Mason, who had come to rely on him to take many of the lay responsibilities of the parish. His death was marked with great respect by everyone; *"... several of the tradesmen closing their places of business, and many of the cottagers and other residents drawing their blinds during the time of the interment"*. His funeral took place on 26 May, *"amid every token of respect for the memory of the deceased, and of sympathy for the bereaved family"*.[41] The funeral procession was of a varied and representative character and a large number of parishioners (and those desirous of paying a last tribute to the memory of one who for many years had occupied a useful and prominent position in the midst of them all) assembled in the churchyard. The procession, consisting of many important local individuals and the staff of the Gas Works and the Local Board of Health, made its short way from Hamlet House to the church where it was received at the gate of the churchyard by Archdeacon Mildmay. The funeral service was conducted by William Lumley and Alfred Mason: *"with more than ordinary solemnity"*. Jabez Church's death left a big hole in the running of the parish. He was survived by his wife Mary Ann who lived for another twelve years. They are buried together in St John's churchyard, in a substantial tomb with arched decoration on the sides and a small coped stone cap. It is located to the south-west of the church, near the path.

'Her beloved Master's cross was laid heavily upon her'

In 1875 St John's lost another stalwart, Louisa Veley, Frederick Veley's beloved wife. Frederick Veley, whose family originated from Yverdon in Switzerland, had married Louisa Curtis at Dorking on 6 October 1840.[42] In her younger days, after the family had started to worship at St Mary's, Louisa Veley had worked tirelessly amongst the poor, the aged and the infirm. She carried on these good works after she and Frederick had moved to Yverdon house in New London Road (now (2018) Kemsley's) and they had transferred their allegiance to St John's. The death of her much-loved eldest son Frederick Arthur Veley in 1866 at the age of 24, not long after his ordination, had deeply affected her, and she became a changed woman, suffering chronic illness for the rest of her life. She bore her ill-health with great fortitude. In March 1875 Frederick Veley had taken her to Bournemouth, hoping yet again that the sea air might bring about some improvement in her symptoms. Sadly, the opposite happened. On Easter Sunday 1875 Louisa was taken very ill, and just a few hours later, she died. Frederick Veley was a very private man, not given to any display of feelings, and he insisted that the funeral be a quiet, private affair. Alfred Mason, however, expressed what must have been the feelings of most of the parish, when he said during her funeral sermon: *"... to my dear friend long years of suffering were appointed. Her beloved Master's cross was laid very seriously upon her ... ... the discipline of sharp pain, the sense of weakness proclaimed by reasons of utter prostration, the sickness of heart by hope deferred, the disappointment of baffled remedies – all these, I am persuaded, were means in God's hands of revealing his dear Son more and more to her"*.[43] It was a very Victorian death. She was buried in the Veley vault, close to the door of the south vestry of St John's, with her eldest son and her other children. St John's was much the poorer for her passing.

'The offertories had of later years decreased markedly'

By 1876 St John's had settled back into its routine ways, memories of Armageddon fading. The vestry meeting that year on 18 April had seen Mr Robert Hanam appointed as the vicar's warden and

Thomas Tidboald elected unopposed as parish warden. In accepting, Thomas Tidboald thanked them for electing him: *"for, he believed, the tenth time. He was in hopes that perhaps they might have found some fresh blood to come in this time, because he was sorry to tell them that the balance sheet was not a very satisfactory one"*. He was correct. He went on the produce the accounts, which showed for the year 1875–76 there was a balance due to the churchwardens of £34 2s. 6d. (almost 10% of the total).[44] The churchwardens of St John's needed quite deep pockets.

The year 1877 dawned, and in spite of the assistance of two devoted curates, it was becoming apparent that Alfred Mason was finding it increasingly difficult to handle the demands of the parish, and that his hand was no longer firmly guiding the tiller. This was illustrated at the 1877 vestry meeting, held on 3 April. Not only was the balance sheet still stubbornly in deficit, but the offertories were beginning to fall away as well. Thomas Tidboald, again having been appointed parish churchwarden, commented that: *"he was sorry to say that the amounts collected at the offertories had of later years decreased markedly. Indeed, on the previous Sunday evening (30 March) they had collected £1 5s. from a congregation of between 400 and 500 persons"*.[45] This is less than a halfpenny per head, a very small sum for a church, even in a parish like St John's.

A further problem arose at the same vestry meeting. St John's required a new organist, and the meeting was called upon to elect an individual to that position. Sadly, this was not to prove a frictionless task. Robert Hanam opened the discussion by saying that Miss Pattison had initially been regarded as suitable for the post, but when the churchwardens had realised that Mr Barnard had also wished to be a candidate, they had determined to give both parties the same opportunity. He continued: *"With regard to Miss Pattison, there had not been fair play. A rumour had got about that the churchwardens had already elected Miss Pattison, and although this was untrue, she, no doubt feeling aggrieved, had withdrawn her name as a candidate, on the grounds that she had heard that no lady would be elected under any circumstances".*[46] The debate had spilled over into the local press, and Thomas Tidboald had complained strongly of a paragraph in the *Essex Weekly News* which contained derogatory remarks about Miss Pattison and laudatory comments about Mr Barnard, both of which were shown to be contrary to fact. William Cutts then delivered the *coup de grace* for Miss Pattison. He said: *"that he should object on principal to a lady being appointed to the post. The organist should be a man well-versed in music and capable of leading and managing the choir".* It was obvious that Mr Barnard was no answer to their prayers, either – the vicar damning him with the faintest of praise: *"he believed that if Mr Barnard took lessons and had good practice, he might make a good organist".* Mr Barnard was duly elected, *faute de mieux*, to the post. Rampant sexism was alive and well at St John's. This 1877 vestry had been Alfred Mason's last at St John's, and after the customary vote of thanks, *"regret was expressed that this was the last time that he would preside over them".* The vicar, too, expressed his sorrow, *"... a sorrow which increased every day ... ... which he felt on leaving the parish".*

As Alfred Mason began to look back over his eighteen years in the parish, he must have thought much about the curates who had shared their duties with him. The gentle Newman Tibbits, who was at St John's when Alfred Mason arrived, must have been a great help with the duties and the little idiosyncrasies of the place when the new vicar arrived. Just after Alfred Mason had been in the parish for a year, George Mallory was licensed to St John's, in August 1860. He came from a distinguished, land-owning family in Cheshire. His mother, Julia Mallory, was the daughter of John Houldsworth Mallory, the rector and Lord of the Manor of Mobberley. Her family had owned Old Hall for generations and she herself succeeded to the title of Lord of the Manor. She married Rev George Leigh, who became rector of Mobberley on the death of his father-in-law in 1832, adopting the surname Mallory as a pre-condition. George Mallory, their only son, was born in January 1833, followed by a sister, Harriet, in 1834. When George was only two years old, tragedy struck, his mother dying at the age of twenty-nine. His father remarried, and George Mallory's step-siblings included George Leigh Mallory, who died on Everest in 1924 and Air Chief Marshall Sir Trafford Leigh Mallory of Battle of Britain fame[47] (it is thus not inappropriate that the Battle of Britain service is held each year in St John's). George Mallory was educated at Brasenose College, Oxford, where he matriculated in June 1851. He received his BA from St Mary Hall in 1857 and his MA in 1858. George Mallory left St John's at the end of 1861, but never took another cure, and was never ordained priest. He died in March 1864, aged only thirty-one.[48]

William Boys Johnston came to St John's at the beginning of 1861. He was the son of William Downes Johnston of Tunbridge Wells and a graduate of Christ Church, Oxford, receiving his BA in 1857 and his MA in 1860.[49] He was ordained deacon in 1858 and priest in 1859 by the Bishop of Carlisle, Henry Villers. He served his title at the little village church of St John the Evangelist, Levens, just south of Kendal in the Lake District. St John's, Moulsham, was his second appointment. He assisted Alfred Mason for just over two years, leaving at the end of May 1863 to take up a curacy in Swaffham.[50]

George Mallory was succeeded after a short break by Frederick Charles Howard Bent, who came to St John's in the early autumn of 1862. He took his Licentiate of Theology from Durham in 1855 and was ordained deacon in 1856 and priest in 1857 by the Bishop of Ripon, Charles Longley. He had married Caroline Hanley Davison in 1850, and as a married man, Oxford and Cambridge would both have been proscribed to him. After curacies in Wakefield, Dunstable and in Bulphan, Essex (near South Ockendon, and in the middle of the Essex 'fens' – surely a very remote place in the middle of the nineteenth century) he came to Moulsham and stayed until September 1865. He seems to have taken up no ecclesiastical appointment after St John's. He died in 1901.[51]

Thomas Guest Forrest was the son of Thomas Forrest of Edgebaston, Birmingham and was born in 1822. He was admitted as a pensioner to Peterhouse College, Cambridge, where he matriculated in 1844. He received his BA in 1849 and was ordained deacon by the Bishop of Manchester (James Prince Lee) in 1849 and priest by the Bishop of Winchester (Henry Pepys) in 1851.[52] After several curacies in the Midlands and the West Country he came to Moulsham in 1864, staying until June 1865. He left to take another curacy at the other end of the country at the newly opened Chapel of Ease of St John the Evangelist, Devoran, in Cornwall. He died in 1902, aged 81.[53]

John Charles Burnside was the first curate appointed to St John's as a result of Alfred Mason's advertisement of 1865. He had studied at King's College, London, where he had qualified in 1857, being ordained deacon by the Bishop of Lichfield (John Lonsdale) in 1857 and priest in 1858. He came to Moulsham in late 1865 following a curacy on the Isle of Wight and was somewhat unusual in being married with a family when he arrived in the parish. He obviously gave Alfred Mason good grounds for selecting a man with a non-Oxbridge education and he appears to have fulfilled the incumbent's exacting criteria during his time at St John's. Alfred Mason's judgement was indeed sound – John Burnside stayed at St John's until late 1869. He moved only as far as Rivenhall for his next appointment, ultimately becoming vicar of Cornish Hall End, near Finchingfield.[54]

Alfred Mason's carefully worded advertisement also attracted another curate, John Peckham Skirrow Woodward, who came from a long-established clerical family, his father and grandfather before him having held the living of Plumpton, near Lewes in Sussex. After attending Marlborough College, John Woodward went up to Emmanuel College, Cambridge, where he graduated BA in 1864, receiving his MA in 1872. He was ordained deacon in 1865 by the Bishop of London (Archibald Tait) and priest by the Bishop of Rochester (Thomas Claughton) in 1867 at St Mary's, Chelmsford. Moulsham was his first appointment, and again he showed how wisely Alfred Mason had been in selecting his curates – he stayed for just short of seven years, sharing a major part of the burden of running the parish with the incumbent.[55] Whilst curate at St John's, he met and married Mary Pearson, the daughter of the rector of Springfield. After leaving St John's in July 1872, he served as curate in two more Essex parishes, before succeeding his father as rector of Plumpton (the family had purchased the advowson some twenty years previous to his succession). He died in 1917.[56]

William Black arrived at St John's in early 1870, having previously served as curate at St Phillip's, Liverpool. He had been born in Dublin in 1846, the son of William Fausset Black, DD, and had gone up to Christ's College, Cambridge, where he matriculated in 1864. He took his BA in 1868 and received his MA in 1895. He was ordained deacon in 1868 and priest in 1869 by the Bishop of Chester (William Jacobson).[57] He left St John's in the summer of 1872 to take up a chaplaincy appointment in Devon. He spent much of the rest of his life serving at St John's Mission, Mazagom, Bombay. He was one of the most intellectual curates of St John's, Moulsham, being widely recognised as an accomplished painter. He spent his holidays in Norway, studying Norwegian poetry, on which he became an acknowledged expert. He died in London in 1929, aged 84.[58]

William Patrick Leonard Hand was another Dubliner. He attended his local university, Trinity College, taking his BA and Divinity Testimonium in 1871. He was ordained deacon in 1872 and priest (in St Mary's, Chelmsford) in 1873 by the Bishop of Rochester (Thomas Claughton). He was licensed to St John's on 25 February 1872[59] (his licence is one of the few from that era to survive) and took his first baptism in May of that year. He served at St John's for just over a year and a half, leaving to become the incumbent of the little village of Great Barrington near to the Gloucestershire/ Oxfordshire border. The parish was shortly afterwards combined with the Oxfordshire parish of Taynton. He remained vicar of the combined parishes until his in 1900 at the age of only fifty-one.[60]

William Black's replacement at St John's was John Benwell Seaman. He arrived in the parish in the autumn of 1872. He was fortunately the only male member of his family to escape the predilection for Biblical names which had bedevilled them for generations – his father had been christened Meshach and his brother Shadrach (perhaps they felt that Abednego Seaman was a step too far). He went up to Queen's College, Cambridge (a family tradition) in 1841, graduating BA in 1847 and taking his MA in 1864.[60] He taught as assistant Master at Cheltenham College for a few years, after which he took the unusual step of serving for seven years as chaplain to HM Convict Establishment in Tasmania. He left St John's at the end of July 1873, and seems to have been very undecided as to where his eventual vocation lay, serving many more different curacies interspersed with spells as a missionary in Canada. He died in May 1900, aged seventy.[61]

William Faithfull Lumley was the second son of Major Lumley of Northampton and was born in India in 1844. He attended King's College, London, where he received his AKC in 1867. He was ordained deacon in 1867 and priest in 1869 by William Connor Magee, the Bishop of Peterborough. After a brief curacy at All Saints' church in the tiny Rutland village of Tinwell, he took up a post as curate in St Edmund's church, Northampton in 1868, staying until 1872.[62] While in Northampton (where his family lived) he met Rosa Maddy, the daughter of a Cambridgeshire vicar, whom he married in St Matthew's church, Ipswich, on 14 January 1869.[63] He moved with his family to St John's, Moulsham in 1873 in the late summer. Here he stayed until he was appointed chaplain of the County Gaol in Springfield in December 1876, and in his New Year sermon at St John's on 7 January the following year Alfred Mason reminded the congregation of how much William Lumley had contributed to the parish during his three-and-a-half years amongst them, emphasising how very fitted he was for the post of chaplain.[64] William Lumley gave his final sermon to the parishioners on 14 January 1877. On his departure he was presented with a set of silver gilt spoons and salts: *"from all in the parish of St John's"*. Sadly, just a few years after he moved to Springfield, his wife Rosa died at the relatively early age of thirty-seven. Their second son, Charles Lumley, born just after the family moved to Springfield, is of note as he was the grandfather of Joanna Lumley, the actress. William Lumley died in 1915, aged seventy. Strangely enough, he is probably best known for his revision of Fulton's Book of Pigeons, on which he was clearly a great authority.[65]

'To know him was to be his friend'

Of all the curates who have served at St John's over the years, few, if any, have had a more tragic life than Alfred Mason's last appointment, Edward Clive. He was born in 1844 to an Army captain, Edward Clive senior, and his wife Elizabeth, in Market Drayton, Shropshire. He was admitted as a pensioner to Corpus Christi College, Cambridge in 1867, gaining his BA in 1874 and his MA in 1877.[66] He was licensed to St John's in September 1874 just after his ordination as deacon, but his licensing was overshadowed by a most tragic event. At the beginning of October 1874 his parents came to visit him in his new parish, together with a young lady, Miss Emily Jane Spiers, the daughter of Benjamin Spiers, Edward's former tutor. For a young woman to travel with an unrelated couple and stay the night in Chelmsford was most unusual, and it almost certainly meant that Emily Jane was Edward's 'intended'. They all went to St John's church to hear Edward's first sermon on the Sunday (4 October). On the Sunday morning: *"Miss Spiers was in apparent health, but she was seized the same evening whilst back at the Saracen's Head hotel, with inflammation, and despite immediate and unremitting medical attendance (Dr Nicholls being called at once) expired on Tuesday morning"*.[67] She was aged just twenty-five. Edward Clive must have been heartbroken. Nevertheless, he threw himself into the work of the parish, and he and William Lumley bore the brunt of the duties. Alfred Mason was increasingly spending time on the continent *"for his health"*. Moulsham was once again proving a hard taskmaster. Edward Clive, by his unstinting efforts to minister to anyone and everyone in the parish, endeared himself to all – it was said of him: *"to know him was to be his friend"*. He stayed in the parish until the next incumbent, Thomas Henry Wilkinson, left. He will be met again in the next chapter.

'If I go on much longer, I shall break down'

So Alfred Mason's days in Moulsham drew to a close. Towards the end of 1876 he realised that he had to make a decision, and so he approached the Bishop, and asked him, quite frankly: *"My Lord, I want you to remove me from a charge which I feel is too heavy for me, and which I feel could better be discharged by a younger man. I think Moulsham itself would be better shepherded by a man who could bring more energy to the work than I can at my time of life* (he was then fifty-eight). *The fact is, My Lord, I think I have done my work here, and if I go on much longer I shall break down, and have to spend the rest of my life at a watering-hole, which is the last thing in the world that I wish to do. I should wish to die in harness. I should like to be in a parish where the work was within my compass – where I could feel that I was not neglecting my parish – where I could take an adequate survey of the whole, and do my work with more satisfaction to myself"*.[68]

The Bishop found Dedham for him. Dedham, which met Alfred Mason's requirements for a parish where the work was: *"within his compass"*, and Dedham, full of happy and lasting childhood memories, was to bring a little more peace to Alfred Mason's soul. He was formally instituted by the Bishop on Sunday 15 April 1877, but curiously did not take his final leave of St John's until Tuesday 1 May. The tributes to him, and their accompanying presentations, were no less than epic. The local press devoted an entire page in each of the Chelmsford papers to reporting the presentations and summarising Alfred Mason's achievements while he had served at St John's. These were, even in summary, impressive: the provision of new schools; the enlargement and beautifying of the church; the increase in the number of services (when he left there were sixteen a week), house-to-house visitation of the sick and needy; lectures for men and night school for adults;

Bible classes and a parochial Church Society – and in addition, Alfred Mason had funded two curates out of his own pocket in order to minister to the needs of the parish effectively. It had all been admirably summed up by William Lumley in a sermon preached just before Alfred Mason's departure: *"His pastorate in this parish has been marked by patient well-doing; his health and wealth have been spent for your good and in the service of the Lord"*. It was a measure of the love that the parish showed for the man that on the occasion of his return to Chelmsford after being absent for some long time to recover his health, he had found it difficult to enter his vicarage, so great was the throng that wished to greet him.

'I ought to call this the proudest moment of my life'

The presentations made to Alfred Mason on his departure came from a wide range of individuals and groups. As Rural Dean, he received a presentation from the clergy of the deanery, presented to him by Arthur Pearson, the rector of Springfield, and by Canon Carey. The clergy of the deanery had subscribed to an address, bound in maroon Russian leather by Messrs Durrant and Co, of the High Street, and having Alfred Mason's personal coat of arms embossed on the cover. This was followed by a presentation on Monday, 16 April from past and present curates of St John's. They gave him an album containing an address and photographs of the twelve curates who had officiated at St John's during his incumbency (these included Rev James Tanner, the headmaster of the Grammar School, who had never been formally licensed as a curate at St John's, but who had helped with many of the services during Alfred Mason's absences). The curates' tribute to him was both moving and heartfelt: *"...we, the past and present curates of Moulsham during your incumbency ...   ...desire to express our deep sense of the great benefit we have obtained from your words of advice so faithfully illustrated by your daily practise"*. Alfred Mason was very moved and spoke warmly of the gratitude he owed to the curates for all their earnest and devoted labours in connection with the parish.

Figure 13 – Alfred William Mason, incumbent of St John's,
Moulsham, 1859–77

But perhaps the most moving and devoted of all the presentations – that of the parishioners to Mr and Mrs Mason – took place in the schoolroom on the evening of Tuesday, 1 May 1877, which, by a happy coincidence, was the anniversary of the day, four years previously, when Alfred Mason had been welcomed back into the parish after a prolonged and difficult bout of ill-health. About five hundred of the parishioners had subscribed and a total of about £175 had been collected. The committee set up by the churchwardens had debated long and hard about the nature of the presentation, and in the end had selected a very chaste and beautiful silver *epergne* (a branched, ornamental centrepiece for a table) with two side ornaments to match. The *epergne* (which was capable of being converted to a candelabra) was of Egyptian design, representing honeysuckle. It bore Mr Mason's crest, together with the following inscription: *"Presented by the parishioners of St John's, Moulsham, as a token of affection and regard to the Rev Alfred William Mason, MA, vicar, on the occasion of his leaving the parish. April 1877"*. The presentation to Mrs Mason consisted of a beautiful and massive gold bracelet, set with diamonds and coral, bearing the inscription: *"Presented to Mrs A.W. Mason, as a souvenir of love and gratitude by the parishioners of St John's, Moulsham. April 1877"*. These tasteful presents were accompanied by a leather-bound album containing the names and addresses of 475 subscribers, which was illustrated by a watercolour of St John's church (which may have been painted by William Black).

At the presentation itself Frederick Veley presided, and he and the two churchwardens (Robert Hanam and Thomas Tidboald) all made long speeches full of tributes to Alfred and Mrs Mason. The vicar then rose to reply. He was almost overcome by emotion, but in his response he was typically self-effacing. He said: *"I ought to call this the proudest moment of my life ... ... and yet I am deeply conscious of so many defects and shortcomings during my administration of the parish"*. But he also paid eloquent testimony to all Mrs Mason had done to aid him in the parish, with a revealing insight into his own character: *"...there are ways in which she has been a helper to me that no-one knows but myself. No-one can tell how she has infused cheerfulness and helpfulness into the heart of a man who is naturally gloomy and desponding – how she has taught me to look on the bright side of things and helped me in difficulty and trial"*. Perhaps this offers a clue as to the true reason for Alfred Mason's absences from the parish due to ill-health.

The last of the presentations (but by no means the least in Rev and Mrs Mason's eyes) was made on Thursday, 3 May, on behalf of teachers and scholars of the school. The testimonial consisted of a very elegant album for *cartes de visite*, with a written inscription in ornamental writing which read : *"Presented by the teachers and scholars of St John's School, Moulsham, as a token of affection for Rev A.W. and Mrs Mason"*. Alfred Mason again thanked everyone: *"in most feeling terms"*. In truth, his cup of gratitude was in danger of running over. Alfred Mason had already preached his last sermon as vicar in St John's on the evening of Sunday, 29 April. The church had, on that occasion, been filled with one of the largest congregations ever to assemble within its walls. Touchingly, he took as his text the same verse from 1 Corinthians iii, 9 – as he had used for his first sermon on coming into the parish in September 1859. He concluded his last address to his parishioners with the words: *"And now, dear friends, the time has come when I must bid this church and this parish my last public farewell. I commend you to God and to the word of His grace, which is able to build you up and give you an inheritance among those that are sanctified"*. So ended eighteen years of dedicated and selfless ministry.[68]

Alfred Mason then moved, as vicar, to his beloved Dedham. Here he laboured for more than seven years, giving what he could, until ill-health made him its victim once again, and he retired finally from active ministry in October 1884. He moved to Church Street in Colchester, where he assisted, from time to time, the vicar of St Mary-at-the-Walls, Rev J.W. Irvine. He also made occasional visits back to St John's, where his name appears in the register of services from 1885 onwards. He died on 3 December 1890, a few days short of his seventy-second birthday. The notice of his death stated that: *"...he had for many years suffered from a weak heart, and this, coupled with a severe attack of bronchitis, was the cause of his death"*.[69] His funeral was held on Tuesday, 9 December 1890, at St Mary-at-the-Walls, Colchester, and was conducted by the Bishop of St Albans, the Rt Rev Dr Festing. He was laid to rest in Colchester cemetery (St John's churchyard had been closed to new burials by this date).[70] At the hour fixed for the funeral in Colchester, his old congregation met in St John's where the vicar (now Rev George St Alban Godson) read the service for the dead, assisted by the curate, the Rev George Collier. Again, the church was well-filled.[71]

The only existing photograph of Alfred Mason (*Figure 13*) shows an intelligent, kindly-looking yet firm man, already worn by his efforts on behalf of: *"All Christ's children"*.[72] He died a wealthy man, leaving over £20,000 in his will.[73]

The next incumbent of St John's would be a very different kettle of fish.

4. THOMAS HENRY WILKINSON

(1877–79)

"An experience of two years has convinced me that with only two clergy, it is impossible to attack with any purpose the mass of ungodliness which exists among us".[1]

If the clergy of St John's were to be described in cricketing metaphors, that for Thomas Henry Wilkinson would easily be found. *"He did"*, it would read, *"not trouble the scorers very much"*. His tenure of St John's lasted for just over two years, and in those two years he seems to have had little impact on the parish. The man himself was something of an enigma - even his origins do not appear to be straightforward.

'He felt that for him to accept their spiritual charge was the will of God'

A Thomas Henry Wilkinson is recorded as being born on 10 March 1828 to James John Wilkinson and his wife Anne of St Pancras, London.[2] These details agree with those quoted in a separate source (his University record) which gives the same year for his birth (1828) to the same father (James John Wilkinson, of St Pancras, London). However, the original entry in the International Genealogical Index (IGI) giving his birth date also states that 'Thomas Henry Wilkinson' died on 16 October 1831, aged three. This suggests that the grieving parents may have adopted another little boy of about the same age and raised him as Thomas Henry.

The young Thomas Wilkinson went up to Brasenose College, Oxford where he matriculated on 2 February 1847, aged 18. He took his BA in 1850 (double honours, fourth class) and received his MA in 1853.[3] He was ordained deacon in 1852 and priest in

1853 by the Bishop of Peterborough, George Davys, and served his first curacy at Holy Cross Church, Daventry. He then served a long stint as perpetual curate at Grosmont on the North Yorkshire moors (1853–63), before moving to the opposite end of the country as vicar of Leusden (now Widecombe-in-the-Moor), Devon, from 1863 to 1871. His next appointment was as perpetual curate at Holy Trinity, Barnes, in west London, before coming to Moulsham in 1877.[4] His appointment to Grosmont in 1853 (a living valued at £300 under the patronage of the Archbishop of York)[5] offered him the possibility of a settled life, so in March 1858 he married Elizabeth Mary Waddington of Leeds. They were to have five children.

Archdeacon Mildmay announced in April 1877 that he had appointed: "... *the Rev Thomas Henry Wilkinson MA who was until recently vicar* (sic) *of Holy Trinity, Barnes, in Surrey*" to be the next vicar of St John's, Moulsham.[6] Archdeacon Mildmay was now in his late seventies, and no longer had the iron grasp on the business of his office that had characterised most of his rectorate. With hindsight, it seems that Thomas Wilkinson was not an ideal candidate for the demanding post of St John's, Moulsham, a fact that he himself acknowledged within a couple of years of his being inducted. He officiated at St John's for the first time on Sunday, 10 July 1877, when he delivered what were described as *"two extempore sermons"*. one in the morning and one in the evening. In the evening he chose as his text: *"God with us"* and delivered a very optimistic message for his future ministry in the parish. *"He dared not,"* he said, *"have accepted their spiritual charge, had he not felt in his inmost heart that for him to do so was the will of God. Whatever trials might be in the future, whatever troubles might oppress them, there was no darkness that the words 'God with us' could not brighten".*[7] This was not how things would turn out. Thomas Wilkinson was formally inducted into the living some three weeks later and was quickly into his stride, taking the St Peter's day service (Friday 29 June) and preaching on behalf of the Society for the Propagation of the Gospel with enthusiasm, although the collection was a meagre £2 5s. 6d.[8]

The new vicar was soon shown how St John's Sunday School could put on a good display. On 6 September, in the afternoon, the children, in number about 180, first of all assembled in the church to listen to a short address from the Rev Francis Cardwell, the vicar of St Mary's, Hoxton. They then formed up in procession outside, headed by the Union band, and marched, *"with banners flying"* to the vicarage grounds, where *"everything had been arranged for their enjoyment"*. Tea had been prepared in a large tent, to which later in the afternoon both children and their parents had been invited, and they both in their turn *"did ample justice to the good things set before them"*. There followed games, and after dark a brilliant display of fire balloons, which *"seemed to afford the youthful spectators the most intense delight"*. A very good time, it would seem, was had by all.[9]

'Loved and honoured by all who had the privilege of knowing her'

In November 1877, Archdeacon Mildmay suffered a great personal tragedy. He had taken his wife to Bournemouth, where she was to stay with her family, and on the Saturday morning whilst alone in her room, she fell into the fire. Being unable to get up, she was severely burned on the shoulder and on one arm before anyone could assist her. Initially it was thought that she was in a critical condition, but reports received in Chelmsford on 23 November suggested her condition *"was thought to be of a more favourable character"*.[10] However, by the beginning of 1878, it was clear that she was gravely ill, it being reported on 4 January that, *"her medical advisors having given up all hope of recovery believe death to be imminent"*.[11] Archdeacon Mildmay and other members of the family were at her bedside when she died on Sunday, 6 January, at the age of seventy-nine. The news was received with shock and deep sadness in Chelmsford, and as a mark of respect, the Essex County Ball (of which Mrs Mildmay was the patron) was immediately postponed. On the Monday after her death, a muffled bell was tolled from St Mary's most of the morning as tribute to her memory. Caroline Mildmay was a daughter of the first Lord Radstock and had been married to the rector since 1830. The tributes to her in the press were both heartfelt and generous. It was noted: *"how well and faithfully she had discharged the duties of her position during that long and happy marriage, as the poor of the county town and the charities of the parish and neighbourhood could bear abundant witness. Loved and honoured by all who had the privilege of knowing her, there will be but one feeling of profound regret at her loss, and of deepest sympathy for the archdeacon and his family in this irreparable (sic) bereavement"*.[12]

The body of Caroline Mildmay reached Chelmsford on the afternoon of Thursday, 10 January and was conveyed immediately to the rectory. At half-past three the sad procession set out from there to the cemetery in Rectory Lane, followed on foot by her grieving husband, surviving daughters and sons-in-law accompanied by the Bishop, Thomas Claughton. The senior curate of St Mary's, Rev John Parmiter, read the burial service in the small cemetery chapel, which the local press described somewhat tactlessly as being: *"decorated cheerfully to bring to the mourners the bright side of the occasion"* (whatever that may have meant). After the burial service the coffin was deposited in the family vault which archdeacon Mildmay had commissioned Frederick Chancellor to build following the unexpected death of his daughter Horatia Glyn, some twenty years previously.

So Caroline Mildmay was laid to rest. She will be remembered at St John's as the person who laid the foundation stone of the Episcopal Chapel of Moulsham more than forty years previously. She would have been proud to see how her handiwork had been (literally) built upon. Yet she is another, like John Crabb, who has no memorial in the church she had helped to create.

In spite of Caroline Mildmay's death, St John's still had its traditional Christmas entertainment, held, as was the custom, after Christmas (this time on 3 January 1878) with Thomas Wilkinson in the chair. The items consisted of a good mix of carols, solos, piano duets and dramatic readings. The press reported that the performances were very good, and singled out for special praise the choir singing accompanied on the piano by the vicar's daughter. The proceeds from the evening's entertainment were to be used as a treat for the choir, so it was perhaps not surprising that the most popular item was the carol: *"Here we come a-wassailing"*.[13]

'All the seats would be free'

It was not long before Easter arrived and Thomas Wilkinson had to chair his first vestry meeting, on Tuesday, 23 April 1878. It started on a relatively optimistic note, with Thomas Tidboald presenting: *"a more satisfactory statement than he had ever before, as in the past the balances had generally been very much against them, but in the year just gone the adverse balance had been reduced to 11s. 11d."* In the year to April 1878 the offertory had increased from £124 5s. to £141 4s. and although this showed *"the liberal pulse of the people"* there were still some grumpy individuals around the table, one of whom expressed the opinion that: *"some of those who occupied a better position in life gave copper, when silver might have been expected"* and there were often times when *"the collections did not average even a halfpenny per head of those present"*. The accounts were, however, quickly adopted.

Thomas Wilkinson then proposed Robert Hanam as the vicar's warden for another year, thanking him for the way in which he had fulfilled the office in the past, and expressing the hope that he would continue to do so in the future. Robert Hanam accepted the office and hoped that: *"they might find a man more effective, but not one who would endeavour to do his duty more correctly"*. Thomas Tidboald was re-elected parish churchwarden, which he accepted in spite of (eleven years previously) being told: *"he might depend upon it, he would not need to be in office for more than a year, but he had continued until this time"*. Some things never change.

Thomas Tidboald then brought up the subject of a new burial ground for Moulsham. The vicar felt that this was a very important issue and action was needed soon. He agreed he would see Archdeacon Mildmay as quickly as possible, and that after any such meeting had taken place, he would call the parishioners together to explore the various options available. Already it was apparent that after forty years of burials the churchyard was very nearly full.

The meeting then moved on to discuss (yet again) the issue of seating in the church. Mr Warrick stood up and complained at *length* that recently: *"on attempting to go into a vacant place in a pew, he had been barred out"*. He had subscribed liberally to the fund that was raised for the building of the church, but he felt that many new people had come into the parish who prevented others from taking empty seats. He had even noticed where: *"a person had been turned out of a pew, and all morning there was nobody put in it"*. When asked by the vicar what he felt should be done about it, Mr Warrick really got into his stride. He replied that: *"All the seats should be free – and in future, he would go into the seat he had referred to – there was no mistake about it. They should not give a seat to anyone, or reserve a seat – they belonged to the parishioners"*. Warming even more to his theme, he was proceeding with, *"remarks that appeared to be personal,"* when there were loud cries of order. Mr Robbins pointed out (trying to pour oil on troubled waters) that no one in the church who held an appropriated seat had, or ever would, object to it being occupied by a stranger after a service had commenced (indeed, a printed notice was fixed in every pew stating that the churchwardens appropriated the seats on the understanding that if not occupied at the commencement of the service, they should be free for the use of any of the parishioners). The meeting became neatly divided, some present feeling that all pews should be free to all, others believing that to have all seats free was to court complete confusion. Appropriations still had financial implications, and to make all pews free in Moulsham could easily adversely affect the balance sheet. The vicar calmed matters down, and in traditional church fashion it was felt best to keep the (unsatisfactory) *status quo*.

After some additional moaning about the collections, one person saying yet again that there were times: *"when the offertory did not average even a halfpenny per head of those present"*, and the suggestion that the choir might look better in surplices (the vicar was not to be drawn on that one), the minutes were signed off and the meeting closed.[14,15]

'He died, surrounded by his family'

In the middle of 1878, not long after the vestry meeting, Archdeacon Mildmay again became unwell. He had not been his usual commanding self for a couple of years, and the death of his wife in January had been to him like a hammer blow, plunging him initially into the deepest grief imaginable. On Palm Sunday 1878, when the renewed chancel in St Mary's was due to be used for the first time, he was, *"under the influence of such emotion and distress as to be unable to attend any but the early morning communion service"*. He did recover a little and was able to chair the Easter vestry meeting at St Mary's as usual, but he was taken ill again on 15 June, just as he was about to travel to Bad Homburg, near Frankfurt, with his two unmarried daughters, one of whom (Miss Evelyne St John Mildmay) was also in poor health. It was felt that a trip to take the waters would benefit her and also her father. By Friday, 21 June the archdeacon felt much better, and so the whole party left for Germany, arriving in Homburg on Tuesday, 25 June. Almost on arrival, his illness returned with greater severity, and from that time up to the time of his death he became worse, and his three surviving daughters and two sons-in-law (his daughter Horatia, who had married Charles Pasco Glyn of the banking family, in 1858, had died within six weeks of her marriage) were summoned immediately. He died at about 5 o'clock on Sunday, 14 July 1878, surrounded by his family. The news reached Chelmsford on the following Monday, and plunged the whole community into the deepest mourning.[16]

Archdeacon Mildmay was a member of the family whose name had become synonymous with Chelmsford over a long and distinguished history spanning some three hundred years. There were said to be no less than forty Mildmays buried in St Mary's churchyard. Carew Anthony St John Mildmay was one of the sons of Sir Henry Paulet St John, the third baronet, and Jane (Dame Jane Mildmay, who donated the land for St John's), eldest daughter and co-heiress of Carew Mildmay of Shawford House, Hampshire. Sir Henry had adopted the name and the arms of the Mildmay family in 1790. Descended from two distinguished families, the archdeacon was born in 1800, and went up to Oriel College, Oxford, taking his BA in 1822 and MA in 1825. He was ordained deacon by the Bishop of Winchester in the cathedral in May 1825, initially serving in the family church at Dogmersfield in Hampshire.[17] He moved to Chelmsford as rector at the comparatively young age of 26 (the patron of the living was his mother, Dame Jane Mildmay) in 1826. At that time, Chelmsford and Moulsham were still a single parish (St Mary's) and as incumbent, the rector had wide-ranging responsibilities, both numerous and varied in their nature. Almost immediately he added a Sunday evening service at St Mary's, and then encouraged and oversaw the building of the Chapel of ease in Moulsham, which is now St John's. He caused subscriptions to be raised for the National Schools (opened in 1841) and contributed greatly to the enlargement of St Mary's, including the construction of a new north aisle and the renewing of the chancel. He married the Hon Caroline, the youngest daughter of the late Admiral Lord Radstock, at Trinity Church, Marylebone on 14 December 1830.[18] They were to have four daughters, Augusta, Caroline, Horatia and Evelyne. Behind the public works, the archdeacon laboured tirelessly at keeping up the religious and moral tone of his parish, as evidenced by the exceptional numbers of confirmations and communicants, and marked especially by the peace and union which existed with regard to church matters in Chelmsford, in distinct contrast to some other parishes where controversy and bitterness ruled. On a personal level, he was described as: *"a man of tall form, with a distinct aristocratic bearing and a meticulous regard for punctuality"*. At vestry meetings, the moment the clock struck the hour, he would begin. Even at the last of his vestry meetings, when he was a minute or so late and had to apologise for his tardiness, he felt that it was not his fault, *"you must blame the gout for it, not me"*. It was a measure of the deep love and affection in which the parish held the late archdeacon and his late wife that on the occasion of the fiftieth anniversary of his incumbency, (which coincided with their forty-sixth wedding anniversary) a large public meeting was held at the Corn Exchange and a handsome testimonial presented. The devoted couple received a magnificent collection of silver plate, a plain, massive gold ring inscribed *"Chelmsford – 1826–1876"* and an illuminated address

Figure 14 – Archdeacon Carew Anthony St John Mildmay, Rector of St Mary's, Chelmsford, and the inspiration behind St John's, Moulsham

to which no less than 800 people had appended their signatures. At this presentation the archdeacon explained that he had endeavoured throughout his incumbency to be consistent in his conduct, remarking that: *"he had come to Chelmsford with the Bible in one hand and the prayer book in the other, and those two it had been his object and desire to keep ever before him"*.[19] His picture (*Figure 14*) shows an aristocratic, firm, yet warm man deeply conscious of his position in life and the standards that he needed to demonstrate to those he came into contact with.

'The day was marked by manifestations of the most widespread regret'

The archdeacon's body, enclosed in a continental-style pyramidal coffin, arrived at Chelmsford station on the Thursday morning (18 July). It was received by the undertaker (Mr Pullen) and the curate (Mr Parmiter) and conveyed immediately to the rectory. The archdeacon's funeral took place on Saturday, 20 July and was a sombre and dignified occasion for the town. The day was marked by manifestations of the most widespread regret at his removal from the place where he had laboured so long. Local sentiment was truly universal. All shops and other places of business were closed, blinds were drawn in houses in every part of the parish, and the sad procession to Rectory Lane cemetery was representative of every class, creed and interest in the neighbourhood, and was the largest funeral *cortège* that had been seen in Essex for many years. The funeral service itself was conducted in the parish church; nowhere else in the parish had as much consecrated space. At half-past two on the Saturday the church was full to overflowing, the congregation for the most part being attired in deepest mourning. The building was decorated with a simple cross of white lilies and ferns located over the reredos, and the altar and all the gas standards were draped in black. The churchwardens and synodsmen carried black wands tipped with black crape rosettes. All the archdeacons and deans of the diocese were present, together with almost all the local clergy including Thomas Wilkinson and Edward Clive. The service was taken by the Rev Parmiter, as the Bishop of St Albans (who would have officiated) was still on the continent; he, too, had gone there to try and improve his health. Miss Evelyne Mildmay (on whose behalf the archdeacon had undertaken the journey to Homburg in the first place) was still too unwell to come back to England for her father's funeral. A cousin of the archdeacon, the Rev Arundel Mildmay, read the lesson. The brass plate, affixed to the top of the coffin read:

"Carew Anthony St John Mildmay
Archdeacon of Essex, Rector of Chelmsford,
Born 2 January, 1800, died 14 July, 1878"

Outside St Mary's the procession formed up and made its melancholy way to the Rectory Lane cemetery. The whole route was lined by mourning parishioners, in some places many deep. The principal mourner was the archdeacon's nephew, Sir Henry Mildmay. The coffin was deposited in the family vault where his daughter and wife already lay.

Special services were held on the Sunday following the funeral at many of the local churches, including St Mary's. Here there was a large congregation, a good many of whom were moved to tears by Rev F. Binyon's sermon. At St John's, Moulsham, in Thomas Wilkinson's morning service, the sermon was an eloquent tribute to the memory of the deceased, the vicar pointing out that it would: *"ill benefit that pulpit to be silent on such an occasion"*. Preaching on the text *"And David himself followed the bier"*, he pointed out that the archdeacon had been a true man, always true to his convictions. He concluded by reminding his hearers of how much they were indebted to the late archdeacon; how, if it had not been for his dedication, hard work and munificent purse, St John's would never have come into existence. Indeed, on the last occasion he (Thomas Wilkinson) had seen the archdeacon, he was engaged on work for their benefit.

So Archdeacon Mildmay left his earthly toil for his heavenly reward. He had, though, not done too badly for his reward on earth. This much-loved, much-revered rector had also been a noted pluralist, sufficiently so to have been somewhat scurrilously taken to task in the pages of Punch:

"AN OPENING FOR AN INDOLENT PARSON"

"A curious question is suggested by an impudent advertisement , quoted by The Times, *which offers for sale:-*

"A sinecure rectory in the Isle of Wight, the annual amount of the tithe rent charge for the last five years being £350, with three and a half acres of glebe, with two cottages producing £30 per annum, the present incumbent in his fifty-eighth year"

As this rectory is a sinecure of souls, there is certainly some reason to doubt that it is a spiritual benefice, and if it is not, ought the sale of it, even if it were sold outright, to be considered simony? Shorwell, near Newport, is the benefice referred to – a material benefice decidedly we should say, not at all a spiritual one; therefore purchasable by any idle person, who wishes to continue to eat the bread of idleness, richly buttered, without occurring the condemnation of Simon Magus. The patroness of this jolly fat living, all rights included, was Lady St John Mildmay, and the incumbent is a St John Mildmay also, The Rev C.A. This St John, the evangelist of Shorwell sinecure, is also evangelist or vicar of Burnham, in Essex, worth £700 a year; and moreover is supposed to preach the gospel at Chelmsford at £800 a year as rector, besides perambulating the highways and hedges for the capture of souls in the capacity of rural dean of Rochester. Notwithstanding this evangelical man is only fifty-eight, the purchaser of Shorwell may easily count on an early succession to that paradise of laziness; for although St John has nothing at all to do there, the highly plural nature of his employments elsewhere renders it tolerably certain that he must very soon be worked to death".[20]

Archdeacon Mildmay's death brought to an end the centuries-long involvement of the Mildmay family with Chelmsford.

Since Thomas Mildmay had first arrived in Chelmsford at the beginning of the sixteenth century, the family had always had an influential presence in the town, but after the archdeacon's death his two remaining unmarried daughters soon moved away and the parish church of St Mary's awaited to see who would be appointed rector.

With the archdeacon's death, the advowson of the living, held since 1563 by the Mildmay family, was relinquished and reverted to the bishop of the diocese (now the diocese of St Albans), the Rt Rev Thomas Claughton. He announced in August 1878 that the next incumbent of St Mary's would be Rev Sir John Caesar Hawkins, Bart. A graduate of Oriel College, Oxford, he had been rector of St Albans prior to its elevation to cathedral status in 1877. He was instituted to St Mary's by the bishop of St Albans on Sunday, 13 October 1878.[21] At the morning service, during which the souls of the congregation were formally placed under the care of the new rector, the bishop himself preached, and at the conclusion of the service the vast majority of the packed congregation received Holy Communion. At the evening service the rector himself preached the sermon, emphasising what a solemn and emotional moment this was, both for himself and for the parishioners of St Mary's. He was in his early fifties when he and his wife Catherine moved to Chelmsford (there were no children). However, his association with Chelmsford was short, as due to ill-health he resigned in 1880.[22]

St John's, Moulsham felt the loss of Archdeacon Mildmay very keenly, and not long after his death a subscription was started to raise a memorial to him in the church. The money collected was sufficient to commission a font to match the pulpit in style. It consists of an octagonal bowl with plain sides bearing the inscription *"One Church, One Faith, One Baptism, One Lord"* around the top edge on a narrow panel bordered with leaves. The bowl itself is set on a short drum and is supported by eight colonettes, each of a different coloured Portland marble similar to the pulpit (these have been painted over). On the base is affixed a brass plate carrying the inscription (in black gothic lettering illuminated with red capitals:

"To the Glory of God and in memory of
CAREW ANTHONY St JOHN MILDMAY, M.A.,
Archdeacon of Essex and Rector of Chelmsford,
a friend and benefactor of this parish
A.D. 1800 – 1878"

'Many people had been much inconvenienced by the temperature of the church'

Thomas Wilkinson chaired his next (and, as it would turn out, his last) vestry meeting at St John's on Tuesday, 15 April 1879. The accounts were presented and briefly discussed. On this occasion there was a small balance against the churchwardens of £2 6s. 9d. Thomas Tidboald noted that there had been a time when the balance due to the officials had been as high as £25, so the previous year had been a positive one. The accounts were received and passed.

Mr William Cutts then brought to the attention of the meeting the falling numbers of people attending the church. He was not sure, but thought that one possible cause was that a good many people had left the parish. Mr Robbins thought that the most likely reason was that the church was so cold in winter (at which there were loud cries of *"Hear, Hear"*). John Saltmarsh agreed with this and said that many people had told him they had been much inconvenienced by the temperature of the church. Thomas Tidboald then pointed out that the warming apparatus for the church, although less than five years old, gave less heat than the old system, and cost a great deal more to run. He had, though, asked Mr Dennis, (the engineer who had installed the system in 1874) to give them an estimate for a new boiler, and he closed the discussion on this subject by expressing the hope that they would have a better state of things for the following winter. The election of the churchwardens (Robert Hanam and Thomas Tidboald) was agreed, and after some desultory discussion about the role and status of synodsmen, these too were duly selected.

Thomas Wilkinson then raised the pressing question of a new burial ground. As a result of the discussions at the previous Easter vestry, he had approached Archdeacon Mildmay and asked him to use his influence with Sir Henry Mildmay to see what could be done. Sir Henry, when consulted, had expressed his willingness to give an acre of ground (which was all that he could give). A number of sites in the parish were in the process of being investigated when the archdeacon's death threw the whole process back into the melting pot. The matter had been left in Mr Gepp's hands, and eventually he and Mr Oxley Parker had recommended a piece of ground near the Pound, opposite Prospect Terrace (Prospect Terrace is the small group of terraced houses at the St John's Road end of what is now Vicarage Road, and the Pound was located on the opposite side of Vicarage Road where the small *cul-de-sac* end of Mildmay Road now stands). Trial holes were dug at the proposed site, and unfortunately: *"they soon came down to the water, and that piece was impracticable"*. They then tried a field at the back of the vicarage (now the site of Oaklands school) lying roughly where St Vincent's and St Michael's Roads now are; this was found to be worse *"coming quickly to water"*. Mr Pertwee (a local surveyor) then suggested the field where the gravel pit had been (it is not obvious whereabouts this was) and this was found to be ideal, there being no water *"down to nine feet"*. Recommendations that this site be used had been made to the new rector of St Mary's, but by the time of the meeting they had received no reply. There then followed some aimless discussion about whether or not legislation would soon be introduced to deal with situations like St John's, where the burial ground was almost full, yet was still being asked to accommodate up to fifty internments a year. Eventually it was decided to postpone any further discussion until the following year. The proceedings then closed with a hearty vote of thanks to the vicar.[23]

'When I needed attention, sympathy and kindness were forthcoming from everyone'

Not long after this vestry meeting, Thomas Wilkinson must have decided that enough was enough and that he was clearly not the man to wear himself out in the service of the parishioners of Moulsham. Of his predecessors, one had died in office and the other had left the parish, fighting ill-health, for a quieter life. For much of 1878 the running of St John's seemed to have devolved squarely on the shoulders of Edward Clive, who had been assisted from time to time by a close friend, Rev John Kershaw, the headmaster of the Chelmsford Grammar school. Whether or not Thomas Wilkinson was away from the parish for prolonged holidays, to recuperate from his labours or for reasons of ill-health is not clear, but there were periods when all the work seems to have fallen on the curates. The strain told on Edward Clive as well, and it was no surprise that in early May 1879 he announced that he too would be leaving the parish. He preached his final sermon at St John's on Sunday, 15 June, taking as his text Peter iii, 4, *"the past time of our life"*. In a moving sermon he spoke, it seemed, almost personally to each member of the congregation, addressing them as *"my dear brethren"*. He was, he said, speaking to them: *"for the last time as curate of your parish. It would be strange, indeed, if I did not feel real regret at the thought of leaving so many kind friends and so much that is dear to my heart in my work here"*. He ended by asking them all for, *"your prayers to God for me, that he will pardon the imperfections of the past, and give me grace to labour more faithfully in the time to come"*. It was said that many of the congregation were in tears at the thought of his departure.[24]

On the following Wednesday evening a good number of parishioners assembled in the girls' schoolroom for the presentation to Edward Clive of a handsome testimonial, to which no fewer than 176 individuals had subscribed. The testimonial consisted of a silver inkstand, ebony and silver envelope and blotting cases, and a letter balance. The silver inkstand bore the following inscription:

> *"Presented to the Rev Edward Clive, M.A.,*
> *from the parishioners of St John's Moulsham,*
> *as a small tribute of their esteem and respect,*
> *and in appreciation of the faithful discharge*
> *of his duties as curate for the past five years".*
>
> June, 1879

In addition to this testimonial, the master, mistresses and children of the national schools had purchased two of Edward Clive's favourite books for him, *viz.* *"The Land and the Book"*, by Dr Thomson and *"Dr Trench on the Gospels"*. Robert Hanam made the presentation, emphasising what an enormous loss Edward Clive's departure was to them all, and that the whole time he had been their curate, he had conducted himself generally so that he had gained the esteem and affection of most (if not all) of the parishioners.

Edward Clive, very deeply moved, reminded people that when he had first come into the parish: *"I remember very well the kind welcome that I received from all of you, and I remember that shortly afterwards, at a time when I especially needed such attention, sympathy and kindness were forthcoming from everyone"*. (This is a reference to the death of Edward Clive's 'intended', Miss Spiers, when the family came to St John's to hear Edward's first sermon). He went on to say that he had: *"intended to pass from home to home, just saying a few words to each one, but I found that everyone was so kind, so anxious to detain me, that it turned out to be a very serious work indeed, and I am afraid that I will not be able to complete it"*. Almost in tears, he concluded: *"Once more, my dear friends, I thank you all very heartily for this handsome present, which I assure you I shall always cherish – always keep – and which will be ever full of pleasant memories for me"*.[25]

'Gentle in manner, kind and joyous in disposition, true and firm in friendship'

It had been Edward Clive's intention, when he left the parish, to take a long holiday, travelling around Europe with a friend, before he took another ministerial charge. So, in the last week of August 1879, some scant six weeks after he had taken leave of St John's, he was at the house of his friend Benjamin Spiers (Emily Jane's brother) in Hertford Square, where the two of them were discussing the proposed holiday. In the early part of that week Edward Clive complained of feeling unwell, but went about as usual until the Friday, when he was taken very ill. By the following Tuesday he was so seriously ill that when his friend Rev Binyon (a former curate of St Mary's, Chelmsford) called to enquire after him, it was not deemed advisable to allow him to visit the sick man. During the day he continued to get worse, and late that evening, although tended to the last by loving and affectionate care, he died. He was only thirty-three years old, and his untimely death was due to: *"rupture of a vessel in his side"*.[26]

His funeral took place on Monday, 8 September, at Norwood cemetery, south London. He was buried in the family grave in which his late father had been interred in early 1878. The principal mourner was his younger brother, Robert, and the burial service itself was performed by Alfred Mason, who had guided and nurtured the raw young curate at St John's. Alfred Mason, compassionate man that he was, *"was deeply and visibly affected throughout the ceremony"*. All who took part in the proceedings were: *"moved with an emotion which fully testified to the loss which they had sustained by the death of their dear friend and companion"*. The previous Sunday evening at St John's, Moulsham (7 September) the Rev John Kershaw (who with the departure of Thomas Wilkinson was acting as *locum tenens* for the parish) preached a very moving sermon, referring to the: *"news which had come so startling a shock that we all say we find it very hard to realise it – the unexpected summons that came from the great Master of Edward Clive, to rest from his labours"*. He remarked that it had only been: *"a little more than a fortnight since many of us had seen him over here on a short visit, to all appearances in his usual good health, and so little anticipating any abrupt termination of his earthly sojourn that he and I were talking about the probability of sharing the care of the parish during the interval. To me, who have often* (sic) *ministered with him at the same altar and in this church, and who, after a comparatively short acquaintance, had become bound by the attachment of a strong friendship, the blow was literally stunning; truly, in the midst of life, we are in death"*. He noted that Edward Clive had become a personal and warm-hearted friend to so many in the parish, and that everyone who had come into contact with him remembered him as gentle in manner, kind and joyous in disposition, true and firm in friendship, considerate and thoughtful to the needy, sick and sorrowing and anxious and painstaking in all his duties. He concluded by reminding his hearers (in true Victorian fashion) that: *"to us survivors, he may yet, from the unseen world, lift his voice and say 'Watch, for ye know not neither the day nor the hour; be ye ready, for the Son of Man cometh at an hour ye think not'"*.[27]

He is commemorated in St John's by the long, shallow brass plate on the north wall of the north transept and the two-light Clayton and Bell window above (depicting 'Deeds of Charity'). The brass work is engraved: *"To the glory of God and in affectionate remembrance of Edward Clive, M.A., who after several years of faithful service as curate of this parish entered into rest on 3 September 1879. These windows are dedicated by his fellow parishioners and friends"*.

Thomas Wilkinson officially resigned as vicar on 6 June 1879[28] and preached his last sermon at the church on the Sunday before Edward Clive's death, 31 August. In this sermon he (somewhat surprisingly) made no reference to his departure from the parish, but he did take the opportunity to point out to the congregation that for the immediate future there would only be two services weekly, both on Sundays, at eleven in the morning and seven in

113

the evening (these being the only times that Rev John Kershaw, as headmaster of the school, was free to take them).[29]

In the *Gospeller* magazine (where perhaps not many of his congregation would have seen his words) Thomas Wilkinson did address his flock. He wrote: *"My dear Parishioners, in addressing you for the last time, it is right that I should explain to you why I am leaving. An experience of two years has convinced me that with only two clergy, it is impossible to attack with any purpose the mass of ungodliness* (sic) *that exists among us. It is not possible to do much more than attend to the Services, Schools and general machinery of the parish and visit the sick and other urgent cases. Under these circumstances, feeling that a stronger man than myself might be able to do more than I (if there were only to be one curate) I resolved sometime since that I would resign unless I were able to provide a second curate".* He went on to point out that the income for the benefice was £370, and as the stipend for a senior curate would be £130, for a junior curate of the order of £120, after paying for maintenance of the vicarage, subscriptions to local charities and his tax bill, he would have less than £50 to live on, and this was obviously not feasible. He explained that: *"Had I been willing to work the parish with only one curate, I need not have left you, but I thought it my duty under Our Lord's Law of Love to sacrifice my own interests* (sic) *in the hope that it might be for your good".*[30]

In October it was announced that Thomas Wilkinson, until recently vicar of St John's, Moulsham, had been appointed to the preachership of the Magdalene Hospital, Streatham. The *Chelmsford Chronicle* noted that: *"the Chapel attached to the Hospital is open to the public and accommodates about 300 in addition to the inmates of the institution".* Thomas Wilkinson was expected to take up his post in a further six weeks, as it was stated that he hoped to be in residence at Streatham in two to three weeks' time.[31] In fact, the financial situation of the parish was not quite as bad as he had reported, as it had been announced in May that the Ecclesiastical Commissioners for England, had agreed to pay the incumbent of Moulsham a further £40 towards another curate; but it was still nowhere near enough to run the parish as Thomas Wilkinson wished.[32]

Figure 15 – Thomas Henry Wilkinson, Incumbent of
St John's, Moulsham 1877–79

So Thomas Wilkinson departed the parish in which he had never really settled (he was never really to settle anywhere during his ministry) and where, in truth, he did not seem to be much missed (in contrast to Edward Clive, there is no record of any presentation to him from the parishioners). His portrait shows a diffident, uncertain man, perhaps never sure of who he was or what he wanted from life (*Figure 15*)

The next vicar of St John's, Moulsham, would need very deep pockets.

5. GEORGE ST ALBAN GODSON

(1879–1900)

*"Had he lived in the dark ages of Christianity, instead of the
reign of Queen Victoria, he would have been enrolled amongst
the army of Saints, as his nineteenth century name signifies,
St Alban Godson, a true and trusty son of God his Heavenly
Father. It will be sometime before we are privileged to look
upon his like again".*[1]

Rev William Gibbens, the sometime rector of Chignal Smealy, was
a close friend of George St Alban Godson, and he penned the
above as part of a heartfelt tribute to the late vicar of St John the
Evangelist, Moulsham, shortly after his death in 1900. It was a
tribute he had found difficult to write, as it was not simple to put
into words what George Godson meant to those who knew him.
But William Gibbens had caught the essence of how George
Godson's incumbency was to be remembered – a good, house-
visiting parish priest, essaying to the end to discharge his duties to
all his parishioners.

'St John's may have appealed to him as somewhere he could use his undoubted talents'

George St Alban Godson was born in about 1832, in Grosvenor
Place, London, in the parish of St George's, Hanover Square. He
was the youngest son of Richard Godson, QC, MP and Mary
Godson. His father was reputed to have bestowed the Christian
name 'St Alban' on him after the parliamentary seat that he (his
father) had at one time represented. George and his two brothers
Henry and Arthur were tutored at home, from whence George
went up to Pembroke College, Cambridge, where he was admitted
as a pensioner in October 1851, aged 19. He graduated BA in

1856, receiving his MA in 1864. He was ordained deacon in 1856 and priest in 1857 in Canterbury Cathedral.[2] After two brief curacies, at St Alphege in Canterbury (1857–58) and near his family home at St John the Evangelist, St Pancras (1858–60), he moved to Shenley in Hertfordshire (near London Colney) where he stayed as curate for almost ten years. Here he met and married Jessy, the daughter of Samuel Preston Child of Woodhall. They were to have no children. In 1869 George Godson moved the short distance from Shenley to the Episcopal Chapel at Arkley, near Barnet. St Peter's, Arkley, was curiously like St John the Evangelist, Moulsham, in its origins. It had been built in 1840, in brick and flint, with freestone dressings, as a chapel of ease to Barnet parish church, most of the money for its construction being donated by Enoch Durant of High Canons, Shenley. It was constructed in much the same debased gothic style as St John's, although it served a much smaller population (only a few hundred) and was accordingly significantly smaller in size, seating only about 170[3]. It is possible that St John's Moulsham, a chapel of ease which came into being in not dissimilar circumstances (but which served a larger population) may have appealed to George Godson as somewhere he could use his undoubted talents to much greater effect, and this may have encouraged him to move to Chelmsford in 1879.

In July 1879 it was announced in the *Essex Weekly News* that: *"The Rev George St Alban Godson has accepted the vicarage of St John the Evangelist, Moulsham. He has been since 1869 the incumbent of Arkley Chapel, near Barnet, Herts."*[4] Three months later the parishioners of St John's received the news they were waiting to hear, that: *"... the Rev George St Alban Godson will, on Sunday next (12 October) be inducted by the bishop of St Albans to the vicarage of St John the Evangelist. The Rev J.A. Kershaw, who has of late conducted the services, on Sunday last gave notice that the vicar designate wished to announce in future, services on the Lord's day would be at 8.30 am (early communion), 11.00 am (morning prayer) followed by an afternoon service at 3.00 pm and an evening service at 7.00 pm"*[5] George Godson was inducted formally to the living on Sunday, 19 October, but the induction was carried out by the rector of St Mary's, Rev Sir John Caesar Hawkins, as the bishop was still unwell. *"There was Holy Communion at 8.30 and at 11.00 the prayers and lessons were read by the rector, George Godson taking the ante-communion service and from the pulpit reading the Thirty-nine Articles"*.[6]

George Godson soon had an impact on the parish. The new pattern of services that Rev John Kershaw had announced just prior to George Godson's arrival was demanding enough on its own, but the new vicar viewed this as only a start. To expand the services, and accommodate all the requests for baptisms and funerals needed assistance, and in late 1879 Rev Harry Percy Grubb was engaged as a curate. With day-to-day running of the parish church and its services under control, George Godson was able to turn his attention to more mundane parish matters. He had not long settled in as vicar when the first of his many vestry meetings was upon him, on Tuesday, 30 March 1880. The meeting did not start on the most promising foot. Thomas Tidboald, on behalf of the churchwardens, produced accounts for the previous year. He regretted that there had been a marked falling off in offertories, those for church expenses and the schools suffering particularly badly. The latter offertory was the smallest it had ever been; for the past year only just over £17 had been received, compared with the normal figure of more than £25. It was felt, after considerable discussion, that in view of the generally depressed nature of business in the town, the figures could have been much worse, and so the accounts were passed. George Godson re-appointed Robert Hanam as the vicar's warden and Thomas Tidboald was re-elected to represent the parishioners.[7] There is no mention in the minutes of the proposed enlargement of St John's church building, but it must have been about this time that discussions started to explore the possibilities. Alfred Mason had repeated his offering of £600 (towards the extension) to the new vicar when he arrived in the parish and George Godson had agreed to carry out these plans to the best of his ability. The estimated expenses in connection with the work were of the order of £1,900, so there was clearly much to do. There would need to be many concerts, sales of work and exhortatory sermons preached before they were able to get anywhere near this sum.[8]

"A little alteration as regards the election of people's churchwarden'

George Godson took his second vestry meeting in 1881 (on Tuesday, 19 April). This was an altogether more lively affair than that of the previous year, when perhaps the meeting had been on its best behaviour for a new incumbent. The financial report was much better – Thomas Tidboald confirmed that: *"the offertories for the past year had considerably exceeded those for the previous two years, being £315 compared to £253 in 1879 and £286 in 1880"*. The accounts were enthusiastically adopted. Robert Hanam was re-appointed as vicar's churchwarden and John Saltmarsh proposed Thomas Tidboald for re-election as people's churchwarden. Then the fun started. Edward Robbins, a well-to-do newspaper proprietor who lived in New London Road, then proceeded to make a point that he had clearly been growing restive about for some time. He asked (as delicately as possible) if: *"he might be permitted to submit to the meeting that the time had approached, or at all events was approaching, when it might be desirable to take into consideration the advisability of making a little alteration as regards the election of people's churchwarden"*. He acknowledged to the meeting that the subject: *"needed approaching with a great deal of care. It was a delicate matter, no doubt; but still, at the same time, he ventured to think that they might, without hurting Mr Tidboald's feelings, or anyone else's whatever – think this matter over calmly and try and see whether or not it would be desirable to have any alteration"*. He continued (beating his way around a whole clump of bushes) by saying: *"firstly that he thought that having regard to the uncertainty of life which they knew did exist it might be more prudent if instead of electing the same gentleman year after year to this office they had an occasional change; secondly, he felt that it was often the case that a little new blood instilled into an institution was*

119

beneficial to that institution, and thirdly, he thought that it was hardly fair to impose year after year on the good nature of any gentleman by continuing to thrust on him an office that he knew involved a large amount of trouble and time". He concluded by expressing hopes that his remarks would be received in the same spirit as that in which they had been made.

William Cutts replied on Thomas Tidboald's behalf. He had, he said: *"been thinking on this subject in the course of Mr Robbins' observations"*. He added, somewhat portentously (as was his nature) that: *"he supposed that Mr Robbins was referring rather to some prospective change"*. He tried to lighten the atmosphere a little by saying: *"So far as Mr Tidboald's appearance went, he seemed to be in tolerably robust health (hear, hear – and laughter) and therefore he (Mr Cutts) preferred to say that while they were doing well they had better remain well"*. There was then some brief further discussion before Thomas Tidboald was re-elected. He then spoke (he had remained silent during the suggestion that he stand down). He said that: *"he would not detain them long by referring to the remarks that had been made by Mr Robbins. He supposed that Mr Robbins thought that he (Mr Tidboald) was on his last legs [Mr Robbins – Nothing of the kind]. He had had an attack of the gout, it was true, and he supposed that Mr Robbins thought that he would not last the year"*. He went on in this vein for some time and concluded, rather sardonically, by saying that he supposed: *"Mr Robbins himself might perhaps like the office"*. The vestry meeting was, unusually, becoming quite heated, and it fell to George Godson to calm it all down by saying that he thought it would be the unanimous feeling of them all that Thomas Tidboald would be the ideal man they wanted for the office if he was willing to serve. Edward Robbins, though, had the last word, pointing out that a Bill was shortly to be introduced into the House of Commons limiting the power of churchwardens and substituting Parochial Boards instead. He reminded them all that the Hon Member who had brought the Bill forward had done so because he had discovered that in some parishes (and he emphasised that this did not include Moulsham) where the office of churchwarden had continued year after year in the same hands, *"certain things had crept in that ought not to have crept in"*. That was enough. The vicar exerted his authority and quickly moved the meeting on to the election of synodsmen, and the meeting closed before any further damage was done.[9] It was a very discrete, and typically Victorian, spat.

'He thought there ought to be a special meeting of the parishioners'

Figure 16 – The West Front of St John's, Moulsham, as it appeared before the tower was built in 1883

With the start of the new year in 1882 attention moved to the need to press ahead with the ideas for the enlargement of the church. Early in the year, a public meeting was held to discuss in overall terms what the objectives were (to provide additional, free accommodation for the poor of the parish to attend divine worship and to improve an uninspiring west end (*see Figure 16*) by the addition of a tower which would provide a visual demonstration of the presence of God in the neighbourhood). The meeting elected a committee comprising George Godson, the churchwardens and a number of prominent individuals associated with St John's. It also agreed that a formal Church Enlargement fund should be set up. The committee worked diligently at its tasks and by Saturday, 25 March, when it assembled at the vicarage to review its progress, it was able to have a preliminary look at Frederick Chancellor's ideas for the modifications. A letter from the architect was also shown to the meeting, stating that a builder had agreed to carry out the proposed works for £1,700. It was unanimously agreed that the work should begin as soon as possible, once the necessary formalities had been complied with. The committee heard that the money that had been collected (or promised) so far fell short of the required amount by about £370 and they agreed that an urgent appeal for the sum remaining should be launched at once. One member pointed out that he hoped that many who previously might have doubted whether or not the undertaking would ever be commenced might now come forward and help to bring the project to a successful conclusion. Not only cash had been received - it was reported that: *"an article of jewellery had been placed in the offertory for the fund and had been valued at £10".*[10]

Early in 1882 St John's had also had an opportunity to demonstrate its patriotic side. On Thursday, 2 March a Mr Roderick MacClean had attempted to assassinate Queen Victoria by firing a pistol at her as she left Windsor railway station for the castle (he missed). On the following Sunday a special service of thanksgiving was held at St John's with appropriate prayers and the playing of the National Anthem on the organ.[11]

By the first week of April Frederick Chancellor's final plans had been completed, in time for the vestry meeting on Tuesday, 11 April. The usual business of the accounts was easily dealt with, Robert Hanam giving detailed figures which showed that the past year had been a good one – the surplus for 1881 was more than £14. He did have to report (although most of the people at the meeting knew already) that: *"with great regret the annual anonymous contribution of £50 in the offertory at St John's had not been given this past Christmas. Though the kind donor who for many years has thus helped the poor of Moulsham is careful that all expense incurred in anticipation of the gift shall be met, the aged and infirm will feel the loss very keenly unless something can be done to supply the deficiency"*.[12] It was never disclosed who the generous donor was, although the finger of suspicion pointed at Frederick Veley (or possibly his daughter Juliana). Each year Frederick Veley regularly entertained about a dozen elderly widows from the parish to a Christmas meal at his house, 'Yverdons' in New London Road.

The vicar again nominated Robert Hanam as his churchwarden and Thomas Tidboald was quickly re-elected to the position of parish churchwarden (this time unopposed), Frederick Veley pointing out that when he had resigned in 1867 Thomas Tidboald had taken over from him. The meeting finished off its routine business by discussing the heating yet again, Thomas Tidboald remarking that: *"Notwithstanding the mildness of the winter eight tons of coke had been consumed in heating the church ... ... as the boiler was very much out of repair and leaked considerably"*. There were also several complaints about the strong draught that appeared from time to time in the north transept (it still does, over one hundred years later). After some half-hearted discussion it was agreed to drop the subject of heating until the following year.

The vicar then moved on to the enlargement of the church. He thought that there ought to be a special meeting of the parishioners to pass a resolution that the plans should be carried out, and that resolution would then enable them to apply for a faculty to carry out the work. Vestry meetings were normally held at ten in the morning, but many of those present felt that an evening meeting at about eight o'clock would enable many more parishioners (most of whom worked) to be present. The vicar reminded them all that the preliminary meeting early in the year to tell everyone about what they intended to do (and when they had appointed the committee to oversee the whole process) had been at eight in the evening. After brief discussion it was left to the churchwardens to call the meeting at the most appropriate time. Robert Hanam reported that subscriptions had already provided a fair sum towards the alterations, so much so, that only between £300 and £400 was still required.[13]

'The alterations contemplated will give additional sittings to 128 parishioners'

The meeting to draw up the petition for the faculty was held (after proper public notice had been given) on 20 April 1882. The petition, addressed to the bishop of the diocese showed: *"that the population of the parish is now 4,956 and increasing out of which it is considered that 4,200 are the poorer class of inhabitants. The church accommodation will at present seat 792 and the alterations contemplated will give additional sittings to 128 parishioners"*. It continued by giving a full version of the resolution passed at that meeting, describing how: *"in carrying out the work it is intended to lengthen the nave – to erect a porch on the south side and to build a tower at the west end of the church (see Figure 17) ... ...that there are no pews or vaults in the said church held under faculty or by prescription, and the estimated cost of the said work amount* (sic) *to £1,900, toward which a sum of £600 has been given by a former vicar, the Rev A.W. Mason and most of the remainder has been received or promised and an account has been opened with the bank in Chelmsford where the sums are paid in as received from the subscribers"*. The petition also confirmed that the works involved in these alterations did not involve the removal of any bodies or remains, and that no monuments, gravestones or any mural tablets needed to be repositioned. The petition was approved on 25 April and the citation issued on 1 May.[14]

There seems to be no information in the local press or in existing church records of when the work started and there appears to have been no formal stone-laying ceremony, which is unusual for such major additional construction. The building work appears to have taken much longer than anticipated. By October 1882 it was reported that: *"The St Alban's church building society have made a liberal grant towards the Moulsham church building fund but*

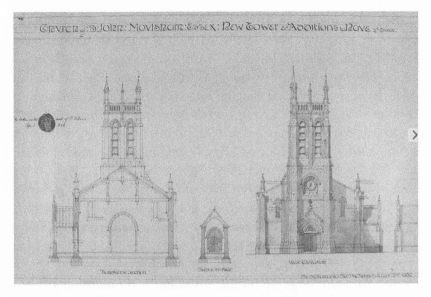

Figure 17 – The proposed tower modifications to St John's, Moulsham, in Frederick Chancellor's 1883 sketches

the amount has not yet been officially stated. The rector of Chelmsford has most kindly increased his subscription to £25 and additional sums had been received amounting to £15 14s. The works at the church are proceeding most satisfactorily".[15] The same report stated that it was planned to hold a sale of needlework in aid of the church building fund, although it was not until June of the following year that this took place. Subscriptions to the fund were still coming in at the start of the new year when the receipt of an additional £68 1s. 6d. was acknowledged. This included substantial donations from two local industrialists, the brewer Frederick Wells of Oaklands and Walter Gray of Phoenix House.[16]

Work continued at a much reduced pace throughout the winter, and by the time of the 1883 vestry meeting on 27 March, it was simply noted, rather hopefully, that: *"when the church was completed, their offertories would be better than before".*[17] Money for the additional construction was still coming in little by little, the *Essex Weekly News* reporting that at the beginning of April the receipt of a number of subscriptions, including the

125

rather odd sum of £6 18s. from Mr Charles Pertwee, the local surveyor who had been trying to help the parish find suitable land for a new burial ground.[18] Work on the tower continued to creep upwards (literally) towards completion and the bishop of St Albans announced that he intended to hold a confirmation service in St John's: *"during the summer, the day of which was uncertain* (the confirmation, not the summer) *pending completion of the church extension and of the building of the tower, which are* (sic) *now far advanced, the tower rearing its lofty head as a prominent feature in that part of the landscape".*[19] Earlier in the year, a new curate, Rev Tom Athorne, had been licensed at St John's, taking his first service at the end of February, but, sadly by the end of April it was reported that: *"we are sorry to hear that the Rev T.B. Athorne will not be able, on account of his health, to continue at St John's, Moulsham. All who have heard Mr Athorne during the short time he has been with us will regret this decision".*[20]

By May separate subscriptions were being collected for a clock to be mounted on the west face of the tower, facing Moulsham Street. The *Moulsham Parish Magazine* reported that month that: *"Miss Phillips has collected 15s. for the church clock. There is now £27 10s. in hand, but the clock will cost between £60 and £70 without the proposed big bell".*[21] On Wednesday, 30 May a service was held in the parish church at Rettendon to celebrate the augmentation, re-hanging and rededication of the peal of bells, at which George Godson preached. The money for the new bells at Rettendon had been raised by subscription, although to add to this money: *"it was hoped that one of the old bells (the tenor bell) would be sold – it was estimated that this might fetch up to £50"* (this bell was later to end up in St John's).[22] A week later, completion was well in sight and the bishop of St Albans was able to announce that he would hold the planned confirmation service in St John's on 15 July at three o'clock.[23] There was, though, still a stubborn £200 to £300 needed to cover the final cost of the building works, and in time-honoured fashion a bazaar was to be held to wipe off this remaining debt.

'Nine large stalls, besides several little *attachés*'

The sale took place in the Shire Hall on Thursday, 28 June 1883 in the ballroom, and such were the scope and the quantity of the articles for sale that (rather like the bazaar to raise money for the building of the church nearly fifty years earlier) it needed to be extended to a second day. The event was fulsomely reported in the local press, and much of that report detailed why the enlargement of the church was necessary and what the impact on the parish would be. The reports pointed out that: *"the enlargement of the church and the addition of a handsome tower at the west end have not been achieved without a heavy expenditure of money, and the hope which has been expressed that by the time the work has been thoroughly completed and the Church formally re-opened, the required funds will have come to hand, stands a remarkably good chance of being realised after the eminently successful labours of the first day of the sale"*. The reports went on to announce that the bishop of St Albans would preach at the re-opening services on 15 July in the morning and would hold a confirmation service in the afternoon. The pressing need for the enlargement was noted, due, it said, to the large congregations that worshipped there and the continued rapid growth in the overall population of the parish. The reports praised the excellent design of the tower: *"with its quartett* (sic) *of pinnacles – which forms a striking and remarkably pleasing feature of the landscape, viewed from any point in the surrounding neighbourhood,"* noting also that this tower: *"will be the receptacle for a much needed public clock, and also, after a short time, the home of a peal of bells, for the installation of the first of which provision is being made"*.

George Godson's visit to Rettendon to preach at the service for the re-dedication of the bells had not simply been a friendly gesture to a fellow vicar but had also had a business purpose as well. The *Essex Weekly News* pointed out that the funds for the enlargement of the church and the installation of the clock and bells were distinct, noting that the raising of the money for the clock: *"is likely to cause but little trouble, for the reason that everyone agrees that one of the chief things that Moulsham lacks is a public chronometer, whose rulings could be taken as a guide for all the other clocks in the neighbourhood. The estimated cost of the new mechanism is £90, of which nearly £60 has been subscribed, the men employed at the Arc works* (Col Crompton's factory in Anchor Street) *being by no means behindhand with their donations. The clock will strike the hours on an 11 cwt tenor bell of good tone, which has hitherto, and for many years, been hung at Rettendon, but has now given place to a complete peal. The bell has just been purchased for Moulsham through the Rev H.A. Cockey for £55; and as the two small bells formally used at St John's Church have been purchased for St Mary's, Chelmsford,* (from whence they originally came) *for £50, Moulsham will not have much trouble to make up the difference. The completion of the peal of eight, as at present suggested, will probably not be undertaken at present"* (It never has).

The bazaar itself had been authorised by a committee comprised mainly of the ladies of the church as well as a number of prominent local individuals including the wife of the rector of St Mary's (Mrs Johnson), Lady Hawkins (the wife of the former rector) and Mrs Pryor of Hylands who had promised to lend their support. The arrangements on the day were impressive. At two o'clock the band of the Chelmsford and West Essex Yeomanry, located in the Grand Jury room, struck up the National Anthem and the sale immediately commenced. The local press had clearly dusted off its French dictionary describing the bazaar as comprising: *"nine large stalls, besides several little attaches, which evidently owed their origins to a superabundance of articles, or to the necessity for making a separate exhibition of some specialité"*.

The range of articles available for sale was quite astonishing. The vicar's wife produced a number of items specially adapted for the aged and infirm, including washing, reading and writing tables for the bedridden (the bedridden were a Victorian speciality). Perhaps slightly less practical was the: *"fly-catcher of muslin, large and airy, to be placed over the feeble one's head and face"*. It was not recorded what the feeble one thought of this technical innovation. A friend of the vicar's wife, a dear lady of over eighty, produced several ornamental pin-cushions, described rather archly as: *"a curiosity in their way"*. Mrs Saltmarsh's stall contained a series of elegant glass cases, some containing skeleton leaves and other seaweeds and there were also innumerable paintings, embroideries, quilts and dried flowers for sale. There seemed to have been sufficient merchandise to furnish most of the parlours of Chelmsford. Trade was brisk and steady throughout both days, and the grand total realised (£230) made a substantial contribution to removing the deficit.[24] One week later the *Moulsham Parish Magazine* was at last able to announce that: *"the enlarged church at St John's will be re-dedicated on Sunday 15 July, when the preachers will be the Lord Bishop of St Albans (who will also hold a confirmation service) and the Rev A.W. Mason"*. The magazine also noted that the revised version of *Hymns Ancient and Modern* would be used for the first time at that service, and went on to detail further amounts which had been collected for the clock, raising another £5.[25]

'It was for people to connect their earthly blessings with the House of God'

The rededication service was held, as advertised, on Sunday, 15 July 1883. By then it was reported that although there was still a balance on the cost unprovided for: *"no trouble ought to be experienced by those who have taken the matter in hand to collect the amount"*. The clock had been subscribed for in its entirety.

At the services on the Sunday large congregations were present throughout the day. The bishop, Alfred Mason and George Godson officiated, and lessons were read by the curates, the Revs Sydney Wilkin and Walter Smith, the latter taking part in his rather daunting first service at St John's, as the replacement for the Rev Tom Athorne. The bishop preached a long sermon on the appropriate text, *"Now, therefore, arise, O Lord God into Thy resting place, Thou and the ark of Thy strength"* (2 Chronicles vi, 41). He used his sermon to criticise the philosophical attitudes of the 1880s, contrasting the association of an individual with God's House of Prayer (as at St John's) with those who thought that they could efface and destroy religion in the land. For those who truly believed: *"Their old faith was their only joy when they came to die, and their only stay and support in the dark days of distress and anguish; and at such times fragments of old songs and hymns that they used to sing in childhood came across their memory, tender and sweet, not like the teachings of that new philosophy – the philosophy which taught that all ended in the grave"*. It must have made a deep impression on many in the congregation.

In the afternoon at three o'clock the bishop held the confirmation service, with candidates from Moulsham, (45), Chelmsford St Mary's, (4), Springfield (2) and Broomfield (1), addressing each candidate personally before the laying-on of hands in his usual fatherly manner.

The day concluded with evening prayer at seven o'clock, when the church was again well-filled. Prayers were read by Sydney Wilkin and the lessons by Walter Smith and George Godson. The service was choral, with the choir giving an excellent rendition of the anthem *"I was glad when they said unto me"* (not by Sir Hubert Parry). Alfred Mason preached the sermon and reminded the congregation that there had been a time when he had looked with an anxious eye on the increasing population of the parish, conscious of the many religious divisions which existed in it, and how he had grieved deeply in his heart for those who had been brought up in the church of England but who had been driven away to other communions through lack of accommodation in their own parish church. This day, he felt, had gone some way to assuaging that grief. There was a good response in the collections, the dedication service in the morning raising over £16 with the total for the day exceeding £23.[26]

'So as to harmonise with the rest of the structure'

The *Essex Newsman* gave a very full description of the alterations and the way in which the building work had been carried out.

It was recorded how: *"the old tower* (sic – there never was one) *at the west end of church and the whole of the west front have been removed, the nave lengthened and a new tower of much larger dimensions has been built"*. This is the existing (2018) tower, now a prominent feature of both the local landscape and the church itself. The tower is twelve feet square internally and the walls at the bottom are three feet thick. The total height to the top of the parapet is sixty feet and the tower itself is divided into three stories. The ground floor forms the principal entrance to the church. The west front boasts deeply recessed doorways with columns supporting the arched mouldings. The carved tympanum (of a later date than the building of the tower) depicts St John's vision on Patmos with the Archangel Michael fighting the dragon Satan in the sky.[27]

The whole composition is surmounted by a gable and a cross. The side walls of the ground floor of the tower are lightened by two windows on the south side and one on the north. The latter is filled with the painted glass window retrieved from the west end after the explosion of 1874 (it is the only glass rescued from that catastrophe). The windows on the south side were installed in October 1883 by members of Frederick Veley's family in memory of the late Mrs Veley and other relations. The windows consist of two lights filled with stained glass, one light featuring Timothy hearing (but not appearing particularly interested in) the scriptures, and the other being him consecrated by St Paul. They were described at the time as being: *"of a very rich colour, and general expressions of gratification have been made by the congregation at the handsome and appropriate nature of the gift to the church"*. The lights were designed by Mr W.B. Simpson and Sons of London.[28] A large archway fifteen feet in height connects the tower with the nave and under this arch is a glazed screen with doors.

The second storey of the tower forms the clock and ringing chamber, the chamber being lit by a number of small windows. The approach to this chamber is by a stone staircase, from ground floor level, contained in a circular turret which is built out from the main part of the tower, and which forms a distinct feature on the north side. The third storey of the tower is the belfry which has on each face two large openings filled with slate louvres, set well apart in order that the sound of the bell may be heard throughout the parish. The upper part of the tower is surmounted by a stone balustrade with pinnacles, that on the north-west corner being larger than the other three, thus relieving some of the harsh formality that might otherwise exist. The whole tower is surmounted by a very short spire with a gilded vane. A new south porch was erected at the same time as the modifications at the west end in order to accommodate the enlargement of the nave and provide an additional access point to the church. The whole of the new structure was erected in white brick and stone so as to harmonise with the rest of the building, and the whole works were carried out by Messrs Brown and Sons of Braintree and Chelmsford under the skilful direction of Frederick Chancellor.[29]

The long-awaited parts for the clock were delivered to the church in early August 1883,[30] and the mechanism was quickly erected by Mr Henry Sainsbury, *"manufacturer of cathedral, church and turret clocks"*, of 12, Curtain Road, EC. The clock was ceremonially started on Saturday, 11 August and was found: *"to keep admirable time"*. The dial plate, when installed, was silvered, and bore the following engraving: *"This clock was erected and fixed in this tower AD 1883, George St Alban Godson, Vicar; Robert Chas Hanam and Thos Tidboald, churchwardens"*.[31] The tenor bell from Rettendon has (most of the time) continued to broadcast the hour to the parishioners of Moulsham, although for many years it has been driven by an electric motor – when it was first installed, it was wound by hand on a weekly basis.

'They had a piece of land offered them for free, but would not accept it'

The 1883 vestry meeting was held on Tuesday, 27 March, and was a lively affair. The accounts and the routine business of the meeting were dealt with relatively quickly, Mr Hanam and

Mr Tidboald being re-appointed to their previous positions. The serious and pressing question before the vestry was what needed to be done about the churchyard (although, with the opening of the Nonconformist cemetery in London Road in 1846, some of the dissenters in the parish had chosen to be buried there). With a parish that included the Workhouse in Barrack Lane and which also initially covered Galleywood Common (Galleywood parish was not created until 1873) and which had been occupied by workmen building the Eastern Counties Railway, the pressure on St John's small churchyard had been considerable. Thomas Wilkinson had attempted, with the assistance of the churchwardens (and the legal skills of Frederick Veley) to obtain a grant of suitable land from the Mildmay family, but efforts had effectively ceased with the death of Archdeacon Mildmay in 1878 (*see chapter four*). The pressure on the small amount of space remaining in the churchyard continued to build up, and in February a local man, Samuel Hunter Cooper, an agricultural dealer, of Hall Street, sadly recorded in his diary: *"Sam Percy Cooper died aged 13 months all but one day – was buried in Moulsham churchyard in a tiny space near the Rectory Lane gate* (this is the gate opening on to St John's Road) *in a coffin made by Sorrell of Hall Street. Fees 9/-* (nine shillings), *Coffin 12/- which was paid for at the time"*. Just a month later he was, even more tragically, writing that: *"at Chelmsford, Moulsham, a son was born 4.30 died at 5.00 Sunday morning – was buried in the same tiny grave as Sam Percy. Just enough room left"*. A shattering comment not only on the condition of the churchyard but also on the perils of being an infant in the 1880s.[32]

Just a few days before the vestry meeting, the Rev George Wilkinson, the minister of London Road Congregational Chapel had chaired a deliberately provocative meeting at the Chelmsford Literary and Mechanical Institute on the subject of 'Why the Church of England should be disestablished and disendowed'. The meeting was held under the auspices of the notorious Liberation Society, and although supported on the platform by a number of eminent Congregationalist speakers, George Wilkinson chose to dominate the proceedings, using his chairman's introductory remarks to take a swipe at Moulsham and its churchwardens over the cemetery question. He pointed out that: *"there was a cemetery in the London Road* (James Fenton's Nonconformist burial ground) *which was bought by Nonconformists. They bought a Chapel, and a house, and had borne all the expenses from that time until this. He was one of the unpaid chaplains of that cemetery, and they had buried hundreds of persons there and never received a single farthing, and some times they had not received as much as thanks".* He contrasted this behaviour with the attitude of the people at St John's, noting that their church friends in Moulsham wanted a cemetery, and it was natural to think that they would do as the Nonconformists had done, and provide it themselves, but, as everyone knew, that was not the case. He pointed out that they were: *"going to make the parish provide the cemetery, and what made the case worse, was that they had a piece of land offered to them free, but they would not accept it. They would rather make the parish buy a piece of land and go to the expense of building a Chapel rather than put their hands in their own pockets and meet their own expense* [Applause]". He went on to say that if their church friends would accept that piece of land and then appeal for voluntary subscriptions, then the Dissenters would help them and he would even preach a sermon in London Road Chapel to help them raise money [Prolonged applause]. He rounded off his argument by stating that he believed that: *"if there was a church that could not stand without being supported by the state, then in his judgement that church did not belong to that kingdom of which it was written 'it shall not be moved'".* After that, Mr Fisher's vigorous address in favour of disestablishment must have seemed something of an anticlimax.[33]

A week after this brickbat, the vestry met to consider their response.[34] Almost all of those present, except for the vicar, felt they had been personally attacked. Robert Hanam summarised (just in case anyone had forgotten) the sequence of events, starting with the approaches made to Archdeacon Mildmay by Thomas Wilkinson some five years previously. He concluded by confirming that he had referred the matter to the Chelmsford Local Board of Health, and that they themselves were in discussion with the Local Government Board to try and decide who was responsible (and for what). The meeting, after some vigorous discussion, agreed that the churchwardens would draft an appropriate response and seek to have it published in the local press as soon as possible. Their letter appeared the following week. They reminded readers that George Wilkinson, as chairman of the meeting, had made a long speech, the whole thrust of which was condemnatory of the Church of England and of churchmen generally, and of the churchwardens of Moulsham in particular, and although he had said at the outset that his object was not to abuse the Church, they felt that his whole speech had been, *"a strange mixture of oily expressions, sinister complaints, subtle suggestions and spiteful insinuations"*. They dealt with the main point of his speech by saying that although Mr Wilkinson stated that they had been offered: *"an excellent and suitable piece of land"* which he had accused them of refusing, they firmly rebutted this charge. They pointed out that: *"they doubted that Mr Wilkinson had ever acquainted himself with the acre of land he had so extolled"*, and if he had, they were at a loss to understand how he described it as: *"excellent and suitable"*. All this, they continued, was against a framework where there was no statutory obligation imposed on churchwardens to provide a burial ground for the parish. They concluded, rather sardonically, by taking the opportunity afforded by writing their letter to suggest to Mr Wilkinson that he studied some standard work on churchyard matters, *"before he returns to make the like onslaught on other parochial officers"*. They added an appendix which was printed with their letter, detailing briefly the history of their attempts to find a burial ground for the parish.[35]

'In nearly every case bones have been disturbed when new graves had been dug'

The churchwardens had, however, been very prudent in this matter, and had, at the time of these exchanges, already written to the Secretary of State at the Home Office. That letter had included a copy of their prior communication with the Local Board of Health, which had stated that the churchwardens wished to draw attention to the state of St John's churchyard which they described as: *"now so crowded that human bones are frequently disturbed in digging new graves, and it has therefore become absolutely necessary that a fresh site for a burial ground in Moulsham should be obtained"*. The churchwardens did not receive a reply from the Local Board of Health for some months, and when that reply did come, it was to state that it was not a matter that they considered to be their responsibility. They therefore forwarded the local board's response, together with an emphatic restatement of the present position of the churchyard, to the Home Office in an attempt to force either the Local Board of Health or the Local Government Board into taking some action. As a result of that letter, sent at the beginning of February 1883, a Dr Hoffman visited St John's on behalf of the Home Office Burials Act Department, in order to carry out an inspection, on Monday, 9 April. He was accompanied around the churchyard by George Godson and his curate, Sydney Wilkin; the churchwardens, by Frederick Veley, and most importantly of all, by George Osborn, the sexton.

Dr Hoffman began by asking the sexton, that if he had, as of that day, to dig half-a-dozen new graves in virgin soil, could he do so? The sexton replied that he considered that impossible. Indeed, as he recalled, the last piece of virgin soil used had been at least ten years previously. Dr Hoffman then asked about walled graves and vaults and the sexton confirmed that there were still some of these that had space for living family members (as was the case for the Veley family vault). The sexton was then asked: *"whether or not bones had often been thrown out in digging graves?"* and George Osborn confirmed that on almost every occasion in recent years when a new grave had been dug, this occurred: *"in nearly every case"*. The Inspector (Dr Hoffman), with gentle civil-service understatement, felt that this was: *"very strong evidence that the graveyard was full"*. He went on to explain that any walled graves and vaults with space in them would be exempted from the Order for Closure (which he would recommend that the Home Office issued) but that any burials in those graves would be restricted to relations of those already interned. This, he confirmed, could be restricted to widows and widowers if that was what the vestry wanted, but: *"it could be any relationship you like; that is left to you"*. This led to a brief exchange, a rare flash of dark humour in the discussions over the fate of St John's churchyard;

> *"Mr Veley: Is a wife a relation? [Laughter]*
> *Rev G. St A. Godson: I should think so – rather close*
> *Mr Veley: Not in point of Law*
> *Dr Hoffman: Well, I am no lawyer [Much Laughter]"*.

Dr Hoffman then moved on to the tricky question of when the churchyard should be closed. It would not do, he argued: *"to close your churchyard and leave you without a burial ground. Perhaps the local board will think better of it when they find that your churchyard is about to be closed"*. George Godson pointed out that they had taken no steps so far, and did not even look like doing so. Dr Hoffman regretted that he had no powers to compel either the Local Government Board or the local board of health to do anything but he did confirm that the former had the power under the Local Interments' Act to get a new burial ground. The meeting concluded, most unsatisfactorily, after about an hour with the whole issue far from resolved.[36]

Meanwhile, the two boards both continued to vacillate and try and shift the responsibility for taking some action on to the other. Neither wished to make a call on the rates to fund the purchase and the laying out of a new cemetery. And if such a cemetery were planned, the even more difficult question then arose as to which parish should pay. Was it to be a cemetery for Moulsham or for the whole of Chelmsford? The arguments and the prevarication continued through the summer of 1883, but the Home Office had by then taken note of what Dr Hoffman had reported, and by September the churchwardens were able to post the official notice that St John's churchyard would be closed for burials (from 31 March 1884) not only on the door of St John's church itself, but also on the doors of all the other Chapels in the parish, as required by law.[37]

The year drew to a close. St John's had seen the culmination of two years' hard work to enlarge the church, resulting in what is basically its present outline shape. It had, though, not been an easy year for George Godson. Tom Athorne had left the parish on health grounds (as mentioned previously) and his replacement, the relatively experienced Walter Smith left quite suddenly, preaching his last sermon on Sunday, 16 September. As he explained to his congregation during that evening service, this was only: *"the tenth Sunday he had ministered in that church, but the congregation would not again see him there. He did not like changes, and he had hoped that he should have a prolonged residence in Moulsham. Since he had been in the parish, he had experienced much kindness, and had made some true friends, but it had not been permitted to him to remain, and he now wished to bid the parishioners farewell. He hoped he should be forgiven for these remarks, which would perhaps make his last words more impressive than they otherwise would be".*[38] Did he jump or was he pushed? It will probably never be known. George Godson had managed to keep up the traditions of St John's, and the Sunday scholars had their annual treat on Thursday, 16 August, on that occasion being entertained in a field kindly lent by Mr A.C. Marriage, near Ingatestone Hall. The treat had been quite an adventure – the boys and girls had travelled, some 200 of them, by the 12.47 train from Chelmsford railway station (for some of the poorer children, this could well have been their first experience of a train journey). The infants had followed in horse-drawn wagons. It was reported that: *"after a very happy evening was spent, the children all reached Chelmsford without any accident".*[39]

'Not gone from memory – not gone from love'

St John's moved into the new year, 1884, the future a little brighter with the resolution of the cemetery problem in sight. Those with family members already buried in the churchyard found that additional family members could still be squeezed in (literally). Samuel Hunter Cooper again recorded in heart-rending terms the funeral of more of his children as scarlet fever made its devastating rounds of the parish. He wrote that: *"Bertie Cooper was born and died on 10 June; was buried with Fred John and Ernest Cooper on 11 June '84 in Moulsham churchyard close to wicket gate. Rev Smith officiated. Father and myself followed. Fred John Cooper died from scarlet fever and inflammation of the brain aged eight years and six months, June 9th 1884 ... ... also Ernest Cooper who died at Moulsham aged three years and six months of Rheumatic and scarlet fever and was buried with his two brothers Bertie and Fred John next to my other children"*. It must have been a shattering time for Samuel Hunter and his wife Helen, with five of their boys all buried in the same tiny grave in St John's churchyard. Samuel Hunter wrote, desperately trying to cling on to his faith, in his little diary: *"Not gone from memory – not gone from love – but gone to their Father's home above"*.[40]

The vestry meeting for that year (held on Tuesday 15 April) had been a slightly subdued affair. Thomas Tidboald was not present and the meeting was quick to express hopes: *"that his health would be restored and his useful* (sic) *spared for a long time"*, and in his absence he was re-elected. Robert Hanam presented the accounts which showed a healthy balance in hand of more than £33, although it was pointed out, rather prosaically, that they: *"would have an opportunity of largely spending it in the next few months"*, as both the organ and the heating boiler required major repairs. The vestry were also told by George Godson that the churchyard, which was to have closed on March 31, would not now do so, but as a result of the churchwardens communicating with the Local Government Board, that date had been extended to 31 July. The meeting felt that they should, yet again, formally record that: *"the present state of the churchyard was lamentable, as they hardly knew where to bury"*. The meeting also paid tribute to their clerk, John Lewis, who had died on 13 November 1883. He had a truly remarkable record, having been clerk for almost twelve years, taking over from Thomas Whiffen, and for the last nine of those years he had not missed a single service at St John's until the Sunday before he died, when George Godson had sent him home before the evening service because he was ill.[41] Also remembered was Mrs Joanna Mott, of the Mildmay Almshouses who had died on 8 January 1884. She had given faithful service for more than thirty years at St John's as a 'pew-opener'. She, too, like John Lewis, had been: *"diligent in the discharge of her duties at the church and had gained the love and esteem of the congregation"*.[42] The meeting readily re-elected John Lewis' son (another John Lewis) as clerk in his father's stead.[43]

St John's continued to host its regular events for active participants in church worship. On 17 January the clergy had given a late Christmas entertainment to all members of the choir, the men's and the young people's Bible class, in the girls' schoolroom. As a special treat, the Rev de Lisle, vicar of Galleywood, brought along his magic lantern and showed views of famous British and Irish beauty spots, many of which he had personally visited. The choir, led by Mr Barnard, expressed their thanks to the speaker in song.[44] The new year continued to see the last dribs and drabs of money trickle in towards the church enlargement fund – some boxes of articles left over from the sale of work had been discovered in a store room in the church and had been sold for £2 9s. 4d.[45] The money was specifically used to provide new gas lamps that were situated on either side of the path at the west end of the church (this part of the church had become inconveniently dark after the tower had been erected.[46] Tragedy also struck the morning service at St John's on 30 March when Elizabeth Barnard, aged 70, the mother of the organist, died suddenly during the morning service. The curate, the Rev J.F. Smith, was said to have: *"presided very effectively"* as a replacement for Mr Barnard on the organ.[47]

The cemetery question was now nearing its resolution because of (or perhaps in spite of) the efforts of the vicar and churchwardens of St John's. Although they had been obliged to seek an extension of the time fixed for closing the churchyard, which had been moved to 31 July,[48] pressure was building on both the Local Boards and throughout the summer of 1884 wheels were turning just a little faster. The 31 July deadline came and passed, obliging the churchwardens to apply to the Home Office for yet another extension (to 31 December)[49] although the Home Office on this occasion made it quite clear that this was absolutely final. This really did at last shove the Local Boards into action. By September they were able to announce that: *"the broad basis on which a proposal to provide a new cemetery for Chelmsford and Moulsham was originally contested has been narrowed down to a question of site"*. At the Government enquiry (held on Thursday, 10 September under Major Tulloch) the Board confirmed that they had in view four sites, one in Wood Street (which was completely unacceptable, according to the surveyor, being unworkable clay); a fourteen-acre site on the Writtle Road; a site in Writtle parish (near Admiral's park) and a site at the back of the gaol offered by Sir Henry Mildmay. The last two, for a range of reasons, were thought to be unacceptable. The Local Board did make a last feeble attempt at delaying, the Rev Bartlett suggesting that: *"the question should really wait a little while longer"*, but the outcome was that the only viable site was the one in Writtle Road (the site of the present Borough Cemetery) and steps were taken to start the procedure for compulsory purchase.[50] Final closure (this time with no possibility of any extension) of St John's churchyard took place on 31 December 1884. After that date, only a small number of relatives of those interred were added to the many bodies in this acre of ground.

'His life was characterised by giving of his time and substance'

One other death was to strike hard at St John's (and Moulsham and Chelmsford) in 1884, was that of Thomas Tidboald. He died at his residence, Tavistock House, New London Road, at midnight on Thursday, 26 September 1884. He had been ill for some months, but was generally thought to have recovered his health, so his death, at the age of seventy-five, came as something of a surprise. A native of Devon, Thomas Tidboald came to Chelmsford at an early age and went into business as a grocer and provision merchant, opening a shop in the High Street. By 1867 he was able to dispose of what was then a thriving business in order to devote more of his time to good works. His life was characterised by giving of his time and substance for the moral and physical improvement of those less fortunate in life than himself. He felt it his duty to bring a supply of affordable energy, in the form of gas, to all individuals in the larger towns of Essex, and to this end he took on a managerial role in many of the local gas companies. He was said rarely to have turned down a genuine request from an institution (particularly if it was concerned with juvenile education) on many occasions making donations to the Essex Industrial school when its future appeared to be uncertain.[51] His funeral took place in St John's churchyard on Wednesday, 2 October in the presence of a large number of parishioners, the burial service being performed by George Godson. At the Harvest Festival service on the following Sunday George Godson referred at length to the life and example of Thomas Tidboald describing his death as: *"the gathering in of one who had been a remarkable example of the fear of God manifested in the world in the life of man"*.[52] The Tidboald family generosity did not end with Thomas' death. He died a wealthy man (he left almost £123,000) and his widow continued his charitable donations, the most important being the provision of a new infants' schoolroom for St John's national school (located just to the north of the boys' and girls' buildings). When it appeared as if promised funding for this expansion was not likely to be forthcoming, Mrs Tidboald gave £1,000 towards the building, sufficient for the entire construction to go ahead as planned. It was opened by Canon Alfred Mason (as he now was) on 28 October 1885.[53] Thomas Tidboald's death created a vacancy for parish churchwarden, and Thomas Saltmarsh was duly elected (unanimously) to the post at a special meeting of the vestry on 18 November 1884.[54]

'They had to be buried in grounds which did not belong to the parish'

The 1885 vestry meeting passed quickly and without incident. A positive balance in hand of just over £14 was reported and both wardens were re-appointed without any debate, Thomas Saltmarsh in particular emphasising the many kindnesses he had received since taking over from the late Mr Tidboald. The cemetery question was still (just) twitching, and Robert Hanam asked if the local board of health had done anything since the Inspector's enquiry the previous September. The minutes recorded that the local board was waiting for the finalising of the loan, but it was hoped work would start by late May 1885.[55] George Godson clearly felt that the local board of health still needed reminding that the need for the new cemetery was pressing. In June, the sanitary committee of the local board of health reported that they had received a letter from the vicar of Moulsham, complaining of the continued delay in the construction of the cemetery. The committee was able to report that: *"the mortgage had been sealed (for £1,100) from the Dunmow Building society"*. It was to be paid back in fifty monthly instalments of £51 4s. 2d. They also recorded in the minutes that the completion of the sale of the land, from a Mr Chevely, was imminent.[56] The delay was causing problems for George Godson and the parishioners of Moulsham. Unless they were fortunate enough to have already secured a burial plot or space in an existing vault, they now had to be buried: *"in burial grounds which do not belong to the parish"*.[57]

The year closed on a happier note for the congregation of St John's. Aleck Barnard, who had been elected organist in 1877 when Miss Pattinson had withdrawn her candidacy under rather acrimonious circumstances (and who had been living alone in Anchor Street since his mother had died in the Sunday service some eighteen months previously) married. His bride was (most appropriately) Miss Cecilia Bond of Mildmay Road, the daughter of a local bootmaker. Their wedding took place at St John's on Monday, 7 December (it was not recorded who played the organ or what music the couple chose). The boys of the choir presented the couple with a marmalade dish and matching spoon. The bridegroom also received a short address from the boys, thanking him: *"for all the pains he had taken in training them and suffering, from time to time, their inattention"*.[58] The adults of the choir gave the happy couple a clock on their return from their wedding tour.[59]

'He did not remember when it was'

Early in 1886 the Church Enlargement fund was finally wound up. The fund committee met in late February at the vicarage when the final accounts for the project were produced and passed. The balance in hand, after paying off all expenses for the enlargement, was just over £200. The committee expressed their collective thanks to Robert Hanam for the competent way in which he had managed the accounts. It was resolved that a major portion of the surplus be used towards the expenditure necessary (yet again) to improve the heating in the church, and also for the stone carving over the doors at the west end that was not provided for in the original plan. The vicar also suggested that a choir vestry be formed in the organ transept by the simple process of erecting a screen. The committee duly agreed with this suggestion.[60]

The 1886 vestry meeting, held on Tuesday, 27 April, was overshadowed by illness. The vicar's warden, Robert Hanam, was not present. Although said to be recovering from his recent indisposition, he was still too unwell to attend the meeting, and prayers were said for his full recovery. Thomas Saltmarsh presented the accounts, and although the balance in hand was an increase on the previous year (just over £21 as against £14), he cautioned against undue optimism. He pointed out that it did not really show a very healthy state of affairs, as there had been five more collecting days in the last year's financial period. If the results from these days were deducted, St John's was left with a deficit of about £26 on the year. Thomas Saltmarsh also told the meeting that as far as he understood the situation, even though the churchyard was closed, St John's had to keep it in repair and charge any costs involved to the overseers of the parish. George Godson clarified this point for the meeting by stating that they were obliged to do this by a provision in the act for closing churchyards. After some brief further discussion the accounts were carried unanimously. The various officers were re-elected (Robert Hanam *in absentia*) and the meeting concluded with the vicar asking if anyone present (particularly if they were a member of the local board of health) could give them any information about the probable date of the completion of the cemetery. Mr Simpson said that he could not tell them that, but that he could assure them that work was going on as fast as possible, and that the contractor involved (Mr Grizzett of Woodham Walter) was a *"capital man"*. When pressed for an exact date, Mr Simpson had to admit that: *"he did not remember when it was"*. There followed a very brief discussion about the poor state of the Rectory Lane cemetery, and the meeting concluded with the usual vote of thanks to the vicar.[61]

In May, a young boy, Arthur Diss, was severely wounded when climbing the railings of St John's churchyard for the purpose of gathering some leaves. He fell, and his leg came into contact with one of the spikes of the railings. After treatment by Dr Bodkin he eventually made a full recovery. The incident is of note because Arthur Diss was the head chorister of St John's, and instrumental in devising the address from the boys of the choir to Aleck Barnard on the occasion of his wedding.[62] St John's continued to hold confirmation services on a yearly basis and 1886 saw the Bishop of St Albans, Thomas Claughton confirm fifty-two candidates (a good average for St John's) on 20 April.[63] He would be back in Chelmsford in August to dedicate the new cemetery on Writtle Road. At that dedication ceremony hope was expressed that the whole site would be completed by the end of October.[64]

'A ghost at night in Moulsham churchyard'

In September 1886 it was reported that much mischief had been done recently in New London Road by nocturnal marauders. The events were described as: *"very fair instances of the amusements of a brainless section of the youth of the town"* (nothing changes).

145

Damage was reported to bells, knockers, gateposts and fences at some of the grandest houses in the area. Coupled with these practical jokes had been strong rumours of a ghost seen at night in Moulsham churchyard, with a truncheon in its hand. The presumption was that the senseless jokers, not content with the destruction of property, were trying to frighten the credulous. However, on enquiry, the press found the story: *"not to have been satisfactorily corroborated"*. The parish constable (PC Watchem, no less) agreed to keep a lookout for anything untoward.[65]

In October, the church clock (not for the last time) showed that it had a personality and a mind of its own. On Tuesday and Wednesday (the thirteenth and fourteenth) it: *"it deviated altogether from the ordinary ideas of time, striking six at twelve o'clock at night and one at six o'clock in the morning"*. Inquiries suggested that this was most probably due to: *"the atmospheric conditions and not to the intermeddling of the Moulsham churchyard ghost"*.[66]

Towards the end of the year the local board of health's Sanitary Committee appointed the new superintendent of the Writtle Road cemetery. After receiving applications from nearly thirty candidates, they interviewed seven and eventually selected William Henry Bird of Lower Anchor Street. He moved with his family into purpose built accommodation on the cemetery site, with free rent, rates, heating and lighting. He was also paid 15s. per week and was expected to act as administrator, sexton, and general repair man. The cemetery was, at long last, open for business.

'The present vicar looks upon a church service as the most mournful thing on earth'

The next couple of years at St John's started very peacefully, but again trouble was simmering just below the surface. The 1887 vestry was a short affair, a balance in hand of just over £20 being reported, and Robert Hanam and Thomas Saltmarsh were speedily re-appointed. There was some brief discussion about Queen

Victoria's golden jubilee, due in August. Disappointment was expressed that St Mary's parish was dithering, unable to reach a decision as to how to commemorate the event, several projects having been suggested and all being eventually rejected. The meeting felt that they should start looking at some specific scheme for Moulsham, and a new organ for the church or a good peal of bells for the tower were frontrunners. Arguments for and against both ideas were aired, but neither received any significant backing, and the matter was dropped. In truth, there did not seem to be much enthusiasm in the parish for celebrating the jubilee. William Cutts then gave a brief hint of the troubles that were soon to beset St John's by suggesting: *"with due respect, that a number of parishioners felt it might be a good thing if the litany were omitted from the morning service when Communion was administered"*. He felt that there was a need to shorten the service, which was too long on Communion Sundays. Indeed, he noted that a number of women had stayed away from this service simply because it was too long, finding it difficult to get their husbands' dinners in time. The vicar said that: *"he was much obliged to Mr Cutts for making the suggestion"*, and agreed to give the matter his earnest attention.[67]

Discontent in St John's was much more deep-rooted than even the pessimistic Mr Cutts had realised, and by the beginning of 1888 a correspondent, daring only to sign himself as 'Z' wrote to the *Essex Newsman* pointing out that although there had been a meeting some six weeks before Christmas to form a choir (in order to enhance the services) those who had joined had done so on the understanding that they would be provided with surplices. Regrettably, no surplices had been forthcoming, and: *"the choir continued to make their entrances and exits dressed in all colours"*.[68] Further correspondence a week later from 'A Moulshamite' suggested that it was: *"nothing less than a solemn farce to witness the choir in various shades of their colours and apparel marching in from the vestry"*. The writer felt that the problems were more deep-seated than simply a question of surplices, as: *"it was well-known that a large number (sic) of the parishioners of Moulsham attend St Mary's simply because they object to the dull and monotonous services at St John's, especially in the morning".*[69]

The vicar took action, and at the beginning of April certain inhabitants of Moulsham received a circular from him asking them to state whether or not it was desirable that the choir should be surpliced. This action arose from the 1888 vestry meeting where George Godson stated categorically that he would not make any alteration in the services unless a large majority of the congregation desired it. The vicar had, though, been somewhat selective in the distribution of his circular, having appeared to have sent it mostly to those individuals whom he felt were opposed to the choir wearing surplices. The result, of course, was no large majority in favour of change. Only three of the thirty members of the choir received the circular. The outcome was great discontent, particularly amongst the choristers, and at the evening service on 29 April the choir absented themselves *en masse*. George Godson was not slow to retaliate and on the Monday he wrote to the absentees pointing out that: *"if their absence from the choir had reference to what had lately passed as to surplices and church music, I regret to say that I am forced to withdraw your name from the list of members"*. The choir members held a meeting that same evening, and wrote to the vicar, saying that in their judgement: *"the so-called poll on the question of the surplices ... ... did not in any way indicate the sense of the congregation"*. This had the same effect on George Godson as that of a red rag on a bull. He angrily exerted his authority and the next day he wrote to the rebellious choristers, apologising that: *"there should be any difference between us"* but stating that, under the circumstances, *"it is best that you should retire"*. St John's had just lost its choir.[70] At the beginning of June 'A Moulsham Parishioner' wrote a stinging letter to the local press, commenting on what he called: *"by far the most efficient part of the choir"* and outlining all that he felt was wrong with the most recent service that he had attended at St John's. That service, he said: *"was past everybody's understanding. The present Vicar looks upon a church service as the most mournful thing on earth"*. He gave free reign to his sarcastic wit when he suggested what might be done: *"perhaps a portion of St John's church should be cut off and placed on the end of St Mary's to provide room for the overflowing congregation that assembles there".*[71]

The situation could hardly continue as it was, and in an attempt to find out what was really going on, the Bishop of St Albans paid an unheralded visit (something virtually unknown in the diocese) to St John's on Sunday, 3 June. He gave George Godson and the churchwardens just under an hour's notice, which brought on a state on near panic at the vicarage. Hand written notices were hastily prepared and sent to those in the congregation who mattered, and at the last minute nearly all the seats were filled. There is, sadly, no record of the sermon the bishop preached (on the text: *"Today, if ye will hear His voice, harden not your hearts"*) or of any of the discussions that he had with the vicar and the churchwardens, but the enormity of an unexpected visit by the bishop seemed to have calmed the congregation – for the moment.

The 1889 vestry meeting was poorly attended and business was disposed of quickly. The only item of significance was that Robert Hanam had decided that he no longer wished to be considered as churchwarden and accordingly George Godson nominated Mr Butler of Summerhill as his warden. Thomas Saltmarsh also no longer wished to stand and Adolphus Maskell was duly elected as parish warden in his stead.[72] The significant event of the year was the opening of a new church room. St John's had, since its foundation, lacked any formal parish hall, most meetings being held in the infants' schoolroom, so this opening fulfilled a great need. On 24 June the new building, in George Street, was opened by the vicar. The building itself was of iron and had been erected by Messrs Crompton and Fawkes of the Arc works on a site let by Frederick Veley at a nominal rent (this suggests the building was located in George Street near the back of Yverdon House, Frederick Veley's residence). The interior of the building was panelled with matchboard and insulated with felt between the matchboard and the iron. The whole was provided with comfortable seats for at least two hundred people. The total cost was of the order of £200, and at the time of opening at least £150 had already been raised. George Godson envisaged the place as being used for a wide range of activities of a more secular nature, although he felt there was also scope for a series of Bible classes, as well as self-betterment classes for the young apprentices in the Arc works just around the corner. However, in his short speech at the opening, he could not resist taking another dig at the rebellious choir. They could, he said: *"meet there to train themselves so that their singing of God's praise might be better than it had hitherto been"*.[73]

'What can be done to increase the attendance at the church?'

The new decade dawned with the issue of falling congregations still looming over St John's head like the proverbial sword of Damocles. At the vestry meeting it was reported that although the previous year had opened with a balance in hand of more than £15, the year had ended with the churchwardens being owed £6 10s. It was clear that the reason for the adverse balance was a drop in the offerings, and this was attributable to a fall in the numbers of people attending the services at St John's. The matter of the falling off in attendance was raised formally by Mr Cutts. He pointed out that: *"time after time he had found that the adults in the un-appropriated seats (exclusive of the school teachers) did not exceed twenty, and frequently the number had been below that. He had attended the church for forty years, and could remember when all those seats had been filled. Could nothing be done to increase the attendance at the church?"* After some discussion he proposed that: *"the churchwardens be requested to convene a meeting of the parishioners of St John's, Moulsham, at the schoolroom, at such an early date as they may deem expedient, to consider the question of the serious decrease in attendance of worshippers at the church, and what steps it may be advisable to take in this matter"*. George Godson was not convinced. He felt it was better that such a matter be considered at a meeting such as the present vestry rather than a public one, as these were often attended by people who: *"perhaps had not in their hearts – as he was quite sure Mr Cutts had – a real earnest wish of something desirable being done"*. After some further tricky discussion about the reasons people went to St Mary's rather than St John's, William Cutts' motion was carried by eight votes to one.[74]

'You are painting the vicar very black'

The proposed meeting was duly held on Thursday, 24 July in the schoolroom with Mr Bond in the chair. There were a goodly number of ladies from the parish present. The purpose for holding the meeting, said the chairman, was to get at the reason why so few people attended St John's church. He pointed out that with a population about 5,500 in the parish, something must be wrong if only 150 attended what was, after all, a good church. Adolphus Maskell revealed that, as a result of what had been said at the last vestry meeting, he had received a letter from the vicar, indicating that he (the vicar) proposed to give up the grant for the second curate, and that he also wished to relieve the parish of expense, by himself engaging and paying an organist. Indeed, Mr Maskell continued, the vicar had (since writing that letter) intimated to Aleck Barnard that his services were to be dispensed with, and the vicar's warden then read out a lengthy and somewhat pained letter from the organist which reminded them that since he had been appointed by the vestry, he felt he could only be dismissed by the vestry. George Godson, it appeared, had made it very clear that whatever this present meeting decided, he would make it his responsibility (and his alone) to employ an organist. Put simply, the vicar said, it did not matter whether the meeting dismissed Mr Barnard or decided to keep him. It would matter not one jot to the vicar. [Cries of *Oh! Oh!*]. William Cutts then took to the floor. He believed that credit needed to be given to Mr Godson for his best intentions, but he felt that: *"the indifference of the vicar to the wants and wishes of the parishioners had led to the present lamentable result"*. This was greeted with prolonged applause, although it was reported that George Godson's supporters at the meeting responded with cries of: *"you are painting the vicar very black"* and *"it's a disgrace"*. Mr Cutts then proposed the resolution that: *"only a twentieth part of the population of the parish attended church, the reason being the dull and monotonous character of the services, requesting the vicar to take steps to introduce a surpliced choir and have the musical portion of the services rendered in a more hearty, cheerful and inspirited character"*.

Mr Hardy then spoke in support of George Godson. He described Mr Cutts as a wayward sheep (because of his leaving the church) and felt that: *"it was the wish of those present to turn the church into a theatre of varieties – they would not get large congregations by that"*. Mr Newton, another supporter of the vicar, proposed an amendment that: *"another meeting be called to give Mr Godson the opportunity to prove or disprove what had been said"*. He believed that Mr Godson preached the truth and that the others wanted to drive him out of his office because they wanted surplices and ritualistic services. Mr Bragg made his position quite clear. Surely, he said, the choir could sing just as well *"without those little rags"*. If they did not make a stand now, he continued: *"next would come the procession and recession and the flag with the cross on it"*. The vote was taken and the motion carried by thirty-one votes to seven. George Godson was not impressed. A copy of his dismissive letter responding to the motion passed at the meeting was sent to the *Essex Newsman,* and in this letter he stated categorically that: *"he cannot regard the resolution as an expression of the wishes of the parishioners at large"*, suggesting that the problem lay with a few non-communicant parishioners who were the cause of the bad feeling. Mr Maskell (who was probably the most significant non-communicant to whom the vicar had referred) replied, stating that because of the open way in which the meeting had been convened, he did not think that: *"the resolution should be entirely disregarded"*. He felt that dismissing Mr Barnard and changing the musical character of the services would not materially affect the congregations, but with the regard to the organist, he was sure that even if the churchwardens convened a meeting with the vicar, the issue was unlikely to be resolved.[76] George Godson, whose standing in the parish had just been enhanced by his appointment as chaplain of the workhouse in Wood Street, as a replacement for Rev W. Buswell, who had just resigned, allowed himself a touch of sarcasm when he replied to Mr Maskell. In a brief letter he stated that: *"if the boat's crew pull together, instead of dipping their oars into the troubled waters at their own sweet will, no doubt they would all make good way".*[77] His sarcasm was probably wasted on the parishioners of Moulsham. It was obvious, too whose side one of the curates was on. In reporting on Rev Ley's sermon in St John's on 10 August, the *Essex Chronicle* noted that he alluded to: *"the beggarly array of empty benches in the church"* pointing out how lucky they were. He reminded them that: *"there were very few churches that had so great an advantage in this respect (having so many seatings unappropriated) as that in which they were now assembled".* The *Chronicle*, ever keen to stir the pot, noted how the congregation appreciated this remark, *"for they turned to each other, and with difficulty suppressed their smiles".*[78]

'He had taken the not very subtle hint, and sent in his resignation'

Aleck Barnard finally succumbed to all the pressure (after fourteen years as organist) and handed in his resignation in September, thus avoiding any confrontation between the churchwardens and the vicar.[79] Arthur Ley felt that he, too, had had enough, and at the beginning of October took the opportunity in his farewell sermon of telling his hearers that: *"three months since he received a communication from the vicar to the effect that the staff of curates was to be diminished by one, and suggesting* (sic) *that since Mr Ley's eyesight was a hindrance to him in church, it was not necessary that he should remain the sole curate".* He had taken the not very subtle hint, and sent in his resignation, although, as the *Essex Chronicle* reported, he was: *"naturally very aggrieved at the manner in which it was brought about".*[80] Later that month it was reported that George Godson had appointed a new organist for St John's church. It was said that his choice had fallen upon a lady who was: *"not of this district"*, and, as he himself had intimated earlier, he would pay her salary.[81] There is no record of any such lady being appointed. As the year approached its end, the rumour mill continued to grind away. In December, the *Essex Chronicle*, often considered the mouthpiece of the established clergy in the county, felt it was able to state categorically that: *"there is no truth in the rumour which has been widely circulated to the effect that an exchange of livings was about to take place between the Rev George Godson, vicar of Moulsham, and the Rev Dr Rogers, vicar of Roxwell."*[82]

The following year was to prove a little less challenging for everyone connected with the parish, (except perhaps Mr William Ripper, who was to be appointed as headmaster of St John's National Boys' school during the course of 1891). In January, Frederick Veley's daughter Gertrude married in St John's, and the happy occasion was enhanced by her choice of bridegroom,[83] as she married the Rev John Albert Kershaw, the former headmaster of the Grammar School, who had shared many of the duties of running the parish with Edward Clive during the last years of Thomas Wilkinson's incumbency in the late 1870s. John Kershaw was now the rector of St James', Colchester. He had lost his first wife, Mary, in tragic circumstances in November 1884. She suffered a stroke, whilst apparently in excellent health, during a visit of condolence to the relatives of Miss Hutchinson (Rev James Hutchinson's daughter) who had just died at her home in Duke Street.[84] Mary Kershaw was only fifty and left seven children motherless when she died. Gertrude Veley, who was only thirty-five at the time of her marriage, would have clearly had her work cut out. George Godson himself suffered a deeply-felt loss in February. His dear friend Edward Newcome, the vicar of Leavesden (near Watford) whom he had known since his first incumbency in Shenley, died suddenly whilst on a visit to Moulsham vicarage for the weekend. The *Essex Newsman* reported, with that peculiar Victorian mixture of sternness and relish, how he had: *"complained of feeling unwell whilst sitting, on the Saturday morning, in Mr Godson's study. Shortly afterwards he fell back and expired."* Mortals, be warned.[85]

In March, Mr Bocking resigned the headmastership of St John's National boys' school and was replaced by Mr William Ripper.[86] It was to be a year to remember for him. St John's had muddled along with whoever they could beg, borrow or steal to come and play the organ after Aleck Barnard's awkward departure the previous year, but William Ripper's arrival in the parish really was God sent. He had previously been the organist at St Mary's, Widford, and in May it was announced that he: *"would in all probability be appointed to St John's"*,[87] and this proved correct. He commenced his musical duties on Sunday, 31 May.[88] In September, secure now in his job at the school and with extra income from his organ duties, he married Miss Martha Madalene Beckett, the daughter of Mr William Beckett, a local horticultural engineer.[89] His cup of happiness must have been full to overflowing.

In April the vestry meeting convened on Tuesday, 31 March and was a relatively genteel affair. At the end of the financial year, Adolphus Maskell reported, the balance due to the churchwardens was just under £3, a distinct improvement on the previous year. George Godson nominated William Butler again as his warden. Adolphus Maskell, having presented the accounts, asked if he could be relieved of the duties of people's warden, and proposed Mr Cutts in his stead. This proposition was carried unanimously. Mr Cutts asked Mr Bolingbroke to present his report on the charities existing in the town which might have some relevance to St John's. Mr Bolingbroke confirmed that he had looked carefully into the matter, and they all seemed to be completely in order. William Cutts was not convinced. He still felt that St John's did not receive its fair share of the monies due to it. Then followed a debate about the Church Repairing Fund. This was a sum of money invested in India Three Per Cents which generated about £28 per year income. The fund was administered by Frederick Veley, who was a stickler for following the letter of the law (he was, after all, a very successful solicitor) and it had been set up to cover any *'necessary repairs'* to the church. What exactly constituted *'necessary repairs'* then exercised the minds of the vestry for the rest of the meeting, and it was not resolved to anyone's satisfaction. It was agreed to return to the subject at a later date.[89]

In August the provisions of the recent Parliamentary Act concerning free education came into force and George Godson called a meeting of the parishioners to explain to them the impact of this legislation on St John's National Schools. He pointed out that St John's would probably be the only school in Chelmsford to offer free education (in fact, this was to turn out not to be the case) and although the financial situation looked promising (the school would be paid 10s. per head per scholar, compared with about just under 8s. at present) that extra money would soon be swallowed up in increased remuneration for teachers and the inevitable enlargement of the building. The meeting agreed that the provisions of the Act would come into force after the harvest time break in October. The newly-married Mr Ripper would have his work cut out, overseeing the introduction of such a radical revision in the operation of the school.[90]

One other, much talked about, wedding took place before the end of the year. Percy Butler, the forty-year-old son of the vicar's warden, married Thomas Tidboald's very wealthy widow Eliza (she was fifty-one). They tied the knot well away from the prying eyes of St John's parishioners in the Chapel Royal, Savoy in the Strand. Rev Andrew Mellis, a former curate of St John's, was best man. It was a society wedding of some note.[91]

The next year, 1892, was to prove a sad year for St John's, as some of the stalwarts who had laboured so hard for the church and parish, died. Early in the year, not long after his son's society wedding, William Butler caught influenza. His condition worsened, turning into serious bronchitis, and he died in the early hours of Saturday, 12 March, surrounded by his family. He had a distinguished history of church service, having been chapel warden of Holy Trinity, Springfield, for some years. He followed this with a twenty-five year stint as churchwarden of St Mary's, Widford, and vicar's warden of St John's since the 1889 vestry meeting. His family had long-standing connections with the parish. His father, James Butler, had been Moulsham parish chief constable for many years.[92] William Butler was much missed, not least of by the vicar, who now needed a new warden. Mr George Sergeant was duly appointed by George Godson within a couple of weeks.[92]

'A beloved and respected inhabitant of Moulsham parish'

A sombre vestry took place on 20 April. Not only was William Butler's death still fresh in everyone's minds, but George Godson brought to the meeting the news of Robert Hanam's death that very morning. William Cutts dealt very briskly with the accounts. Although a balance in hand to the churchwardens of more than £20 was recorded, a legacy from Mr James Warwick of £25 meant that effectively the year had operated at a slight deficit. There was a brief mention (again) of surplices, the vicar saying that he understood that the question had been brought up during the preceding twelve months, and he personally wished to say that: *"he had no objection to the choir wearing surplices, providing that it was the wish of the congregation, and that the adult members were communicants, and that the churchwardens must see their way to paying the necessary expenses"*. Mr Cutts reassured the vicar on the last point, stating that he had authority to confirm to the meeting that any required funds would be provided outside church expenses. A resolution of their adoption was carried without anyone voting against it, although Mr Bragg had stated that he personally was opposed to their use in St John's. It was a quick and unexpected resolving of such a long-standing and contentious issue.[94]

Robert Hanam's funeral was held in St Leonard's, Sussex, on Tuesday, 26 April, when he was buried in the same grave as his wife Caroline. The burial followed a memorial service the previous day in St John's, conducted by the Archdeacon of Essex assisted by

George Godson. Robert Hanam had been a widower for twenty-seven years and had no children, but the church was crowded with his personal friends and his fellow governors of the Grammar School and the Discharged Prisoners' Aid Society.[95] In his will he left substantial sums of money for his numerous godchildren and his two domestic staff who had looked after him devotedly for many years at his home in Lancaster House, Mildmay Road (now the St John Ambulance headquarters). In October a beautifully inscribed marble tablet was placed on the east wall of the south transept of the church in memory of Caroline and Robert Hanam, referring to him as: *"a beloved and respectable inhabitant of Moulsham parish for over twenty years and for fourteen of those years vicar's warden of the church"*.

On 1 September, Frederick Veley died at his home, Yverdons, in New London Road (now Kemsleys). He had been a prominent member of both Essex and Chelmsford society for more than fifty years and had been a prime mover in the creation of the Chelmsford and Essex Dispensary and Infirmary. Frederick Veley was born in 1810, son of Dennis Veley and Susannah Cunnington. As a young man he had been very interested in his family's history and had visited Switzerland to try and find out more about his ancestors. He discovered that the family originally came from Yverdon just north of Lausanne and that their name had originally been *de Veley*.[96] He was reported to have said that *de Veley* was too difficult for English people to pronounce easily, so he decided to keep *Veley* as his surname. He married Louisa Curtis at Dorking in 1840 and they had a happy marriage, with eight children, until Louisa unexpectedly died in 1875, aged sixty-two. He remarried in 1876, to Harriet Langley Hall, who was some thirty-five years his junior. Frederick Veley's funeral took place in St John's churchyard on Tuesday, 6 September where he was buried in the family vault (near the present clergy vestry door) along with his first wife and some of his children who had predeceased him.[97] He (and other members of his family) are commemorated on a series of wall plaques which are located in the Veley Chapel, in the south-west corner of the church. He died a very wealthy man, leaving over £27,000 in his will, along with the advowson of Aythorpe Roding church which he passed to his newly-married daughter Gertrude. She was later to confer the living on her husband, Rev John Kershaw, who had been associated with St John's for many years. Frederick Veley, though, in his will, left no bequests to St John's.[98]

There was a moment of light relief during what had been a sombre year. In September, it was recorded, with just a hint of amusement, that: *"during the morning service at St John's, Moulsham, a large, well-kept Persian cat entertained itself by noiselessly jumping over the pews between the choir vestry and the clergy vestry, passing across the chancel in its journeys. The pulpit was occupied at that time by the Rev J.F. Smith, a former curate, who during his sermon urged the necessity for being prepared for death, and made a fitting allusion to the suddenness with which it had overtaken Mr Stanley Copland.* (Stanley Copland, the son of a prominent dissenter, had drowned in August while trying to rescue a child from the sea at Walton-on-the-Naze. He was posthumously awarded a certificate by the Royal Humane Society). *The cat was again in evidence in the evening, when it joined in the choral service by mewing. Mr John Lewis, the Church Clerk, tried in vain to dislodge it from the corner in which it had ensconced itself, and in the end had to keep guard over it with his synodsman's wand."*[99]

'She was greatly loved by the poor, to whom she extended a kind liberality'

The following year's vestry saw little that was difficult or contentious. The accounts were presented by Mr Matson (William Cutts was ill) and showed a positive balance of just under £11, a relatively healthy state of affairs. George Godson was not able to re-appoint George Sergeant as his warden, as Mr Sargeant was no longer resident in the parish, and so he nominated Mr R.F. Hayward in his stead. Mr Cutts was re-elected unanimously. There was some half-hearted discussion about the internal walls of the church as they would need some attention in the near future, and again the question was raised of what funds might exist (held in trust for Moulsham church) that could be used for repairs. The churchwardens and the vicar agreed to investigate and make their findings public. The meeting closed, as usual, with a vote of thanks to the chairman.[100]

Early in the year, George Godson's wife, Jessy, had been very unwell, but the *Essex Chronicle* was able to report at the end of June that: *"Mrs Godson, the wife of the vicar of Moulsham, has been lying seriously ill for some weeks, but is now, we are glad to say, recovering"*.[101] Sadly, that report on the Friday, raised false hopes in the parish, as on the following Monday she died. George Godson, a very private man as far as his own feelings were concerned, simply posted a brief bulletin on the vicarage gate which said: *"Asleep in peace. 7.50 a.m. July 3. G.St A.G."*[102] Jessy Godson was almost seventy years old. She deeply felt her attachment to her Hertfordshire home (she was born at Woodhall, near Shenley) and her funeral took place very privately in St Martin's churchyard on 7 July 1893. A memorial service was held in St John's at the time of her burial in Shenley. She was much missed by the parishioners. It was said of her that: *"she was greatly loved by the poor, to whom she extended a kindly liberality in a quiet, unostentatious manner"*.[103]

George Godson did not allow his private grief, which must have been considerable, to impact on his duties as a parish priest. He always had a strong interest in helping the working class to improve their educational standing, and in 1873 had written a small book (which he had published at his own expense) entitled *'Night Schools, their Use and Management'*.[104] He followed this up in November 1893 by calling a meeting to consider the advisability of starting evening classes (under the Continuation Code of the Elementary Education Acts). He pointed out that classes could be held on any subject that a group of individuals wished to study, and that adults of whatever age, and of both sexes, could attend the classes. His approach was enthusiastically endorsed by Mr Bemays, HM Inspector of Schools, who also provided a very helpful explanation of the workings of the Continuation Code. The meeting resolved that the classes should proceed as outlined.[105]

The following year the vestry was dominated by the need to discuss the churchyard and its upkeep. George Godson stated that the law relating to the management and repair of closed churchyards was in a state of transition, and the Town Council was in the process of taking over the powers previously held by parish councils. When this process had finally been completed, the Town Council, on receipt of a certificate detailing the expenses incurred in the management and repair of the churchyard, would be obliged to meet this expenditure. However, the question of control of the churchyard (by churchwardens or Town Council?) was still not clearly defined and William Cutts advised that at the moment no certificate of expenses should be submitted. An intriguing item in the reports of the meeting noted that: *"Mr Frederick Chancellor had prepared some designs for the decoration of the church which would involve expenditure of about £80"*. The designs were clearly not to everyone's taste. Mr Bond said that: *"he thought that the expense of the suggested decoration of the Church was heavy and that he for one would not like to see any elaborate decoration of the building"*. George Godson agreed to send Mr Bond the plans for him to make further comment on them. The accounts were then presented and explained by Mr Cutts. He pointed out that they had ended the year with a positive balance (of just under £1) but in view of the money they had needed to spend to keep the churchyard in order, this represented a satisfactory result. The vestry meeting had also, yet again, to deal with grumbling from the congregation about the services. They were still felt to be far too long (often concluding, when there was Communion, as late as a quarter to one) and several of the vestry meeting felt they could do with 'brightening up' The vestry was on the verge of another vigorous discussion when Mr Cutts weighed in. The conduct of the services, he said, rested firmly with the vicar, and the vicar alone. The meeting was put in its place and the subject quietly dropped.

June 1894 saw the death of Mr Unwin of St John's Road. He had for many years acted as the organ blower at St John's (at the princely sum of £1 per quarter). In paying tribute, George Godson said that: *"his efforts, together with the skills of Mr Ripper on the organ, had raised the quality of the music performed at St John's to a very high level"*.[106] At Christmas the same year, the usual special gift of a £50 note appeared on the collection plate for the poor of the parish. On this occasion, though, the identity of the donor was at last revealed. It was Arthur Pryor, of Hylands House.[107]

The following year saw a long and difficult vestry meeting take place on 16 April. Routine business was quickly dealt with at the beginning of the meeting, a balance of £5 10s. in hand being reported. William Cutts was able to tell those present that the porch erected during the year at the east end of the church (the small room used at present for flower arranging) had been built at a cost of £45, paid for out of a long-established fund set up many years previously. The fund (which was now exhausted) had also been used to install a series of ventilation pipes throughout the church. It was thought that these had made a positive contribution to the removal of the persistent and annoying draughts from certain areas of the church.

'The vicar thinks he could get them back with entertainments'

Mr Bond felt that he had to state, yet again, that there were problems with the services. He quoted examples of a not insignificant number of newcomers to the parish who had initially worshipped at St John's and then expressed their disappointment with the services. They had 'tried' the services at St Mary's and found them much more to their liking, and had become regular worshippers there. When asked why he thought they preferred St Mary's, he replied rather feebly that: *"he didn't attribute it to anything"*. Pressed by Mr Cutts to explain himself a little more fully, he said that some of those who had gone to St Mary's had

told him: *"we go to St Mary's because we like the services better –*
it is a brighter and more attractive service." William Cutts was not
impressed. *"It might be,"* he said, *"a more attractive service, but*
what has that to do with devotion I fail to see". George Godson
then made it quite clear where he stood. He felt that if, on Sunday
mornings, they could get up good entertainments (whatever that
might mean) they could, no doubt, get them all in. This caused
considerable amusement at the meeting, and was unfortunately
seized upon with glee by the newspaper reporters in attendance,
the *Essex Independent and Farmers' Gazette* using the somewhat
mischievous headline 'THE VICAR THINKS HE COULD
GET THEM BACK WITH ENTERTAINMENTS'.[108] Perhaps
not knowing how serious (or not) the vicar was in his comments,
the vestry meeting felt that any further discussion was unnecessary
and after the customary vote of thanks to the chairman the
meeting closed.[109]

The following year's vestry, on 8 April, was poorly attended, with
only ten individuals present in addition to the clergy. Routine
business was again dealt with speedily, Thomas Saltmarsh being
persuaded by the vicar to act as his warden again and the vestry
re-electing Mr Cutts. The previous year had shown a small
balance of just over £2, but it was pointed out that there were
significant items relating to the fabric of the building that needed
urgent attention, including improvements in the lighting (it was
agreed that incandescent lamps should be installed), thorough
cleaning and repairing of the walls , and at the same time the
opportunity would be taken to alter the west end doors so that
they opened outwards. Disappointment was once again expressed
at the general level of the offertories, but this was tempered by
favourable comparisons with St Mary's on a *per capita* basis.
It was revealed that at the previous Sunday evening service at
St Mary's, the church had been filled, with people standing, yet
only £5 had been collected from such a large throng.[110]

On 10 August, in accordance with the decisions taken at the
vestry meeting, work started on the repairs and improvements to

St John's. In order that the work could be completed as quickly as possible, it was decided to close the church for three weeks, the services being held in the schoolroom during that period.[111] A local plumber and painter, Henry Parkhurst, had his tenders accepted: just under £140 to cover the repairs to the exterior of the roof, including the fitting of three of Ridge's ventilators, cleaning down the interior of the church and colouring it with 'some decoration' and staining the tops of the benches. A separate tender from Mr Parkhurst for £22 10s. covered improvements to the lighting arrangements (including fitting additional incandescent burners).[112] The work was completed and the church re-opened in September, and in November it was revealed that the total cost of the repairs had: *"involved an outlay of £258. Subscriptions amounted to £120 so together with the balance in hand from the repair fund (just over £139) a small sum was left on the credit side"*.[113]

'I am deeply touched by your kindness'

Two other events of note were recorded relating to the parish in 1896. James Dace died on 3 September at his home in Colchester, having caught a chill a few days earlier during a visit to Clacton. He was the founder of the well-known musical firm (which in its heyday had a number of shops throughout Essex) and was connected with St John's through having been appointed as the first organist of the church. He left St John's in 1858 (when the organ was moved from the south transept) and became the organist at London Road Congregational Chapel.[114] Also, at the close of the year, the Men's Bible class (a class that George Godson had supported vigorously during all of his time at St John's) presented the vicar with a cushioned armchair (for him to use in the church rooms in George Street) together with an illuminated address to which they had all added their signatures. George Godson was very much moved. An intensely private man (and perhaps more so since the death of his wife) he did on this occasion attempt to express what he felt, saying: *"I am deeply touched by your kindness. It is a comfort to the heart to anybody who is in earnest to meet men, who, as he knows, come to the class simply because they like to come, and who knows by his long experience of men that their hearts are in the work that he is doing".*[115]

Uncertainty and dithering with regard to the churchyard continued to dominate the vestry meetings at St John's for the rest of the century. It was no help that there was considerable disagreement over the exact provisions made in the Local Government Act over the transfer of certain powers from vestries to Parish or Town Councils. Chelmsford was a perfect example of that uncertainty. William Cutts, for St John's, stated his firm belief that if the churchwardens certified their expenses then their control over the churchyard ceased. However, Mr Duffield for St Mary's, thought precisely the opposite. It was by no means clear who was right and who was wrong.[116] At St John's, successive vestry meetings drew attention to the deplorable state of the churchyard, but the only decisions that they ever reached were to have the wall fronting Moulsham Street repaired and the plain fence along the south side of the churchyard replaced. The church clock and the bell were again giving concern. The clock could now be relied upon to be erratic and a growing number of parishioners were unhappy about the 'funereal' sound of the bell when it was rung for services. After some inconsequential discussions, it was felt that little could be done to rectify either of these problems until the financial situation of the church was substantially changed for the better.[117]

The new century dawned, but it dawned at a difficult time for the parish of Moulsham. At the last vestry meeting in 1899, both William Cutts and Thomas Saltmarsh had felt that they could no longer bear the burdens of office as churchwardens, and Thomas Saltmarsh had stood down (there were some hints that his health was beginning to fail). The vicar had managed to persuade William Cutts to carry on as parish warden for a little longer. George Godson, too, was ailing, the arduous round of parish duties that he had set himself taking their toll on his now precarious health. In January 1900 he had suffered from a bad attack of influenza (which at that time was often fatal) and in February he had been obliged to travel to Folkestone to try and recover his health.[118] By March he was back in the parish and was able to attend what would turn out to be his last vestry meeting, on 17 April. It was a sombre affair. Thomas Saltmarsh had died the previous June, at the age of 72, and in addition, the church had lost its clerk, John Lewis, who had served faithfully since his father's death in 1883. William Cutts resigned as parish churchwarden, but agreed to serve as vicar's warden, which was (by 1900) a less demanding post. George Taylor was elected as the choice of the parishioners. The latter (who was also the deputy mayor of the Borough of Chelmsford) accepted the office on the understanding: *"that the vicar's warden would render him as much assistance as he could"*. George Taylor was seconded for the post by Adolphus Maskell, who was at that time the mayor of Chelmsford. St John's clearly had friends in high places. The meeting then discussed the clock again. A report from an expert had shown that the condition of the clock was very poor and it would require substantial expenditure to put it right. The meeting was not impressed and the subject was dropped. George Godson, in closing the meeting, paid tribute to: *"those two dear men"* (the curates, George Collier and Francis Sear) who had effectively run the parish during the vicar's illness.[119]

'He was quick to involve himself with local community organisations in Chelmsford'

George Godson had indeed been well-served by curates during his ministry at St John's. When he arrived in 1879, Thomas Wilkinson's departure had left the parish church with only two services each Sunday (all that the Rev John Kershaw could find time to take, given his commitments as Headmaster of the Grammar School) and the new vicar speedily appointed the first of many curates who would come to share the duties of the parish with him during his incumbency. Harry Percy Grubb was born in Ireland and came from a family who were originally Quakers.

He was the seventh child and fourth son of Richard and Maria Grubb and was the first member of the family to take holy orders. He took his BA at Trinity College, Dublin in 1871 and was ordained deacon in 1872 and priest in 1874 by the Bishop of Down and Connor. After various curacies in Ireland and at Potter's Bar, Middlesex, his appointment at St John's was announced in November 1879[120] and he took his first service in the church on 14 December.[121] He was quick to involve himself with local community organisations in Chelmsford, and as early as January 1880 he was addressing the Chelmsford Temperance Society (a somewhat incongruous fellow-speaker of the platform was St John's arch-nemesis, the Congregationalist minister, George Wilkinson). By the end of 1880 he had been elected president of the Chelmsford Mutual Improvement Society. He was described as: *"an Irish clergyman with strong evangelical leanings"* when he spoke at a Biblical Conference in Halberstadt, Germany, in 1909[122] and his evangelical leanings seem to have characterised his time at St John's. He was in great demand as a guest speaker throughout Essex for the temperance movement although it is not clear how he administered the Eucharist at St John's if he believed in total abstinence. On 24 September 1882 he preached his last sermon as curate of Moulsham. The church was crowded and included many people from other parts of Essex who would never normally come to St John's. In that last sermon Percy Grubb reminded his hearers that *"the God of all grace"* was able to give them strength to resist even the severest temptation. St John's was sorry to see him go, and the ladies of the Bible class presented him with a travelling clock and a gold pen.[123] In 1892 Harry Percy Grubb married into the aristocracy, his bride being Margaret Adelaide Crichton-Stuart. He died at Poole, in 1925, aged seventy-six.

Percy Grubb's departure meant that George Godson needed a replacement almost immediately to help with the considerable parish duties at Moulsham, and in December 1882 Sydney William Wentworth Wilkin was ordained deacon at the traditional St Thomas' day ordination at St Mary's, by the Bishop of St Albans, being licensed at the same time to St John's.[124] He preached his first sermon on the first Sunday in 1883 and quickly settled into the routine of the parish. Sydney Wilkin was born in Paddington in late 1859, the eldest son of Sydney Wilkin, a Master Mariner, and his wife Sarah. He went to King's College, London, graduating in 1881. St John's was his first parish. He took his last service there on 27 September 1885, leaving to take up the post of curate-in-charge of the new district of Groombridge, near Tunbridge Wells (where the church was still to be built). After two more curacies in Hampshire he was appointed a chaplain to the forces in 1887.[125] In September 1888 he married Annette Robins and was posted overseas to Egypt in 1894. After a distinguished career in the forces, particularly in the Great War, he was placed on half-pay (on account of ill-health) in September 1918. He died in retirement near Brighton in 1927, aged sixty-eight.

Tom Beverly Athorne was born in 1847, the son of George Athorne, a York grocer and his wife Lavinia. He attended St Peter's School, York, where he was elected the best classical scholar and in 1866 won an Open and an Ellerton scholarship to the University of Durham at the same time as a University Mathematical scholarship.[126] He graduated from Durham with a first class degree in both mathematics and classics in 1868. He was commissioned as a lieutenant in the eleventh Worcestershire Rifle Volunteer Corps but after his ordination as a deacon by the Bishop of Worcester in the cathedral on 21 December 1877[127] he resigned his commission on 23 January 1878.[128] He was then appointed curate at Upper Mitton, Worcestershire, where he became a noteworthy member of the local community, in considerable demand as a speaker and a local thespian. Someone of such a considerable talent who was looking for a post may have caught George Godson's eye, and he came to St John's, preaching his first sermon there on 25 February 1883, when it was reported that: *"he made a good impression on the congregation"*.[129] However, he seems to have suffered from very poor health, and as described earlier, took his last service at the end of April that same year. Strangely, though, he continued to live in the parish. During his brief curacy he had married Annie, the eldest daughter of the late George Robinson, of Summerfield, Hartlebury, at Holy Trinity, Stourbridge, on 4 April 1883.[130] They returned to Chelmsford to live at Grove House (in Grove Road?) where a son, Alwyn Spencer was born on 12 January 1884.[131] In the intervening period he continued to take an active part in the social life of Chelmsford, and was even recorded as taking the funeral of a non-conformist in the New London Road cemetery in August 1883.[132] Did he have too much sympathy towards nonconformists for George Godson's taste? He was, fortunately, an individual of independent means and was able eventually to move to Dover (perhaps to try and improve his health) where he died in 1889, aged only forty-two.

After the strange, short curacy of Tom Athorne, George Godson quickly sought a replacement, and perhaps he felt that a more experienced (and even married) curate might meet his requirements. Walter Edward Smith was born in about 1856 in Westminster. He went up to New College, Oxford in 1874 and obtained a first-class BA in 1878, being awarded the University Cobden Essay prize in 1879. He was ordained deacon in 1880 and priest in 1881 during his curacy at Harpenden (1880–83) where he had married Margaret Rose Vaughan in 1881, and George Godson clearly felt that here was a more experienced priest who could well prove to be just what was needed at Moulsham. Sadly, it was not to be. Walter Smith first officiated at St John's on 17 July 1883 but by September he was (as described earlier) already taking leave of the parish. The *Chelmsford Chronicle* of that week carried an advertisement to the effect that: "*No.1 Osborne Place, New London Road, was to let at Michaelmas, Unfurnished. Three good reception rooms, six good bedrooms dressing room, box room, convenient kitchen, cellars and other offices; garden, stables. Apply Rev W. Smith, address*". This suggests that he had bought himself a substantial property in Chelmsford, with the intention of living in it in some style and for some time.[133] His reasons for leaving St John's and Moulsham are shrouded in mystery. He then moved to the small village of Corton, just south of Lowestoft, as the vicar, eventually becoming vicar of the relatively prosperous living of Andover in Hampshire. He died at Stroud, in Gloucestershire in 1935 aged 80.

John Francis Smith was born in 1855, the son of James Smith, a shipbroker, and his wife Elizabeth. He graduated from the University of London in 1880 and was ordained deacon at the traditional St Thomas' day service in St Mary's, Chelmsford by the Bishop of St Albans, being licensed at the same time to St John's, Moulsham. At his ordination he was described as a 'literate'.[134] He took his first service at St John's in 1884 and was ordained priest in December of the same year. While at St John's he married Mary Mackenzie of Dunvegan in Scotland on 12 August 1885.[135] The parishioners of St John's clubbed together and presented the newlyweds with a substantial cheque for £34. John Smith seems to have been a musically-gifted individual, deputising on the organ at St John's in an emergency. Among the wedding gifts was a piano from the bride's uncle. He preached his last sermon at St John's in 1887, and left to take up a curacy in the London docks, followed by a brief spell at East Ham. He then moved to Glasgow where he was rector of St Luke's in the city for a number of years.

'The parish is deprived of the services of a zealous and fruitful promoter of the gospel'

Andrew Mellis was ordained by the Bishop of St Albans in St Mary's, Chelmsford on Sunday, 20 December 1885, receiving his license for St John the Evangelist at the same time.[136] He was a foundation scholar of Hatfield Hall, Durham, where he was awarded a second-class BA in mathematics[137] although at his ordination he was described as 'BA, Merton College, Oxford', a degree he may have been awarded *ad eundem* (a process whereby one university awards a degree to an alumnus of another). He took his first service at St John's on 10 January 1886, and soon made an impact, quickly endearing himself to the parishioners as an able and caring priest. It was announced in October of the following year that he would shortly be leaving the parish[138] and on Thursday, 3 November it was reported that: *"The numerous friends of the Rev Andrew Mellis in Moulsham greatly regret the fact that he is about to leave the parish. His ministrations in St John's church have been greatly appreciated by the congregation and it is felt by many that by losing him the parish is deprived of the services of a zealous and fruitful promoter of the gospel. Friends and the poor have subscribed a sum of money, which was presented together with a Venetian purse. He was also given an address acknowledging his services and expressing regret at his leaving the parish"*,[139] After leaving Moulsham he became a curate in Herne Bay, Kent, before moving to Reculver. He was then appointed as chaplain to the Blean Union workhouse in 1894. He spent most of the rest of his life in Kent.

George Alfred Thomson was born in Kennington, Surrey on 26 July 1859, the son of George Thompson, a shopkeeper and his wife Martha. He migrated to St John's College, Cambridge, in 1883, obtaining his BA (junior optime) in 1885 and his MA in 1889. He came to Chelmsford as the Second Master of the Grammar School, being appointed in the early summer of 1885. He was ordained deacon by the Bishop of St Albans in 1886 and was licensed to officiate at St John's on 20 June (his annual remuneration was £4, reflecting the paid position he already had at the Grammar School). Before his arrival in Chelmsford he had married Augusta Burton in 1884 and they settled in the town, moving into the little cottage on the corner of St John's Road and Mildmay Road, which they named 'Nonpareil Cottage'. Here their eldest daughter Gertrude was born in 1887. He took his first service at St John's on 11 July 1886, and was soon taking his part in the running of the parish, although with his commitments at the Grammar School he was really only able to help on Sundays. In April 1887 it was announced at a meeting of the Governors of the Grammar School that the Rev G.A. Thompson had been successful in his application to become headmaster of the Hipperholme Grammar School, Halifax, and that he would take up his duties in December of that same year.[140] In August 1887 it was reported that: *"a few of the head boys of the Grammar School waited on the Rev G.A Thompson at his residence, Nonpareil Cottage to present him with a testimonial. The presentation took the form of a massive oak and brass inkstand, with the usual equipment, and it has a plate stating that it was 'to the Rev G.A. Thompson, BA, from the boys of the Grammar School, Chelmsford, July 1887".*[141] He preached his last sermon in St John's in the summer of 1887. He went on to serve as headmaster at Hipperholme until 1890, when he was appointed headmaster at Horsham Grammar School in Sussex.[142] In 1891 he was awarded the degrees of LlB and LlD by Trinity College, Dublin. He continued at Horsham until 1917, when he was appointed rector of Tidworth and Shipton Bullinger in Hampshire, a post he held until 1922. He retired to Bournemouth where he died in January 1923, aged seventy-three.[143]

William North Surridge (William North Andrews) was the son of a prosperous Essex solicitor, North Surridge, and his wife Anna. He was born at Romford Hall on 5 November 1858, and went to school at Charterhouse. He was admitted to Trinity College, Cambridge, as a pensioner on 31 May 1877, matriculating at Michaelmas of that same year. He was awarded his BA in 1881 and MA in 1887. He was ordained deacon (as William North Surridge) on Wednesday, 21 December 1881 (St Thomas' day) at St Mary's, Chelmsford, by the Bishop of St Albans, being licensed to a curacy in Tring at the same time.[144] He was licensed as priest (as William North Andrews, having accepted the surname Andrews *in lieu* of Surridge on 20 September 1882) at the corresponding service in 1882. His curacy at Tring lasted from 1881 to 1886, then it was announced in September 1887 that: *"The Rev W.N. Andrews, who has been appointed curate at St John's, will shortly move from Writtle to Chelmsford. Mr Andrews has taken the house ('Nonpareil') at the corner of St John's Road, recently vacated by the Rev G.A. Thompson".*[145] He took his first service at St John's on 2 October 1887 (which as a priest licensed in the diocese he was able to do). He was officially licensed to St John's on 3 December the same year. He took his last service in the parish church in 1889 and shortly afterwards was appointed to Diss, in Norfolk, as curate where he married Edith Emily Manning, the eldest daughter of the rector. After becoming vicar of Paston in Norfolk in 1891 he moved to Erwington in Devon as sinecure rector. He died in 1922, aged sixty-four.[147]

The splendidly named Arthur William Benjamin Walmesley Watts was born on 18 April 1864 to the Rev Henry Watts and his wife Emma in the vicarage at Tichborne, Hampshire. He was educated at Trent College, Long Eaton, Derbyshire and went up to Selwyn College, Cambridge in 1882 where he graduated BA in 1885. He was ordained deacon by the Bishop of St Albans, again at the traditional St Thomas' day service at St Mary's on 21 December 1887, being licensed at the same time to St John's.[148] He took part in his first service at St John's on Christmas day of the same year and preached his first sermon on 1 January 1888. Just before he arrived in the parish he had married Elizabeth Brooke at St Saviour's in London. While in Chelmsford he revealed himself as a talented cricketer, playing frequently for the town side as a very effective bowler. He was ordained priest at St Mary's on 21 December 1888, again by the Bishop.[149] In March 1889 it was announced that: *"Moulsham – the Rev A.W.B.W. Watts; this gentleman, who is the second curate of St John the Evangelist, Moulsham, has accepted the curacy of St John's, Woolwich"*.[150] He left Moulsham at the end of the month. In fact, he went to Holy Trinity, Hounslow, until 1891, and after a series of other posts, (including, at one stage, a chaplaincy to the Ongar Union workhouse) he became vicar of Nunkeeling with Bewholme and Atwick in Yorkshire. Here, just north-west of Beverly, he stayed from 1904 until his death in 1933 at the age of sixty-nine.[151]

'The church was packed to overflowing'

Arthur Baynes Merriman Ley was born in Bishop's Stortford in April 1846, the son of William Merriman Ley, a solicitor, and his wife Ellen. He was admitted as a sizar to St John's College, Cambridge, where he matriculated at Michaelmas 1867, and obtained his BA in 1871 and his MA in 1875. He was ordained deacon in 1872 and priest in 1873 in the diocese of Norwich and his first appointment was as curate of Great Yarmouth from 1872 to 1874.[152] After two further curacies (one, at Barmer, in Norfolk where he married Harriet Walford) George Godson must have felt that here was an experienced parish priest who could be just what St John's needed. Arthur Ley was licensed to St John's on 30 July 1889, but he had already officiated at a baptism in St John's at the beginning of April (his previous curacy had been in the diocese of St Albans). With the departure of Arthur Watts, Arthur Ley briefly became the sole curate, becoming senior curate when George Collier arrived. For a little while matters seemed to run very smoothly, but less than a year after his licensing the local press felt it had to: *"contradict the rumour that the Rev A.B.M. Ley, the senior curate at St John's church, Moulsham, was about to leave the parish"*.[153] Any respite was brief. Just two weeks later the same newspaper carried an announcement saying it had learned that: *"the rumour that was current a fortnight ago with regard to the departure of the Rev A.B.M. Ley, was a true one, and the Rev gentleman was about to leave St John's Church, Moulsham, where he is senior curate"*.[154] And so he left the parish. His thoughts and comments have already been noted and it is clear that he was much appreciated in Chelmsford and its environs. Just before his last service at St John's, he was invited to preach at the Harvest Festival at St Paul's, Highwood, where it was reported that: *"the church was full to overflowing"*. His departure from Chelmsford did not mean that he cut his links entirely with the town, and he was listed amongst the clergy present at the 21 December 1890 ordinations in St Mary's.[155] He moved from Moulsham to Layer Breton as curate in 1891, becoming vicar of White Colne in 1896. He remained there until 1913, when he retired to Bishop's Stortford, where he died in 1922 aged seventy-five.

'My hands are full, and my heart also'

Of all the curates that served George Godson, none became such a prop to him as George Victor Collier. In a very long and devoted curacy (George Collier stayed in Moulsham almost twelve years, longer than any other curate) which meant towards the end that he took almost total charge of the parish during

George Godson's last illness, he endeared himself to the parishioners in a way that few of the clergy associated with St John's were ever able to do.

George Victor Collier was born on 13 April 1864 in Edinburgh, the son of William Francis Collier, DD, (a Master in the Edinburgh Academy) and his wife Mary Ellen (she was Irish).[156] He studied Theology at Trinity College, Dublin, where he graduated BA in 1888. He was ordained deacon by the Bishop of St Albans on Sunday, 16 June 1889 at the cathedral in St Albans and was licensed to St John's as a curate at the same time.[157] He took his first service at St John's shortly afterwards and his first baptism in September the following year, when Arthur Ley was preparing to leave, after having been ordained priest in June 1890 at Great Berkhampstead church by the Bishop of St Asaph's, acting under commission from the Archbishop of Canterbury, as Thomas Legh Claughton was unwell.[158] He quickly settled into the life of the parish, living at St John's Road (number fifteen) and taking on what must have been a heavy burden of visiting, as with the departure of Arthur Ley there was only himself and Edward Parkinson (who also had responsibilities at St Mary's, Widford) to assist George Godson, whose health was already beginning to fail. George Collier proved to be a talented young man, frequently in demand at many parish social functions. Edward Parkinson left in 1893, and although two other curates did come in later on to help in the running of the parish, George Collier was clearly George Godson's right-hand man, virtually acting as vicar from the summer of 1900 onwards. He preached his last sermon in St John's on Sunday, 3 February 1901 (after George Godson's death) paying fulsome tribute to the friendliness and help he had received from all the parishioners.

He was instituted to the living of Theydon Bois by the Bishop of St Albans on the following day (Monday, 4 February) and inducted to the living by the Bishop-designate of Barking on Friday, 9 February.[159] He came back for his presentation from the parishioners on Monday, 15 April, in the schoolroom, when he received a purse and a cheque for 100 guineas, an illuminated address and a book containing the names of all the subscribers. He was much moved. In acknowledging the gifts, he said: *"I thank you, Mr Cutts, for the kind words you have said concerning me. My hands are full and my heart is full also. Never have I had to face an ordeal which I have looked forward to with more anxiety than this, for I feel that I would like to do justice to the occasion and my good friends"*. During his thank you speech, someone called out: *"Well done, Mr Collier!"* *"No,"* George Collier replied, *"It should really be well done, Moulsham!"* It was not to be complete severance from Moulsham, because he returned from time to time to take special services at St John's.[160] While at Theydon Bois he married a widow from Ongar, Mary Elizabeth Usborne, in 1903. She was 31, and already had a son, Michael Thomas Usborne , whom he formally adopted. They had a daughter, Frances Elizabeth Collier who was born in 1907. He died in 1936, in Wallingford, Oxfordshire.

Edward Parkinson was born near Manchester in 1848. He went to New College, London, where he studied theology. He was ordained at the 21 December ceremony held at St Mary-at-the-Walls, Colchester, by the Bishop of St Albans in 1879. Edward Parkinson also read the Gospel at that service.[161] He was licensed at the same time as curate to Waltham Holy Cross (Waltham Abbey). He was ordained priest in 1880, continuing as curate at Waltham until 1886, moving into the parsonage house as senior curate in 1882. He then moved as curate to Elstree in Hertfordshire, where he stayed until 1889.[162] He was appointed curate at St Mary's, Widford, to assist the rector in August of that same year,[163] but when he came to Chelmsford he took up residence in 'Nonpareil Cottage' on the corner of St John's Road and Mildmay Road. The cottage was by then owned by one of St John's churchwardens, Robert Hanam.[164] He was licensed formally as one of the curates of St John's on 18 December 1889, being paid a generous stipend of £150, but latterly he can have spent little time officiating at Moulsham. When the rector of St Mary's, Widford, Rev William Buswell died in February 1893 (he had been in poor health for some time, and his sight was failing) Edward Parkinson had been effectively running the parish for almost two years.[165] The rector had been appointed to Widford in 1840, and had thus been almost a contemporary of Christopher Muston. Edward Parkinson relinquished his duties at Widford in June 1893, having been presented by the parishioners with an address and a folding table.[166] He left St John's the following August, moving to Storrington, Sussex, as curate. He never married and died in about 1908, aged about sixty.

William Louis Benthall was born on 1 August 1868 at Marylebone in London. His father, William Henry Benthall was private secretary to the Duke of Argyll. Like his father and grandfather John, William went up to St John's College, Cambridge after attending Uppingham school under the Rev Thring. He graduated BA in 1890, obtaining his MA in 1904.[167] He was ordained deacon by the Bishop of St Albans on Sunday 20 December 1891 at St Mary's in Chelmsford, being selected as the reader of the Gospel at this service. He was licensed at the same service as curate of St Stephen's, Walthamstow.[168] He was ordained priest on 18 December 1892 at Cheshunt.[169] He stayed at Walthamstow until 1893, moving to Chelmsford, where he was licensed to St John's on 29 June 1894, although he had already preached at St John's on behalf of the Bishop's Fund.[170] During his time at St John's he became a prominent and very successful member of the Chelmsford Lawn Tennis Club. He took his last baptism in the parish in June 1898, moving to a curacy in what was the very challenging parish of Spitalfields in London. After further curacies in the London area he moved as chaplain to Dusseldorf from 1907-10, but went into retirement early due to ill-health. He had been admitted to the Bethlem Royal Hospital for almost a year in 1902 and again in 1908, where he was detained suffering from a severe persecution complex (he believed the Freemasons were trying to murder him because of his love for an unnamed, aristocratic German woman). He died in a private mental hospital in 1953, aged eighty-four.

'He had a firm interest in the Church Lads' Brigade'

Francis Charles Sear (he is recorded in Crockford's Clerical Directory as Frederick Charles Sear) was born in Southsea in 1875, the son of John Sear and his wife Elizabeth. John Sear was one of the Royal Navy's principal Inspectors of Machinery, and in Francis Sear's youth the family frequently moved around the country, living close to different naval bases. He attended King's College, London, becoming an associate in theology (AKC) in 1896. He was ordained deacon by the Bishop of St Albans in 1898 and licensed to St John's as a curate until the end of the year. He quickly immersed himself in parish work taking (with George Collier) his share in the clerical responsibilities during George Godson's now increasingly frequent absences through illness. Francis Sear had, like the vicar, fallen ill to a severe bout of influenza early in 1900, from which he had recovered rather more quickly than the incumbent. Francis Sear clearly had a firm interest in the Church Lads' Brigade and it was reported in April 1900 that: *"a brigade is being started in connection with St John's church. At a meeting to consider the project, 52 youths attended, who heartily entered into the idea. The Rev F.C. Sear will be in command of the company, with the rank of captain."*[171] Francis Sear left St John's officially on 29 December 1900 but returned early in the new year to receive a presentation from the parish.[172] He left St John's to take up a curacy at Prescot, Lancashire, marrying Ellen Mabel Gardener at a village near Great Yarmouth in the late summer of 1901. After several years at Prescot he moved to Harrow-on-the-Hill where he stayed for many years. He died near Exeter in 1950, aged seventy-five.

'Words will not come to do even a faint justice to his long life of faith and service'

As the century drew to a close, George Godson was struck down just after Christmas with a severe bout of influenza. His continued and selfless devotion to all the parishioners of Moulsham in all weathers and in all circumstances, visiting the sick and the dying at all hours of the day and night, had taken their toll and he struggled bravely to recover from this painful and debilitating illness. Although he more or less recovered, it left him with a serious weakness of the heart, and for the remainder of his life he suffered from asthma and periodic congestion of the lungs. In the last year of his life he was only able on three or four occasions to preach at St John's. In September 1900 he went to Brighton, hoping that a prolonged stay and the sea air might alleviate his symptoms, but while he was there he became worse and quickly returned home to Chelmsford, being confined to his room for more or less the rest of his life. He died on Saturday, 1 December 1900 at the vicarage, at about two o'clock in the afternoon surrounded by his relatives including the Rev Arthur Gordon, the vicar of All Saints, Gordon Square, London. The impact on the parish and the wider town of Chelmsford was profound. There was an intense sense of loss and pain on the following Sunday, at St John's, and generous and heartfelt tributes were paid in surrounding churches and Chapels. George Collier, who had been one of the closest associates of George Godson, was eloquent in his testimony, saying that: *"words will not come to do even faint justice to the long life of faith and loving service which yesterday came to an end on earth ... ... if we look at the lives we have known we shall find none that have more faithfully striven than our dear vicar and succeeded in the carrying out of this dear precept of the loved and loving disciple of Him who went about doing good"*. Francis Sear in the evening service paid his own tribute, saying that he found him to be: *"the most self-sacrificing, kind and considerate of men ... ... many a small corner of the little world in which he moved has been made brighter and happier than when he found it"*. The Rev H.A. Lake, the rector of St Mary's, Chelmsford, made touching reference to George Godson's death on that same Sunday, describing him as a man: *"whose chief characteristics were self-forgetfulness and kindness of heart"*. Perhaps one of the most telling tributes of all came from George Godson's friend, Rev W. Trimmer, vicar of St Mary's, Broomfield, who gave details of a touching incident: *"which truly showed the kindness of heart that characterised the deceased.*

179

Figure 18 – George St Alban Godson, Incumbent of
St John's, Moulsham, 1879–1900

Being asked to undertake the Sunday duty at Broomfield, he readily consented – and it was not for some considerable time afterwards that he found out that his friend had had to provide help for his own church in order to allow him to get to Broomfield. Fulsome tributes were also paid in the pulpits of London Road Congregational Church, Baddow Road Congregational Church and in the Baptist Chapel.[173]

'He found what he required in the work of helping the poor, the sick and the suffering'

George Godson was buried, not in Shenley, with his wife Jessy, but in the Writtle Road cemetery, as: *"it has been thought by his friends that it will be more fitting for the late Vicar of Moulsham to be laid among his old parishioners*". His funeral service took place at St John's on Saturday, 8 December 1900, presided over by the Bishop of Colchester and attended by no less than twenty-three clergy (including the Unitarian minister, Mr E.J. Harry, one of the few people with whom George Godson had clashed in public debate). An open landau had to be used to carry all the wreaths as there were so many. The tributes to him continued on the Sunday after the funeral. At St John's the Rev Bartlett said that the late vicar had been: *"a man possessed of sufficient means to enable him, had he so chosen, to live a life of ease and enjoyment – to lead, as people would say, an independent life. But that was not his choice. He preferred a life of toil in a sphere, not brightened by many attractions of some obscure and thankless task, and he found what he required in the work of helping the poor, the sick, and the suffering"*. In his service at St Mary's, Great Baddow, the Rev A.N. Colley added his own tribute, and at the Baptist Chapel, Pastor H.S. Boulton said that: *"Chelmsford was much the poorer for the death of a well-known and respected Minister"*, and he continued, giving a brief physical description of the man himself, *"Frequently in our streets might have been seen a tall, thin figure hurrying to and fro on errands of mercy – and though we differed theologically, we esteemed him as an Evangelical preacher of the Gospel"*. Mrs W.H. Beckett of Chelmsford was moved to put her thoughts into very Victorian verse, which the *Essex Chronicle* felt was worth publishing:[174]

IN MEMORIAM

Silent for aye that kindly voice,
And cold that helpful hand;
The spirit's flown to the far-off home,
In the bright and better land.

Thine the unselfish Christian love,
Apart from sect or creed,
Ever ready, ever sure,
To aid in times of need.

181

Many a wan and aged soul
By thee hath brightened been;
Wher'er the hand of sickness pressed
Thy kindly thought was seen.

Now thou art gone! Though hearts will weep,
Our Father knoweth best.
Thou hast fulfilled his loved commands
And now hath entered rest!

'He was full of good deeds; his graceful hospitality was inextinguishable'

Amongst St John's parishioners thoughts quickly turned to ways in which they might provide a tangible memorial to their late vicar. George Godson's Men's Bible class clearly felt the loss as deeply as any group, and at their first meeting after the vicar's death, William Cutts advocated a permanent memorial to him. After some brief discussion, it was agreed that a brass tablet should be erected in the Church room in George Street and that this tablet should be placed on behalf of both the Men's and Women's Bible classes. By the middle of January 1901 sufficient money had been collected and at a meeting on the 14th it was decided that the tablet should be engraved: "*The Rev G. St A. Godson, MA. This tablet was erected by members of the Bible classes in loving memory of their late leader*". George Collier, who chaired the meeting, was charged with the task of finding a suitable text of scripture.[175] Shortly afterwards the clergy, churchwardens and synodsmen gathered in the church itself to decide how best to commemorate the late vicar's incumbency. It was quickly agreed that there should be a memorial, and after some brief debate about what form it should take (initial suggestions included a peal of bells or a new organ) it was decided to recommend to a full meeting of the parishioners that: "*a stained glass window should be erected in the south transept*".[176] Subscriptions were called for, and such was the response that sufficient money was raised (about £116) to provide two large windows. These were commissioned from Charles Eamer

Kempe (in his most pearly and feathery style) with one representing Ezekiel and the other (not surprisingly) St John the Evangelist. They were dedicated at a special service on 8 March 1902 in the presence of a large congregation.[177] Each of the windows bears at its foot the same inscription:[178]

**'George St Alban Godson, Priest,
Vicar of Moulsham MDCCCLXXIX – MDCCCC
In recollection of his faithful ministry his friends and
parishioners dedicate this window'**

George Godson died a relatively wealthy man, leaving over £6,000 in his will, details of which were published in February 1901.[179] His close friend, the sometime rector of Chignal Smealy, William Gibbens summed him up perfectly when he wrote: *"he was a good, patient house-visiting parish priest, showing, in his parochial labours no distinction between rich and poor in his somewhat diversified flock. He was full of good deeds, his graceful hospitality was inextinguishable, kind to the sick, the mourner, the erring, the sufferer, and a true comforter of the distressed and the afflicted soul, yet not forgetting as a faithful shepherd of his divine master to shake his pastoral crook over the heads of the disobedient, the godless and the profane"*. His passing was deeply mourned in the parish, perhaps more than that of any other incumbent, except possibly Alfred Mason (although he, of course, died some years after he had left St John's). George Godson's portrait shows a slightly gaunt, devoted figure, one that must have been easily recognisable around the parish (*Figure 18*).

The next incumbent would bring a whiff of the English Church Union to St John's.

6. ROBERT TRAVERS SAULEZ

(1901-06)

*"He has been Vicar of Belchamp St Paul in this county
for something like fifteen years, and we have never heard
anything but good of him.
We have not the slightest doubt that he will make a
faithful and zealous Vicar of Moulsham. He has shown not
a little courage in taking this post, which implies plenty
of work and scanty pay".*[1]

So, in 1901, the *Essex Chronicle* greeted the news that Robert
Travers Saulez was to be the new vicar of St John the Evangelist,
Moulsham. It is not easy to see what would motivate an intelligent,
talented priest in his early fifties to leave a quiet, beautiful well-
endowed rural parish where he would have known most of his
seven hundred or so parishioners by name to come to a parish with
many more social problems and to minister to what was often an
ungrateful flock. Yet come he did, and his ministry in Moulsham
was to be a challenge that he did not always master. To follow
George Godson was no easy task (particularly as Robert Saulez was
by no means a wealthy individual, and the problems that dogged
Thomas Wilkinson were also to hang around the new incumbent's
neck) but he left his impact upon the parish too, and many had fond
memories of him when he finally left Chelmsford.

Robert Travers Saulez was born 19 September 1849, in Naini Tal,
a popular hill station in the Indian province of Uttarakhand, at the
foot of the Himalayas.[2] His father, Rev George Alfred Frederick
Saulez was employed as a chaplain in the Bengal Principality, and
his mother, born Mary Eliza Cookson in Jamaica in 1861 had
been sent to the much healthier, cool hill station to give birth.

Robert's two eldest siblings, having been born in the heat of Bengal, had both died in infancy. Robert was the sixth child of thirteen, and the fifth boy. He was sent back to England to be educated at Heversham School in Westmorland. He was admitted as a sizar to Trinity College, Cambridge, on 14 October 1870, matriculating at Michaelmas in the same year. He suffered a severe blow when his much-loved mother died in November 1871, while he was still up at Cambridge, but he continued his studies, spending as much time as his could with his father, who by then had moved back to England as rector of Exton in Hampshire. He graduated BA in 1874, obtaining his MA in 1877. On 1 March 1874 he was ordained deacon in Chester cathedral by the Bishop, being licensed at the same time a curate of St George's, Everton.[3] Just under a year later, the same Bishop ordained him priest; again the ceremony was in Chester cathedral.[4] He stayed at St George's, Everton, until he was appointed secretary to the Chester Diocesan Finance Association in October 1876,[5] a post he held for just under a year. His next appointment was at the iron church of St John the Evangelist, Walton, to which he moved as priest-in-charge in August 1877.[6] While at Walton, he married Margaret Schofield Hunt, the daughter of a Hampshire gentleman, in his father's church at Exton (his father may have taken the service). His eldest son, Robert, was born in January 1882 while the family was living at Warbeck Moor House, Aintree.[7] In 1883 it was announced that he was moving to his father's parish, Exton, as curate-in-charge.[8] His father was by this time almost seventy years old, and in poor health. Here his second son, Arthur Travers, was born in 1884. He stayed at Exton for another year (during which time his father died) and then caught the eye of the Hon and Rev Robert Henley, MA, the vicar of Putney, who offered him the post of his curate.[9] Here he moved in influential circles, and it was no surprise that when he next moved it was at the behest of the Dean and Chapter of St George's, Windsor, who in 1886 offered him the living of Belchamp St Paul, a wealthy and relatively undemanding parish where he succeeded the Rev William Tindall-Atkinson, MA, as vicar.[10] Belchamp St Paul, in the north-west tip of Essex (not far from Haverhill) at that time had an income of just under £400 a year, and with a population of just over 600, was indeed a comfortable post. Two more children were born to Robert and Margaret, another son, Alfred, while the family were at Putney and a daughter, Margaret, was born after the move to Essex in 1888.

In Belchamp St Paul Robert Saulez showed that he had lost none of those organisational skills he had acquired while acting as the secretary to the Chester Diocesan Board of Finance, and shortly after his arrival in the parish he was appointed to the position of Diocesan Inspector for schools for the Deanery of Yeldham.[11] He was obviously keen to improve the education of his rural and isolated flock, and in 1890 it was reported that he gave: *"in the schoolroom at Belchamp St Paul an account of the holiday he had spent that summer in Paris. He was able to illustrate his talk with a Magic Lantern show."*[12] To his parishioners, such tales of faraway places (he might as well have been talking about the moon) must have seemed magic indeed. He continued to work hard in his parish, in 1892 seeking the opinions of everyone as to what needed to be done next to restore the church. The tower was in a 'dilapidated' condition (literally) and after parish meetings it was felt to be the next candidate for serious work. It was restored as a memorial to Mr G.W. Eagle, who was eighty-four that year (he was still alive) and had worshipped at the church for seventy-seven of those years, and been churchwarden for forty-six of them. The cost of the restoration was £500 and already by November 1892 almost £200 had been raised.[13] Even in such a quiet and peaceful parish, the strain could sometimes tell. Early in 1892 Robert Saulez had a serious attack of influenza,[14] then often viewed as a fatal illness, and its effect continued for some time. In February 1894 it was reported that: *"the vicar of Belchamp St Paul, the Rev R.T. Saulez, has been compelled through illness, to leave the parish for a period of four months. This is the result of overwork."*[15] and later that same year he felt that he had to resign from his position as Diocesan Inspector for Schools.[16] In 1899 his talents were further recognised at a Diocesan level when he was appointed Rural Dean of Yeldham.[17] This, then, was the man who would be the next incumbent of Moulsham.

'Promising and well-received'

On Thursday, 10 January 1901 the rector of St Mary's, Chelmsford, the Rev H.A. Lake, who was the patron of the living of St John the Evangelist, Moulsham, received a letter from Robert Saulez, accepting the position of vicar of Moulsham. The *Essex Newsman* commented, without a hint of irony, that: *"Mr Saulez, however active himself, will doubtless find it necessary to keep at least one curate in Moulsham."*[18] This announcement meant that there would still be something of a gap in providing services at Moulsham, as it would be two or three months before a new incumbent could be installed. Early in February it was announced that the Rev William Davis, the vicar of North Fambridge, would take up residence in Moulsham in order to act as *locum tenens* until Robert Saulez was in post.

Even before Robert Saulez had been installed, the antennae of the Protestant Press Agency, in the person of their ever-vigilant secretary. Mr Le Lievre, had caught a whiff of something a bit unsavoury. As soon as he was aware of the appointment, Mr Le Lievre started firing off his usual letters to the local press, standard practice for the Agency whenever there was a hint of High Church Tendencies in a clergyman newly appointed to a post. The *Essex Chronicle*, although it received a missive from Mr Le Lievre, felt itself under no compulsion to publish it, quickly dismissing it by saying: *"No sooner is a clergyman of the High Church school appointed to a living than down comes a letter from Mr Le Lievre to the local paper, which latter, in our opinion, is calculated to annoy or embarrass him (the clergyman) and more or less frustrate him in his efforts to begin his work as a Christian Minister ... ... quite apart from the side which may be taken, such a mode of warfare is unfair and un-English".*[1] In spite of these storm clouds, Robert Travers Saulez was instituted and inducted by the Bishop of Barking on Sunday, 24 March 1901 at the evening service in the presence of a large congregation.[19] Robert Saulez had made a previous brief appearance at St John's, when he gave an address at the regular Wednesday evening service on 6 March (which he could do as a licensed priest in the Diocese of St Albans). His discourse on the outlines of the Christian Life was described as: *"promising and well-received"*.[20] And so Robert Saulez came to Moulsham. It is difficult, more than one hundred years later, to identify what might have been his reasons and motives for moving to such a diverse and extensive parish, with its singular history of wearing out incumbents. But come he did, and one of the first items which needed his attention was to provide (out of his own stipend) additional priestly support in the form of a curate. Both George Collier and Francis Sear left the parish early in 1901, and Robert Saulez turned to an old friend, the Rev John Banks Beers, who had been the curate at the little village church of Sturmer, in north Essex (between Haverhill in Suffolk and Belchamp St Paul) and who was living in semi-retirement at Great Ouse, near Ely, to come as his assistant at St John's. John Beers was licensed to the parish on 15 July 1901 with a generous stipend of £163 a year.

'Hold your tongue!'

Just two short weeks after his installation as vicar, Robert Saulez had to chair his first vestry meeting, on 11 April 1901. It was a fraught affair, even by Moulsham's standards. It began in a relatively calm and sombre attitude, with the minutes recording the sense of loss of the parish at the death of George Godson. The financial position was recorded as being less than satisfactory, the very small deficit with which the year had begun rising to more than £41 by the end of March 1901 (although about £20 was due to come from Henry Guy's charity which would significantly reduce the debt). The financial outlook was not particularly promising as the parish, Mr George Taylor pointed out, would now have to pay the organist's salary (George Godson had always paid this out of his own pocket) and substantial expenditure would be required on the churchyard. Robert Saulez then continued by explaining to the meeting that the laity were being given a more defined and formal role in the running of the parish church, although he pointed out that: *"he did not believe in the synodsmen being called Parochial Church Councillors at present:*

he preferred them being called a consultative committee". He
emphasised again that the work in the parish was too much for one
person to carry out satisfactorily, and said that he hoped that they
would soon provide him with an assistant, as it was his view that
the responsibility was that of the parish and not the vicar. Then the
fun started. George Bragg, a self-made painter and decorator who
lived at the town end of Baddow Road, started off as he meant
to go on, addressing the vicar directly (and it is worth quoting in
full from what is as near a verbatim transcript as possible, in the
Essex Newsman):

Mr George Bragg: *"I should like to ask you, sir, a question.
I read in the public press that you are a member of that illegal,
law-breaking, notoriously Romanising society, the English Church
Union* [Loud cries of 'order']. *I ask you if it be so?"*

The Vicar: *"It is quite true, I am; and if anyone wants to
know anything about me, if he will give me a chance and wait and
see, I think he will see"*.

Mr Bragg: *"I don't think you ought to be allowed that chance,
and I think it is a disgrace for the Rev. Mr Lake to appoint a
gentleman who is a ——"* (the remainder of the sentence was
drowned in uproar and cries of 'order').

Mr Cutts: *"The discussion of this question is no part of the
business of this meeting, and if I may say this"*...

Mr Bragg: *"You are putting the closure into force"*. ('Oh, Oh'
and 'Order').

Mr Cutts: *"Oh No! We are not here to discuss the English
Church Union, ceremonial, or doctrinal matters.* ['Hear, Hear!']
*I am quite sure of this, that if any gentleman in the congregation
felt that there was anything he could legitimately object to, if he
would bring it before the churchwardens they would feel their
duty to inform the vicar. If there was anything in the services, or in
the order of services that was distasteful to the majority of the
congregation, the vicar would give way in a moment.* ['Hear,
Hear!'] *I think it is a great pity, that without any occasion, you
should bring these questions up connected with the English
Church Union, or matters of ritual, ceremony or doctrine"*.

Mr Bragg: *"That is your idea. There are things which are distasteful to many of the congregation"*. [Interruption]

Mr H. Hardy: *"Our vicar has not had a chance yet"*. [Applause]

Mr Taylor said this cross-examination was entirely out of order. [Hear, Hear!] He was sure Mr Bragg would see the desirability of not giving the vicar a bad send-off at the start. [Applause]

Mr Bragg: *"I will do anything to assist the Church if we have a faithful protestant clergyman"*. ['Order']

The vicar rose and said: *"I think it will be very easy for anyone here who has feelings of hostility towards the English Church Union to wait and see. I think that is sufficient answer to Mr Bragg"*. ['Hear, Hear!']

Mr Bragg: *"It won't satisfy me!"*

Mr H. Hardy: *"You must wait and see"*. [Applause]

Mr Bragg: *"Hold your tongue!"*

Mr J.G. Bond: *"Why does Mr Bragg come here – he never comes to Church?"*

Mr Bragg: *"I support the Church as much as you do!"*

Mr Bond denied this, and then asked again why Mr Bragg came there.

Mr Bragg: *"I come to support my wife and family"*.

Mr Bond: *"You are the last man who ought to come here and ask these questions"*.

The Vicar: *"Don't you feel you have had enough?* ['Hear, Hear!'] *This discussion helps me to feel that there is still some life in the parish and some hope"*. [Applause]

These remarks, spoken pleasantly and calmly, restored the meeting, which then terminated.[21] The cracks had been papered over, and the *Essex Newsman* reporter must have worn down his indelible pencil in the excitement.

'He had wondered how he might become known to the men'

In October 1901 John Beers, having helped Robert Saulez accustom himself to his duties in his new parish left to return to his home parish in the diocese of Ely, and Robert Saulez made arrangements for clergy from St Mary's-at-the-Walls in Colchester to assist him with the demanding Sunday timetable at St John's.[23] By the end of the year the vicar was feeling much more comfortable with his duties in the parish and with his parishioners. In the run up to Christmas 1901 the Arc Works club in Anchor Street held their smoking concert in the recreation room of the works on 30 November. Robert Saulez was present, telling the assembled throng that: *"he had wondered how he might become known to, and make the acquaintance of, the men and had thought that he could not do it better than by singing them a song"*. He then proceeded to sing 'The Drummer Boy's Motto' and 'The King's Highway' for which he was enthusiastically encored. The local press reported that: *"the rev gentleman's manner created a great impression, and just before he left he was accorded musical honours and three hearty cheers"*.[23]

Just a few days later Robert Saulez was officiating at the funeral of Miss Emma Shambrook, the Headmistress of St John's Infants' School, who had died on 27 November at the house she shared with her elderly mother in Mildmay Road. George Collier, who had moved in April to Theydon Bois, came back to assist with the funeral; he had known Miss Shambrook well. She had died from cancer, after a series of operations to remove the tumour had been unsuccessful. She had been Headmistress of the Infants' School for twenty-seven years. Curiously, she was (at her own request) buried next to George Godson. At the end of 1901, on 22 December, the Bishop of St Albans held an ordination at the parish church in Rickmansworth. Edward Morton Bartlett was ordained deacon and licensed at the same time to St John's. Robert Saulez now had a full-time curate to assist him in the running of the parish.[24]

'The vicar had to rise from his sickbed'

Robert Saulez continued his social duties at the beginning of 1902, when the parish tea was held on 22 January. Over 200 people enjoyed the event which took place in the schoolroom. Both the vicar and his new curate attended – the latter acquitting himself well by rendering a number of songs that were well-received by the appreciative audience.[25] Even with a vicar and a curate, illness could still cause problems with the services; at the beginning of February, both the vicar and his curate were confined to bed with severe colds, and although strenuous efforts were made to find another clergyman to conduct the services on the morning of Sunday, 5 February, none was available. The vicar had to rise from his sick-bed and struggle through the Eucharist as best he could. It says much for his character that on a bitterly cold February morning he should make such an effort (fortunately his cold did not develop into anything worse). In the evening, St John's was lucky. The rector of St Mary's, Rev Lake had already agreed to take that service, and Robert Saulez was spared another trial with the elements.[26] Wednesday, 2 April 1902 saw the annual vestry meeting take place in St John's Girls' School. Such meetings now took place in the evening, and on this occasion there was a good attendance.

The accounts were dealt with first, Mr George Taylor (the parish churchwarden) had begun with a deficit due to the churchwardens of just over £41 and ended substantially worse, that debt rising to just under £72. He pointed out that the increased deficit had been due to exceptional expenditure (which was not detailed in the minutes) but on a more positive note he was able to record that the offertories (at just under £396) were the highest they had been since 1889. The accounts were adopted. The vicar then expressed his thanks to the congregation for their liberality in the Easter Offerings (these were traditionally presented to the incumbent to supplement his stipend) and pointed out that he could not have been anywhere near as effective as a vicar without the support of his two wardens, Mr Cutts and Mr Taylor. Robert Saulez than proposed Mr Cutts as his warden for the following year and Mr Taylor was elected to represent the parish. It was reported that the windows which had just been installed in the church to commemorate the ministry of George Godson had cost £115 and 'a few shillings' and had been fully paid for. The vicar concluded the discussion by congratulating the parish on collecting almost

£133 for the Curates' Fund. The Additional Curates Society had made them a grant of £40 (to be renewed annually) and he hoped this would act as an inducement for them to provide him with an extra curate in 1903.[27]

'This new scheme came like a bolt from the blue'

Later in the year St John's (and the vicar's churchwarden in particular) suffered a great loss when Mrs Cutts died in May. She and William had lived quietly in a house in Manor Road ('Carisbrooke') and the contribution they had made between them to St John's had been enormous. Her funeral took place on 20 May and was conducted by Edward Bartlett.[28] Her husband lived for a few years more but the vigour with which he had carried out his duties as vicar's churchwarden was markedly diminished. Her death was a great loss to the parish. In June the Boer War ended, and a service of thanksgiving was held at St John's to celebrate the peace. Robert Saulez then sprang his next surprise on an unsuspecting parish. In the October issue of the *Moulsham Church Magazine*, the vicar announced that he had selected a thoroughly experienced choirmaster for St John's in the person of Mr Douglas Smith of St Gabriel's, Pimlico and St John the Baptist, Kensington. In the same issue of the magazine he went on to praise Mr W.H. Ripper highly for all his good work in training the choir, but said that he believed that it was his duty to find a choirmaster who made the training of choirs his sole profession (it seemed to have escaped everyone's notice that Mr Douglas Smith came from a marked high church background, and that Robert Saulez may have had other motives in replacing Mr Ripper). In addition to the existing choir of men and boys at St John's, the vicar announced that Mr Douglas Smith would also form a choir of probationers and a choir of ladies. *"It is a bold solution,"* said the vicar, *"and I have taken it entirely upon my own responsibility. I have told my churchwardens and I am informing my synodsmen"*. It was clear that this announcement did not meet with universal approval (especially from Mr Ripper) and it was no surprise to see that there were some fairly caustic letters in the local press. 'A Parishioner' wrote in obvious indignation that: *"you can imagine my surprise on opening our parish magazine to read of the alteration to be made respecting Moulsham Church Choir ... ...having been advised from the pulpit that no alteration or change in anything connected with the church would be made without the knowledge of the parishioners, this new scheme, arranged in secret and flashed* (sic) *to us through the magazine, came like a bolt from the blue. When we take into account the deficiency of funds, which is being constantly brought to our notice, and various expenses with which the parishioners have been saddled just to maintain the present order of things, it is not surprising that a feeling exists that we should first endeavour to decrease our liabilities before engaging in an unnecessary and expensive venture. We shall be glad to have a reasonable explanation on the subject, and to hear what our churchwardens think of it"*. The *Essex Newsman* was even moved to comment editorially on the vicar's announcement and the resultant response of the parishioners (although it used the opportunity to have its own dig at St John's), saying: *"the vicar of Moulsham announces a programme of musical reform in connection with his church, including the formation of a choir of ladies ... ... there is one thing Mr Saulez's programme does not comprehend, and that is the stopping of the melancholy church bell with which the parish is so severely afflicted. If only he would have that dreadful instrument of torture broken up, or given to a prison for use only on the occasion of executions, he could do much not merely for the promotion of music but also for the suppression of profane swearing. We know of many people who use the big D* (sic) *every time the dismal bell begins, and we have a fancy that it shortens the general average life of the inhabitants of Moulsham"*.[29]

Mr Ripper ceased his duties as organist of St John's on Sunday, 23 November. On the Thursday prior to this he received a presentation from the men and boys of the choir to mark his twelve years of service as organist and choirmaster. The gift consisted of a furnished rosewood smoker's companion (Mr Ripper was presumably a smoker), a pair of brass candlesticks, two silver mounted briar pipes in a case and a silver matchbox. Robert Saulez, in making the presentation, said he was sorry to part with Mr Ripper(!) who had taken infinite trouble with musical matters at the church and the welfare of the choir. Mr Ripper, in reply, said he thanked the choir for the gifts and said he left them as a friend with nothing but good feeling for them. Stuffing his tongue firmly in his cheek he added that he would watch with great interest the progress of the choir.[30]

'It has indeed, said one wag, gone on strike'

The following year, 1903, was a much calmer one for the parish church. The ill-feeling over Mr Ripper's departure had been forgotten by the time the year started with the social tea at the beginning of January. So successful had this become that it had been found necessary to hire the Corn Exchange (near the Shire Hall) to accommodate all those who wished to attend. No less than 486 people were served food and drinks. The evening finished with a 'capital entertainment' which was well received.

The vestry meeting that year was a much more orderly and business-like affair than that of the previous year. The Mayor, Alderman George Taylor, presented the accounts which showed that the year started with an adverse balance of just under £72 and ended with a reduced deficit of about £47. The total offertories for the year had been £361, a very satisfactory state of affairs, and Mr Taylor expressed the hope that by Easter 1904 the account would be in surplus. The vicar expressed his gratitude to the churchwardens and synodsmen (particularly praising Mr Taylor for the enormous support he had been to St John's) and thanked the congregation for the generosity of their Easter offering (£31). He nominated Mr Cutts as his warden. In accepting, Mr Cutts could not resist mentioning that he had been connected with St John's for more than thirty years. Mr Gripper proposed the re-election of the Mayor as parish warden, and emphasised that everyone who came to St John's would heartily endorse what he vicar had said about Mr Taylor. The Mayor, in returning thanks (and accepting his office) expressed the hope that the vicar might regain better health, and added that, although he and the vicar might sometimes agree to differ, he felt bound to say that the vicar was about the most tolerant churchman he had ever met. This remark was greeted with prolonged applause.

It was reported that the church clock was broken and would not strike (it has indeed, said one wag, gone on strike) and it was thought it could cost as much as ten pounds to repair it. It was left to the churchwardens to explore how permanent any such repair might be. The vicar then raised the problem of the additional clerical help that the parish might need. He pointed out that the Assistant Clergy fund was proceeding well. He thanked the Rev R.F. Cobbold for the assistance he had given him over the past year, and said that he would review the position with his churchwardens when he (the vicar) returned from holiday. Rev Cobbold reminded the meeting that he was one of the unemployed clergy, and as long as he was resident in Chelmsford, he should be glad if the vicar and the parish would accept such help as he could give under the vicar's direction. A hearty vote of thanks was accorded to the Rev Cobbold for all the assistance he had rendered the parish. The vicar then stated that the church organ was in a very poor condition, and the parish would soon need to investigate the provision of a new one. The meeting concluded with the churchwardens being authorised to move the pulpit from its existing provision so that it: *"it avoided obstructing the chancel"*. The vestry then closed with a vote of thanks to the chair.[31]

In spite of the vicar's comments about the organ, it was used for a recital on 14 May, given by Mr Ripper's replacement as choirmaster, Mr Edward Douglas Smith. He was described as the 'Choirmaster of St John's and organist of St Gabriel's, Pimlico' but it was not clear how he divided up his time and his duties between the two locations. Collections at the recital raised just under £3 for choir expenses.[32] In spite of the organ being (presumably) adequate for this recital, the parish was starting to explore the possibilities of getting a new instrument. In August a well-attended parish meeting was held to explore possible schemes to replace the present organ. Robert Saulez read a letter from Messrs Norman and Beard stating that: *"the present organ was on its last legs, in a very dilapidated condition and worth no more than its breaking up price of £25"*, They advised that a new organ should be erected in the south transept. The cost would be about £946 and the necessary electric blower (which was to be located in the side chapel) would add another £150. Mr Cutts proposed that a committee be set up to oversee the whole process, and Mr Franklin proposed that such a committee be composed of clergy, churchwardens and synodsmen. The vicar agreed and said that they had no doubt that the parish could raise the sum required.[33] In November Mr Douglas Smith's engagement at St John's came to an end and he was able to return to St Gabriel's, Pimlico. It was stated by the vicar that the ongoing training of the choir would now be undertaken by the organist.[34]

By 1904 the first rumblings of the storm that would overtake Moulsham began to be heard. The year, though, started well. The social tea was going from strength to strength and on 18 January no less than 587 people descended on the Corn Exchange for their feast. Robert Saulez gave a brief speech, saying that: *"he looked forward to future social teas in a building in their own parish, which had yet to be erected"*. He emphasised that his two and a half years in Moulsham had been a very happy time, and pointed out that the past year had been a record as it had seen the joint efforts of St John's and St Mary's working together for the Master. He added that they all looked forward to an individual being as generous to St John's as one had been for St Mary's. He regretted that they would soon be losing their curate, Mr Bartlett, but thanked him for his considerable contribution to the parish.[35]

Friday, 15 April saw St John's 1904 vestry meeting take place in the absence of the vicar, who was kept at home by influenza. As vicar's warden, William Cutts took the chair and (possibly because for the vicar's absence) the meeting proceeded quickly and smoothly. George Taylor, as parish warden, presented the accounts, which showed receipts of just a shade under £436. The year, which had opened with a deficit of £47, closed with a deficit of just a few shillings less. Mr Taylor complained that: *"too many special offertories were given away, and as long as that was the case, they would remain in debt"*. As an indication of how much money was involved, Mr Taylor pointed out that the special offertories had increased from £27 in 1902 to more than £90 in the year just ended. On the proposal of Mr J.G. Bond, the accounts were adopted. The vicar had written to the meeting, nominating Mr Cutts as his warden, and, in the same letter, had expressed his sincere thanks to the churchwardens for their unfailing courtesy and their devotion to duties. Mr Taylor was re-elected as the parish warden. The chairman then read a further letter from the vicar, thanking all the parishioners for their generous Easter offering. The chairman asked that it be recorded in the minutes that: *"the parish owed their thanks to the choir for the great improvement in the singing – and that improvement reflected great credit on Mr Burrell, the late organist"*. A vote of thanks was recorded to the choir and to Mr Burrell.[36] (Mr S.J. Burrell, ARCO, left St John's to take up the post of organist at St Mary's, Broomfield, on 1 May 1904).[37]

On the Sunday following the vestry meeting, Robert Saulez arose from his sickbed to take the morning service, but in doing so, was 'overcome by weakness'. He was unable to proceed after pronouncing his text, but gave out a hymn after which the service ended. The following Monday he was in better health and was able to go away on the Tuesday to recuperate. He had recovered sufficiently in order to return for Sunday, 24 April, when the Rev John Lansbury Dutton commenced his duties as the new curate of Moulsham.[38] In May the Bishop of St Albans came to Chelmsford and consecrated a further three acres of burial ground at the Writtle Road cemetery. The replacement for St John's churchyard was filling up fast and would continue to do so until cremation became a regular feature of Church of England funeral arrangements.[39] In July, Robert Saulez received some rare good news. An anonymous parishioner had sent him a cheque for the exact sum required to clear the debt that George Taylor had reported at the recent vestry meeting.[40]

In October the first, few, heavy drops of rain from the approaching storm began to fall. The *Essex County Chronicle* reported that: *"The Rev R.T. Saulez, the vicar of St John's, Moulsham, wishes to put two candlesticks, with two candles, to be lit at all services, on the altar of the church"*. In his sermon on the previous Sunday (22 October) the vicar had announced this decision, saying that it was not only legal, but plainly ordered, and he added that he felt: *"it would add to the dignity of the worship being performed"*.[41] He qualified his remarks by adding that: *"he noted the laity in St John's regarded the introduction of lights as unwise"*. Towards the end of the nineteenth century the Church of England had become much concerned about the creeping introduction of ritual, and there had been some very public and difficult decisions taken about what could be done and what was specifically forbidden. It is, however, slightly surprising (certainly when viewed from the twenty-first century) that there should have developed so much feeling at St John's about altar lights. A survey in 1901 showed that of just under 9,000 churches, mostly in England and Wales, well over half were using candles on the altar.[42] The vicar had both his supporters and detractors in the press. A 'Broad Churchman' wrote: *"I hope the attempt to introduce 'altar lights' to St John's will be strenuously resisted .. .... St John's has always been regarded as an evangelical stronghold – long may it continue so"*.[43] Other contributors suggested that altar lights were derived from purely pagan worship, whilst a supporter of the vicar commented that if candles were legal in the great cathedrals (such as St Paul's) then surely they would be legal in St John's. The Bishop of St Albans had obviously got wind of what was going on and he made an unexpected visit to Chelmsford on Sunday, 30 October,[44] preaching two sermons, one in the morning to the whole congregation and one in the afternoon for men only (no less than 330 attended).[45] Reports on the sermons in the press suggest that there was no reference in either of these services to 'altar lights' (one sermon was devoted to temperance and the other to the role of the prophet Nehemiah) but the subject was certainly discussed on Wednesday, 16 November when a special 'annual conference' was held to discuss the matter.

'Was the Bishop's visit a check on enterprise?'

Robert Saulez opened this 'annual conference' by describing how, over the past three years of his incumbency: *"wardens and synodsmen had been brought together and every single change in the arrangements had been laid before them"*. He continued by saying that the introduction of altar lights had been considered, and reminded the meeting that: *"if there had been a curb on his wishes, that curb had been put there is a most friendly way"*. He said that the visit of the Bishop to the parish had certainly been a check on enterprise, but as a result of the discussions, the Bishop had confirmed that an uncontested faculty would be required for the use of any candles on the altar. The vicar pointed out that this meant the matter rested in the hands of the parishioners, and since this was so, he (the vicar) would be prepared to wait. He ended by reiterating that: *"he should never forgive himself if he let a pair of candlesticks dampen his ardour for Christ and His Church."* The discussion then moved on to the subject of a church council, in which Mr George Taylor, Mr Cutts and Mr Hedley Osborn took part. Mr Gripper asked the vicar (after the vicar had outlined the way in which he saw the church council operating) if he was still going to form a council after everything that had happened? When the vicar replied *"certainly"* Mr Gripper said that he felt the vicar ought to consult the parishioners, to see if they agreed. Robert Saulez seemed to think that this was unnecessary. *"The Council,"* he said, *"would be a body of voluntary workers which the vicar could explode* (sic) *at any moment"*. The meeting, suffering from a sense of anticlimax, subsided, and in a calm but slightly simmering atmosphere Mr Martin gave a brief talk on 'Sunday: A Modern Problem' (Sabbath observance was already, by 1904, in marked decline) and the meeting ended with the chairman pronouncing the benediction.[46]

'This meeting protests against the ordinary morning service not being held at eleven o'clock'

And so 1905 dawned, the year that almost finished St John's. The storm soon broke. The Bishop of St Albans had to make a special visit to Chelmsford on Saturday, 18 February to meet with the vicar and the two churchwardens to try and resolve the issues, spending the afternoon with them on neutral territory in St Mary's vestry hall in New Street. The Bishop was not in the best of moods, and the first problem that confronted him was that of the Sunday services. Robert Saulez had announced on 22 January from the pulpit that the services on the last Sunday of each month would change. There would be a choral celebration of Holy Communion at eleven o'clock, followed by mattins at a quarter past twelve. On the Friday after this announcement (27 January) the churchwardens and synodsmen met under the chairmanship of Mr J.G. Bond and passed a resolution that: *"this meeting protests against the ordinary morning service not being held at eleven o'clock on the last Sunday of the month, as usual, and earnestly invites the vicar to reconsider his decision in this matter, and requests him to send his reply to this resolution within a week"*. In reply the vicar stated that he had been guided by his conscience, and that, in addition, on his way home from church, discussing this with Mr Cutts, full approval of his suggestion had been given by his warden. He had, he felt strongly, done the right thing, and he emphasised that: *"when I stood at the altar and heard our choir with all their hearts offering up a service with which God must have been well pleased - when I saw the communicants coming up in larger numbers than had ever been the case except at the three great festivals – I knew it was the answer to many prayers and that the Spirit of God had moved on the face of the waters"*. The churchwardens were not impressed. They wrote to the press, explaining that as the vicar had published, in the *Moulsham Parish Magazine*, only a portion of the correspondence that had taken place between vicar and churchwardens they wished to put the record straight, particularly on two points. Firstly, they pointed out that they had already written to the vicar to say that his statement that Mr Cutts had fully approved the innovations was not correct and that Mr Cutts himself had subsequently written to point out the erroneous nature of the vicar's remarks; and secondly, noting that in his remarks the vicar spoke of the meeting of the churchwardens and synodsmen being a 'private' one, they had expressly written to the vicar and the curate (Mr Dutton) to invite them to the meeting. Mr Dutton had a prior ecclesiastical engagement and the vicar stated that he did not wish to attend on his own, explaining his absence to the congregation by saying the churchwardens had wished him to attend 'on terms'. The wardens both emphatically denied this suggestion, and decided that it was their duty to place all the facts of the case before the Bishop of St Albans, and to seek his guidance and advice.

The churchwardens had submitted a list of six questions to the bishop. These were:

1) Whether or not it was possible for the innovation complained of (the displacement of the ordinary eleven o'clock service) to be reversed?
2) Whether or not mattins could be said at a quarter past twelve?
3) Whether or not the invitation for the non-communicants to attend the service was expedient?
4) Whether sentences from the *Benedictus* and the *Agnus Dei* introduced into the Communion Service were permissible?
5) Whether or not the mixing of the chalice as part of the ceremonial at Holy Communion was legal?
6) Whether or not the bishop would direct the vicar to re-instate the original form of service on the last Sunday of the month?

The bishop dealt with the disputed points very quickly. He said that there was no doubt that it was not legal to have mattins after twelve o'clock, but since the vicar had now abandoned that idea, there was no need for him to give any further direction on it. The question of inviting non-communicants to the service was entirely at the discretion of the vicar. He (the bishop) admitted that he personally did not think it expedient under ordinary circumstances but he noted that: *"many good men thought differently"*. It being a matter in the discretion of the vicar, his lordship declined to pronounce on it. He went on to state that the singing of the *Benedictus* and *Agnus Dei* was quite legal – this had been confirmed by the judicial council of the Privy Council. With regard to the mixing of the chalice, it had been decided (in Read *v.* the Bishop of Lincoln) that this was legal but that mixing it during the ceremony was not. Robert Saulez had ceased doing this and had given his lordship an undertaking that he would not do so in future. With regard to the remaining questions, the bishop stated that this was the first time he had encountered these during his episcopate, and therefore he carried out a thorough investigation of the legal position. He could, he explained, be setting a precedent, and he wished that precedent to be correct. He said that he would give a firm directive on the question that evening, but while he was present at the meeting he would take the opportunity to hear other views on the subject. He referred to a petition which had been delivered to him, signed by more than a hundred communicants, supporting the vicar. There followed a discussion and a vote, the meeting deciding that morning prayer would take place at 10.30 a.m. on the last Sunday of the month. The bishop said he was happy to sanction this arrangement, and, indeed, was critical of the vicar for not consulting his wardens and synodsmen before changing the time of the service. Robert Saulez, it was reported: *"appeared to be considerably affected by the Bishop's decision"*. He felt a strong objection to any interference with his control of the services and stated quite bluntly that if the bishop issued a direction (as he had indicated he would), he (the vicar) would feel it his duty to resign. The bishop concluded by pronouncing the Benediction and confirmed that he would send his direction to Robert Saulez by post that same evening (Saturday).

On the following Sunday (19 February) Robert Saulez was preaching at Boreham and so the curate, Rev John Dutton, read a letter from the vicar just before the end of the service. It read: *"With a sorrowful heart I write to announce that I have placed my resignation of this living in the hands of the Bishop of the Diocese"*. The *Essex County Chronicle's* sympathies clearly lay with the vicar. *"We trust,"* they said, *"that the Bishop will think more than once before he accepts it. He would be greatly missed in the parish, and by none more than the sick and needy"*.[49]

'Every time he opens his mouth, he puts his foot in it'

This announcement was followed a few days later by the 1905 annual vestry meeting. Of all those meetings for which details have been recorded, this was probably the most fraught, by some margin. It took place on 28 April, in the Girls' schoolroom, and was packed, with people standing in the aisles. Robert Saulez, in the chair, asked George Taylor to read the accounts. He set the tone of the meeting by saying that: *"it was his determination, before he sat down, to render them all to you, in a true and unadulterated statement and to show you the way in which the vicar has accused me in a wrongful manner. He cared,"* he went on, *"not one jot for slander (and there has been plenty of it circulated in the parish lately with reference to myself) but I will allow no-one, man or woman, to assail my honour"* [Applause]. Mr Taylor then read a summary of the accounts to Easter 1905. The offertories amounted to just under £128, markedly down from the previous year and seriously less than in 1903. He pointed out that the sum of £47 from an anonymous donor had been given expressly to wipe out money due to the people's warden from the previous year. The contributions to the sick and needy fund only amounted to £34, but he explained that this was due to the lapsing of the £50 Christmas donation from Mr Arthur Pryor of Hylands House, who had recently died. The additional curates' fund had totalled £184. In spite of the donation to pay off the debt to the people's warden, there was still a balance due to himself of, curiously, almost exactly the same sum, £47. The total liabilities of the church were about £184. The meeting then moved on to discuss the clergy fund. The year had started with a balance of £47 and balancing income and expenditure, the church, he said, would need to find £82 for the rest of the year. The reason, Mr Taylor said, that the fund: *"had got into that condition"* was because the vicar, notwithstanding presentments both verbal and written, had spent a considerable sum on the Church Army man who had come to St John's. Because of this the churchwardens had felt justified in retaining half of the Easter offering (traditionally it was all given to the vicar). In response to a question he said that the Church Army man had cost almost £44 and Mr Taylor reiterated that he had told the vicar that the church was unable to afford that expense. The vicar complained that they had no balance sheet for the fund, and said he would like to hear all the details, including a list of subscribers, read to the meeting. Mr Taylor responded vigorously. *"I am delighted,"* he said, *"that the vicar has raised this point. Every time he opens his mouth to speak, he puts his foot in it – he says there has been no balance sheet issued – and yet he has got all the money paid to him for 1903 and part of 1904"*. With respect to the clergy fund, Mr Taylor said he knew why it had been passed to him. When this dispute had cropped up he had received a letter from the bank saying the account was overdrawn by £73. This account had been opened by the vicar and his (Mr Taylor's) name had been given as a guarantor. He had never, he went on, been consulted and had never drawn a cheque on this account. Mr Taylor continued: *"he thought it a mean and contemptible thing for a Christian minister to come to a vestry meeting and suggest that he (Mr Taylor) had not issued a balance sheet"*. He concluded by addressing the vicar to his face: *"You have no excuse to say that I have been dabbling in the fund in a wrong manner!"*. The vicar was immediately on the defensive, replying rather lamely that: *"I did not say anything. I feel as a man who has been abandoned by his wardens and his synodsmen"*. (This was greeted with loud cries of 'Hear, Hear'). Mr Taylor pressed the vicar further about the overdraft, and the vicar explained how it had come about. He had brought down a man from London to improve the condition of the choir [A voice: *"It did no good"* and another *"it was not necessary"*] and it cost, he said £50, money which he had paid himself [Applause]. Mr Taylor reiterated that he was not saying that the vicar had used the money for any object but the church, but he stressed again that the vicar had no right to give Mr Taylor's name as a guarantor at the bank without mentioning it to him. The vicar denied that he had done so, but Mr Taylor read a letter from the bank, dated 26 January 1905 and relating to that account, clearly stating that the wardens were responsible for it. Mr Cutts chimed in, saying that: *"on the face of it, it is perfectly clear that the wardens are responsible for the overdraft on that account"*. The vicar attempted to draw this uncomfortable discussion to a close, begging someone to move and to second that the accounts be passed. There were no takers.

'Is there any man who is perfect?'

A Miss Browning tried to deflect the attacks on the vicar by changing the subject, suggesting it would be *"rather nice"* if they could all know more about the clergy fund, as she had heard that subscriptions were falling off dramatically. Mr Taylor agreed and said that he knew of one case where a lady had shown the collector the door. Mr Darby (the collector) confirmed that this was true. Miss Browning then attempted to put the participants at the vestry meeting in their place. *"Ought we not to do better?"* she asked, *"with Mr Mason and Mr Godson we had become unused to giving – we are constantly being told that we are in debt, but in my view it is the fault of the parishioners, not the bankers. Our vicar,"* she continued, *"is not perfect – is there any man in this room who is perfect?* [Voices: 'No, No'] *"Do we ever hear of a clergyman who understand accounts?* [Brittle laughter] *–You, Mr Taylor, have been brought up as a man of business"*. Mr Taylor acknowledged this fact, but said that he wished they had let him guide them more. Miss Browning was, however, now well into her stride: *"Cold water,"* she said, warming to her theme, *"has been thrown on all our vicar's schemes – we want to pull together more, as there are some half-a-dozen people pulling the other way"*. Mr Taylor rose to the bait and pointed out that Miss Browning was not a parishioner, and added that he felt she had already said enough. She was not to be deterred. *"I have,"* she snapped back, *"worked in this parish a great many years, when you were at the Chapel"*.(This was a dig at Mr Taylor's nonconformist origins). The redoubtable Mr Bragg sprang to Mr Taylor's defence, saying that this remark was quite uncalled for ['Hear, Hear'].

'There are many people who would be glad to see the back of me as people's warden'

The meeting was becoming very heated. Mr Gripper, realising that tempers were fast running out of control, spoke up as a peacemaker (as he often did). After paying tribute to the wardens for their service to the church, he appealed for a spirit of unanimity, and proposed that the accounts be adopted. Mr Bragg seconded and the motion was carried. The meeting then moved on to discuss the tricky matter of the election of wardens. Mr Cutts said that his duties as warden were now ended, and it was also clear that Mr Taylor no longer wished to act as parish warden. When asked by Mr Gripper what would happen if nobody was nominated, it was said that churchwardens remained in office until successors were appointed. Mr Bragg proposed (and Mr Markham seconded) the election of Mr Taylor as people's warden and the motion was carried unanimously. Mr Taylor would have none of it. He thanked Mr Bragg and Mr Markham for his re-election, *"but,"* he said: *"anyone who has any common sense can see tonight that there are many people here who would be glad to see the back of me as people's warden. I am going to give them the opportunity of doing so, because I will not hold an office in which I do not appear to possess the confidence of the churchgoing people"*. He ended with a dig at Miss Browning, saying that: *"I can promise you that if there is any attempt at Romanism in St John's, I shall be the first to come to the fore, and the old Nonconformist instincts which have been sneered at in a cheap way by Miss Browning will assert themselves"* [Applause]. Mr Cutts added that if Mr Taylor would not stand for office, then neither would he. The vicar pointed out that under the Canons of the Church, where there was a dispute between a vicar and a warden, the people could elect a warden, so again Mr Gripper proposed and Mr Markham seconded the election of the two wardens, Mr Taylor and Mr Cutts. This was carried *nemine contradicente*. George Taylor, though, insisted on having the last word, emphasising that: *"he did not feel disposed to take this office. I have been insulted and maligned – and even tonight I have been reminded that I was brought up a Nonconformist. I hope that it is understood that I will not accept office".* Three of the synodsmen also declined to stand for office, and after some half-hearted votes of thanks (the meeting was neatly split, some thanking the vicar, and some the wardens) the meeting, which lasted more than two hours, was finally closed. William Cutts wrote to the press that same evening, saying that he had thought long and hard after the meeting about what he should do, and he felt in all conscience that he could not accept the office. Accordingly, on the following Saturday morning he had telegraphed the Rev Pressey, (with whom the Rev Saulez was intending to exchange livings) to say that he (Mr Cutts) would not accept the office of churchwarden.[51,52] So did St John's have churchwardens or not?

Worse was to come. Robert Saulez had to write to the press on 15 May to let his parishioners know that there was yet another hitch to his plans. He pointed out that: *"Up to 10 May everything was practically settled for an exchange of livings between the rector of Foxearth (Rev William Pressey) and myself, but on that day the legal trustee wrote that he declined to entertain the proposed arrangements unless I had an independent income of my own of £600 per annum".* He went on to say that he had immediately written to the Bishop of St Albans to say that he would have to stay in Moulsham. The Bishop had heartily endorsed this course of action. He concluded by saying that he would: *"go forward with a fixed determination to forget all the sad experiences of the last few months, and I urge my people to do the same".*[53]

Things very much calmed down for a little while after that. Both George Taylor and Robert Saulez were biding their time, and the option of the vicar moving to another parish had disappeared for the moment. So the parish muddled along through the summer of 1905, really neither at peace nor at war. Toward the end of the summer, John Dutton announced that 18 August would be his final service at St John's. He had been ordered by his doctor to take a prolonged rest, and he planned to have a holiday of at least

two months' duration.[54] Shortly after that it was announced that
he would move as rector to Aspenden in Hertfordshire.[55] Robert
Saulez was to have some assistance in his last few months at
Moulsham as in November the bishop confirmed that the Rev
W.W. King Ormsby would be coming to St John's *"for an indefinite
period"* to act as assistant priest. He had previously been chaplain
at Boulogne.[56,57] His arrival at St John's coincided with another
outbreak of Christian ill-feeling in the parish.

'I have tried to trap you, and I have succeeded'

The problem of the accounts and the deficit would not go away,
and by the end of November it was felt necessary to have an extra
vestry meeting to try and resolve everything once and for all.
A crowded attendance came to St John's schoolroom on 28
November to try and clear the air. Memories of the vestry meeting
on 28 April were still very much to the forefront of everyone's
minds. George Taylor started by reading a letter he had written to
the vicar asking for particulars relating to certain accounts. The
vicar replied, in a spirit of optimism, saying: *"I am exceedingly
glad and thankful that the end of all this sad trouble is in view and
I shall be willing to fall in with any suggestion which may bring
about peace and the restoration of friendship"* [Voice: 'a very
gentlemanly letter']. That was the good news. The meeting went
downhill rapidly after that. Mr Taylor continued by pointing out
that the vicar, instead of sending him the accounts, had only sent
him the totals, and in order to explain them, he (the vicar) had
wanted a private meeting of vicar and churchwardens. George
Taylor had refused, and given as his reason a confidential letter he
had received from the vicar saying that he (the vicar): *"had tried
to trap you and now I have succeeded"*. There was then an ill-
tempered argument between those who wanted the confidential
letter read out at the meeting and those who felt it should remain
completely private. Mr Taylor (apparently oblivious to the fact
that he had already revealed some of the letter) stated that unless
the vicar (who had written the letter) gave his consent, he would
make no statement about it, and when Mr Bowyer attempted to

speak, Mr Taylor rounded sharply on him, saying: *"You are such a little upstart I cannot discuss it with you"*. The meeting was coming nicely to the boil.

The essence of the churchwardens' complaints, according to Mr Taylor, was the vicar's spending of money that the church did not possess. He felt that the vicar's attitude could be summed up in the phrases: *"if they spent £200 or £300, it would come from the clouds and they need not trouble themselves about it"*. The vicar tried to hit back. He said that he would like to ask Mr Taylor, a 'financier', about the altar wine for the church. Mr Bragg's antennae twitched, *"It is,"* he shouted angrily, *"a communion table. We want no such thing as altar wine or sacrificing priest!"* In the excitement the money for the wine was forgotten, and the vicar was able to put his finger on the nub of the problem – because the churchwardens had refused to stand at the last Easter vestry (although the vestry had tried very hard to elect them), he (the vicar) had, completely against his will, been forced to do the accounts, and he complained bitterly that Mr Cutts and Mr Taylor had placed him in this invidious position. The rival parties were just gearing up to spar again when a newcomer, Mr Thomas Thompson, got up to speak. He said: *"I do not wish to sail here under false colours. I am not a member of the congregation of St John's church, nor have I attended church very often, but I am a parishioner and a baptised and confirmed churchman. I will"*, he continued, *"tell you why I have taken scarcely any part in church work in this place. When I came here, something more than thirty-five years ago, Chelmsford was socially a very different place from what it is today. A sort of small-beer aristocracy* (a reference to the Mildmays and their immediate circle) *dominated everything, and if a stranger went to church he simply got kicked about from pillar to post, and by that conduct I was utterly chilled. But what I want to do is to appeal especially to this meeting by asking whether or not the time has come that this unhappy condition of things that has prevailed for so long in Moulsham should be put an end to?"* [Prolonged applause]. He continued in a more optimistic vein, saying; *"We are approaching Christmas – the season of peace and goodwill – and I do hope that this quarrel, if quarrel it be, will not be carried over that season, and into the new year. I think that there ought to be a new start in the parish. Some of the things that have taken place I have viewed with wonder and with pain – with wonder at the small questions that have given rise to this strife and with pain at some of the things that have been needlessly said. But I do think that Mr Taylor and the vicar should shake hands over this business. He pointed out that the Bishop of Colchester, in a recent visit to the parish, when talking of the miracle of feeding the five thousand, said the people sat down in an orderly manner, received what was offered to them, and followed Jesus in the way. That, the Bishop added, was an example to everyone".* Mr Thompson concluded by pointing out that he was: *"an outsider, but I hope soon to become a worshipper at St John's* [Applause] *and I trust I may have a little influence, even tonight, in bringing about peace".* He sat down to prolonged and loud applause, and there was a real sense that his words had hit home. Both Mr Cutts and Mr Taylor grudgingly acknowledged Mr Thompson's little speech, and felt that peace was the right answer, but both were adamant that they would never serve as churchwarden again.[58]

There remained the question of what was to be done with the keeping of the accounts, and by whom. The curate, the Rev W.W. King Ormsby, agreed to take over responsibility for them. Bearing in mind what had been said at the December vestry meeting about debt, he took the opportunity when preaching at St John's early in January 1906, to make an appeal for the parish to try and clear the outstanding debt.[59] By Sunday, 3 February he was able to announce that only £21 of the debt remained, and he was able to tell his congregation that: *"a comparative stranger, who was interested in the vicar and the work at St John's had agreed to give £5 if the rest of the debt was cleared by 10 March."*[60]

'My mistakes were made through you sending me the wrong figures'

Robert Saulez's last hurdle in the parish was the 1906 vestry meeting, which took place on 20 April in the Girls' schoolroom, as usual. It soon became clear that the parish was exhausted with all the bitter wrangling that had completely overshadowed everything else throughout the last few years, and the meeting proceeded in a calm and orderly (and at times, almost humorous) fashion. There was (of course) a quibble (from George Taylor) when the minutes were read. He took exception to the paragraph which stated that he made no objection to being proposed as people's warden until after the resolution had been put and carried. The vicar agreed to strike out the offending sentence. Mr Taylor then went through the mistakes in the accounts (simply restating what he had said about the accounts at the last November vestry) and the vicar expressed his thanks to Mr Taylor, saying that although a good many mistakes had been made by both of them, he was exceedingly glad that it had all been cleared up. Mr Taylor leapt to his own defence *"There is just one thing I want to make clear. You said we had both made mistakes. I think you said that my mistakes were made through you sending me the wrong figures"*. At this there was 'nervous laughter', but no further comment from Mr Taylor.

The Rev King Ormsby then presented the accounts, and what amazing figures he had to give to the meeting. They had turned the previous year's substantial debt into a surplus of almost £135. this had come about mainly through the curtailing of the vicar's liberal approach to expenditure. The accounts were speedily and wholeheartedly adopted. Robert Saulez proposed Mr Barker as his warden, a proposal that the meeting accepted rapidly, and Mr Spurgeon put forward the name of Mr Franklin as people's warden, a proposal that George Taylor also supported, but with something of a *caveat*. He supported the proposal because Mr Franklin was: *"a sound businessman and also a man who would protect the best interests of the parish ... ... and because* *he was the gentleman who moved the resolution opposing the service which brought us so much trouble in the parish* [A Voice: 'We don't want that'].*" Mr Franklin's election proposal was seconded by Mr Wackrill and carried unanimously. Mr Franklin accepted the office on two conditions. Firstly, that he should serve for only one year, until the following Easter, and secondly, that he should have no clerical work in connection with the accounts. Fifteen synodsmen were elected, and the meeting closed with a vote of thanks to the vicar.[61]

George Taylor, as befitted one who had been the Mayor of the Borough and was now an Alderman, had the last word. The press published a copy of the letter that he wrote to Mr Franklin some two months after the 1906 vestry meeting. He had submitted the previous year's accounts to Mr Wackrill and Mr Spurgeon (the latter had been Messrs Barclays chief of staff in Chelmsford for many years until his retirement) and their audit had completely vindicated Mr Taylor's stance. He concluded his letter with one last swipe at everyone, summarising by saying: *"In the face of the facts just stated, I hope that those parishioners that were deluded into thinking that I was making unfounded statements from time to time as to the incorrectness of the figures placed before them will now see that I was fully justified in the course which duty compelled me to adopt".[62]* So there.

'We hope that Mr Saulez will find at Willingale a not unpleasant Patmos'

George Taylor had had his last word, but by the time he had written the letter to Mr Franklin, the situation in the parish had changed completely. At the end of May 1906 it was reported that Robert Saulez, who by then had been at St John's, Moulsham, for more than five years, had accepted the rectorship of Willingale Doe, which had recently fallen vacant through the death of the previous incumbent, the Rev J. Swayne. Willingale, a small village just to the north of the road from Chelmsford to Ongar, was unusual in that it had two churches, St Andrew's, Willingale Doe, and St Christopher's, Willingale Spain, located close to each other in the same churchyard, and until 1929 each church had its own incumbent.[63] The report gave the value of the living as £480, a substantial sum in 1906, and significantly greater than Moulsham, and added, somewhat portentously: *"We hope that Mr Saulez will find at Willingale a not unpleasant Patmos".*[64]

At the end of June it was announced that Robert Saulez and his wife would take a holiday preparatory to his leaving Moulsham for his new parish, and while he was away Rev King Ormsby would be in charge of the parish until the arrival of the Rev William J. Pressey. The latter, it was stated, would bring his own curate with him. There was felt to be great sympathy for Rev Ormsby who had come from Stafford to St John's at considerable expense, and had taken a house in New London Road for three years. The press hoped that: *"he will find some congenial duty so that his services will not be lost to the neighbourhood".*[65]

Robert Saulez wrote his valedictory letter to his parishioners in the July issue of the *Moulsham Parish Magazine*, saying: *"No man can have had such friends, such support, such kindness, such loyalty – and willing and easily separate from all of this – and yet the strain has been very great indeed ... ... this new work (at Willingale Doe) opens up before me, and grasping the situation as I believe rightly, my own impaired health, the need for full energy in Moulsham – the directing of God's Holy Providence have made me feel that a lesser sphere of work, a life of quiet pastoral work with the beautiful example of one of the most striking figures of a village parish priest (John Keble) before me, might be the Master's Will".* The reference to John Keble is telling, and reading between the lines it is clear that he was a considerable influence on Robert Saulez. John Keble, who became a leader of the Oxford Movement, in spite of his great intellectual skills, was content to spend most of the latter part of his life simply as vicar of the small parish of Hursley, near Winchester, until his death in 1866, asking (and receiving) no ecclesiastical preferment. The same issue of the magazine also announced that the bishop would institute Robert Saulez to the new living on 1 August.[66]

Robert Saulez preached his last sermon to a crowded congregation at St John's on Sunday 29 July. *"He had come to Moulsham,"* he said, *"regarding it as his last sphere of work, but things had turned out otherwise. He had tried,"* he went on, *"to feed his congregation raw meat* (sic) *when they could take only milk. He would, though, not leave them without deeply thanking them for their generosity and kindness".*[67] And some of the people in the parish had been kind and generous. The members of the Men's Bible Class (he had made Bible study one of his priorities) presented him with a handsome travelling bag together with a morocco handbag and purse for Mrs Saulez. The *Essex Newsman* reported rather smugly that: *"a purse containing £35 was also presented to Mr Saulez from a few of the parishioners as a token of their appreciation for his work among them. There have also been some other presents from some other parishioners".*[68] The Rev King Ormsby also preached his final sermon in the same weeks that Robert Saulez received his gifts – and he could not leave without reminding the parish that: *"they must stand by their committee of finance and work in such a manner as to ensure a freedom from the worries of finance for those who minister in St John's".* So the old order was done away with.

The parish must have read of the rather meagre presentations to their former vicar in the press, and perhaps consciences were stirred a little. Towards the end of September it was reported that a handsome marble clock, subscribed for by no less than eighty-eight of the parishioners of Moulsham, had been forwarded to Robert Saulez at his new parish, in recognition of his pastoral work amongst them.[69]

Robert Saulez had been served well but sparsely by the curates that he had been able to employ through the additional curates' fund. However, the fact that he had no independent means ensured that he had never been able to have more than one curate at any time to assist him in the running of a difficult and populous parish. This was in stark contrast to St Mary's. He had, though, been able to attract some good men to assist him, and, unusually, not all of his curates were young men, fresh from ordination.

John Banks Beers came to St John's as a short term stopgap, it being announced in July 1901 that his services had been engaged (as assistant curate) for St John's church to cover July, August and September 1901.[70] John Beers was a graduate of Trinity College, Dublin, receiving his BA in 1865 and his MA in 1868. He was ordained deacon in 1866 and priest in 1867 in the diocese of Carlisle. He was fifty-eight when he came to Moulsham, after a number of curacies around England, and he was licensed at St John's on 15 July 1901. He assisted Robert Saulez in the parish until the end of September when it was announced in the local press that: *"the Rev J.B. Beers, who has done good work as a temporary curate of St John's Church for the last three months, is leaving for duty in the Ely diocese".*[71] The same short article also pointed out that Robert Saulez would be assisted until the end of the year by clergy from St Mary's, Colchester.

Early in 1902 Robert Saulez was able to engage as a curate a deacon newly-ordained at the St Thomas' day ordination by the Bishop of St Albans, which in 1901 took place in the parish church in Rickmansworth.[72] The Rev Edward Morton Bartlett was born on 21 August 1877, the second son of James Joyce Bartlett, an agricultural engineer of Wimborne, Dorset, who sadly died when Edward was a young boy. He was educated at Wimborne Grammar school, and his mother's remarriage (when Edward was only eleven) to a local squire, William Whittle of Merly Hall, Canford presented Edward with seven step-siblings. His cannot have been an easy childhood. He was admitted as a pensioner to Pembroke College, Cambridge, matriculating at Michaelmas 1897. He obtained his BA in 1900 and his MA in 1904.[73] After further training at Wells Theological college, on his ordination as deacon he was also licensed to St John's. He took his first service there in early January 1902. He was ordained priest by the Bishop of St Albans at Hitchin in December 1902.[74] He was soon playing his part in the life of the parish. At the social tea in January 1902, with over two hundred people present, the new curate acquitted himself well when he sang a selection of popular songs that were: *"well received."*[75] He took a prominent part in the service held at St John's to mark the postponement of King Edward VII's coronation but after two years in Moulsham he felt that it was time to move on, and in November 1903 it was announced that: *"the Rev E.M. Bartlett, the curate of St John's, has accepted the appointment as senior assistant curate at St Mary's, Ipswich and will leave Chelmsford at the end of January 1904. Whilst in Moulsham over the past two years, Mr Bartlett has been deservedly popular. He has taken a great interest in the welfare of youths, for whose benefit he did a great deal in starting the 'Saturday Lads' Recreation Room'. He also personally undertook the duty of installing the electric light in the George Street church room. His brother Ernest is a doctor in Ipswich."*[76] When the united Men's and Women's Bible classes met in January 1904, they presented Edward Bartlett with a handsome stationery case.[77] Whilst in Ipswich he married Miss Evelyne Margaret Foster at St Matthew's church on 21 November 1906, shortly before his installation as rector of Woolpit in Suffolk.[78]

John Lansbury Dutton was the son of John Dutton of Curbridge Hall, Witney, Oxfordshire and his wife Martha. He was born in 1862 and went up to Trinity Hall, Cambridge, matriculating at Michaelmas 1881. He took his BA in 1884 and received his MA in 1892. He was ordained deacon in 1885 and priest in 1888 by the Bishop of Peterborough.[79] After two curacies in Northamptonshire followed by spells at Ipswich and the challenging parish of All Saints, Forest Gate, he came at the age of forty-three to St John's,[80] taking his first service in Moulsham on Sunday, 24 April 1904.[81] He quickly endeared himself to his parishioners in spite of his slightly eccentric habits. In October the *Essex Newsman* reported that: *"The Rev J.L. Dutton, curate of Moulsham, whilst tricycling down Manor Road last Thursday (4 October) evening, was thrown from his machine owing to it skidding. He sustained an injury to his left knee, which will keep him indoors for several days."*[82] He preached his last sermon in St John's on Sunday, 13 August 1905 after which he took two months' holiday (under orders from his doctor). During this time it was announced that the rector of Aspenden, Hertfordshire, had: *"after fifty-four years,*

217

first as a curate and then as a rector, resigned his benefice from 30 September, owing to advanced age and enfeebled health. He will be succeeded by the Rev J.L. Dutton, the curate of St John's, Moulsham, Chelmsford."[83] John Lansbury Dutton stayed as rector at Aspenden for twenty-three years, retiring at the age of sixty-six. He died at Newmarket in 1944.

'Slander hunts down its quarry in Essex'

The Rev William Watson King Ormsby was born in Dublin in about 1849, and attended Trinity College where he took his BA in 1871 and his Divinity Testimonial in 1876. He received his MA in 1880. He was ordained deacon in 1869 and priest in 1872 in the diocese of Down. After spells at churches in Carlow he became assistant to the Bishop of Down and a minor canon of St Peter's cathedral in Dublin, where he stayed from 1880 to 1886. After two posts in England, he was appointed vicar of St John the Evangelist, Boulogne, in 1895. He resigned from this post in 1901.[84]

Of all the priests who have been officially associated with St John's, William Ormsby was far and away the loosest cannon. A strong-minded man, not slow or shy to take on the establishment, he had a life-long love affair with litigation, rather like that of his great hero, Bishop Henry Philpotts of Exeter, in the previous century. His resignation from St John the Evangelist in Boulogne demonstrates how ready he was to use the law when he felt that he had good chance of winning. On the evening of 10 December 1899 he was returning from France to England for his Christmas holidays on the South Eastern and Chatham Railway (SECR) steamer *Mabel Grace*. In fog off Folkestone the *Mabel Grace* collided with the Swedish steamer *Lisa*, and William Ormsby was: *"thrown violently on the deck"*. In court he pleaded that this had caused a severe shock to his nervous system and brought about significant 'spinal concussion' (*sic*), resulting in his having to resign his chaplaincy in Boulogne. He argued his case successfully (in spite of the SECR's counsel suggesting strongly that the injuries were *"all in his head"*) and was awarded £900 in personal damages.[85] The injury incapacitated him for some considerable time, and it was not until November 1905 that it was announced that: *"the Rev W.W. King Ormsby, who has been licensed by the Bishop to officiate in the diocese of St Albans, had come for an indefinite period to assist the vicar of Moulsham in his parochial work"*.[86] He took his first baptism at St John's on 2 December but was not formally licensed as curate until Saturday 17 February 1906 at Woodford by the bishop, reading the Articles in Moulsham church on the following Sunday. His stay in the parish, as noted before, was unexpectedly brief, but on his departure in August 1906, he took on a number of temporary duties in the diocese, deputising for sick or absent incumbents. He was always much liked by those to whom he ministered, but his attitudes and opinions often seemed to clash with those in authority over him. His story subsequent to his departure from St John's is not without interest. He left as a licensed priest in the diocese of St Albans, and extended this by being licensed also for the diocese of Norwich in 1909, and then for the diocese of Chelmsford when it came into being in 1914. By this time he was already sixty-five years old, but still combative enough to prove a thorn in the side of the new Bishop, the Rt Rev John Edwin Watts-Ditchfield, a leading Evangelical, who has been said to over-compensate for his methodist past by strong assertion of episcopal authority. In 1916 William Ormsby published extensive correspondence in the local press between himself and the Bishop which perhaps might have been better left unseen. His real champion was his biographer, J. Randolph Coverdell, who in 1919 published an extraordinary book: *"Might versus Right in the Church of England"* which dealt mainly on responses to the question: *"What had the Bishop of London against me?"* (the bishop had withdrawn his licence). The book contains a curious chapter entitled: *"Slander hunts down its quarry in East Anglia"* which deals with William Ormsby's time in Essex. The author champions William Ormsby's cause, saying: *"His own merits attracted strong friendships, but the friendships grew cold when by an underground passage from an unknown source the old lie came along – something against him"*. This culminated in an episode in Chelmsford in 1916 when the Bishop summoned him (apparently from the sickbed where he lay ill with bronchitis) to answer an accusation that he (a life-long abstainer): *"had been guilty of taking a surreptitious drink on his way to church"*.[87] The bishop dealt leniently with him on this occasion, but William Ormsby felt that the whole world was against him. The local press also reported, towards the end of 1919, that his elder son Robert George Ormsby, who had been reported as missing at the battle of Ypres in 1915, had: *"lost his life saving that of a wounded man at the same battle"*.[88] William Ormsby

Figure 19 – Robert Travers Saulez, Incumbent of
St John's, Moulsham, 1901–06

was clearly not one of life's lucky people (although, curiously, there seems to be no reference to his son's death in any of the official sources of the First World War). William Ormsby laboured for a few more years in Essex, never being appointed to a permanent benefice, until he died on 23 December 1925 at Little Waltham, aged 77. His brief obituary in the local press suggested that the family were of ancient and noble lineage, being descended from the Viking chieftain Orm, who invaded England in AD 877.[89]

He was cremated at Golders Green crematorium on Monday, 26 December, his only surviving daughter at home, Miss Beatrice Ormsby taking the ashes to Dublin for burial in the family vault. In his will, details of which were published in 1926, the gross value of his estate was no more than £683. His will contained the unusual clause: *"that I desire to put on record and protest in this my will against the way in which I have been treated by the authorities in the Church of England over the last twenty or so years; which treatment had resulted in my work as a Church of England priest having been hindered and my prospects ruined"*.[90] St John's, Moulsham, would not see his like again.

So Robert Saulez moved to Willingale Doe. His duties also included the parishes of Shellow Bowells and Berners Roding, and here he ministered in a rural environment where, in truth, he felt much more at ease. Over the next ten years, he endeared himself to his flock, but, by then, the difficulty of travelling to a relatively remote church, significant problems with the church building and lack of parishioners led him to resign as vicar in 1916.[91] He was presented in February 1917 with an illuminated address together with a purse of money, by James Glasse of Berners Hall to mark his departure.[92]

Personal tragedy was never far from the Saulez family throughout the latter part of Robert Saulez's life. In 1917, his second son, Major Arthur Travers Saulez, who was in command of 'D' Battery, 64th Brigade, Royal Field Artillery, was killed on 28 April.[93] He had been twice mentioned in Despatches, and his grieving parents commissioned a stained-glass window in his memory in

St Christopher's, Willingale Doe.[94] Just four years later his third son, Captain George Saulez, RASC, died: *"in hospital in Baghdad, owing to the extreme heat. Aged thirty-five years, he leaves a widow and two children aged five years and three-and-a-half months."*[95] He is buried in the Baghdad (North Gate) War Cemetery.[96] Robert Saulez continued his ministry at Willingale Doe (though no longer as incumbent), and in 1926 was writing to the local press to try and raise the issue of help for small parishes like the one he assisted in, which, he felt, were neglected by church and state authorities alike.[97] He and his wife moved to live in Twinstead rectory when Robert Saulez finally retired from active ministry on 26 April 1927.[98] Even then, he felt that he had to continue to do the Lord's Will, moving to Twinstead only on the condition that he could help with 'light duties' in the parish, in spite of his advancing years (he was now seventy-seven years old). He died on Sunday, 29 January 1933 at Twinstead rectory.[99] He was eighty-three years of age. He and his wife had been able to celebrate their golden wedding anniversary in 1931 (on 28 April, the day on which they had been married in the British Embassy in Paris) but for the last couple of years of his life he had taken little part in the affairs of his adopted parish and its parish church. His funeral took place in Twinstead church on 31 January. Margaret Saulez lived to a ripe old age, celebrating her one hundredth birthday on 14 November 1946.[100]

Robert Saulez was never really at ease in the parish of St John's, Moulsham, during his time as vicar. He never found it easy to work with lay people in authority, particularly when their ideas clashed with his own; yet he was much missed by a significant proportion of the parish when he left. His portrait *(Figure 19)* shows a strong, determined individual, with just a hint that his strength might sometimes prove to be his weakness.

In what direction would the next incumbent take the parish?

7. WILLIAM JAMES PRESSEY

(1906–18)

*"Mr Pressey is very musical, and possess talents of no mean order.
Whilst at Salisbury Theological College,
he won the position of First Organ
Scholar, and he was organist for three years at his college in
Oxford. With regard to ritual, Mr Pressey does evidently not
hold extreme views, but at services in the church the cross is
carried in procession before the choir. In the village of Foxearth,
unbounded regret is expressed at Mr Pressey's departure".*[1]

So the *Essex County Chronicle* described the man who came in June 1906 to take up the challenge of steering St John's, Moulsham through the next decade and a half, including the very difficult period of the First World War. As with Robert Saulez, it is not easy to see what would motivate a talented, musical priest in a comfortable well-off rural living (and with time and resources to devote to his extensive antiquarian interests) to move to a difficult and populous parish with a wide range of social and economic problems. In his farewell speech to his Foxearth parishioners, William Pressey simply said that: *"he and his wife were going, not because they were not happy, but because a call had come, and that was the right thing to do".*[2]

'He and Mrs Pressey were much loved by the parishioners of Foxearth'

William James Pressey was born in Hackney, in east London, in late 1858, the second son of Arthur Pressey, a Colonial Merchant, and his wife Rebecca Cecil Shaddack, whom Arthur had married in Lewisham in 1853. William Pressey went up to Wadham College, Oxford, where he graduated BA in 1884, subsequently attending Salisbury Theological College prior to his ordination as deacon on Trinity Sunday (31 May) 1885 by Bishop Kelly in Salisbury Cathedral (Bishop Kelly was acting on commission for the Bishop of Salisbury).[3] At the same time William Pressey was licensed as curate to the nearby parish of Wilton. He was ordained priest by the Bishop of Salisbury in June 1886[4] having received his MA at a congregation held in Oxford on 17 June 1885.[5] In 1887 he moved as curate to the prosperous parish of St Mary Magdalene at St Leonard's-on-Sea in East Sussex. His next appointment came when the Bishop of St Albans offered him the post of curate in the parish of Foxearth, in north-west Essex (the parish is only a couple of miles from Long Melford in Suffolk, and is right on the county boundary). This post carried a substantial stipend, and William Pressey felt that he could now take the important step of marrying and having a family. On Thursday 17 April 1890 he married Grace Maria Lemoine, the daughter of Mr William Lemoine (of an old and distinguished Sussex family) at the church of St Mary Magdalene where William Pressey had been curate.[6] They moved to Foxearth, where William Pressey acted as curate to the noted High Church rector, Rev John Foster, who had been in charge of the parish since 1845. His curacy was to last only a couple of years, as in March 1892 Rev John Foster died. The report of his death said: *"He had been rector for forty-seven years, and was one of the pioneers of the High Church movement. He spent a considerable sum of his own money beautifying his own parish church, dedicated to SS Peter and Paul"*.[7] The Bishop and the other patrons (one of whom was the widow of the rector) did not waste any time looking for a successor and the curate was appointed rector at the beginning of August the same year. The *Suffolk and Essex Free Press* announced that: *"Mr Pressey has been curate for some time and is very popular ... ... he came to Foxearth from St Leonard's-on-Sea. The living is valued at £443"*.[8] During his time at Foxearth he not only continued to endear himself to his parishioners, but did not neglect his musical duties and interests. He continued to compose, and the setting of a 'Hunting song' that he made in 1894 brought forth favourable comments.[9] He also defended lesser known composers whose work he appreciated, writing a long letter praising the output of Lefebure Wely and Batiste after stinging criticism of them both at an international festival lecture.[10] He and Mrs Pressey were both much loved by their parishioners at Foxearth, and the local press recorded numerous small acts of kindness by the rector and his wife, particularly for local children.

The formal announcement was made in June 1906 that: *"The Rev William James Pressey, the vicar (sic) of Foxearth, had been appointed vicar of Moulsham, Chelmsford. It will be remembered that some time ago negotiations took place between the rev gentleman and the Rev R.T. Saulez with the exchange of livings, but the exchange was not effected. The Rev R.T. Saulez goes to Willingale Doe and Mr Pressey comes to Moulsham".[11]* On their departure from Foxearth, both the Rev and Mrs Pressey were the recipients of handsome presentations, showing the respect and esteem in which they had been held in the parish. At a meeting in early August 1906, chaired by one of the churchwardens (Mr Ewer) the rector received a massive silver salver, inscribed: *'Presented to Rev W.J. Pressey, M.A., by the parishioners of Foxearth, with sincere gratitude for his sixteen years of pastoral work among them. 2 August 1906'.* The meeting congratulated Moulsham on gaining such an incumbent and his wife, and the other churchwarden, Mr Ward, asked Mrs Pressey to accept, in the name of the parish, a case of silver-backed hair brushes, clothes brushes, comb and back glass.[3] The rector also received a silver penholder, together with a letter signed by all the children who had contributed to the gift, thanking him for the hymns and songs he had written for them over the years.[12]

'The new incumbent came to Moulsham with excellent credentials'

The Rev William James Pressey was instituted as vicar of Moulsham by the Bishop of Colchester in the parish church on Tuesday evening, 7 August 1906. The Rev W.W. King Ormsby conducted the first part of the service, the lessons being read by the Rev H.M. Burgess, the vicar of Highwood, and the Rev Canon Lake, the rector of St Mary's and the patron of the living. The bishop, in his address, remarked that the new incumbent came to Moulsham with excellent credentials, and the only reason that William Pressey had given for leaving his former parish (which he had served faithfully for so many years) was a desire for a more strenuous ministry.[2] The new vicar read himself in on the following Sunday morning (12 August) when, instead of a sermon, he read the Thirty-Nine Articles. He gave his first sermon at St John's at the evening service, choosing as his text: *"For I am determined not to know anything among you save Jesus Christ, and him crucified"*. He appealed to the congregation to help him in his work, saying no ministry could be successful without personal sympathy between minster and people. A religion, he felt, that was merely of emotions, was no use, but religion must be something that would help to solve all the troubles of daily life.[13] Mr and Mrs Pressey quickly settled into parish work, and made considerable efforts to get to know their flock. Already, by the beginning of September, they were said: *"to be rapidly making themselves popular in the parish. On Monday (3 September) entertaining members of the Mothers' Union and the Bible class at a social gathering in the vicarage"* and on the following Thursday: *"the Men's Bible class went to the vicarage for bowls – it was hoped to raise a good team".*[14] The fund raising was not forgotten, either. In December William Pressey and his organist (Mr H.A. Parker) held a sale of work and two concerts in order to raise funds for St John's, The concerts were much appreciated and the whole day raised no less than £40 for the church.[15]

William Pressey had been described, when his appointment was announced, as: *"not holding extreme views with regard to ritual,"* although it was noted that at services in Foxearth church, the cross was carried in procession before the choir.[16] However, as pointed out before, William Pressey's predecessor as rector had been a noted high churchman, and one of the principal projects on which he had spent his own money had been the painting of frescoes throughout the interior of the church. At the time that they were commissioned, the local press announced that: *"The Ecclesiastical authorities at Foxearth have decided not only to introduce scriptural figures, emblems and subjects in the stained glass windows, but also as polychromatic designs on the wall, etc."*[16] Photographs taken at the end of the nineteenth century show a church where every square inch that could be painted seemed to be crowded with biblical scenes and texts. It must, indeed, have been a riot of colour and the visual impact on the rural population must have been considerable.[17] This is where William Pressey ministered for sixteen years, and it would be strange if some of that beauty had not left its mark on him and given him ideas. St John's, Moulsham, was a very plain and undistinguished church and had plenty of flat wall space. So it is perhaps not surprising that the new vicar started to plan ways in which he might beautify his new charge. Sadly, no plans or schemes seem to have survived relating to the first phase of the decoration, but the report of the Easter Sunday services at St John's on 31 March 1907 states that: *"The chancel of this church has been beautified by the painting of frescoes in the panels between the three lights in the east window, the gift of Miss B. Wackrill. The painting is the work of Mr E.O. Hemming, who recently carried out the decoration of the chancel of St Mary's, Chelmsford, and the frescoes in St John's represent Our Lord as the Bread of Life and the True Vine. A carpet and fittings for the chancel, a gift of the Guild of the Ascension, were used for the first time on Easter Sunday. The floral decorations for the festival were very effective, being composed mainly of spring flowers. There were large attendances at all the services on the Sunday, and the offertories, which were (as is the custom) given to the vicar, amounted to just under £29".*[18] In a photograph taken in about 1910 these paintings can just be distinguished between the stained glass windows. They were to be just the start of the decoration that William Pressey had in mind, but there seems to have been no reaction recorded either in the parish or from the congregation. If a similar scheme had been carried out in the chancel at St Mary's and there had been no ecclesiastical flak, St John's may have taken this as a cue and gone ahead with their own similar project.

'Thanks was expressed to the vicar for his able guidance which had brought harmony to the parish'

In the 1907 vestry meeting, William Pressey's first, held on Friday, 5 April, there is no mention of the new decorations, other than a brief acknowledgement of Miss Wackrill's generosity. There was, however, plenty of sweetness and light. A much improved financial situation must have contributed to the good atmosphere which prevailed throughout the discussions. It was pointed out right from the start that there were a number of items in the accounts (which had been presented by the Rev W.W. King Ormsby) which had been disputed, and as a result the accounts had been re-audited by Mr Spurgeon and Mr Wackrill, and it was agreed that the corrected values should be entered in the minutes. The accounts for the year ending March 1907 were then presented. They were very satisfactory, and the adverse balance of £85 with which the year had begun, had been converted into a surplus of just over £3. The vicar re-nominated Mr Barker as his churchwarden, and Mr Franklin continued as parish warden. The vicar then presented the accounts of the charities, which he had clearly examined meticulously. Income from the Bond and Pollard charities, which had apparently laid untouched since 1895, now amounted to about £40, and he had also discovered that through a misunderstanding the parish had not received for the previous five years tickets for the infirmary and dispensary to which it was entitled under the will of the late Mr F.T. Veley. The arrears of tickets had now been obtained. Thanks were expressed to the auditors, and the synodsmen were then re-elected together with the addition of Messrs J.G. Bond, E.C. Gray, R.E. Wackrill, W. Rist and H. Winterflood. The meeting ended with a vote of thanks to the vicar followed by the benediction.

The vestry meeting was followed after a short break by a meeting for all the congregation. The vicar thanked everyone present for their great kindness on Easter Sunday and then gave details of the clergy fund, which had a balance in hand of more than £125. He thanked Mr Darby and the ladies of the church for all that they had done to collect money for the fund. Mr Darby reciprocated.

He thanked the vicar for the way in which he had kept the accounts, pointing out that it was sometimes stated that vicars were not business men, but Moulsham's vicar had turned out to be a very astute business man indeed [Applause]. There were other votes of thanks, in addition to that for Miss Wackrill, who paid for the frescoes; one for the Guild of the Ascension, for the carpets; to Miss Barker, for a set of alms bags for use at Festivals, and to Miss Franklin, for a set of altar linen. All round thanks were expressed to the vicar for his able guidance which had brought harmony to the parish, and the meeting ended on a more positive note than for many years.[19]

Later in the year, the parish suffered a severe blow with the death of William Cutts. He died on Saturday morning, 5 October, at his residence, 'Carisbrooke' in Manor Road, Chelmsford. He had not been well for some time, the *Essex Newsman* describing how: "*he had to resort first to a slow trap, then to a wheelchair*". William Cutts had been born in Braintree, the son of a well-known schoolmaster, and had initially been apprenticed to a miller, but finding the work uncongenial, went into the office of a local solicitor, Mr Land. At the age of nineteen he came to Chelmsford, and joined the office of Mr John Copland, where he remained for the rest of his working life, rising to the post of Managing Clerk. He had served as churchwarden at St John's for no less than sixteen years, and had always provided a strong, if somewhat obdurate hand on the church's tiller. He had been married twice, and left seven grown-up children. He had been a great supporter and benefactor of the Chelmsford Infirmary and Dispensary and also of the Mechanics' Institute. His funeral took place on Friday, 11 October at St John's and was followed by interment at the Writtle Road cemetery. His contributions to the church over the years had been immense.[20]

'He did not want to wipe out the commandments'

The new year (1908) dawned. Mrs Pressey had been unwell over the Christmas period, and at the end of January she and her husband went to St Leonard's-on-Sea to recuperate.[21] The winter was harsh, and there was much destitution in the parish. St John's, with William Pressey's encouragement, took the lead by setting up a soup kitchen in the George Street church room.[22] By March the Presseys were back in the parish, and William Pressey wanted very much to finish the decoration of the chancel. On Friday, 13 March he called a special meeting to discuss the next phase of the painting of the frescoes and texts. Messrs E.O. Hemming and Co. provided copies of the proposed designs, and the vicar presented them to the meeting, suggesting that: *"as the scheme had been commenced the previous year, paid for by Miss Wackrill's gift, he felt it would be a nice thing to complete it before this coming Easter."* He went on to point out that some friends of his had already offered to pay for part of the work, the Guild of the Ascension had agreed to fund a dado and the churchwardens themselves had guaranteed the cost of the decoration of the two brackets to be located where the commandments were at present. The total cost had been estimated at £30, of which only £12 remained to be raised. Mr J. Barker proposed and Mr Wood seconded a resolution approving the scheme. When asked where the commandments would go if they were removed from the east end, the vicar said he wished it to be understood that he did not want to wipe out the commandments, and that they could be put up in another part of the church if required. The resolution was unanimously carried and the vicar and the churchwardens were authorised to petition for a faculty.[23] The faculty application was submitted on 26 March and was quickly approved. A deposit of £14 was paid to E.O. Hemmings and Co. on 14 April.[24] The work was executed rapidly, and by the end of May William Pressey was able to publish a balance sheet showing that the required sum of money had been raised from friends and parishioners. The decorations were most impressive and were to enhance the chancel area for many years to come.

William Pressey's brief balance sheet (*Figure 20*) is of interest, as it does give some small clues as to the original composition of the decorations. There were 'Four Archangels', although the balance sheet (and other surviving documentation) gives no indication of

MOULSHAM VICARAGE
CHELMSFORD
6 MAY, 1908

My Dear

I enclose herewith a Balance sheet of the account for the Easter Decorations with my very sincere and hearty thanks for your most kind help. It has made me very happy to feel that the East End of our church is now really worthy of a House of Prayer.

With kindest regards, Very truly yours, W.J. Pressey.

St John's, Moulsham

Balance Sheet for the Account for East End Decorations
EASTER 1908

Dr		Cr	
Mrs Chappell	£1 0. 0.	By Messrs Hemmings account	
Mrs Foster (Foxearth)	2. 2. 0.	as under:-	
Mrs Walter Gray	2. 2. 0.	Cost of 4 Archangels and	
Mrs Van Holmrigh	2. 2. 0.	accompanying decoration	£8. 8. 0.
Miss Lister	2. 2. 0.		
Mr J.H. Martin	1. 1. 0.	Cost of two figures as painted	
Mrs Meeson	0.10. 6.	in panels complete	£16.16.0.
Mrs Neane	2. 2. 0.		
Miss Palmer (per Vicar)	2. 10. 0.	Cost of 2 medallions in splays	
Rev. W.J. ands Mrs Pressey	2. 2. 0.	in East Window	£4. 4. 0.
Mrs Rowley	1. 1. 0.		
Miss Wackrill	2. 2. 0.	Cost of Dado (to floor of	
Miss B. Wackrill	8. 8. 0.	sanctuary)	£1 10. 0.
The Guild of the			
Ascension	1.10. 0.		
Balance paid by Vicar	0. 2. 6.		
	30 18. 0.		£30 18. 0.

Figure 20 – William Pressey's balance sheet for the east
end decorations at St John's, Moulsham

which archangels were painted. Christian tradition normally recognises Gabriel, Michael and Raphael as foremost among the archangels[25] and it seems likely that Uriel was added as the fourth. Reference is made to 'two painted figures' and these have been identified with St Peter and St Paul (the saints to whom Foxearth church was also dedicated). At some subsequent stage the whole of the chancel decorations were (probably) simply painted over and (very poor) archangels reproduced in approximately the same positions. It is not clear what state the original 1908/09 frescoes are in if they could be recovered.

Not long after his arrival in the parish, William Pressey had expressed his dissatisfaction with the state of the organ at St John's. By this time it was almost fifty years old and had never been a particularly distinguished instrument. So it was no surprise in June 1907 that he started a New Organ fund to replace the existing instrument. At the 1908 vestry meeting, after the routine accounts had been dealt with (the sick and needy fund had had a demanding year – the soup kitchen in the church rooms had been heavily used throughout the previous winter, although it had managed to make a slight profit) the vicar reported at length on the New Organ fund. After nine months' collecting from sales of work and concerts, plus some donations, about £453 had been raised. This was a significant sum, as poverty in Moulsham had been extensive during the previous winter. The meeting then moved on to the normal business. Both the existing wardens (Mr J Barker and Mr R. Franklin) were re-elected. William Pressey concluded the meeting by mentioning at length all those who had contributed to the parish in money or time over the past year, and after a vote of thanks to the vicar, the meeting closed.[26]

Sales of work and concerts continued throughout the summer, the substantial sum which had already been raised (and which was reported above) giving a boost to the efforts. A typical sale of work in the vicarage garden on 2 July (at which the faithful Mid-Essex band yet again toiled away all day)[27] raised more than £65, which, considering that the event took place on a Thursday afternoon, is astonishing (was it early closing?) and with sums of money rapidly accruing towards the New Organ fund, a special vestry meeting was held on Thursday 10 September in the choir vestry, chaired by Mr Barker (William Pressey was on holiday) to consider the various schemes for the improvement of the church. These included the New Organ fund, the enlarging of the choir vestry, improving the lighting of the church (either by gas or electricity), the extending of the interior decoration that had already been started in the chancel, and the furnishing of what is today (2018) the Veley chapel. Mr Pertwee produced the relevant plans and estimates for all those projects and explained to the vestry meeting how they would be implemented. He agreed that he would act as honorary (i.e. unpaid) architect for the various alterations. A resolution was passed unanimously that: *"the Vicar and the churchwardens be forthwith empowered to sign the petition for the faculty to carry out the improvements to St John's Church"*.[28] The faculty was swiftly granted and by October it was announced that: *"Messrs. Abbott and Smith of Leeds have secured the contract for the new organ for St John's Church, Moulsham. The same firm built the organ for St Albans cathedral, Leeds parish church and Leeds Town Hall"*.[29]

Work started immediately and continued over Christmas, so that the new instrument was ready by the beginning of February 1909, and on Wednesday 17 February the church was crowded with a large congregation for the dedication of the new organ and the side chapel by the Bishop of Barking. He preached an appropriate sermon on the text: *"it came to pass, as the trumpeters and singers were as one, to make sound to be heard in praising and thanking the Lord"*. After the sermon, the service continued with a short organ recital given by Mr H. Davan Whetton, the organist of the Foundling Hospital, and the service concluded with the hymn: *"Angel voices ever singing"*.[30] The fundraising had been very successful, and some eight weeks later, at the 1909 vestry meeting, it was reported that the New Organ fund showed a credit balance of just under £3 after paying £247 towards the total bill of Messrs. Abbott and Smith.[31] The same vestry meeting briefly discussed the question of free seating in the church (yet again) but attempted to postpone any decision-making by agreeing that: *"the opinion of the congregation on the matter should be obtained by inviting them to express their wants on circulars distributed in the church"*. In the end, the matter was left to the vicar and churchwardens to decide.[32] Additional funds were still required to complete the organ, and sales of work and bazaars continued throughout 1909, a typical one in July raising more than £67, part of which was also to go the vestry enlargement fund.

'Singling out those who had assisted with the Band of Hope'

St John's was now looking forward with enthusiasm to the new year (1910). The church building itself had been greatly enhanced, the new organ was an outstanding success, and a settled clergy team (of William Pressey and Edward Hort) was giving the parish a stability and a sense of well-being that it had sought ever since the difficult departure of Robert Saulez in 1906. William Pressey showed his appreciation of the contribution that the laity made to the running of the parish by giving his usual dinner at the vicarage on 3 January to churchwardens, sidesmen, organist and the adult members of the choir. The guests responded to the vicar's hospitality with enthusiastic and repeated toasts to the host and Mrs Pressey.[33] In March, the newly-consecrated Bishop of Colchester, Robert Henry Whitcombe, held a confirmation at St John's. A total of eighty candidates were present, of whom no less than forty-eight were from St John's. The clergy's ministrations were bearing good fruit.[34] The Friday in Easter week saw a short but very positive vestry meeting (even though it was held on 1 April) where the parish warden, Mr Franklin, produced accounts showing a small credit balance of 8s. In view of the considerable expenditure that had taken place over the previous twelve months, this was, he said, to be regarded as a very positive result. Fifty-one pounds was still owed on the organ fund (with only £36 in hand) but the vicar was confident that the difference would soon be made up.

The two wardens (Mr Barker and Mr Franklin) were re-appointed and the meeting concluded with the vicar expressing his deep thanks to all those who had helped in the running of the church, singling out particularly those who had assisted Edward Hort in the running of the Band of Hope, which had clearly been a great success during the previous year. A special mention was made of those whose gifts had continued to enhance the interior of the church. Miss van Holmrigh had produced a beautifully worked fair linen cloth for the altar, and Miss Bond had made a new credence cloth. The Guild of the Ascension, too, had made their contribution in the form of a handsome bound and printed book for use on the altar during services. A St John's vestry meeting would not have been the same without some reference to the church clock, and this meeting did not disappoint. Mr C.J. Simpson felt that the clock in the tower should be made to strike (presumably at the time of the vestry meeting it was silent) but Mr Franklin disappointed many present (and those poorer people of Moulsham who could not afford a watch) by saying that they had received expert advice that: *"with the present clock it would not be practicable"*.

Although the younger choristers had not been invited to William and Mrs Pressey's dinner for adults in January, they were not forgotten. The choristers, together with the Sunday School teachers and the magazine distributors, were all treated on 18 June to a *"delightful water picnic"*, starting from Brown's wharf (on the Chelmer and Blackwater navigation) in a barge, from whence they were towed to Baddow Mill lock. Here they all disembarked for a picnic tea, courtesy of the vicar, before arriving back at Brown's wharf, just as dusk was falling. A good time was no doubt had by all.[35] Being a vicar in Moulsham, though, was not without its hazards. On the afternoon of Tuesday 14 July Mr Pressey was riding his bicycle along the newly metalled Moulsham Street, when, no doubt to his consternation, the handlebars came off. The machine skidded, and Mr Pressey was thrown heavily from it, sustaining severe bruising. The unfortunate vicar was helped home by Mr Ripper (the accident occurring close to St John's school) whereupon Mr Pressey promptly fainted. He was immediately seen by Dr Martin, and although no bones were broken, he was stated to be: *"severely bruised and suffering from shock"*.[36] The vicar, though was made of stern stuff, and a few weeks later it was reported that: *"The Rev W.J. Pressey, vicar of Moulsham, was able to preach at St John's on Sunday morning (31 July) for the first time since his somewhat serious bicycle accident. Although still feeling the effects of his fall, the Rev gentleman is making a steady recovery"*.[37]

'The choir "with great zeal" set to work to try and extinguish the outbreak'

The new organ was attracting considerable attention locally, and when Mr Herbert Parker, the organist, gave a recital in July, the church was said to be packed. The programme was designed to show some of the merits of the organ, and included a gavotte by Dr Elgar, which had been written to demonstrate the use of the tremulant stop. Mr Parker was assisted in the recital by Mr Henry Bailey, bass, who was a regular recitalist at the Royal Albert Hall, and who enhanced the proceedings with a fine rendering of 'Sun of my Soul' which he himself had written. A collection was taken on behalf of the choir fund, and it was perhaps some of those funds that enabled adult members of the choir to enjoy themselves (and support local industry) by hiring a Clarkson bus. Clarkson was a well-known maker of steam-powered cars and buses whose factory was located opposite St John's church, on the site of the present-day Albion Court. The bus was used in July for a trip to Cambridge. The whole experience turned out to be far more exciting than any of them could have dreamed of when they set out from Chelmsford just after seven in the morning. With Mr Pressey's influence (but not his presence, as he was still confined to his bed after his bicycle accident) they were entertained by Mr D. Ward, of Lower Hall, Foxearth.

They left Foxearth to continue their journey to Cambridge, and while passing through the village of Hundon, on the Essex-Suffolk border near Haverhill, they saw a cottage on fire. The bus was immediately stopped, and the choir *"with great zeal"* set to work to try and extinguish the outbreak. As was reported in the press: *"a lack of water rendered the extinguishing of the fire impossible, so the choristers helped by removing furniture from the blazing building, in addition rescuing a number of chickens from a burning shed and run. In the end all the furniture was safely piled up, and the chickens went about clucking their thanks to the choir in chorus* (sic) *while the inmates of the cottage also expressed their gratitude"*. A convenient brook was located for the singers to clean themselves up, and after an *al fresco* luncheon, the party resumed its journey to Cambridge, reaching their destination in the early afternoon. After visiting several colleges, the choristers returned to Chelmsford, with the churchwardens and organist serving supper on the bus, eventually reaching St John's, just before midnight. All felt they had enjoyed the day immensely.[38] 1910 had indeed turned out to be a fun year for St John's.

'The parish would have to be entirely self-supporting with respect to the Clergy Fund'

In 1911 the vestry meeting was held as usual in Easter week, in this case on Friday 21 April. The meeting started briefly in the choir vestry, where an adjournment was proposed so that everyone could move to the girls' schoolroom. The large attendance meant that it could no longer continue in the vestry. The parish warden, Mr Franklin produced the accounts for 1910–11, which after payment of all outstanding bills, showed a credit of between £1 and £2. These accounts were speedily adopted. The two wardens were re-elected and the synodsmen re-appointed *en bloc* with the substitution of Mr Mason for Mr Wood who had left the parish. This terminated the formal business of the vestry meeting.

The vicar then produced the other relevant accounts, Clergy Fund, Sick and Needy account, Parochial account and those accounts related to the Mildmay charity. After a brief discussion, all were passed, but William Pressey had an important announcement to make with respect to the Clergy Fund. He reminded the meeting that the grant received from the Assistant Curates' Society had ceased at the previous Lady Day, and pointed out that the parish would in future have to be entirely self-supporting with respect to the Clergy Fund (the Assistant Curates' Society was itself chronically short of funds). Mr Franklin then produced accounts for the Free Will Offering fund and the New Organ fund. The former was substantially in credit, and was proving a valuable source of income to St John's, and the Organ fund was now closed. All bills relating to the organ had now been paid, and because the last sale of work had produced much more income than expected, the fund had ended up with a positive balance of more than £36. It was decided to transfer £25 to the Clergy Fund and the remainder to the Free Will Offering fund. The vicar went on to thank the congregation for their splendid Easter Offering which amounted to almost £34. He then singled out those subscribers whose generosity had enabled the church to complete the decoration of the side walls of the chancel (on 10 February an estimate: *"for decorating the side walls of the chancel per designs submitted and approved, £35"* had been received from Mr E.O. Hemmings and Co., and the work had started on Monday, 27 February and had been completed on 30 March). Thanks were also expressed to Mr Pace, for his kind donation of a print of Moulsham Hall to hang in the vestry; to Mrs Gripper, for working the Band of Hope Banner, and all those who undertook the various departments of church work so regularly and efficiently. A hearty vote of thanks to the vicar, proposed by Mr J.G. Bond and seconded by Mr Harden, terminated the proceedings.[39]

The choir, however, had not had as exciting a year as the previous one, with its firefighting episode. Indeed, it had been involved in a rather more sombre outing. On Sunday 25 June they had sung anthems as part of that afternoon's service at Chelmsford Prison, being entertained afterwards by the Prison Chaplain, the Rev H.C. Pigot, to tea.[40]

'The church, in advocating temperance, was doing God's work'

Towards the end of 1911, Julia Matson (the last of the family of three sisters and a brother, all unmarried, who lived in New London Road) died, and in her will, published early in 1912 she left £100 each to St John's, Moulsham and St Giles, Mountnessing (where all the Matsons were buried in the family vault): *"to augment the livings of these parishes"*.[41] The whole family had been involved with St John's for many years, and the brother, Mr A.K. Matson, had been one of the mainstays of the vestry for some considerable time, although never taking any prominent office in the church. Mr Ripper, the headmaster of St John's schools, was also taking an increasingly important part in parish life. In March 1912 he was the principal speaker at a meeting of the St John's branch of the CEMS, an unusual honour for a lay person. His presentation on 'Religious Education' was well received, Rev Pressey in particular commending it. A vigorous discussion ensued, with many participants condemning the *'apathetic attitude'* of churchmen with regard to religious education.[42]

Later in the year, Mr Ripper, who was the secretary of the Moulsham Bowling club, was presented with a framed photograph of himself to commemorate his tenure of the secretary's post. In the subsequent match, held on the vicarage bowling green, William Pressey's team beat the club team by twenty-three points.[43] Edward Hort, too, was making his mark to some degree as a speaker locally; strangely, for a Church of England priest, he was another strong advocate of total abstinence. His work with the Band of Hope has already been noted, but in March he addressed a packed public meeting of the Chelmsford and Essex Temperance Society in the Mechanics' Institute. He pointed out that the church, in advocating temperance, was doing God's work, and it was most important that everyone present should do all that they could: *"to get rid of this national sin"*. Ex-Sergeant-Major Watkin (late of the Gordon Highlanders) then delivered a lecture on the evils of intemperance. That must have contained some real gems.[44]

'Wanted, £180'

The annual vestry meeting, on Friday, 12 April, proceeded to deal with the routine business very quickly, although on this occasion it was necessary to replace Mr Franklin, who no longer felt he could act as parish warden. Mr W.H. Ripper was proposed for the vacant position by Mr Mason and seconded by Mr Green. Mr Ripper thanked the vestry for the honour it had done him and said he would always strive to do all in his power for the good of the church and the parish generally. Mr Franklin produced the accounts and pointed out that they were still in credit – but only to the extent of one penny. All the accounts were speedily passed. The meeting then moved on to discuss much more weighty matters. The parish added its penn'orth to the debate on Welsh disestablishment, by carrying the resolution that: *"The Parishioners of St John's, Moulsham, in Easter Vestry assembled, strongly protest against the proposal to dismember the Church by cutting off from the Province of Canterbury the four Welsh Dioceses and to despoil it by confiscating to secular uses endowments consecrated to the service of God – and that this Vestry urges on all Christian people irrespective of political party to unite in uncompromising resistance to any bill embodying such proposals"*.

The vicar then dealt with the charity accounts, including the newly set up 'Church Hall account' for which £87 had already been collected. The most pressing matter, and one which could impact heavily on the parish, concerned St John's schools. The parish had been pressed by the authorities (in this case, the Board of Education) to do certain things towards improving the standard of the school building and facilities. William Pressey pointed out, that as far as St John's was concerned, the Board had asked for some things to be done which seemed to him to be perfectly reasonable and correct; all the cloakrooms were inadequate and needed considerable improvement to their sanitary arrangements, and he felt that it was not unreasonable to enlarge some of the windows. However, he felt their suggestions regarding the playground to be very unreasonable indeed, and in truth they could not see their way to enlarging the playground without the greatest difficulty and expense, if at all. If the Board did not insist on the playground being enlarged, they would be ready to try and achieve the remaining items. Mr Pertwee had estimated the cost as between £150 and £180. He suggested that they set up a three-thousand shilling fund to try and meet the lower figure. Mr Franklin pointed out that if they acceded to this request from the Board, they might find the Board imposing further demands on them in a year or two's time. He also felt that to do this work now meant that fundraising for the new church hall would have to be put on hold. In the end it was decided that the vicar would call a public meeting to seek out the wishes of the parish, but on balance he felt that it would be bad policy to part with a school they already possessed. In the end, at the vicar's suggestion, it was agreed that a public meeting would be held to discuss how best to respond to the Board's suggestions. The vicar brought the meeting to a close, again offering Mr Franklin heartfelt thanks for all his contributions over the previous six years.

'Offley suddenly burst into flames'

Services at St John's in 1912 were not without their more dramatic moments. It was reported in September that: *"an extraordinary incident occurred at St John's church, on Sunday afternoon, 22 September, while a christening service was being conducted by the Rev E.A. Hort. A Mr Offley, of Lower Anchor Street, was attending the church with his little son Lesley Walter, for the purposes of Baptism, when to great amazement and alarm of all present, Offley suddenly burst into flames. Fortunately, these were quickly extinguished and Mr Offley was not injured, except a little about the hands, but his waistcoat and trousers were considerably damaged. It appears that a box of safety matches in his pocket was ignited by the friction of some sulphur of potash* (sic) *tabloids which he carried as a remedy for a sore throat. Mr Offley suffered from shock somewhat at the time.*[45]

Money continued to be given towards the cost of the modification of the schools. A steady trickle of donations was added to the fund throughout the rest of the year, augmented from time to time by gifts such as those of £10 each from Miss Lister and Mr Martin. By the beginning of October the total in the fund was more than £153, although the overall cost was now estimated at £200.[46] Just before Christmas Alderman Cramphorn died, and at St John's, on Christmas day, William Pressey paid fulsome tribute to him, saying that: *"only yesterday we laid to rest one who for some years past had been Mayor of this Borough and one who occupied that position with credit to himself. One who was always ready to*

241

undertake what he felt to be for the good of the community, and who in many ways was in active and whole-hearted sympathy with the poor".[47]

'Altar lights were legal, but were they expedient?'

The new year kicked off with the usual round of thank-you dinners at the vicarage, the choir being entertained on the first Monday (6 January) to a meal, followed by a whist drive.[48] At the vestry meeting on 28 March 1913 the vicar bit the bullet and gently informed those present that: *"some members of the congregation"* were desirous of placing a memorial in the church, and they would like that memorial to be in the form of altar lights. The proposition had been made to the vicar himself the previous year (1912) but he felt it was not a matter that the clergy could accept on their own responsibility, and he felt that the best course of action was to put it before the vestry meeting and seek the views of all the parishioners. It was a brave move on William Pressey's part, because although the climate was very different from ten years previously, the subject of altar lights was one of the main issues that had caused Robert Saulez to resign from the parish. William Pressey pointed out that altar lights were already in use at Chelmsford, Springfield, Boreham and even Chelmsford Prison. On the motion of Mr Wallis, seconded by Mr Bickmore, it was resolved that, subject to the wishes of the congregation, a faculty be applied for in order to accept the gift of parishioners of two altar lights. There were two dissentients. One of them, Mr W. Howes, said: *"altar lights might be legal, but were they expedient?"* He felt that the aim of the congregation should be to encourage others to come to church, but he was anxious in case anyone stayed away because of altar lights. The other, Mr Mott, was more gloomy. He was sure, he said, that the question was going to cause trouble, even though he agreed that if there was a clear majority in favour, then that was the end of the matter.[49]

The rest of the meeting, covering the general business of St John's, proceeded in a brisk and orderly fashion. All the accounts showed healthy credit balances, and the 1911–12 surplus of one penny had been turned into a better figure of almost £2. The vicar confirmed that the Church Hall fund now stood at £105, and as they had a site (presumably the present site of the church hall). All the parish had to do was collect funds for the erection of the building.

'Things are getting on up Moulsham Way!'

The fact that the vicar of St John's had felt that the congregation should decide on the question of altar lights was not lost on the editorial team of the *Essex Newsman*. The comment written under the pseudonym *'Reflexions by Reflex'* made a cheeky observation on the Moulsham vestry meeting. The writer said that: *"How some people do seek trouble, to be sure! I see that there is a proposal to have altar lights at St John's, Moulsham. At the Easter Vestry, on the question being introduced, two good men and true raised objections. I congratulate the good padre, the Rev W.J. Pressey, on the democratic attitude adopted by him. In the end, he said, let the congregation decide. That's the way. Things are getting on up Moulsham Way!"*[51] The Band of Hope continued to go from strength to strength. On Wednesday, 4 June a sale of work was held in the vicarage, together with a concert of songs and recitations. The whole event was most successful and £6 was raised for the Band of Hope funds.[52] The other major fundraising events of the year were also successful, particularly the winter sale held in the Infants' schoolroom, on Thursday, 4 December, when no less than £35 was raised for the all-important Clergy Fund.[53]

Those who worked hard for St John's were sometimes surprised by a generous presentation from the congregation to express their appreciation of all that the individual had done. Mrs J. Barker, the wife of the vicar's warden, was astonished to receive a gold watch brooch and a plain gold brooch to commemorate the many years of service that she had given as honorary secretary of the St John's working party. The whole presentation had been devised by her good friend, Mr Wykeham Chancellor, who had managed to keep everything well under wraps until the day of the actual presentation, 25 November – no mean achievement in those days.[54]

'It is difficult to find words adequately to thank them for their kindness'

And so to 1914, a year which, although the storm clouds were starting to gather over Europe, began with such promise for Chelmsford and Essex, with the gazetting of the Order in Council creating the new diocese on 23 January.[55] St Mary's, in Chelmsford, was to be the new cathedral and the patronage of St John's would now be the responsibility of the bishop. On 27 January, the vicar of St James the Less, Bethnal Green, John Edwin Watts-Ditchfield, received a letter from the Prime Minister, Herbert Asquith, offering him the newly-established bishopric. He was consecrated in St Paul's on 24 February at ten o'clock by Archbishop Davison. At eleven o'clock on the same morning, a service of Holy Communion was held in St Mary's, at which William Pressey was the preacher.[56]

The beginning of 1914 also saw an important change in St John's. At the end of 1913, on 29 December, the annual supper given to the adult members of St John's choir took place in the vicarage, and when Mr Ripper proposed the health of the curate, Edward Hort, he congratulated him on his new appointment as vicar of Chadwell Heath, near Romford, whilst at the same time voicing the regret of the whole congregation of St John's that they would be losing such a devoted priest.[57] Edward Hort was instituted into his new incumbency on Tuesday 6 January, being formally welcomed by his new parishioners on Saturday 17 January.[58] On the following Wednesday he took his final farewell of Moulsham. The Girls' school was packed to overflowing and the Rev Hort was presented, on behalf of the parishioners, with a cheque for fifty guineas and an album containing the names and addresses of no less than 470 subscribers. William Pressey paid Edward Hort a fulsome tribute, emphasising how the curate had left his mark on

St John's with the re-organisation of the Sunday School, his transformation of the Band of Hope, his devoted work with the CETS (the Chelmsford and Essex Temperance Society) as well as by preaching and by example. He then handed the departing curate the cheque, the list of subscribers, and the following address: *"To the Reverend Edward Arthur Hort – we, whose names are hereto subscribed, ask your acceptance of this purse of gold, as a slight token of our sincere appreciation of you in your role of assistant priest of St John's, Moulsham, over the last seven years. We assure you of our heartfelt wishes that every blessing and success may attend you in the important sphere of work which you have been called to undertake as Vicar of Chadwell Heath"*. Edward Hort was deeply moved. It was, he said: *"difficult to find words adequately to thank them for their kindness. The book he would value and keep although he did not need anything to remind him of the time he had spent at Moulsham – it had been a very happy time. He did not take any credit for the work that had been done amongst the children because he felt that it had been done by his helpers quite as much as by himself, and he took this opportunity for publicly thanking them for all the assistance they had rendered him"*. He sat down to prolonged applause.

His curacy of almost seven years had been second only in length to that of George Collier, and almost equal in terms of his impact on the parish. It was clear that he would not be easy to replace.[59] The new curate, though, was already at the meeting. Alfred Braund, who had previously been working in the diocese of Exeter, had been appointed to St John's at the beginning of January and had taken his first services on the Sunday prior to Edward Hort's departure.[58] He was not to settle comfortably in the parish. For St John's, January was to be a very busy month. The infants of the Sunday school had been given their usual treat on 7 January, and on 15 January Mr A.S. Lugg, who for many years had toiled away as CEMS secretary, was presented with a silver inkstand and a handsome clock on the occasion of his forthcoming marriage to Miss Florence Cable.[60]

'I want the Diocese to be won for Christ'

With Chelmsford now the diocesan centre for Essex and legislation having changed, there was a financial impact to be considered for St John's. A meeting was held in the schoolroom on Wednesday, 4 February to consider the parish's contribution to the Diocesan Finance scheme. Bishops, their cathedrals and chapters did not come cheap. William Pressey said that the amount to be provided by the parish of Moulsham would be of the order of £50 a year, a significant extra burden on the parishioners who were already having to raise money to provide a curate. After much discussion it was agreed that two hundred people should be approached to see if they could give one shilling a quarter. The inevitable committee was put together to oversee the whole proceedings.[61] This, though, was a time to rejoice. On St George's day. 23 April, Chelmsford was *en fête* as the new bishop was enthroned in his cathedral and the 450 or so of his clergy assembled to hear him tell them: *"I want the diocese to be won for Christ"*.[62] William Pressey and Alfred Braund must have reacted with enthusiasm to his words.

A tragic death occurred at Frinton in late May. The Rev Louis Butler, the vicar of St James in Clacton, a new parish which he was trying to build up from nothing, died, probably from an accidental overdose of sleeping pills, although he had been chronically ill for several months. He died in most pathetic circumstances. Having walked from Clacton to Frinton-on-Sea, he was found dying, at lunchtime, on a seat overlooking the beach. He had left a very sad note, saying: *"I fear that I am never likely to be well again – I cannot allow myself to become a burden to others, especially my darling wife and children"*. He was only forty. Once again an Essex clergyman had worked himself to death. He had previously been a curate at St Mary's in Chelmsford and had often helped out at St John's. William Pressey paid him a very moving tribute from the pulpit at St John's on the following Sunday.[63]

Alfred Braund's tenure of the curate's position at St John's was to be brief. In June the *Essex Newsman* reported that: *"the Rev A.A.*

Braund, the curate of St John's, left on Wednesday, 24 June for fresh fields of labour near Southampton". There was no hint of why, after only six months, he had departed, and there was no report of any presentation to mark that departure. He was succeeded almost immediately by a local priest, Leonard Wright, who had been curate of Bocking for the previous two years, and whose parents lived at Great Leighs.[64] The worsening situation in Europe did not put off the adult members of the choir from having their usual summer jolly, which on this occasion comprised another trip to Cambridge, but this time by National autos (rather than by Clarkson steam bus) although they did stop again in Foxearth for lunch. On this outing, though, there were no fires to distract them.[65]

On 4 August war was declared. There was a rapid response from the churches in Chelmsford. On Saturday 8 August a United service of all the local churches was held in the High Street, in front of the Shire Hall. The service was directed by Canon Lake, the Rev William Pressey and the Rev T.M. Mundle. The Mayor and corporation were present, and the cathedral organist, Mr F.R. Frye, was responsible for the music.[66] This was followed by a service of supplication in the cathedral on 19 August at eight in the evening, when Rev Pressey himself was the preacher.[67] With the country now on a war footing, temperance seemed to be even more on people's minds as the year drew to a close. In October, William Pressey presided at a Chelmsford and Essex Temperance Society meeting where there was a long and serious debate about temperance meetings for the troops, although those present were unable to reach a consensus as to how any such meetings could be organised.[68] Even the war, though, would not be allowed to interfere with a St John's Sale of Work. The winter event, on 2 December, went ahead as usual. On this occasion the takings were well down and only £17 was raised for the Clergy Fund.

'Only doctor's orders would have kept him at home'

By early 1915 the toll of almost ten years at Moulsham was beginning to tell on William Pressey. With all the movements of troops from the battlefields of the Great War to England (and *vice versa*) new and vigorous strains of influenza were beginning to make their mark on the population at home, and William Pressey was taken very ill early in the year. By the end of February it was reported that his convalescence at St Leonards-on-Sea had been highly beneficial and that he had returned to Moulsham *"much improved in health"*.[70] The respite was only temporary, and by 6 March he had suffered a relapse.[71] By April he had left again to try and recover his health at the seaside.[72] These bouts of illness meant that he, for the first time in his life as a priest, missed an annual vestry meeting, which on this occasion had to be chaired by Mr Barker. The vicar sent a long letter to the meeting, regretting his enforced absence, saying that: *"only doctor's orders would have kept him at home"*. He re-nominated Mr Barker as his warden and Mr Ripper was re-elected parish warden. Mr Ripper presented the accounts, which showed greatly improved offertories (probably because of the number of troops who attended services in St John's during this period). These offertories had led to: *"substantial credit balances on all funds, and all payments had been discharged"*. In fact, the various balances stood at an impressive £216, and the Church Hall fund was in credit to the tune of almost £513. The ruridecanal representatives were elected *en bloc*, but this was a pointless exercise, as all meetings were held during the daytime and nobody from St John's had been able to attend any of them in the last year. Mr Barker concluded the meeting by proposing that a letter be sent to the vicar regretting his absence, and this was carried unanimously.[73]

St John's clearly looked after those troops billeted in Chelmsford (and particularly those in locations like the schoolrooms and the church rooms) and it must have been gratifying for the church to receive, as a mark of appreciation of the time spent in the parish, from the Royal Berkshire regiment (which by May 1915 was at the front) some: *"beautiful glass and silver cruets"* which bore the inscription: *"St John's, Moulsham. Presented by the 4th Royal Berks regiment, Easter 1915"*.[74] Later in the month Mr Franklin finally severed his long and devoted association with the parish, moving to Gidea Park to be near his family.[75] By August, food shortages were beginning to make themselves felt, and at a meeting of the Chelmsford and District Vegetable Products Committee (the *"Fruit for the Fleet"* group) William Pressey announced that the site of the future church hall had been planted with cabbage plants, donated by a Mr Fulcher.[76]

'Skulking at home in their armchairs or in the sunshine'

By the spring of the following year, disillusionment with the conduct and the aims of the war ('the war will be over in a few months, or at least by Christmas 1914') was starting to set in amongst some individuals in Chelmsford. In the first few months of 1916 the number of reports of tribunals (for those who wished to be exempt from military service) in the local press escalated significantly. Although most were individuals refused exemption, the number of those who thought that they might be able to avoid fighting for their country was worrying some people deeply. Prominent among those concerned with this trend was Leonard Wright, the curate of St John's. On 19 March 1916 he preached a sermon at the evening service, which the *Essex County Chronicle* felt was worth quoting almost in its entirety (it chimed with many of the paper's editorial views). It is interesting because it shows the attitude of much of the established church to the war (and to the concept of war) and the convoluted reasoning that was often used to justify that position. Under the headings: *'Clergyman's condemnation of certain Objectors to Military Service'* and *'Stirring Sermon at Chelmsford'* the transcript of Leonard Wright's sermon made his own position abundantly clear. Using the text: *'And a mixed multitude went up with them'* he started by suggesting that: *"Bad tendencies remain quite dormant if no spark is applied to them, but if a spark was applied, mischief immediately followed"*. He alluded to the mixed multitude of the Israelites, good and bad together, and the influence of the bad on the good to the eventual detriment of all. He then quickly moved on to relate that situation to the society in which they all lived. He went on: *"As we look around and read the signs of the times, we cannot fail to see a mixed multitude today in our midst – a very mixed multitude who are unwilling to assist their country in its present great need. There are still those – I am certain of it – who only think of themselves, and to whom the nation's need and the nation's peril mean nothing".* He went on to describe such people as: *"skulking at home in their armchairs, or in the sunshine, content, while their brothers are defending them and their homes with their lifeblood".* All good, patriotic stuff, but when he tried to demonstrate, on biblical grounds, that England's action was right in God's eyes, his reasoning and his logic were less coherent. He pointed out that: *"When a man says that he would not defend his mother because it would mean not killing a German, he has broken God's command – Honour thy father and mother and that is how he would honour his mother – the mother that brought him into the world, fed him, nursed him, and who would willingly lay down her life for him".* The *Essex County Chronicle* loved it[77] and just two weeks later the *Essex Newsman* praised it and reported very favourably the interest it had generated in the county town.[78]

After all of that, the vestry meeting, held late in the year on 28 April, was quiet and relatively uneventful. Mr Ripper, as parish warden, presented the accounts. The past year had begun with a balance in hand of just over £25 and ended with a positive balance of just under £19. He was able to report that the Church Hall fund stood at £471, and £400 of this had now been invested in Exchequer Bonds. Mr Wallis was able to confirm that £27 had been contributed to the Diocesan Fund, although William Pressey noted that this compared poorly with St John's true quota, which was £50. The accounts were speedily adopted. Mr Barker and Mr Ripper were confirmed in their existing posts, and the meeting passed a warm vote of thanks to Mr Spurgeon, thanking him for his services in auditing the accounts and expressing the fervent hope of all those present that he would speedily be restored to health.[79]

'One of the most valuable of churchworkers'

Sadly, the sentiments expressed in the final resolution of the April vestry meeting were not to be realised. George Spurgeon, who had been ill for some considerable time (and whose illness had occasioned his retirement from the bank where he worked) died on Saturday, 12 August, at his home (Granville House) in Mildmay Road. In addition to his auditing of St John's church accounts, which he had carried out for a number of years, he had been Honorary Secretary of the Free Will Offering scheme and had done much to encourage its use since its introduction in Moulsham. At his funeral service, William Pressey, who appeared much moved by his death, described him as: *"one of the most valuable of churchworkers"*.[80]

In September of 1916 Rev Leonard Wright left St John's to take charge of the mission church of St Mark's in Southend. He had served St John's with great devotion and diligence during his two years in the parish, ably deputising for William Pressey on many occasions. One of his last responsibilities had been when he took 115 children from the Sunday school on an outing to Southend, coincidentally meeting up with Rev E.A. Hort, a former curate of St John's, the pair of them assisting with the school tea in the Victoria restaurant.[81] Leonard Wright was replaced by Rev John Alexander Livingstone, who took up his duties at the beginning of October 1916.

January 1917 saw a warm and generous gesture of appreciation to Mrs Pressey (who so often lived in her husband's shadow) from the Ladies' working party. They gave her a beautiful Russian leather handbag as a heartfelt token of appreciation for all she had done for them.[82] The annual vestry meeting was held on Friday 13 April. A small credit balance was reported for the previous year of £3. The two wardens were again re-elected. Mr J. Foster was publicly thanked for the assistance he had given as organist during Mr Parker's illness (from which he had now recovered) and Ambrose Darby's generosity in providing cassocks and surplices for the choir was also gratefully acknowledged. Mr Mason, who had taken over from Mr Spurgeon on the latter's death as auditor, was commended for his efforts, and after a statement by Mr C.H. Wallis, on the Diocesan Finance account, the meeting concluded with an enthusiastic vote of thanks to the chairman.[83]

On 10 August the *Essex County Chronicle* announced that Captain Leonard Gray of the Essex Regiment, a well-known solicitor practising in Chelmsford, had died of enteric fever (dysentery) in Egypt on 31 July, aged 45. He was not married. He was the son of Ellen Mary Gray of Laurel Grove, Chelmsford and the late Charles Harrison Gray (of the brewing family). Leonard Gray was associated with the cathedral and its Sunday school, but also with St John's, his parish church.[84] He left £1,000 to: *"the vicar of St John's, to dispose of as he likes"*. There is no memorial in the church to commemorate Leonard Gray's death or his generosity.[85]

'The burden on William Pressey increased markedly'

The following year, 1918, was to prove William Pressey's final year in Moulsham, and it started on a sombre note. George Osborn, after many years' service as sexton (until the effective closing of the churchyard) died after a stroke at his home, Woodbury Villas, Elm Road at the age of eighty. His funeral took place at the Writtle Road cemetery on 23 January, with William Pressey and Canon Lake officiating.[86]

William Pressey presided at what would turn out to be his final St John's vestry meeting on Friday, 7 April. Mr Ripper presented the churchwardens' account. The balance for the previous year had risen slightly, now standing at over £4. The accounts presented by Mr Pressey were all in credit, and included the Assistant Clergy fund, which stood at just under £114, the sick and needy fund which had a credit balance of more than £51, and the Church Hall fund which recorded a balance of £58 as well as £450 invested in War Bonds. The parish had not been able to meet its full commitment to the Diocesan Finance Board, contributing only £3 when their allocation had been £50, and the meeting expressed strong feelings that more should be done to raise this sum. Mr Barker was re-appointed vicar's warden and Mr Ripper was unanimously elected as people's warden. After the meeting had expressed its deep sympathy for the Bishop of Barking, whose wife had recently died, the proceedings closed with a vote of thanks to the chairman.[87] Shortly after this meeting, Mr Barker was relieved to receive news that his only son, second-lieutenant Barker of the Royal Fusiliers, who had been reported missing, believed killed, was in fact in a Surrey hospital, recovering from severe gunshot wounds.[88]

As the year, and the war, ground on, the burden on William Pressey increased markedly. With no curate, and the need to help at Widford (whose vicar was serving as a volunteer in the forces) services had to be reduced at St John's until the Rev C. Cornish was made available by the Norwich diocese to assist William Pressey for three months (he does not appear to have ever been formally licensed as a curate at St John's).[89] He was reported as assisting William Pressey at a well-attended Harvest festival service at Widford on 4 October.[90] His arrival in the parish meant that things started to move for William Pressey, and the *Essex Newsman* was able to announce, on 26 October, that: *"The Rev W.J. Pressey, vicar of St John's, Moulsham since 1906, has been offered by Mr Frank Grubbe, and has accepted, the vicariate of Margaretting, vacant by the appointment of the Rev W.S. Smith to be vicar of Billericay. The appointment of a new vicar of St John's rests with Canon Lake, the Rector of Chelmsford"*.[91] In fact, there was to be little delay in the making of this announcement, as the *Essex County Chronicle* was able to report on 22 November that: *"The Rev R.F. Burnett, the Rector of Runwell, has, subject to the Bishop's permission, accepted the living of Moulsham, Chelmsford, and will begin his duties at the start of February"*. The delay was due to Robert Burnett's service as a temporary chaplain to the forces in France.[92]

There still seemed no end in sight to the war, and St John's held its usual All Saints' memorial service for all those fallen in battle on the evening of Friday 1 November, with the Rev Cornish conducting the proceedings and William Pressey giving the address.[93] However, relief was at hand. The first public notice of the cessation of hostilities was posted in the window of the *Essex*

County Chronicle offices at 10.30 on the morning of 11 November. The newspaper stated that: *"the information had been in possession of the office but no publication was made until the Premier's announcement afforded confirmation at 10.20"*. Soldiers and civilians shook each other by the hands, and everyone, it was reported: *"wanted to laugh, cheer and shed a tear at the same time"*.[94] The cathedral bells rang at regular times throughout the day and Canon Lake conducted a thanksgiving service in the building in the evening, with many people having to stand outside. There seems to have been no corresponding service at St John's to celebrate the Armistice.

'He never had one opinion for the rich and another for the poor'

When William Pressey came to Moulsham in 1906, he brought with him a curate, Edward Hort, from a neighbouring parish, who had clearly caught his eye. It was to prove a wise and far-sighted choice. Edward Hort stayed at St John's for over seven years, and was loved and trusted enough to be able to take over the effective running of the parish when William Pressey was away on holiday or recuperating on the south coast.

Edward Arthur Hort was born in Reigate in 1870. He obtained his AKC (first class) from King's College, London in 1896 and was ordained deacon the same year on 4 October by the Bishop of London in St Paul's Cathedral, being licensed to St John's, Limehouse, at the same time.[95] He was ordained priest by the same bishop on 19 December 1897.[96] In 1905 he moved to a curacy at Willingale Doe with Shellow Bowells and Berners Roding (the parishes to which Robert Saulez moved when he left Moulsham).[97] It was announced in 1906 that Edward Hort would be coming to St John's, Moulsham, where he was licensed on 18 August.[98] He took part (as listed earlier) in a wide range of activities in the parish and there was considerable disappointment when his departure was announced. Mr Franklin, in paying his own personal tribute to Mr Hort, stressed that one of the best features of his work had been the firm manner in which he held to his opinions. He never had one opinion for the rich and another for the poor. He left St John's for Chadwell Heath[99] and was formally welcomed by his new parishioners in January 1914.[100,101] After Chadwell Heath he moved to St Paul's, Goodmayes, in 1917. He never married and died in Hitchin, in 1942, aged 73.

Alfred Augustine Braund was born in Woolwich in 1873, the fourth son and youngest child of Marwood Braund (a solicitor) and his wife Eliza. He took his AKC in 1900 and was ordained deacon by the Bishop of St Albans in St Mary's, Chelmsford, on Sunday, 30 September the same year, being licensed at that service to a curacy in East Ham.[102] He was ordained priest in September 1901 at the parish church in Saffron Walden.[103] After serving in East Ham, he moved to Stockland with Dalwood in Devon in 1903 (his father's family came from Exeter) followed by a curacy at Heavitree from 1908 to 1913.[104] His last position before St John's was Upton. In June 1914 the *Essex Newsman* was able to report that: *"The Rev A.A. Braund, AKC, who was ordained in the St Albans Diocese some time ago, and has been working since in the diocese of Exeter, has been appointed to succeed the Rev E.A. Hort, and will take up his duties on 18 January 1914"*.[105] He came to St John's as a replacement for Edward Hort, but obviously did not settle as it was announced just six months later that: *"The Rev Braund, the curate of St John's, Moulsham left the parish on 24 June 1914 for fresh fields of labour in Southampton"*.[106] His curacy had been much shorter than expected. Perhaps he found the task not to his liking, or perhaps William Pressey thought he was not up to the demands of the job. After further curacies, Alfred Braund ended up in Andover, where he died, aged only fifty-seven, in 1930.

'He is well-known for his fine tenor voice'

Alfred Braund was followed as curate by a young man from Great Leighs, Leonard Wilcher Wright, whose talents and attitude chimed more closely with those of William Pressey. Leonard

Wright was born in 1883, the seventh and last child of Walter Wright, a well-known local farmer, and Lavinia Wilcher. Leonard took his AKC in 1912 and was ordained deacon the same year at the Advent service at St John's, Leytonstone, by the Bishop of St Albans, being licensed to Bocking (under Dean Brownrigg) at the same time.[107] He was ordained priest at the St Thomas' day ordination on 22 December the following year, in the cathedral at St Albans.[108] He had married Miss Woodleigh Emma Marshall (she was twenty-three years older than him) at Dunmow parish church on 17 July 1907 (in other words, he was a married student when he attended King's College). The *Essex Newsman* reported that: *"In the musical profession the bridegroom is especially well-known for his fine tenor voice, and he has also been organist at Dunmow parish church for the past two years."*[109] It was announced in May 1914 in the local press that Leonard Wright had been offered the curacy of St John's, Moulsham, and that he had accepted, and hoped to commence his duties there in the middle of June that year.[110]

It must have been a very congenial appointment for William Pressey, whose musical talents and inclinations were widely known and appreciated. Leonard Wright stayed at St John's for more than two years, and proved himself a great supporter of the war effort, working with young people (setting up a rifle club) and giving the striking sermon (directed at those who sought to avoid having to fight) which was mentioned earlier in this chapter. He preached his last sermon as curate of Moulsham on Sunday 24 September 1916, and that very same evening he was presented with a cheque for £23 and the fervent good wishes of the congregation. He left to take charge of the mission church of St Mark's in Southend. His stay there was to be relatively brief, as at the beginning of 1918 he was in France, serving as temporary chaplain to the forces. He maintained his close connections with the forces throughout much of the remainder of his life, being commissioned as a Chaplain (fourth class) in 1918. After a curacy at Stansted Mountfitchet (from 1920–21) he was appointed rector at Wyddial in Hertfordshire in 1921, of Sharnbrook in Bedfordshire in 1927 and finally Irthlingborough in Northamptonshire in 1932. The parishioners of Sharnbrook were so grateful for his work among them that they bought him a car as his leaving present. He died, after a short illness at the rectory in Irthlingborough on 1 May 1941, leaving a widow, but no family.[111]

With so many young priests away in France serving with the forces, William Pressey must have wondered if it would even be possible to get anyone at all to assist him in the parish. However, he was able to attract John Alexander Livingstone to St John's for a short period of four months in 1916–17. John Livingstone was born in Westminster in 1881 and attended Queen's College, Birmingham where he graduated in 1905. He was ordained deacon in December 1905, being licensed at the same time to St Giles', Colchester.[112] He was ordained priest in 1906 in West Ham parish church. He stayed at St Giles' until 1908, moving to Edmonton that year and then to Hillingdon in 1912. He came to St John's in September 1916, shortly after the departure of Leonard Wright, and although by the time of his arrival in the parish he was a relatively experienced priest, he seems not to have settled in Moulsham and by February 1917 it was announced that he had left to work with the Church Army in France.[113] He worked with the Church Army on the continent until 1919 when he returned to England to take up the post of chaplain with the Selly Oak Infirmary, where he stayed until 1924, becoming vicar of St Matthew's, Smethwick.[114] He remained in this post until he died in early 1939.

The late war period (particularly from the spring of 1918) was a time when the position of curate was becoming very difficult to fill in many parish churches, and as stated, St John's was no exception. The struggle to maintain some semblance of normality must have told on William Pressey, and a photograph taken towards the end of his incumbency (*Figure 21*) shows an intelligent, motivated man, perhaps showing the strain of trying to run a difficult parish almost single-handedly for the period of his last few years in charge.

'He had never realised what tremendous help was going to come from the parishioners'

William Pressey concluded his ministry as vicar of St John's, Moulsham on Sunday, 8 December 1918. His last sermon, preached on that Sunday evening, was based on the text: *'Building for God'* and he pointed out that much had been done to improve the physical building that was St John's Church, but far more had been done to build up each individual in the church so that they might take their part in the spiritual fabric of God's kingdom. On the following Monday, in the Girls' school, with Mr Ripper in the chair, a cheque for £100 was presented to Mr Pressey, together with the inevitable album containing the names of all those who had contributed to the magnificent gift. There were many tributes from prominent local worthies, including Alderman George Taylor and Canon Lake, and it was telling that Mr F.A. Wells, the most prominent local nonconformist, was also keen to add his tribute to Mr Pressey's work in Moulsham.

William Pressey, in reply, said that this was the hardest task he had had to do since he had come to Moulsham, as many things had been said that were far too kind. He had made himself a promise, twelve years earlier, that he would do all that he could for the parish, but he had never realised what tremendous help was going to come from the parishioners themselves. He felt, though, that the parish was in good hands, and that his successor, he was sure, had a very happy time in store if they worked with him as happily as they had worked with him (Mr Pressey). He had been lucky, he said, in his choice of wardens – in Mr Barker and Mr Ripper he had two of the finest wardens any parish could ever have had. In a voice almost breaking with emotion he thanked them for all their kindnesses to him and his wife. Mr Pressey also received from Mr Ripper (on behalf of the children of the schools) a cycling suit and a bag. From the Mothers' Union, Mrs Pressey received an electric lamp and bottle of scent, together with a scent spray from the Mothers' meeting.

William Pressey was inducted into his new living in Margaretting on Wednesday, 11 December by the Bishop of Barking, the

Figure 21 – William James Pressey, Incumbent of
St John's, Moulsham, 1906–18

institution being performed by the Bishop of Chelmsford. A large
number of parishioners from St John's was present.[116] William
Pressey stayed at Margaretting as vicar until he finally retired in
1928, aged seventy. Margaretting had been a much less demanding
post, and he was not only clearly happy there, having time to
devote to his antiquarian interests, but he also much endeared
himself to his parishioners. He and his wife retired to Worthing (to
be near her family) where they celebrated their golden wedding
on 17 April 1940.[117] Another war came as a hammer-blow to
William Pressey – the Great War had convinced him that mankind
should never have to endure such a conflict again – and he died on
24 August at his home, 'The Croft', Panters Lane, Worthing at the
age of eighty-five. He left his widow, Grace, and two daughters,

Nellie and Margaret.[118] Mrs Pressey did not long survive him, dying in their family home on 3 February 1945. They were both buried in the little churchyard as West Tarring, near Worthing.[119] In his will, for which probate was granted on 5 November 1943, William Pressey left £4,195, but this included no bequests to St John's[120].

The next incumbent of St John's would certainly have strong and sure foundations upon which to build.

8. ROBERT FREDERICK BURNETT

(1919–30)

"He had done his very best in trying to put the affairs of the parish on a satisfactory basis, and that he had succeeded in so many ways must have meant a great deal of extra work for both him and his wife – and they had done it with a kindliness and enthusiasm that had earned the deepest respect and thanks of everyone ... ... and they were losing a real friend who had always been ready to promote any good thing in the parish, and they would particularly remember him for all he had done towards getting that Parochial Hall, and for improving the church".[1]

The above were just some of the fulsome comments made by the parishioners of Moulsham when Robert Burnett finally left St John's after nearly twelve years of demanding toil in the parish. He had, indeed, put the affairs of the parish on a very sound and satisfactory footing, providing probably as his most lasting memorial the commodious (and much needed) Parochial Hall, to replace the iron building that George Godson had caused to be erected at the back of Frederick Veley's plot in George Street. Robert Burnett was the first vicar of St John's to have served in a theatre of conflict, and his harsh experiences there were to stand him in good stead during the immediate post-war period and the difficult days of the 1920s.

'He expressed the hope that if they criticised him, they would do so to his face'

Robert Frederick Burnett was the son of Richard Alfred Burnett, the rector of the little church of Graigue with St Mullin in Kilkenny, Ireland, and a minor canon of the diocese of Leigh, and his wife. He was born at Kyle Cross, just over the border in

Wexford, in 1882. He followed in his father's footsteps and went up to Trinity College, Dublin in 1900, taking his BA in 1903, his Divinity Testimonium in 1904 and receiving his MA in 1907.[2] He was ordained deacon by the Bishop of Peterborough in the cathedral on Sunday 25 September 1904 and priest the following September, again in the cathedral.[3] At the same ceremony at which he was ordained deacon, Robert Burnett was licensed to a curacy at All Saints', Peterborough where he stayed until 31 December 1906, when he left for a curacy at St Mary's, Brighton. All Saints' was sorry to see him go – he was presented with a marble clock, together with a cheque, along with all the good wishes of his parishioners.[4] On Tuesday, 9 April 1907, back at All Saints', Robert Burnett married Sarah Barton, the only daughter of the manager of the local gas works, who lived in Park Road, Peterborough. Robert Burnett stayed as curate at St Mary's, Brighton for a year, then moved to the little parishes of Buckworth and Woolley near Huntingdon as rector. He then came to Essex in 1912 as rector of Runwell, taking up an additional post in 1918 as temporary chaplain to the forces (TCF), staying in France until February 1919. He was instituted to St John the Evangelist as vicar on the evening of Wednesday, 26 February 1919 by the Bishop of Chelmsford, the induction being performed by the Rural Dean, Rev F.B. Paynter. He was presented by the patron, Canon Lake. St John's regular standby, Rev W. Davis, who had been acting as unofficial curate-in-charge, also took a significant part in the service. The bishop, in his address, stressed the duty of the parishioners to their parish priest as well as the vicar's responsibility towards his flock. After the service in the church, many of the congregation met in the Infants' School to welcome their new vicar. Robert Burnett, in addressing those present, thanked them for their welcome, and expressed the hope, that, if they criticised him, they would do it to his face and not behind his back.[5]

'Choir boys are generally choir boys – but ours are a real good lot'

Robert Burnett had only a brief few weeks to settle into his new vicarage before his first vestry meeting was upon him, on

Friday, 25 April 1919. Mr Ripper submitted the churchwardens' accounts, showing a much improved balance in hand of £35 compared with sum of just over £4 in hand at the end of the previous year. The various other accounts reported good balances – Free Will Offering, £63 (as against £49); the Assistant Clergy fund, £99 as against £113; the Sick and Needy, £65 compared with £52, being the more important. The accounts were speedily adopted, and Mr Barker and Mr Ripper confirmed as wardens. The vicar then proposed that the church workers met three times a year (January, July and October) and this was agreed. Robert Burnett, concluding the proceedings, said he was thoroughly in love with the parish, and with the people, and was really enjoying himself. He had persuaded the churchwardens to take all the accounts off his hands, so as to leave him free to attend to the spiritual side of the parish.

He said that he would shortly confirm the arrival of two assistant curates, one of whom had just been demobilised after five months as a prisoner of war. They could, he thought, manage the two men on £440 a year, of which £340 would have to be raised by the parish. They could not, he suggested, get good men without paying for them. Ambrose Darby could not resist adding his penn'orth: *"And you don't get good money"*, he said, *"without getting good men"*. Chelmsford's leading auctioneer had had his (commercial) say. Robert Burnett ended by giving the choir some unexpected praise. *"Choir boys,"* he added, *"are generally choir boys – but ours are a real good lot and they do behave themselves extremely well"*. His remarks were greeted with widespread laughter.[6]

Later, in the following month, the vicar was able to announce that he had secured the services of his 'two good men'. The Revs E. Herbert and A.P. Daniels, both of whom had seen distinguished service in the Great War. Edward Herbert had been captured by the Germans in their major offensive of March 1918, being released just after the armistice in November 1918 and Alec Daniels had been awarded the MC for his bravery in Mesopotamia, Egypt and France. Mr Herbert, he stated, was already in the parish, and Mr Daniels would be arriving on 28 May.

'The memorial would be a parish one, not a denominational one'

Robert Burnett was also faced with two major issues in the parish which needed resolving. William Pressey had left for Margaretting just a few weeks after the declaration of the armistice, and the problem of commemorating those from the parish who had given their lives in the Great War had implicitly been left to his successor. Robert Burnett was no slouch, and as soon as he had placed the parish on a sound pastoral footing, he turned his mind to the question of a war memorial and to the other important issue, the erection of a parochial hall.

He tackled the first of these issues by calling a meeting, not just of members of St John's, but of all those who lived in the parish of Moulsham, on 21 July 1919, to decide how best to commemorate Moulsham's fallen, saying, in the advertisement detailing the meeting: *"All those who are willing to assist in furthering this object, or who are in sympathy with it, are invited to attend"*.[8] Large numbers of people were present at the subsequent meeting, and the vicar, who presided, said that no one disagreed that some kind of memorial should be erected. He outlined the suggestions that he had so far received, which included placing a tablet, which included the names of all those who had made the supreme sacrifice, in the church, as well as the installation of a new clock. This would replace the current clock and would: *"... go properly without being tied up with string and wire, as the present one was, and would strike the hours and half-hours"*. He felt that the striking would recall the sacrifice those men had made. He apologised to those present, saying he ought to have called the meeting earlier, but there had been much talk of a Borough memorial, and he had not wished that anything Moulsham planned to do should clash with the Borough's plans. However, as nothing seemed to be happening on the Borough front, he had spoken to the mayor, who had expressed the opinion that Moulsham were quite justified in carrying on, and any plans they (Moulsham) had would not interfere with what the Borough was doing. Mr Ripper then proposed formally that the memorial be a brass tablet, inscribed with the names of the Moulsham men who fell in the war, and that such a tablet be placed in the nave of the church, and in addition a new clock be installed in the tower.

The motion was seconded, but some of the ladies present at the meeting felt that whatever form the memorial took, it should be placed outside the church where it would be easier for the public to see it. It was agreed by everyone present that the memorial would contain the names of all fallen men, irrespective of creed, as the memorial should be a parish one and not a denominational one. An estimate had been received for a new turret striking clock, with one dial, and the price was £150 to £160. Including the tablet, they ought to be able to complete the project for £250. After some further discussion, it was agreed that a stone tablet (or tablets) should be placed on the front of the tower and it was thought that probably from sixty to seventy names would need to be included. A small committee, chaired by the vicar, was formed to oversee the whole process.[9]

Money was quietly raised, and, by the time of the next public meeting in March 1920, the target had almost been reached. The vicar reported that the total sum now stood at £215, and the purpose of the meeting was to take a final decision on the form of the memorial. There had been, he said, initial suggestions that the church should have a new clock in the tower, but very few people were now in favour of that, and the majority of subscribers had suggested a cross which they felt would better represent the sacrifice of those who fell in the war. Mr Wykeham Chancellor had proposed a plan for a cross, and it was suggested that this should be erected on the left-hand side of the footpath, between the Moulsham Street entrance gates and the church door. The cross would be supported by a slightly tapering shaft, standing on an octagonal plinth, the total height from the ground being seventeen feet. The monument would be of Portland stone. The vicar also pointed out that the railings on the left-hand side of the footpath would need to be re-arranged so that people would be able to walk around the cross. So far, eighty-five names of those from the parish who had fallen in the war had been passed to him. He emphasised that the subscription list was still open, although at the present moment almost all of the cost of the memorial had been met. It would be some time before it could be completed, as there were significant problems associated at the present time with finding transport for large loads of stone.[10]

'Through danger and hardship reached the highest standards of Christian virtue'

The memorial was finally made ready for its unveiling and dedication on Sunday, 7 November 1920, and was, indeed, in the shape and dimensions of Wykeham Chancellor's earlier proposed design. In addition to the names of eighty-seven men from the parish of Moulsham who fell in the Great War, the base of the cross bore the inscription: *"In memory of the men of Moulsham who fell in the Great War 1914–1918"*. As this was the first war memorial of a public nature to be erected in the Borough, the unveiling ceremony attracted a large number of people. The vicar conducted an impressive service in the church, wearing his uniform as chaplain to the forces. Canon Lake assisted and at the same time dedicated the Clergy stall, which had been given by the Darby family. It bore a brass plate with the inscription: *"Presented by Ambrose and Alice Darby in memory of their sons killed in the Great War – Stanley Edward, 1915; Harold Edgar, 1916. Also Henry Arthur, accidentally drowned, 4 August 1903"*.

The unveiling ceremony was carried out by Major-General Sir S.W. Hare, KCMG, CB, who was the commanding officer of the 54th East Anglian Division. He said that he looked upon the brave fellows who had given their lives as individuals who would continue to teach a great lesson of duty and self-sacrifice, and who through danger and hardship reached the highest standards of Christian virtue. Canon Lake added a few words on the present state of the country, and the service concluded with the 'Last Post' and 'Reveille'. After the service, Major-General Hare inspected those Old Soldiers from the Comrades' Club who were present.[11]

An editorial in the following day's *Essex Newsman* took the Borough Council to task for having done nothing so far (there had been a long and slightly futile debate about the best form a memorial might take) saying: *"Surely, if Moulsham can put up £200 or £300* (sic) *in honour of the brave boys who are no more, that other part of Chelmsford, which has so far put up no sign, ought to be able to put up an equal, if not larger, sum, than the Cinderella parish. Now – whose move?"*[12]

'Why, then, is this Hall being erected?'

Much, if not all, of the money for the parochial hall had been raised by the previous vicar, William Pressey, and as soon as practical after the ending of the Great War and the efforts devoted to the funding and erection of the Memorial, attention turned to the building of the hall. On Wednesday, 16 February 1921 the Bishop of Chelmsford (John Watts-Ditchfield) laid the foundation stone of what was seen as the first phase, a building comprising an entrance hall with a commodious classroom on either side. It was reported at the time, that the cost of this work (£1,000) had already been met by the parishioners, though this heartening news was tempered by the thought that the rest of the scheme would still need a further £2,000. A substantial proportion of this latter sum still needed to be raised. The foundation stone was laid on a site: *"which has been selected adjoining the vicarage gardens and which occupies a most convenient position"*. (The vicarage plot at that time extended to where Oaklands Crescent is today). The plans (produced by the architects Messrs C. and W.H. Pertwee (who were to waive their professional fees) included a main hall seventy-two feet by twenty-four and a half feet incorporating a stage and dressing rooms at the further (east) end. Mr F.J. French had been selected to undertake the construction work.

The stone-laying ceremony was preceded by a service in St John's church, conducted by the vicar. The Bishop of Chelmsford was attended by his chaplain, the Rev F.A. Redwood, and other clergy present included Canon Lake and the Rural Dean, Rev R.S.

Paynter. The curate of St John's, George Twist, was also in attendance together with the Mayor and Mayoress of Chelmsford, Alderman J.O. Thompson, OBE, JP, and Mrs Thompson. In the course of his short address, the Bishop congratulated the vicar, and all those associated with him, in undertaking such a project during the difficult period that the country was going through. People, he said, might ask why this hall was being raised. He believed that over the last sixty of seventy years a great change had come over the activities of the church. No longer was church activity confined to a service on a Sunday and perhaps one meeting during the week. Now it was almost impossible to lay down any limits for parochial activity. The church was entering into every phase in the life of men, women and children, and the parish church on its own was insufficient to meet these needs. A building such as the one now contemplated would encourage the right forms of recreation, but they must always remember that such forms of recreation should always lead to the spiritual tone and atmosphere of God's house. The procession from the church, led by the choir, made its way to the vicarage field, where the bishop: *'well and truly'* laid the foundation stone. The inscription on it read: *"This stone was laid by the Lord Bishop of Chelmsford, February 16th 1921"*. People were reminded that bricks could be laid by subscribers, and that any such subscriber could then have their initials inscribed upon them.[13]

'He wished the Borough Council could build homes in Chelmsford as quickly'

Moulsham Parochial Hall reached the first stage of its completion on Wednesday, 22 June 1921 when a well-adapted room just inside the main entrance doors was opened by Alderman Thompson. The cost of this first phase of the scheme had been met in its entirety. The first room, of brick, with an asbestos roof and distempered walls was capable of accommodating about one hundred and fifty people. The eventual plan was to divide this room into two with a passage in the centre leading from the entrance doors to the hall. The vicar, chairing the proceedings, congratulated everyone on the hard work necessary to complete this phase of the project in just over four months, but reminded them all that money still had to be raised towards the main hall, which when finished, would be capable of holding over four hundred people. He also expressed his gratitude to the architects and builders for their sterling contribution.

The mayor said he felt deeply honoured at being asked to perform the opening ceremony. He reminisced at length about his days as a solo chorister at St John's and how a photograph of him taken as the time had become famous. He congratulated the parish on the speed with which the building had gone up, wishing that the Borough council could build homes in Chelmsford as quickly. He pointed out to the parishioners something which they probably already knew, that their vicar was a personality of spiritual experience and broad sympathies, and he was backed up by a curate of like characteristics, and he hoped that the place that he was declaring open would always be a home of good cheer, working for the maintenance of the spiritual power of the church. Canon Lake, in moving thanks to the mayor, said he often wondered how his worship managed to get through his busy days – but the Borough was fortunate in having a mayor who managed to do almost everything. He congratulated Moulsham on their excellent effort and hoped they would soon see the completion of their scheme. Having got a (semi) captive audience, the parish was determined not to let them go without extracting some money from them, so it was no surprise to see that the opening ceremony was followed by a fête held in the vicarage grounds, and, later in the evening, by a concert held in the newly-opened hall. The day was rounded off with a dance on the vicarage lawn.[14]

'They would have the best organ in the neighbourhood'

Money quickly started to be raised for the second phase of the project, which was completed the following year. In addition to these substantial sums, there had been other significant demands on the church purse during 1921. In April, a report was received from the committee which the vicar had appointed to raise funds for the restoration of the organ (even though it had only been in use for twelve years). The committee proposed that the organ should be thoroughly cleaned, the reeds re-voiced, and as well as a complete overhaul of the action, four new stops should be added. After consultation with the parishioners and an organ expert, it was decided not to move the instrument, as any such removal would be costly and would serve no useful purpose. The cost of the whole scheme was about £410, and by 29 April just over £395 had already been raised, over £100 by the choirboys themselves. The vicar explained that he hoped that the work would be completed in no more than eight weeks, and then they would have the best organ in the neighbourhood. At the same meeting the vicar mentioned that he had received a faculty for altering the north transept, so that seat holders, while retaining their seats, would no longer be able to enter the area directly (from outside) but in future would have to use either the south or the west door.[15]

Robert Burnett had, of course, to continue the normal business of the parish as well as these two major projects. One of the curates, the 'two good men' (the Rev E. Herbert) only stayed at St John's for about three months, the *Essex Newsman* reporting that he had retired from his position at St John's and returned to London: *"owing to his inability to obtain a residence in the district"*. That, at least, was the official line.[16]

Not long after he had taken up the reins at St John's, Robert Burnett had a sad duty to perform. On 14 July 1919, after a few hours illness, Juliana Veley died at her home, 'Bleak House', in New London Road.[17] Her funeral took place at St John's church on the following Friday, 18 July, with Robert Burnett and William Pressey officiating at a full choral service. The principal mourners were her brother, Dr V.H. Veley, and her sister, Mrs J.A. Kershaw. The church was completely full, the majority of the congregation being women. Juliana Veley had been a substantial benefactress to the poor of the parish. As William Pressey said in his tribute: *"countless numbers in this parish will miss her great kindness and her bounty"*.[18]

Robert Burnett presided at his second vestry meeting on Tuesday, 6 April 1920. The meeting was held in a good atmosphere – the war memorial and the parochial church hall had become realistic and viable propositions. The vicar began by thanking the parishioners for their handsome Easter offering. The churchwardens accounts showed a buoyant income of almost £561, and after money had been set aside for a thorough cleaning of the church there was a small profit (£7). Mr Barker finally felt that he had to step down after fourteen years' service as vicar's warden, and Robert Burnett paid fulsome tribute to him, emphasising what exceptional help he had received from Mr Barker when he had first arrived in the parish. Mr Stamp Wortley was appointed to the position. Mr Ripper, who had been parish warden for the previous eight years, after being re-elected, also proposed a vote of thanks to Mr Barker, which was carried unanimously. Free will offerings were reported to have brought in over £94, and the Assistant Clergy fund showed a very healthy balance of over £150. It was also agreed to apply for a faculty for a marble tablet to commemorate Juliana Veley, who had died the previous summer, and this was agreed unanimously. The vicar concluded by expressing his deep appreciation for the contribution made by all church helpers.[19]

Alec Daniels, the second of Robert Burnett's 'two good men' left St John's later in the year, accepting a curacy at Holy Trinity, Harrow Green, Leytonstone, at the beginning of October. As might be expected of someone with a strong military background, he had taken a prominent part in the cadet movement and his work had struck a chord with the many disillusioned young people in the parish. He would be greatly missed, not least by the vicar. George Cecil Twist, who in May 1918 had left his position as vicar of Castle Hedingham, to assist clergy in the cathedral, where he was appointed priest-in-charge at St Peter's, Rainsford End, had moved to Osborne Place in St John's parish on leaving Castle Hedingham.[20] He found travelling to the cathedral (and even more so, to St Peter's) very onerous, and in August 1919 he accepted with alacrity the curacy of St John's when Robert Burnett offered it to him, officially replacing the Rev Herbert.[21] In May 1921 it was announced in the

Essex Newsman that: *"Parishioners of St John's will learn with interest that Mr Gerald Wace, of Ely college, who is due to be ordained at the Cathedral on Trinity Sunday by the Bishop of Chelmsford, will begin his duties at St John's immediately after his ordination. Mr Wace, who graduated from Queen's college, Cambridge, served as a combatant during the war, and was wounded".*[22] However, his name does not appear in the list of ordinands at the cathedral that Trinity Sunday, and there is no record of him ever appearing at St John's.

'The collection was the largest of any organisation in the town'

On Good Friday of 1921 (25 March) the weather in Chelmsford was quite exceptionally mild, and Robert Burnett decided to hold the evening service outside the church. This unusual departure from the normal procedure was much appreciated by the congregation.[23] The church was well-filled for the Easter day services, and on the following Tuesday (29 March) St John's held its vestry meeting. Robert Burnett started proceedings by expressing his grateful thanks for the exceptional Easter day offerings, which on this occasion amounted to no less than £53. Mr Ripper then presented the accounts. He stressed that the meeting would not be surprised to learn that the year had been an expensive one. Receipts totalled £726, which included £223 from special offertories and £228 from collections for church expenses. Major expenditure included £38 for coke and £58 for thoroughly cleaning the church, and after all these had been deducted, there remained a balance in hand of just over £10. The chairman, commenting on the satisfactory nature of the accounts, pointed out incidentally that the collection that they had taken at St John's for the Chelmsford hospital was the largest of any organisation in the town. The free will offering fund, which the vicar described as one of the most useful funds in the church, showed a balance of £86. The Assistant Clergy fund stood at £116 and more subscribers had recently been recruited. The Mildmay charity account, which provided Christmas gifts for the inhabitants of the almshouses, was in credit at almost £20.[23]

The vicar again nominated Mr Wortley as his warden and Mr Ripper was re-elected as people's warden. The vicar expressed his thanks to all who had contributed to the smooth running of the church over the past year, and on the proposition of Mr Ripper, a hearty vote of thanks was accorded to the vicar and Mrs Burnett, and also to the sole curate, George Twist. The vestry meeting was followed by a short Parochial Church Council, where Mrs Russell and Mr Burton were elected to fill the two outstanding vacancies at the ruridecanal conference.

In late July, members of the Chelmsford and Essex Temperance Society (CETS) held a grand sports day at Theydon Bois, at which more than five hundred adults and children were present. The Bishop of Barking (the Rt Rev Thomas Stevens) was present to distribute prizes to those children and adults who had gained distinction for work done during the winter 1920–21, and St John's, Moulsham, won the Diocesan Challenge Shield, the first time it had been won by a county branch.[24] In August Robert Burnett and his wife went (as would become their custom) on a long summer break, this time for almost six weeks. During this time, Canon Arthur Sacre, the retired vicar of All Saints' East Hanningfield (who in the Great War had served as a chaplain at Gallipoli, though well over fifty years old, and who had been invalided home)[25] was described as the 'acting priest in charge of St John's' where he was assisted by George Twist.[26] It was also announced, in the Advent ordination services held that same year in Chelmsford cathedral, that: *"Sydney Gelder Farrar, who has studied at Chichester Theological college, was ordained deacon, and at the same time licensed to St John's, Moulsham. He will take up his duties immediately after the ordination"*.[27]

'Funds at Moulsham – but active churchmen needed'

Moulsham's 1922 vestry meeting was held on Tuesday, 18 April, and the headlines of the reports in the press were: *"Funds at Moulsham – But active churchmen needed"*. Robert Burnett opened the meeting, as was his custom, by thanking his parishioners for their generous Easter day offerings. He next welcomed the Rev Sydney Farrar as the recently-appointed second curate. The vicar went on to thank the church workers, saying how gratified he was that they all gave their time so willingly and in such good spirit. However, he considered that the small attendance at this year's meeting was: *"a disgrace to the parish"*. The vicar again appointed Mr Wortley as his warden and Mr Ripper was re-elected as parish warden. At the subsequent Parochial Church Council, the vicar stated that there were now four hundred and thirty-eight names on the electoral roll, and of those, forty-four had been added this Easter. The wardens' accounts showed a balance of £30, the Assistant Clergy fund £42 and the parochial fund £33. Miss Highes had left a legacy to the church which had enabled them to purchase a new carpet for the chancel. Mr Wortley then gave a full explanation of the uses of the parochial fund, which basically, was used to pay the working expenses of the church. This, he said, put the whole of the church finances in the hands of the laity, and it was up to them to see that the clergy did not need to become involved in financial matters. About £900 a year was needed for the efficient operation of the church, and he stressed that if eight hundred people contributed just 6d. a week, it would bring in over £1,000 per year. If they went to a cinema, they enjoyed it, and they enjoyed it the more because they had to pay. He proposed to transfer £100 from the parochial fund to augment the vicar's stipend, because of the smallness of his income. He even suggested that if the fund were properly supported, it might be possible to do away with the collections entirely. There was little support for this idea at the meeting, which seemed to think that both would still be necessary. The meeting closed with the routine vote of thanks to the vicar and his curates.[28]

By July, Rev and Mrs Burnett had decided to have their long holiday again, and Canon Sacre on this occasion moved into the vicarage to provide cover. This year, he had two curates to assist him and seems merely to have acted *in loco parentis* for the parish.[29] One of these curates, George Twist, took the St John's school pupils on their annual outing to Maldon by train (this must have been an interesting journey). A beautiful day (2 August) meant that they all had a most enjoyable time.[30] The luxury of having two curates was, however, too good to be true – in late September it was announced that Rev George Cecil Twist, curate of Moulsham since 1919 had been presented to the perpetual curacy of Highnam in Gloucestershire, rendered vacant by the resignation of Rev Canon P.L. Park.[31]

The appointment was not without its Chelmsford connections – the patron of the living, Major Gambier Parry was the brother-in-law of Mr Oxley Parker (and brother of Sir Hubert Parry).[32] George Twist left Moulsham on 6 December, and was presented prior to his departure with a Royal Sunbeam bicycle and a pair of gloves (from the parishioners, together with a book containing the names of all those who had subscribed). He also received a handsome ebony walking stick from the teachers of the Boys' Sunday school and a suede wallet from the staff at the hospital, where he had been a keen worker.[33] Alfred Darby had endeavoured to sell George Twist's house ('Barton', London Road), an imposing residence standing in an acre of ground, by auction on 3 November, but the house was withdrawn at £2,500.[34] It was sold by private treaty a week later (George Twist was clearly a man of some substance).[35]

'Progressive Moulsham'

Early in 1923 a new curate arrived to bring the number of Robert Burnett's assistants back up to two. Rev Alexander Colvin, MC, curate of Loughton was appointed curate of Moulsham, and it was announced that he would take up his duties at the end of April. He had connections with the area, having served as a company commander with the 5th Essex, when he had been awarded his MC. He was a keen hockey player, and over the next eighteen months his name was frequently to be found listed as a member of various Chelmsford hockey XIs.[36]

Robert Burnett presided at the annual vestry meeting on Tuesday, 3 April. He began the meeting by announcing that Mr Stamp Wortley, who had been his vicar's warden for the past three years, had realised that he must relinquish the position. He felt that Mr Wortley had been the key to helping them through a difficult transition period, and he extended his warmest thanks to him for all his hard work. He said that Lt-Col Horace Cocks, a keen churchman, who had recently come to live in the parish, had consented to be vicar's warden for the coming year. Mr Wortley then proposed the re-election of Mr Ripper as people's warden for the twelfth consecutive year and this proposition was carried unanimously. Mr Wortley then presented the accounts. He stated that although the parochial fund showed a credit of £47 they were about £30 down. There had been no special appeals, and the scheme for one fund had proved satisfactory. He was also able to tell the meeting that the hall building fund, after the final payment to the builders, had a small sum in hand. The Mildmay charity had a small credit balance. Repairs and improvements had been carried out at the almshouses using the £100 received from the sale of surplus land.

Robert Burnett spoke of the great improvement in volume and tone resulting from the fitting of a sound board over the organ. The funds for this had been donated by Mr and Mrs Whistance as a memorial for their late daughter. At the subsequent Parochial Church Council, representatives to the ruridecanal conference and new members of the council were elected. The vicar confirmed that a tenancy agreement had been secured at 83, New London Road, for their new curate, Alexander Colvin, who would shortly be taking up his new post. He pointed out that Mr Colvin knew Chelmsford well, having previously been a master at the Grammar School. Like the vicar, he said, Mr Colvin was Irish [Laughter]. The vicar concluded by thanking all the church workers, especially the choir and the Sunday school teachers.[37]

On Sunday, 13 May, two new flags belonging to the First Mildmay troop of Boy Scouts were dedicated at a special service at St John's church. One of these flags was the Union Jack, and the other the scout flag in which the Mildmay cross had been worked by Mrs Gusterson. Alexander Colvin conducted the service, laying the flags on the altar and saying a series of special prayers over them. Sydney Farrar also assisted with the service in his capacity as scoutmaster.[38]

'I found them at Galleywood in a half-box'

On 9 June, Robert Burnett was awoken in the early hours of the morning by the frantic barking of his dog. He went downstairs and found a young man prowling around in his stockinged feet, in the back hall of the vicarage. The young man, Arthur Howard Grant, aged twenty-two, was apprehended and then released. Later that month, he was arrested on an unrelated charge, when five pairs of scissors were found on him, as well as other suspicious items. He was then charged with breaking and entering the vicarage on 9 June and the Parochial hall on 5 June, and with stealing the scissors and one and a half pound of biscuits. Evidence was given by users of the hall that the items in question had been taken from a trunk and two collecting boxes in the building. The prisoner, in his defence, simply stated that: "He didn't know anything about it". (He seems not to have been a very bright young man). PC Weller, who had questioned the young man at the station, had asked him where the scissors had come from. The prisoner replied that: "He had found them on the road to Galleywood in a half-box". The prisoner, who had nothing else to say, was committed on both charges to the Quarter Sessions.[39] When he appeared in court, on Wednesday 4 July, he pleaded guilty to all the charges against him, and was sentenced to a total of six months' hard labour. It was revealed that he had a number of previous convictions.[40]

In October, St John's held its customary Harvest Festival service, and on this occasion decided that the collections for the day would go to the Chelmsford Hospital and the Clacton Convalescent Home. Almost £32 was raised from a well-filled church for these two good causes.[41] The church was crowded to overflowing on 28 October when the Bishop of Chelmsford (Rt Rev Guy Warman) paid his first visit to St John's (the previous bishop, John

Watts-Ditchfield, had died on 14 July). His sermon was well-received by the assembled throng.[42]

'The accounts were in a very healthy state'

Robert Burnett and his wife were, as has been previously pointed out, in the habit of taking a long break in the summer, and many of those holidays were in Cornwall. In January 1924 the vicar gave an interesting illustrated lecture on his tour of the county the previous year to the Moulsham Guild of St George.[43]

The 1924 vestry meeting was held in the parochial hall on Tuesday 22 April with the vicar in the chair. Mr Ripper presented the accounts which he described as being in a very healthy state. The parochial fund was £16 in credit and the Mildmay charity account £45 to the good. The Church Hall building fund had a favourable balance of £88, but the vicar pointed out that there was still a bond of £50 in the bank, so the true balance was £138. The accounts were unanimously passed. The wardens (Lt-Col Cocks and Mr Ripper) agreed to serve for another year. A brief Parochial Church Council (PCC) meeting made one change to the secretaryship of the PCC itself, and the vicar concluded by thanking everyone as usual.[44]

In May it was announced that a licence had been granted by Chelmsford magistrates for the staging of occasional plays in the parochial hall. It was felt that this would prove a great benefit to the parish, both in terms of additional fundraising and also raising the social activity of St John's within the parish.[45]

'Parochial Church Councils are as silent as the grave'

In July, the Essex Newsman's gossip columnist, 'Reflexions by Reflex' was having another dig at St John's. Whitewash, it stated, was a very good thing, and the 'columnist' had received a letter from a correspondent who had suggested whitewashing St John's church clock. It is worth quoting in its entirety: "While you, dear

Reflex, are on the Biblical stunt, it is, I think, an opportune time to draw your attention to the clock face of St John's church. You see, old dear, it is black with gold figures (maybe brazen) and while this sounds impressive – well, it is more impressive than legible, especially as the sun has the habit of getting behind the church, so shining in the eyes of the enquirer after truth and time – What? Now, only if it were whitewashed, it would show up much better. It might need cleaning more often, but think of the cuss words it would save". Reflex provides the reason for the little jest; he suggests that the request be passed on to the church council for their consideration (if they would consider it) and he goes on to say that he supposes we shall never know whether they do or not: *"for theirs are secret meetings. The Parochial Church Councils are as silent as the grave".*[46]

In June, it was announced that Alexander Colvin's time as curate at St John's would shortly be coming to an end[47] and in late September it was confirmed that he had accepted a chaplaincy in Puerta Arenas, in the diocese of the Falkland Islands. At a meeting of St John's discussion society on 24 September he was presented with a set of theological books and a fountain pen as gifts from the parish, and the vicar praised his work and wished him Godspeed. The same article also stated that Rev Thomas Henry Pimm, the curate of St Mark's, Camberwell, had been appointed curate of St John's, and confirmed that he would take up his appointment shortly.[48]

'He stated quite categorically that this would be for the last time'

The combined vestry and PCC meetings for 1925 were held on 21 April in the Hall, and were relatively brief affairs. The vicar nominated Mr Godfrey Sykes as his warden who thanked the vicar for his nomination and reminded members present of the parlous state of the free will offering fund. The meeting then proposed Mr Ripper (yet again) as people's warden, but was then much surprised to find that Mr Ripper wished to be relieved of that position, saying that he felt it was time for someone else to come forward. There was a deafening silence, and after much cajoling Mr Ripper consented to be re-elected, but in doing so, stated categorically that this would be for the very last time. The PCC then elected sidesmen, ruridecanal representatives and PCC members with one or two minor changes. Mr Ripper presented the accounts, showing that the total receipts had risen to £1,170 and although there was a balance in hand of almost £208, he stressed that this would be taken up by bills becoming due in the near future. The vicar concluded by informing them all that the electoral roll now contained 448 names, but expressed his disquiet that so few of those were present at the meeting.[49]

In early June it was announced that the second phase of the parochial hall (the large hall to the south east of the completed part of the building) had been started. In addition to the hall proper, it would include a kitchen and a crockery store. It was hoped that this phase would be completed in the next few months.[50] The contractors were true to their promise and the Bishop of Chelmsford was able to open the extended premises on 29 September. The new extension had been made possible almost entirely thanks to the generosity of Capt Leonard Gray (the firm of solicitors in Chelmsford is named after him) who had died at Alexandria in 1917 during the Great War. He had left a legacy to St John's (as mentioned in the previous chapter) to be used for the benefit of the parish. Robert Burnett welcomed the bishop, reminding everyone that this was not the first time his Lordship had visited the parish as he had preached at St John's church some eighteen months previously. Capt Gray, he continued, had left them a legacy in his will (for which probate had been granted shortly after he had died) but the money itself had only come to them on the recent death of Capt Gray's mother. The bishop, in reply, said he was glad to join with them in realising the extraordinary contribution of the parish hall to the welfare of the parish. It had been his experience, he went on, that people once they had got a parish hall, wondered however they had managed without one. It offered, too, he thought, a rewarding way for people in the parish to get to know one another, something that was not always easy when individuals only met in church.

Mr Ripper then presented a short financial statement. The contract price for the hall had been approximately £1,197. They had already paid on account and had 1s. 6d. under £597 in the bank. About £30 more would be required to complete everything, and he stated that Capt Gray's legacy, with interest, had contributed £1,085 to the project. The mayor, Alderman Fred Spalding, then proposed a vote of thanks to the bishop, and the event concluded with a bazaar (with the usual wide range of stalls), some musical contributions and an evening of dancing and whist, the whole day raising about £60 for the project.[51]

In October the PCC met again to consider how the hall could best be heated during the winter months. After a brief discussion it was agreed that they would install two anthracite stoves in the main hall. The same meeting also agreed that it would be a good idea to advertise the hall for hire in the local press.[52]

Also in October it was confirmed that Thomas Pimm would be leaving his curacy at St John's, having obtained a similar position at Minehead in Somerset. He had decided to move in the hope that Rev Pimm's young son, whose health was not good, would benefit from the sea air.[53] Just four weeks later the *Essex County Chronicle* announced that his replacement at St John's was to be Rev Frederick Arthur Stroud who would take up his duties on 29 November. Thomas Pimm received a handsome present on his departure from a collection made by the Women's Bible class.[54]

'He thought they were in for a bumper congregation'

The parochial hall was already beginning to prove its worth. In 1926 the First Mildmay Scouts held their annual social party on 16 January. During this event the scouts district commissionaire (Major Magor) presented badges and stripes, and after a camp-fire singalong there was dancing (it was not clear who danced with whom). Arrangements for the evening were made by the vicar, the curate and the scoutmaster, Mr F.G. Carlton.[55] Other scout troops also found the hall a convenient venue for events. In April the First Springfield troop found it worth their while to hire the building for a rummage sale to raise funds for their annual camp at Walton-on-the-Naze.[56]

The usual Easter vestry meeting was held on 7 April in the parochial hall. Robert Burnett told the meeting that Mr Godfrey Sykes had again consented to act as his warden throughout the coming year. Mr Ripper reminded the meeting that he had served as people's warden for fourteen years, and really felt that he could not do the job for another year. Mr Edgar Cheverton was unanimously elected, but was adamant that he could not accept the position due to pressure of work. Someone suggested that a lady might be appointed, but the chairman (rather dismissively) pointed out that the size of the parish necessitated a lot of work. Mr H.P. Sheldrake kindly offered to look after the accounts (and thereby some of the people's warden's work) but it was still not enough. One or two other gentlemen present at the meeting were nominated for the post, but they all declined. Robert Burnett was completely stumped. *"I do not know"*, he said, *"quite what to do or to say about it. Here you have a man who has served the parish for fourteen years and nobody seems anxious to take the job on. After all, it is a job for the church"*. Eventually Mr Cheverton said that if Mr Ripper continued for a further year, he was willing to assist Mr Ripper all that he could. Mr Ripper was therefore re-elected, with Mr Cheverton as his assistant.

At the parochial meeting which followed, the vicar, as usual, thanked all those in the parish whose hard work had been such a great help to him. With regard to finance, he had to say that they had kept their heads above water, but only just. They had completed another section of the parochial hall, which now gave them a fine building, but they hoped soon to press on with the completion of the scheme. Mr Ripper, in presenting the accounts, said that the total receipts for the year came to £1,201 and they had a balance in hand of just over £74. On the parochial hall fund there was a balance in hand of just under £48 after more than £1,127 had been spent. Mr J.A.R. Pitts said he thought it was a general wish that a photograph of the late Capt Leonard Gray (whose generous bequest had largely enabled the parochial hall to be built) should be hung up in the hall. Mr Sykes agreed to provide a suitable frame for the portrait. The meeting then discussed the inconvenience caused by members of the Chelmsford and District Motorcycling club assembling for their runs outside the garage opposite the church. The chairman said that when he saw such a large crowd outside the church the previous Sunday morning he thought they were in for a bumper congregation until he saw that the objects of interest were motorcycles. The meeting agreed that the churchwardens would write to the club suggesting that they arranged to meet at another location. The chairman closed the meeting by announcing that the electoral roll now stood at a total of 547.[57]

St John's summer fête was held in the gardens of the vicarage on 7 and 8 July. It was opened by the local MP, Sir Carne Rasch, Bt. In spite of it clashing with the patronal festival events at the cathedral, a substantial sum was raised by the Thursday evening for parochial funds.[58] At the church council meeting held in November, the vicar reported a positive balance on all funds. All debts relating to the parochial hall had been paid off and the fund had a credit balance of £60.[59] The year ended on a sombre note. The death was announced, on 22 December, of Charles Byford, who had been organist of St John's for a period of eight years. He was ninety-one years of age.[60]

'There were nearly 3,500 houses in the parish'

The following year, 1927, was a relatively quiet one for the parish. Early in the year there was another change in the musical life of the church when Mr H. Wheeler was appointed organist of St Mary's, Great Baddow, in succession to Mr A. Burton, who had resigned after eighteen years' service.[61] The 1927 Easter vestry meeting was held on Wednesday 20 April with the vicar as usual in the chair. The meeting started with a formal vote of thanks to Mr Gerald Gray for a photograph of his late brother, Capt. Leonard Gray, which was to be hung in the parochial hall. Mr Godfrey Sykes had provided a suitable frame for the portrait, as promised. The vicar nominated Mr Sykes as his warden. Mr Pitts then proposed Mr Cheverton as people's warden, stressing that gentleman's considerable organising ability (he had chaired the committee that had overseen the building of the parochial hall) and he went on to say how grateful the whole parish was to Mr Ripper, whose contribution to the church over the past decade and a half had been quite outstanding. Mr Cheverton thanked everyone who had elected him and his proposer for the kind words which had been said on his behalf, before pointing out to the meeting that there were significant items of expenditure that would have to be considered in the following year - the re-decoration of the church, the possible removal of the boiler and the building of a new house for the curate to replace the one which Frederick Stroud now rented. The parochial meeting, which followed, elected the usual number of officers, with a few minor changes from the previous year.

Mr Sykes presented the accounts in their usual format. The church hall account showed a healthy balance of more than £171, but he stressed that a number of bills (totalling £156) would have to be met by the following January. The parochial account at the end of the year showed a credit of only £11 and he also noted that they had paid only £12 of their quota of £87 to the Diocesan fund. The chairman appealed for more subscriptions to the free will offering fund, and ended by expressing his thanks to all who had assisted him throughout the year, singling out the Rev Frederick Stroud, who had worked so loyally. He concluded by saying that he did not think people realised how much there was to do – there were now nearly 3,500 houses in the parish.[62]

In July the young people of the church took part in a game of 'living whist' where each individual took the identity of a playing card, forming teams to represent hands that had been 'dealt'. The event took place at Chelmsford football ground in New Writtle Street, and was organised by Mrs Stroud, the curate's wife. In spite of very poor weather, a substantial sum was raised for church funds.[63] November saw the commemoration of Armistice day with a two minutes' silence around the war memorial outside the church. There was an impressive turnout.[64]

The PCC held its autumn meeting on 16 November, at which Mr Ripper's long and faithful service to the church was recognised by the presentation of a gold watch chain. The vicar praised the enormous contribution Mr Ripper had made as warden over the previous fifteen years. Mr Ripper said he felt that his work had never been a chore to him and he only regretted that his health had not permitted him to carry on any longer. An update on the accounts was presented at which it was stated that funds were down by about £70 in the current year, and again a special appeal was made for money to build accommodation for the curate. It was agreed that the vicar and wardens would look at the various ways available to them to raise the money. Mr H.A. Parker (the organist) had his salary raised from £80 to £100.[65]

'A new school for 800 scholars, to be located in Lady Lane'

Robert Burnett, towards the end of his time in Moulsham, suffered severely from rheumatism (Mrs Burnett often had to drive him to meetings) and in January 1928 he consulted a London specialist. The specialist recommended a lengthy treatment at Bath, and so it was announced that from 23 January the vicar would be away for at least a month and that during that time Frederick Stroud would be in charge of the parish. The planned January confirmation service was postponed until the summer.[66] The vicar, though, was just about well enough to chair the 1928 vestry meeting, which was held on Wednesday, 18 January. He felt that St John's had 'gone ahead' the previous year, but he was disappointed that the church was not as full as he would have liked. He believed that such low attendances were now the general trend in society.

All the parochial organisations, though, had flourished and he hoped that the coming year would see the church go ahead by leaps and bounds to higher things. Mr A.J. Beckett was appointed vicar's warden in place of Mr Sykes, who resigned after four years' service, and Mr Cheverton was re-elected as people's warden. The sidesmen and ruridecanal officers were all re-elected *en bloc*, with the addition of Mr Sykes. The accounts up to 31 December showed receipts of £1,272 and expenditure of £1,305, leading to a deficit of £33. Various late payments reduced this figure to £12, which a parishioner had agreed to pay anonymously. With a deposit of £50 in the bank, this meant that the church faced the new year effectively free from debt. The PCC were then re-elected, with the addition of one new member, Mrs Thackeray.[67]

In March, some of the problems which had much bothered William Pressey concerning improvements to St John's school had resurfaced. In 1912 the managers of the school had been able to deal with most of the minor requirements which the Board of Education had stipulated needed to be carried out to the buildings, but some of the demands (such as the provision of a greatly enlarged playground) had been seen as completely impossible. The school managers had hoped that all the outstanding issues had been quietly forgotten, but this, alas, was not the case. At the meeting of the Borough education committee in late March, it was revealed that the managers of both St John's and Victoria schools had been meeting to discuss proposals that the two schools be merged. St John's was to provide an Infants' and Junior mixed facility and Victoria school a mixed seniors' establishment. These meetings had come about because the Board of Education had sent a letter to the St John's managers informing them that immediate steps had to be taken to comply with the Board's requirement for improved accommodation at St John's. The education committee's recommendation was that the borough engineer be instructed to prepare a sketch plan for a new school, to house 800 scholars, to be located in Lady Lane, and that this information be passed to the Board of Education. A motion that this scheme be postponed to see what the managers (of St John's and Victoria boys) could come up with was narrowly defeated.[68]

St John's was nothing if not inventive in its fundraising activities. The parochial hall hosted a 'flannel dance' (where individuals who attended could be dressed very casually) on 9 May, which made a useful contribution to church funds.[69] Frederick Stroud's stipend was still very modest, in spite of the considerable contribution he made to the running of the parish, so it was no surprise to see that the offerings on Pentecost Sunday (25 May) were presented to him (in the same way as the Easter offering was given to the incumbent). He received about £21.[70] The Sunday school teachers had their annual outing on 9 June. The curate organised a trip to Thaxted, which was much appreciated.[71]

Toc H held their first initiation service at St John's on 5 July. The service started with the 'Pilgrim's Hymn' and continued with the Ceremony of Light, conducted by the chairman Mr C.R. Passmore, at the entrance of the choir. The Hon Sec. (Mr M.R. Morris) and the Jobmaster (Mr A. Bloman) presented Padre Robert Burnett to the chairman. The vicar, who was holding the Group's Rushlight, was duly admitted to the Toc H fellowship. The Padre was then able to admit another sixteen members to the fellowship. The 'Supreme Sacrifice' was then sung by all, standing in a semicircle, with each person holding a lighted taper.[72] Toc H was to make considerable use of the parochial hall over the next few years.

The year also saw a significant death and a retirement. On 10 July, Catherine Swayne, the widow of the late rector of Willingale Doe, died. Since her husband's death, Mrs Swayne had lived in Moulsham and had become a devoted and hard-working member of St John's. A requiem mass was sung in her memory in the church before her body was interred in Willingale churchyard. Robert Burnett, Edward Hort, William Pressey and Alexander Colvin, all of whom had worked with Mrs Swayne in the St John's bible classes, assisted with the services.[73] On the last day of the summer term (27 July) Mr Ripper retired after a headmastership of thirty-seven years at St John's Boys' school (he had been appointed to this position when George Godson was vicar). He had previously been assistant master for six years. Robert Burnett presented him with an armchair on behalf of pupils, past-pupils, managers and friends. Coupled with this was a gift of a fountain pen for Mrs Ripper. Mr Ripper made a suitable response: *"I would like to take this opportunity to remind the boys to take as their motto through life the word 'Duty'"*. After the presentation the school broke up for the summer.[74]

'There ought to be at least five times as many'

The annual vestry meeting for 1929 was held on 23 January with the vicar in the chair. Robert Burnett took the opportunity to express his feelings about the conditions of his parish, and it is worth repeating some of the things he said in full. He began by stating that much of the work of a church, in any parish, was purely spiritual and unseen, and it was very difficult to assess in terms of cold statistics. However, for St John's over the previous year, it was pleasing to be able to report that the collections made for various organisations outside the church had been £31 higher than those for 1927. He struck a less enthusiastic note when he said, though, that: *"In a parish the size of Moulsham it was quite hopeless to think that the work should be carried out with only two clergymen, the Rev Stroud and himself. I would like to take this opportunity of saying what a tremendous help Mr Stroud has been – he is absolutely wholeheartedly in the work of the parish and is totally loyal to me."* He then went on to quote some figures relating to the spiritual work in the parish, saying that there had been during the course of the year some 5,029 communions made in the church, almost one hundred per week, which perhaps might sound good, but when he took into consideration the size of the parish, he felt that there ought to be at least five times as many. He then continued with the more routine business of the meeting, saying that on this occasion they had to say goodbye to Mr Edgar Cheverton, who had been their peoples' warden for two years, and whose business commitments forced him to relinquish the position. He thanked Mr A.J. Beckett for his work as vicar's warden, and then paid particular thanks to two people whose work for the parish was often unappreciated. Mr and Mrs Sheldrake. He reserved his highest praise for the Sunday school teachers, saying that: *"The finest body of people in England were no doubt these teachers – theirs was no doubt a very thankless and onerous task which they carried out at St John's without any supervision from the clergy"*. They were also lucky at St John's, he stressed, in that they had under Miss Swain, the very best Band of Hope in the diocese (and they had the shield on the wall of the parochial hall to prove it). Of the social clubs, he held upon as an example (of how they ought to be run) the billiards club, which over the previous quarter had handed over £12 for church funds.

The meeting then turned to the necessary items of business. The vicar renominated Mr Beckett as his warden, and Mr W.J. Finch was unanimously elected as peoples' warden. The various officials were then elected without any changes. The accounts were presented. They had begun the year with a debit balance of £33, but two anonymous donations had cleared this figure so effectively they started the year with a clean sheet, but they had still been in debt at the end of the year to the tune of £66. It was pointed out that this was not as bad as it appeared, as there were cheques outstanding and an amount due from the overseers that would just about even things up. They had almost reached their quota (£104) for the Diocesan Board of Finance, having managed £80. There was one brief moment of gentle humour – the church had been obliged to pay a charge of £178 towards the making up of Vicarage Road. A fund had been opened with a cheque for £50, and after six months it stood at £51. This announcement was accompanied by much laughter.

The vicar reported that at present they rented a house (in New London Road) for the assistant priest at just under £45 a year. They needed to find £550 to build a house for him (although it would cost £1,600 to build). They had £340 of land, and the Ecclesiastical Commissionaires would make them a present (*sic*) of half the cost. The meeting closed with the usual vote of thanks to everyone present.[75] In spring of the same year technology came to the aged and infirm of the parish. On Wednesday 13 March a wireless set was delivered and installed in the Mildmay almshouses. The set was presented (and was to be maintained by) the Chelmsford Rotary club. Robert Burnett received the set on behalf of the parish.[76] In April, Mrs Stroud showed her artistic skills by organising a production of *"The Quaker Girl"* in the parochial hall. It drew considerable praise from the local press.[77]

One of the main fund-raising events of the year was a Grand Olde English Fayre held in July in the grounds of Oaklands (by kind permission of Major and Mrs C.J. Flower). Colour was added to the scene by many of the stallholders, who were dressed for the most part in Victorian costume. The money raised was to go towards the church's share of the cost of making up Vicarage Road. The mayor, Alderman Thompson, who opened the Fayre, donated a wristwatch to be the top prize in the raffle. There were some gentle mutterings in the crowd when the watch was won by the vicar.[78] This was one of the last times that Major Flower was able to let an organisation use the grounds of his house – as on 13 July it was announced that Chelmsford Borough Council would buy (subject to the consent of the Ministry of Health) Oaklands mansion, with cottages and upwards of eleven acres of parkland, for £6,500. The council had clearly got a bargain, as the sale included almost seventy freehold building plots fronting Vicarage Road and Moulsham Street.[79]

The fundraising continued with a bazaar on 9 October in aid of the Assistant Clergy fund (in other words, raising the money for Rev Stroud's stipend), the road (making-up) fund and for the re-decorating of the church, the need for which was now becoming pressing. The new rector (and sub-dean) of the cathedral (Canon Morrow) and Miss Morrow were present.[80] The autumn PCC meeting was held on 6 November, when the treasurer (Mr W.J. Finch) reported that finances were in a satisfactory condition. The new curatage was paid for, and thanks to an anonymous gift of £200, the whole of the road charges had been paid. A fund for the redecoration of the church had now formally been set up.[81]

'Beyond that he was unable to say anything at present'

So Robert Burnett entered upon his last year at Moulsham. He had, during his incumbency, periodically suffered from severe bouts of rheumatism, and these returned with a renewed intensity at the beginning of 1930. He was too unwell to attend the First Mildmay Scout troop's annual social gathering on 25 January[82] or Mrs Stroud's well-supported production of *"The Sunshine Girl"* in the parochial hall on 19 February.[83] Attempts to postpone the annual vestry meeting (usually held in January) until Robert Burnett had recovered sufficiently were eventually abandoned and a simplified meeting was held on 12 February when the financial position of the church was reviewed and found to be satisfactory.[84] By 30 March the vicar had recovered enough to preach at the church for the first time since his illness, although it was still reported that: *"the rev. gentleman is making steady progress towards complete recovery, but has not yet been fully able to resume all his duties"*.[85]

May 1930 saw the opening of Oaklands Park as a public open space for the Borough (which presumably meant that it might be easier for St John's to hold events there)[86] but the 1930 summer fête took place in the vicarage grounds on 20 August, and very fine weather brought a huge turnout. There was the usual range of stalls and the day's festivities were rounded off by a dance in the parochial hall in the evening. A total of £55 was raised for church funds.

The rumour mill surrounding Robert Burnett was still steadily grinding away, and it was no surprise when the *Essex Chronicle* of 12 September cornered the bishop and was able to report: *"Regarding the rumour that the Rev R.F. Burnett, MA, MC, vicar of Moulsham was contemplating retirement from the living to take another elsewhere, the Bishop of Chelmsford said to the Chronicle last evening that he had written to Mr Burnett, but beyond that he was unable to say anything at present"*. Robert Burnett was at that time on holiday and could not be contacted, so his decision *"could not be ascertained"*.

However, the absent vicar (he had moved from Hunstanton to continue his holiday in Peterborough, where his wife's family lived) did not keep his parishioners in suspense much longer. On Sunday, 21 September, Frederick Stroud read a letter from the vicar, in which he said that he had been offered by the bishop (and had accepted) the living of Great Yeldham. He stressed that, as far as he was concerned, it had not been an easy task to be a vicar of a parish the size of Moulsham, but by tact and co-operation that task had been made as easy as possible. He carried on by pointing out that none of us knew what the future had in store, but whatever happened, he was confident that they would all acquit themselves well and be strong.[89] So Robert Burnett announced his departure from the parish. He had found running St John's, Moulsham, with only one curate, a real strain, and clearly felt it was the right time to move to a less challenging parish. During his time in Chelmsford he had been helped by having some devoted (and in some cases, very experienced) curates to assist him. Robert Burnett had been very impressed by the integrity and courage shown by chaplains during his service in the Great War, and when he came to Moulsham he felt that this was just the right kind of person to assist him in his work. It had therefore been no surprise that when he arrived in 1919 he quickly announced the engagement of Rev E. Herbert and Rev A.P. Daniels.

Edward Herbert's time in Moulsham is shrouded in mystery. His entry in *Crockford's Clerical Directory*[90] contains no reference to St John's, Moulsham, at all, and there is no reference to his being formally licensed to the parish as a curate. He is recorded as assisting in the choir for Juliana Veley's funeral. When he left Chelmsford (giving as his reason his inability to find a suitable residence) he returned to London and accepted a curacy at West Holloway. A year later he had accepted a post with the African Church Railway Mission, which he held until 1924, then becoming rector of Middleburg in the Transvaal.

Alec Percy Daniels was born in Cambridge in the spring of 1890, the seventh child and second son of William Daniels, a master tailor and robe maker (he worked for Ede and Ravenscroft) and his second wife Clara. After reading classics at Clare College, Cambridge, he graduated in 1911[91] being ordained deacon by the Bishop of St Albans at All Saints', Witham on 21 September 1913[92] and priest by the Bishop of Chelmsford at St Mary-by-the-Walls, Colchester, on 4 October 1914.[93] He was gazetted as Temporary Chaplain to the Forces (TCF) on 7 September 1915[94] being sent to France where he won his MC on the Somme in 1916. Whilst at St John's, he met his future wife, announcing his engagement to Phyllis Pomeroy, the daughter of Mr and Mrs G.F. Pomeroy of Rosebery Road at the end of 1919.[95] In October 1920 Alec Daniels accepted a curacy at Holy Trinity, Harrow Green, Leytonstone. The *Essex County Chronicle*, commenting on his departure, said that: *"during his comparatively short stay at St John's, Mr Daniels became greatly esteemed, and was a favourite with the young people, in whose welfare he was closely interested, taking a prominent part in the cadet movement"*.[96] He stayed at Holy Trinity, Harrow Green, for just over a year, then moved shortly after his marriage (which took place at Christ Church, Westminster, in April 1921[97]) to take up the post of Missioner with the Clare College Mission in Rotherhithe. At this time he lived in Bermondsey, where their only child, Alec William Pomeroy Daniels, was born.[98] His subsequent career took him to Western Australia. He died at St Neots in 1957.

George Cecil Twist was the son of John James Twist and Katherine Dewes, who were married in 1863 in Coventry. George was born at the beginning of 1869 and baptised by his clergyman father at the parish church of St James', Birch in Rusholme, on 10 October.[99] After studying at Trinity College, Oxford, from 1888 to 1891, followed by a year at Cuddesdon, he was ordained deacon by the Bishop of St Albans in Cheshunt parish church on Sunday 19 December 1892.[100] He was licensed at the same time to St Peter's, Coggeshall, where he commenced his duties on 21 December. He was ordained priest at Hertford on 21 December 1893,[102] and remained in Coggeshall until accepting a curacy with his father at Castle Hedingham. In 1898 his father, Rev John James Twist died, and it was reported that: *"general satisfaction was felt in Castle Hedingham that the Rev George Cecil Twist, MA, son of the late vicar, has been offered (and has accepted) the vacant living of the parish. He has been acting as his late father's curate since 1895"*.[103] With a good, secure income, Cecil Twist now felt that there was degree of permanence in his life, and on Thursday 7 November 1911 he married the second daughter of the local doctor in Castle Hedingham. The happy couple travelled for their honeymoon to the south of France.[104] By 1918, for whatever reason, he was finding his position at Castle Hedingham no longer very attractive, and by May of that year he had moved to Osborne Place in Moulsham and was assisting clergy at the cathedral.[105] There is no record of his departure from Castle Hedingham, or of any presentation (which seems unusual, given how highly the family was respected in the town). Did he leave under a cloud, or did he feel that he needed a more challenging position? We shall probably never know. Cecil Twist found it almost impossible to obtain any suitable accommodation near the cathedral, and after he had been there just a few months he left the cathedral and took up the position of curate-in-charge at St Peter's, Rainsford End, a mission church established in 1883 to serve the western part of Chelmsford.[106] With Edward Herbert's departure, however, St John's was down to a single curate, and Cecil Twist was offered (and rapidly accepted) this position, taking his first service at St John's in September 1918. He stayed as curate for more than four years, until he was licensed to his next post by the Bishop of Gloucester on 20 December 1922.[108] He subsequently moved to Ashton Somerville, also in Gloucestershire, in 1925.[109] He died in 1944.

Sydney Gelder Farrar was born in South Shields on 18 May 1892 and baptised at the little church of St Hilda's, South Shields where his father was vicar, on 2 June 1892. He was the third child of Rev Herbert William Farrar and his wife Florence Margaret. He found employment initially as a bank clerk, but at the age of twenty-one he felt that he had to join the army, signing up in March 1916 with the 6th (cyclist) Battalion, Royal Sussex regiment (by this time his father had moved to Barcombe in Sussex as vicar). He was severely wounded in the war, and devotedly nursed by a young VAD, Matilda Agatha Wolverson (the daughter of Dr and Mrs Wolverson of Wolverhampton). Matilda and Sydney Farrar were married at St Anne's church, Brighton, on 28 June 1918.[110] His experiences in the Great War had much influenced him, and he decided to attend Chichester Theological College to study for the priesthood, being ordained deacon in December 1921 and priest in May 1923, in Chelmsford Cathedral.[111] Almost immediately after being priested an opportunity arose for him to move back to Sussex and he was licensed as curate to Rev Canon Wilson at Cuckfield on 4 June 1923.[112] He stayed there for seven years, moving to his own incumbency at Barton Hartswode-with-Chestwode in August 1930.[113] He moved to Great Coxwell in 1934, and died in 1970.

Alexander Colvin was born in Dublin in 1884 and studied theology at King's College, London, receiving his AKC in 1909. He was ordained deacon in the parish church at Saffron Walden by the Bishop of St Albans in 1910, being licensed at the same time to St Mary the Virgin, Loughton.[114] He was ordained priest by the Bishop of Barking (acting under commission from the Bishop of St Albans) at Cheshunt on 24 September 1911.[115] Although an ordained priest, he joined the Essex regiment not as a chaplain but as a soldier, fighting in the Great War. Towards the end of the war he married Laura Agnes Foster, the daughter of a local builder, Charles Savin Foster, at St Mary the Virgin, Loughton on 25 September 1918. He chose to be married in his uniform as captain (rather than as a priest) and listed his occupation on the marriage certificate as 'soldier'. Whilst at Loughton, Alexander Colvin was one of the four clergymen shortlisted for the prestigious and well-paid post of chaplain to the local workhouse. Repeated voting, and finally the chairman's casting vote, resulted in the post going to one of the other candidates.[116] There seems to be no explanation as to why, after a year at St John's, he felt that he had to take up a post on the other side of the world in a remote part of Chile, but after a few years away, he returned to Essex and it was announced in April 1927 that he was to be the successor at

Willingale Doe to Robert Saulez, who was retiring on the grounds of ill-health.[117] He was instituted by the Bishop of Chelmsford in December of the same year, although the ceremony almost did not take place, due to a heavy snowfall in Essex on that day.[118] He stayed in Essex for much of the rest of his career, becoming responsible also for Willingale Spain and Shallow Bowells churches. He died in north London on 4 September 1974.

Henry Thomas Pimm was born in Newington, London, in 1891, the son of Frederick George Pimm, a professional scene painter and his wife Mary Anne. Henry Pimm went to Canada as a lay evangelist in 1911, and on the outbreak of the Great War, came back to England with the first Canadian contingent in 1914. He served in France for three and a half years, initially with the 85th Canadian infantry and then with the fourth battalion on the Canadian machine gun corps.[119] He took his Licentiate of Theology after the war and was ordained deacon in 1919 in St Paul's cathedral by the Bishop of London, being licensed at the same time to St Mark's, Kennington as curate. After being ordained priest in 1920 in Southwark Cathedral, he went to Sherborne College as history master, later returning to London as curate at another St Mark's, this time in Camberwell. He married Alice Browne in 1920 and they had one son and one daughter. He came to St John's in 1924 and left in 1925 for Somerset.[53] On his departure to Somerset he was presented by Mrs Wade with an inscribed study clock on behalf of the Women's Bible Study class, on Thursday 2 November 1925.[120] He remained in Minehead until April 1928, when he moved to the small parish of Selsey in Gloucestershire.[121] Selsey was much to his taste, as he stayed there as incumbent until 1942, eventually exchanging livings with Rev A.W. Collins, the vicar of Potton in Bedfordshire, in November of that year (Rev Collins felt he had to move to a less challenging parish on account of his health, which was poor).[122] Subsequent incumbencies saw him officiate at Stopsley (1946–51) and Meppershall. He died in Ipswich in 1976.

Frederick Arthur Stroud was born at St Leonard's-on-Sea, Sussex, on 9 September 1896, the son of Edward Bracy Stroud (a hatter's porter) and his wife Mary, an upholstress. He served in the Great War, with the Honourable Artillery company in Egypt, Palestine and Syria. He was one of the survivors of the torpedoing of the P&O steamship *Arcadian* in the Aegean sea. He was rescued after three hours in the water when a searchlight picked up his frantic waving. Before the war he had matriculated at Leeds University and after the conflict he resumed his theological studies at the College of the Resurrection, Mirfield. He was ordained deacon by the Bishop of Birmingham in the cathedral in 1922 and was licensed at the same time to a curacy at St Agnes', Cotteridge.[123] He was ordained priest in 1923, also in Birmingham cathedral.[124] He married Dorothy Maud Cannon in 1923, and their first child, Graham Frederick Stroud, was born in 1924. In 1925 the *Essex County Chronicle* announced that he would shortly take up duties as curate at St John's, Moulsham.[125] He remained as curate at St John's for five and a half years, increasingly taking over a share of Robert Burnett's duties as the vicar's rheumatism plagued him more and more. He then moved to St Chad's, Chadwell Heath, where he replaced the vicar (who had become seriously ill) on Friday 1 May 1931.[126] Both Frederick and Dorothy Stroud had been much-loved and devoted workers in Moulsham. Frederick had cared tirelessly for the ordinary people in the parish and Dorothy had founded the St John's Theatrical society and made it into a very successful organisation. It was no surprise, then, that on their departure from Moulsham, they received handsome gifts: a mother-of-pearl and gold clock for Mrs Stroud and a mahogany clock (as well as a combined wallet and pocket-book) for the curate.[127] Frederick Stroud's time in Chadwell Heath was to be neither prolonged nor untroubled. He found it a very difficult parish, with another level of problems all together from Moulsham. He had only been there a few months when the church was broken into, twice. On the second occasion a silverware box was stolen, the communion wine drunk and the aumbry prised out of the wall and taken away.[128] In February 1932, the vicar of Greenstead Green, Rev William Duckworth, died suddenly, and six weeks later it was announced that Frederick Stroud had accepted the living.[129] He remained at Greenstead for five years before accepting another challenging parish, St Andrew's, Romford, where he was instituted in 1937. Here he served for many years, retiring to Chingford, where he died in the cottage hospital in 1970, aged 73.

Although Robert Burnett had announced his departure from the parish, life at St John's had to carry on, and the responsibility for much of this fell on Frederick Stroud. At the harvest festival in 1930, on 5 October, bearing in mind the difficult conditions in the country at the time. it was no surprise that he preached a sermon on 'economy'. *"There can be no selfishness"*, he began, *"where God's goods are concerned. On those who are well-off, and have an abundance of good things, God places the responsibility of*

Figure 22 – Robert Frederick Burnett, Incumbent of
St John's, Moulsham, 1919 – 1930

recognising the needs of those who are not so fortunate as themselves". It was a very political message.[130] The St John's Theatrical Society continued to thrive, the *Essex County Chronicle* praising (again) Mrs Stroud's efforts in producing 'A Chinese Honeymoon' and commending the society for thinking about 'The Vagabond King' as its next production.[131]

'Moulsham is a parish of great possibilities and great difficulties'

Just a week later Robert Burnett published his farewell letter to the parish in the *Moulsham Parish Magazine. "I cannot but help feeling tremendously grateful"*, he began, *"for all the help I have had from all the workers in the parish and the assistant priests. Moulsham is a parish of great possibilities and great difficulties... ...but by your help I am able to leave the parish well-equipped in every respect. You have a good parochial hall which I had hoped to see completed before I left, but even as it is, it is a tremendous help to the parish. I may say that a hall the size of ours cannot run on nothing. We have got a house for the assistant priest which is a great help for any parish. The organisations of the parish are in good health as far as numbers are concerned, but do not rest content with numbers – the spirit of them is the great and important matter"*.[132]

St John's parochial hall was filled on Wednesday, 19 November for the presentations to Robert Burnett and his wife. Robert Burnett was given a cheque for £66 and an illuminated album containing the names of all the contributors (contrast this with the 100 guineas (£105) that George Collier, a curate, received when he left in 1901). The churchwardens, Major Doe and Mr Beckett made the presentation, and in his speech, Major Doe said that: *"Mr Burnett had done his very best in trying to put the affairs of the parish on a satisfactory basis, and he had succeeded in so many ways through sheer hard work"*. Robert Burnett was much moved, and in responding said that he felt that the parish had grown tremendously, and one thing that he would take credit for was that he had put the right people at the head of the various parochial organisations. It was to these people that the credit was really due. Other presentations included an oxidised silver ashtray to the vicar and a tweed travelling case and matching scarf to Mrs Burnett.[133] The vicar preached his last sermon at St John's on Sunday, 22 November.[134]

Robert Burnett was instituted to the rectory of Great Yeldham on the evening of Tuesday, 2 December 1931. The ceremony was performed by the Bishop of Chelmsford (Dr Henry Wilson) who was assisted by the Rural Dean, Rev T.H. Curling, of Chelmsford.[135] Great Yeldham was a sharp contrast to Moulsham. Robert Burnett was moving from a parish with a population of 8,500 to one with only 580 individuals, yet his stipend at Great Yeldham was £527, almost doubling Moulsham's £300. Robert Burnett had earned his reward. He stayed at Great Yeldham until 1936, moving back nearer to Chelmsford at Great Waltham. After ten months in this new parish, the *Essex County Chronicle* reported on Friday, 28 January 1938 that the vicar of Great Waltham's condition: *"continues grave and gives great cause for anxiety"*, and he in fact died that very evening, aged only fifty-six.[136] He died a relatively wealthy man, leaving over £7,500 in his will.[137] Although he was only in his last parish for a relatively short time, it is tempting to think that his impact was considerable – his much loved verger, Frederick Wilkin committed suicide shortly after Robert Burnett's death. The inquest was told that he was: *"completely devoted to his vicar"*.

Robert Burnett had overseen, and, indeed, engineered many of the positive changes that had taken place at St John's during his incumbency. His photograph (*Figure 22*) shows a mild-looking, shy and perhaps very private man (there was no record of his funeral service in the local press) but a man with a strong determination to do what was right and to see his ideas through to their conclusion. He had left St John's in good shape for the years ahead.

The next incumbent would take St John's up to its centenary. How would he cope with the legacy of the first one hundred years?

9. WILLIAM STANLEY BROWNLESS

(1931-50)

"How well I remember, towards the end of January 1931,
coming to Chelmsford at the invitation of Provost Morrow, to
view the living of Moulsham. It was a gloomy day. I was not at
all taken by the church and had almost made up my mind to
go back home again and refuse the living.
Then we went on to look at the vicarage. That looked very
depressing that day, and I felt I must refuse it".[1]

Stanley Brownless was clearly not impressed with his first glimpse of St John's, Moulsham, and the vicarage, when Provost Morrow (the patron of the living) showed him around that January day in 1931. So what changed his mind? He and the provost had arranged to meet the two churchwardens (Major Doe and Mr Beckett) at the provost's house, near the cathedral. That meeting changed everything. The two churchwardens were able to put forward very positive suggestions for Stanley Brownless' ministry, and he agreed to meet with the church council a week later. He travelled down from Chesterfield and outlined his vision for the parish. The church council pledged its complete and unequivocal support for everything he had put forward. *"And"*, he said, *"immediately I accepted"*.

'He had done splendid work and become popular amongst all classes'

William Stanley Brownless was born at 18, Poplar Road, Oxton (near Birkenhead) in 1880. He was the son of Captain William Perse Brownless, a Master Mariner, and his wife Sarah Stanley, whom he married on 12 December 1872, at Christchurch, Moreton, in the Wirral. Stanley Brownless grew up in a family where his father was frequently absent on long sea voyages, but his mother had strong links with her local church, and it was no surprise to see that Stanley spent much of his childhood as a chorister (he was well-known during his time a Moulsham for his fine singing voice). He left school at fourteen and went initially into the drapery business as a salesman. Just after his twenty-first birthday he felt a call to the priesthood, and after studying at St Aidan's Theological College, he was ordained deacon in Chichester Cathedral by the bishop on Sunday, 18 June 1905.[2] He was licensed at the same time as curate to St Mary-in-the-castle, Hastings.[3] He was ordained priest (again by the Bishop of Chichester, in the Cathedral) on 23 December 1906.[4] He remained in Hastings until 1910, leaving to go as curate to St Matthew's, Kingsdown, Bristol, departing from St Mary-in-the-castle on 30 July (the presentation ceremony marked a big change for this church, as both curates were moving to new livings and the vicar was retiring).[5] He stayed a year at Kingsdown before moving to Battersea as curate (1911–13), then as priest-in-charge at Fishponds (1913–19). His final move before St John's was to Holy Trinity, Chesterfield, where he ministered for just under three years. Here he was said to have done splendid work and become popular among all classes.[6] Whilst at All Saints', Fishponds, he had announced his engagement to Miss Harriet Mellish Flint, the daughter of Mr Joseph Flint of Battle,[7] and later the same year they were married on 14 August in Battle parish church, by a friend of Stanley Brownless, Rev F. Shippam, the vicar of Christchurch, Hertford. His move from Chesterfield to Moulsham was announced on 13 February 1931[9] and his acceptance published a fortnight later.[10]

He was instituted as vicar of St John's on Wednesday evening (29 April 1931) by the Bishop of Chelmsford (Dr Henry Wilson) and inducted by the Archdeacon of Southend, in front of an overflowing congregation, with many other local clergy present. After the ceremony, at the reception for the new vicar, the bishop presented a cheque to the Rev Frederick Stroud (who had been present at the institution as priest-in-charge) upon his departure to

Chadwell Heath (he had preached his last sermon on Sunday 26 April). With Stanley Brownless now at the helm, St John's was looking forward positively to the future.

'The semi-paganism which prevailed throughout the country'

During the period between Robert Burnett's departure (22 November 1930) and Stanley Brownless' institution as vicar, Frederick Stroud was made priest-in-charge and was effectively vicar of the parish. The last few months of Robert Burnett's incumbency had already resulted in a lot more work falling on his shoulders. It was no surprise to see him chairing the annual parochial meeting for St John's which was held on Wednesday, 29 January in the parochial hall. After a formal vestry meeting, where Major Doe and Mr Beckett were re-appointed to their respective wardens' positions, Mr Stroud pointed out that regret at Robert Burnett's departure had not been tempered by the appointment of a new vicar. Speaking of the parish, he said that it was always up against the financial problem of ways and means. The real problem facing the parish was, he said: *"a need for the re-organisation of their methods of obtaining contributions. There should be better recognition by the church people of their duty and an obligation to support the parish church by systematic and regular offerings, proportionate to each one's ability"*. If the church was only half full, it was not due to any fault or defect in their services but to the semi-paganism which prevailed throughout the country and which carried with it an utter disregard for Sunday observance.

Major Doe then presented the accounts, which showed a debt for the previous year of just over £57, compared with more than £72 for the year before that. Once again St John's had failed to meet its quota for the diocesan fund (£98) on this occasion managing only to pay £51. Frederick Stroud also pointed out that one of the more pressing items of expenditure was the decoration of the interior of the church, which was in a poor state. Major Doe said that he had estimated that this would need £300 (in fact, it was to cost considerably more). In his last duty before he resigned as church council secretary, Mr Edgar Cheverton announced that sixty-four names had been added to the electoral roll. It now stood at 430. The meeting closed with grateful thanks to Frederick Stroud for all his efforts as priest-in-charge.[11]

'With delicacy and a kindly spirit'

When Stanley Brownless and his family first arrived in Moulsham vicarage, they had a very pleasant surprise. Mrs Brownless found: *"the kitchen cupboard stocked with all manner of articles, a gift from the women of the parish"*. It was a simple gesture, but it made a considerable impact on the new vicar. *"It was a kindly act,"* he said, *"and one which shows the true spirit of welcome. It is not just the gift that appeals to us, but the kindly thoughts which must have brought the act into being"*.[12] Stanley Brownless also made it quite clear early on how he wished to run his parish. In his first letter to the parishioners, in the *Moulsham Parish Magazine*, he referred to some of the changes he wished to make, although he stressed that he wanted to do so: *"with delicacy and a kindly spirit"*. These changes (all of which had been communicated to the church council before Stanley Brownless had accepted the living) included no more wearing of vestments as long as he was vicar, daily celebrations were to be discontinued and replaced by celebrations on Wednesday at eight and Friday at seven-thirty. Among other changes were discontinuation of the ten o'clock Eucharist on Sundays and its replacement by eleven o'clock mattins to the Benedictus. Altar lights, coloured stoles and servers would be retained.[13]

In November of that same year, the Diocesan Architect, Mr Wykeham Chancellor, carried out a thorough examination of the fabric of St John's. His report made difficult reading. He suggested that over £1,000 would be required to put the church externally in a sound, watertight condition and to render the stonework safe. The whole of the inside, he thought, would need reconditioning.

The complete cost of all the work would total about £1,600. St John's (the *Essex County Chronicle* reported) served a population of more than 12,000 people (*sic*). Stanley Brownless and the churchwardens promptly opened a restoration fund, emphasising to the whole parish that expenditure over the previous ten or so years had been high (a parochial hall and the curate's house among other items) and that parish resources were now strained.[14]

It was not just the parish financial resources that were now strained. Since Frederick Stroud's departure at the end of April, Stanley Brownless had been running the parish single-handedly, and he lost little time in appointing a curate to assist him. At the end of May, the *Essex Newsman* reported that: *"The vicar of Moulsham, the Reverend William Brownless, has appointed Mr Sydney J. Burling, of King's College, London, to be his curate. Mr Burling's home is in Seven Kings; he is a bachelor aged twenty-four and has had a distinguished college career".*[15] Sydney Burling was ordained deacon by the Bishop of Chelmsford in the cathedral on Sunday 27 September 1931 and licensed to St John's at the same ceremony.[16]

The following year, 1932, started on a very positive note. St John's amateur theatrical group, in spite of the departure of the Strouds (who had been the driving force behind the group's formation) put on a performance of the Japanese musical play 'The Geisha' in the last week of January. *"They had,"* said the local press, *"survived a difficult year with honours".* The Rev and Mrs Stroud came from Chadwell Heath to see the performance: they were clearly impressed with their legacy.[17]

'It was a remarkable experience, and one which I shall never forget'

By the summer Stanley Brownless and his team had really got their teeth into the fundraising, and their efforts were already bearing fruit. In July the vicar (who believed in taking a practical part in the efforts) erected a brightly coloured tent in the churchyard, and made himself available from seven in the morning until nine at night in order to receive any and all gifts that parishioners might wish to contribute. *"It was a remarkable experience"*, he said afterwards, *"and one I shall never forget. I had a celebration of Holy Communion at six-thirty and was on duty in the tent at seven. Mrs Brownless brought me breakfast, lunch and tea. Scores of well-wishers came to see me and leave donations, relays of collectors were on duty outside the church receiving contributions from passers-by and children brought in and filled up feet of pennies"*. He emphasised that great kindness was shown by everyone, even (his words) the Salvation Army. The bishop and the mayor of Chelmsford visited him throughout the day, and the whole event raised £180 for the restoration fund.[18] This was followed up in December by a very successful church bazaar (in spite of the condemnation such events had received at the previous ruridecanal conference) which raised a grand total of £274 for the church restoration fund.

The church council meeting to report on 1932 took place on 10 February 1933 in the Parochial Hall. After the formal business of the vestry meeting (in which Major Doe and Mr Beckett were re-appointed) the main business of the council concerned the restoration project. Mr Wykeham Chancellor's report in 1931 had shown the magnitude of the task facing the parish, but the report of the church council secretary (Mr C.W. Shepherd) showed the success that the parish had had in raising funds for the repairs. He started off by emphasising that, in his opinion, the church was full of real enthusiasm for the project in hand, and he believed that this enthusiasm had created a sense of real, vigorous life in the church. The general overall financial position of the church was extremely sound, and the results of the appeal for the restoration of the church had been better than anyone had dared to hope. The total raised in the previous year had been no less than £1,240. One of the most rewarding aspects, he continued, had been that in addition to the special events (the vicar's day in the tent, the Christmas bazaar) much of the sum had been raised by contributions from various church organisations (billiard club, theatricals, scouts, etc.). He concluded by thanking the vicar, the curate and the congregation. *"Let us therefore,"* he ended, *"show our appreciation by supporting them all to the best of our ability and by shouldering our responsibility in the life of the church"*.[20]

'He praised the flourishing state of the parish organisations'

As 1933 moved into 1934 the problems of the completion of the church fabric restoration still hung over the parish. In the middle of February the vicar hosted the now customary tea and entertainment in the parochial hall, and over one hundred and fifty parishioners were present. After the usual entertainments (arranged by Mr Shepherd) and a sumptuous tea (paid for by subscription) the vicar gave a pep talk to all those present. He praised the flourishing state of the parochial organisations and congratulated everyone on their hard work in completing repairs to the exterior of the church itself. Now, he reported, they would be able to start work on what could be a daunting task, the redecoration of the whole of the interior. The pound scheme, and its associated 'feet of pennies' scheme for the children would be wound up and they would be able to see how much of the interior they could decorate as a first phase. He was, he concluded, deeply moved by their loyalty and dedication.[21] The pound scheme came to an end on 20 March and the vicar was able to report that the results had been very satisfactory. The vicar had made himself available in the church in both the afternoon and the evening, and by the end of the day a total of £161 had been collected. When a number of other gifts were added in, a total of almost £250 was available to spend on the interior decoration of the church.[22] However, in the parish magazine the following September the vicar had to write that a lack of money meant that they were unable to contemplate completion of the restoration straightaway. *"We have always tried,"* he explained, *"to pay for each portion of the work as it was completed, and not run up a big debt"*. At the time of writing, and because of additional work required on the heating, and a bill for the architect's fees, the amount outstanding was of the order of £350 and the church had only £200 in hand to cover this. *"Work on the side chapel, vestries and chancel,"* he continued, *"would have to be postponed but the money for us to complete the work would come before long"*.[23]

'St John's had become a very progressive parish'

The following year (1935) started with a very satisfactory vestry meeting held on a Friday evening (8 February) in the parochial hall. Stanley Brownless presided. The two wardens were re-elected and the vicar commented on how harmoniously the three of them had worked together, and what great support he had received from the two wardens since he had come to the parish. The secretary (Mr Foxwell) in his report stated that under the guidance of the vicar and the curate (Rev Burling) St John's had become a very progressive parish. The well-established youth conferences now attracted a wide range of young people, and the Sunday school, under the curate, was doing outstanding work. He was able to report that the previous year had seen the main body of the church redecorated and the seating converted (at last) to a central aisle. The rest of the interior decoration had to be postponed because of unexpected expenditure on the heating system, which had again been giving trouble.

The secretary also reported that the verger (Mr Samuels) had retired, but that he and his wife had now been allocated an almshouse and a weekly grant until Mr Samuels received his old age pension. The meeting appointed Mr W.F. Gowers as the new verger. Mr Foxwell concluded his report by thanking the vicar and Mrs Brownless, Mr Burling and Miss Read (the lay worker) for the considerable contribution they had made to the running of the parish over the past year. Major Doe then presented the accounts noting that the debit balance of just over £65 with which the year had started had been reduced to £49 by the end of the year. The final count for the pound scheme had been £176 and a collection of farthings by the children had raised just over £5 (counting of these must have been fun). The parochial hall account had a small deficit, brought about by the provision of new curtains and chairs. The diocesan quota, as usual, remained stubbornly in deficit to the tune of £45. The vicar concluded the meeting by noting that the electoral roll now contained 440 names.[24]

This happy combination of vicar, curate and wardens was not to last much longer. In July, the Bishop of Chelmsford announced that Sidney Burling was to be the first priest-in-charge of the new district of St Barnabas, Hadleigh, where a mission church was being erected. The new priest-in-charge, the Bishop added, would take up his duties at the end of September.[25] The new church was dedicated by the Bishop on 1 October,[26] shortly after Sidney Burling's marriage at St John's to Miss Minnie Thurgood, a church worker. It was the first wedding to bless the new central aisle of St John's.[27] Sidney Burling and his wife took their leave of St John's on Monday 7 October with a handsome presentation in the parochial hall, the curate receiving a cheque for just over £41.[28]

Later that October, Stanley Brownless was stricken with a septic foot. With the vicar incapacitated (and with no curate) services at St John's could only be kept going with the help of the Rev W.H. Davies (now an assistant priest at the cathedral) and the Rev M. Behr, the vicar of Margaretting.[29]

'So down each side he placed an aisle'

So the vestry meeting the following year (the penultimate one in this history, 1936) was held on Friday 28 February with the vicar presiding. He re-appointed Mr Beckett as his warden, and Major Doe was re-elected as people's warden. The vicar expressed his appreciation of the excellent support given to him by the church officers and others throughout the year, and added: *"I hope that the time will soon arrive when matters other than financial will have to occupy our attention. At the moment, our chief worry is that connected with finance. We shall, I hope, soon get rid of that worry and then we can all go forward to further effort"*.

Mr Foxwell, the church secretary, then presented his report of church activities throughout the year, which had seen many changes, and had been a period of hard work and difficulties for some in the parish. In spite of all these obstacles, progress continued and he, Mr Foxwell, believed that their church life was full of happiness. Mr Foxwell pointed out that they had lost Rev Burling on his appointment to St Barnabas but that they now had the services of Rev William Getliffe in his stead. The church had organised a very successful bazaar in 1935, raising just under £200 for church funds. The electoral roll remained unchanged at 440. Major Doe then presented the accounts, pointing out that the debit balance had now risen to nearly £52. After the routine election of church officers, the vicar closed the meeting with the Benediction.[30]

William Brownless was not going to be able to count on the services of a curate for very long. In July, it was announced that William Getliffe was appointed to the curacy of Thundersley and that he would take up his duties in the following October. The vicar would, however, for a short while have to run the parish single-handedly, because although he had secured the services of the Rev Dudley Johns as curate, he would not take up his duties until after his ordination towards the end of the year.[31] The fête and bazaar held in 1936 were both markedly less successful than the previous year, this time only raising just over £50 for church funds, in spite of the dance after the bazaar being *"very well attended"*.

The *Moulsham Parish Magazine* that July produced a humorous comment on the alterations that had taken place inside the church building over the last couple of years. The author (perhaps wisely) chose to remain anonymous:

> *"In the bad old days of long ago,*
> *About a hundred years or so,*
> *A church was built – a noble pile,*
> *But in a somewhat unusual style,*

For those who had this church erected,
One thing sadly they neglected,
(and this I think will make you smile)
They clean forgot a central aisle,
Two paths they put along the nave,
Which to many disappointment gave,
For when arrived each festive day,
On which the bride was given away,
Most people had no chance to see,
The bride in all her finery.
When, the marriage service done,
They left the church, not two, but one,
What should have been the best of views,
Was naught but pews – and then more pews,
(and they were only brown ones, too)
Then to the place a vicar came,
And some, no doubt, could guess his name,
he said, "Good gracious, this won't do –
We want three aisles, not merely two".
So down each side he placed an aisle,
Where choir could walk in single file,
And down the centre, one much wider,
Where bride could walk, her gown beside her,
(Though down the aisle the groom would have to slip,
right through the middle he has to trip)
So out they go, in perfect order,
Bride like a lady – you the herbaceous border,
Now you've had this information,
Help your church's restoration
The bride is seen, the vicar's happy,
Now – don't be mean – and make it snappy!"[32]

In September, the Rev Dudley Johns was duly ordained deacon by the bishop in Chelmsford cathedral. He was licensed the same day to St John's, Moulsham, where his stipend (£150) was supplemented by the use of the glebe house.[33]

'Moulsham, he felt, would now enter a new phase of service'

So 1937 dawned, the year of the centenary of St John's consecration in 1837. The Bishop was not available for the exact date of the consecration, in April, so the decision was taken that the church would celebrate the completion of its restoration and would be re-dedicated at the beginning of the year. Accordingly, this significant service was held in the evening of Wednesday, 20 January. The exterior of St John's was floodlit throughout the whole of the proceedings. The bishop, accompanied by a good selection of the local clergy (including Robert Burnett and Sidney Burling) arrived at the west door of St John's, upon which the bishop knocked three times with his pastoral staff. The churchwardens opened the door, whereupon the bishop, accompanied by the attendant clergy, entered. The procession, preceded by the choir, went to the altar. The bishop then pronounced the celebratory prayers for the restored fabric, and then blessed the new banner for the St John's branch of the Mothers' Union (the cost of which (£21) had been met by individual members). Stanley Brownless then outlined how the money for the restoration had been raised, emphasising how generous the parish had been on that day he had sat in his tent in the churchyard, collecting gifts. In total, in the past five years, over £2,700 had been raised towards a total cost of £3,000. He then went on to detail all the work that had been carried out in that period. All the stonework on the top of the tower and all the stone facings had been renewed, a new electric clock had been installed on the west face of the tower, most of the roof had been re-slated and all the guttering had been replaced. New plain glass windows had been substituted for the dilapidated 'tinted glass' windows, and the whole of the brickwork had been repointed. The pews had been re-arranged and the seating now incorporated a much appreciated central aisle. New red tiling had been incorporated throughout the building together with a marble pavement (the gift of an anonymous donor) in the sanctuary. The whole church had been painted, including pews, wall and ceilings. New altar frontals and hangings had been fitted. The side chapel had been floored with orange tiles and the walls of the church panelled in wood.

The bishop then replied to Stanley Brownless, saying that he believed that this service was an historic one in the records of Moulsham, in that it marked the conclusion of five years' work to beautify the house of God. It had been a mighty task carried out in the face of many difficulties and they must all join together in heartfelt thanksgiving for all that they, under God's blessing, had been able to accomplish. Moulsham, he felt, would now enter a new phase of service, and he was glad to be there to pay his personal tribute to a hard working vicar and a happy and loyal people. A collection was made during the final hymn which provided an additional £14 towards the deficit in the restoration fund.[34] The following Sunday (24 January) the mayor of Chelmsford (Alderman J. Thompson, OBE, JP) and the Corporation visited St John's for a commemorative service at which the preacher was the Archdeacon of Southend, the Ven Percy Bayne.[35]

'I have never been happier in my life'

After all these impressive celebrations, the annual vestry meeting (which was held on Wednesday 31 March) was something of an anticlimax. Mr Beckett and Major Doe again agreed to continue in their positions as wardens. Mr Foxwell, in his report as secretary, pointed out that under the able guidance of the vicar, the spiritual life of St John's had deepened, along with the tremendous task that they had set themselves with regard to the fabric of the church. He felt that the vicar was a true leader, was always full of optimism, and that optimism had been fully justified by the scale of their achievements. Major Doe then presented the accounts, and was pleased to announce that the deficit had been reduced by £10 to a figure of £64. The vicar then took the floor. "*I have never been happier in my life than I have been at St John's,*" he observed, "*since I have been vicar here I have been happy because I have felt all along that I have had the support and backing of the congregation as a whole*". He concluded the meeting as usual with the Benediction.[36]

The weekend that was nearest to the anniversary of the consecration seems to have passed with few (if any) events to celebrate it. There is certainly no record in the church archives or in the local press of anything taking place, which is itself unusual. The anniversary year was noteworthy for two other incidents which some may have construed as the Almighty's comments on what went on in His parish of Moulsham. In July, Rev Dudley Johns, the curate, appeared before the mayor (in his *ex-officio* capacity as Justice of the Peace) on a charge of using a motor vehicle without a road fund licence (on 1 April, no less). The Mayor: *"I did not expect to see you here this morning, Mr Johns"*. "No," replied the defendant, *"but I had a suspicion that I would see you, Sir!"* (Laughter). This light-hearted approach clearly worked – the case was dismissed. The defendant admitted that it was his fault, as he: *"did not think clearly about the matter"*. He was fined 4s. and had to pay 12s. to cover the missing period of the licence.[37] On Wednesday 26 May the verger, after checking the copper house (next to the boiler house on the north wall of the church) was just on his way to the west door when there was a terrific flash of lightning and a deafening crash of thunder. He turned to see that the heavy stone cross at the end of the north transept had been struck. Substantial portions of the cross had fallen, tearing large holes in the roof of the copper house, where he had been standing just a few moments before. He had indeed had a lucky escape. There had been damage to the roof of the north transept itself and much of the electrical circuitry of the church itself no longer functioned. The clock had stopped (although that in itself was not a particularly unusual event) but in this case needed extensive repairs, even though it had been replaced as part of the restoration programme. The report of this incident in the *Essex County Chronicle* was cheekily placed next to an advertisement for the local ironmongers, Gripper's, offering to supply and fit lightning conductors. It was truly an ill wind.[38] However events in Europe and the shadows of war were beginning to overtake local events in the press and there is nothing more recorded about St John's in its centenary year, even in church sources. So, with some uncertainty, the parish looked forward to the next one hundred years.

Stanley Brownless had been well served by curates in his first seven years at St John's. Frederick Stroud had left just before the vicar's installation in 1931, and the vicar had to wait until 27 September of that year before Sidney Burling was licensed to St John's after his ordination in the cathedral, although his appointment had been confirmed at the end of May.[39] Sidney Burling was born in Leytonstone in 1907, the son of a wholesale druggists's assistant Henry Burling and his wife Elisabeth Julia. Sidney Burling was educated at King's College, London, where he distinguished himself academically. At the time of his licensing, he was living at Seven Kings. After his year at St John's he was ordained priest in Chelmsford Cathedral on Sunday, 18 September 1932.[40] St John's clearly had attractions (other than his curacy) as on Saturday, 21 September 1935 he married Miss Minnie Tyrell (Trixie) Thurgood, the eldest daughter of Mr and Mrs W.T. Thurgood of 'Beacons', Wood Street. The bride was a prominent church worker at St John's, being the leader of the Women's Bible class. She had also been, for some years, a member of staff at County Hall. After the reception in the vicarage grounds, the couple left for a honeymoon in Devon. Sidney Burling's days at St John's were drawing to a close – the Bishop of Chelmsford had already announced that the Rev Burling would be the new priest-in-charge at St Barnabas, Hadleigh. He stayed at St Barnabas for some years, moving to the united parishes of Tilty and Broxted (near Colchester) in 1961, when he was fifty-four.[42] He died in Colchester in 1987. Minnie died in 1997.

William Atherstone Getliffe came to St John's from the diocese of Exeter. He was born in the little village of Wymondham, near Melton Mowbray, at the end of 1899, the eldest son of Richard and Mary Getliffe. He served in the army for a short time in the Great War, joining up at the age of seventeen and a half and fighting in France with the second Essex regiment. After the war he went to Canada, being educated at the University of Emmanuel College, Saskatoon. He was ordained in Canada in 1929 and subsequently worked in a remote part of the country as a missioner. When he came back to England he was on a list of special service clergy in the diocese of Exeter for just under a year. He came to St John's in November 1935, leaving less than a year later to go to Rayleigh. He was appointed curate at St Peter's, Thundersley in 1936 until in January 1945 he was instituted as vicar of Christ Church, Warley, near Brentwood. After a period of working for the Colonial and Continental church society, he joined the Church Army for the remainder of his life. He married Dorothea, probably during his time in Canada, and eventually they retired to Weston-super-Mare in Somerset. Here William died on 16 May 1964 and Dorothea on 17 February 1968.[43]

James Dudley Johns was born at 27, the Drive, Walthamstow in spring 1909 to James Johns (a stock exchange jobber) and his wife Bessie Phillips Johns. He took his BA at Cambridge in 1934 and trained for the priesthood at Ridley Hall. He was ordained deacon by the Bishop of Chelmsford at Michaelmas on 20 September 1936, being licensed to St John's at the same time.[44] He soon

Figure 23 – William Stanley Brownless, Incumbent of
St John's, Moulsham 1931–50

became much loved by the parishioners of Moulsham, and his work amongst the children with whom he came into contact endeared him to everyone. He moved on from St John's in September 1939 to a curacy at Grays, where his friend Rev Neville Welch had just been appointed vicar.[45] In 1941 he moved to be vicar at All Saints', Forest Gate in succession to Rev Vaughan Edmunds. In 1954 he wrote a little book entitled: *"Belief, Life and Worship – A book of Anglican teaching for senior groups and Bible classes"*.

William Stanley Brownless remained at St John's, Moulsham until September 1950 when at the age of seventy, he decided to retire. In his last letter to the parish, he wrote: *"I leave Moulsham with the happiest remembrances of a grand people. The work here has been carried out well and has been most fruitful. Our services have been well-attended – the congregational singing has been remarked on by many a visiting clergyman, as has the careful listening to the sermons. All the church organisations have been living things and fruitful in spiritual growth. I thank God for all His blessings and mercies during my ministry"*. He preached his farewell sermon on 17 September 1950. Initially in their retirement he and Henrietta moved to Yeovil in Somerset. William Stanley Brownless died in Manormead nursing home, Hindhead, Surrey on 7 January 1965.[47] His portrait, taken while he was at St John's, shows a kindly man with a strong inner drive (*Figure 23*). He was much missed when he left the parish.

What would the next one hundred years hold for St John the Evangelist, Moulsham?

APPENDIX 1

REFERENCES

CHAPTER 1 – A CHAPEL IS BORN

1. *Chelmsford Chronicle*, Friday, 11 April 1834
2. *Chelmsford Chronicle*, Friday, 18 April 1834
3. *Chelmsford Chronicle*, Friday, 2 May 1834
4. *Chelmsford Chronicle*, Friday, 30 May 1834
5. *Chelmsford Chronicle*, Friday, 13 June 1834
6. *Chelmsford Chronicle*, Friday, 20 June 1834
7. *Chelmsford Chronicle*, Friday, 27 June 1834
8. *Chelmsford Chronicle*, Friday, 25 July 1834
9. Malcolm *Johnson, Bustling Intermeddler? The Life and Work of Charles James Blomfield*, pages 104 *et seq., (*Gracewing, 2001)
10. *Chelmsford Chronicle*, Friday, 20 February 1835
11. *Chelmsford Chronicle*, Friday, 8 April 1836
12. *Chelmsford Chronicle*, Friday, 1 January 1836 (page 3)
13. Hilda Grieve, *The Sleepers and the Shadows*, Vol. 2, pages 298 *et seq.*, (ERO 1994)
14. *Chelmsford Chronicle*, Friday, 1 January 1836 (page 1)
15. *Essex Standard*, Friday, 12 February 1836
16. *Chelmsford Chronicle*, Friday, 4 March 1836
17. *Chelmsford Chronicle*, Friday, 18 March 1836
18. *Chelmsford Chronicle*, Friday, 1 April 1836
19. Essex Record Office (ERO), D/DO/Q1
20. Hilda Grieve, *The Sleepers and the Shadows*, Vol. 2, page 293 (ERO 1994)
21. *ibid.*, page 306 *et seq.*
22. *The British Magazine and Monthly Register of Religious and Ecclesiastical Information*, Vol. IX, pages 559–560 (1836) (accessed on Google Books, 23 May 2010)
23. *Chelmsford Chronicle*, Friday, 24 March 1837

24. *Chelmsford Chronicle*, Friday, 14 April 1837

25. *Chelmsford Chronicle*, Friday, 21 April 1837

26. *St John the Evangelist Baptism Registers*, Vol. 1 (1837–51) (ERO D/P511/1/1)

27. *St John the Evangelist Burial Registers*, Vol. 1, (1837–50) (ERO D/P511/1/8)

28. J.A. Venn, *Alumni Cantabrignenses*, Vol. III, page 504 (Cambridge University Press, 1947)

29. *The Annual Register of World Events: a Review of the Year*, Vol. 69 pages 194–5 (1827) (accessed on Google Books, 30 September 2010)

30. Essex Record Office, Q/SBb 498/32 (1830)

31. *Chelmsford Chronicle*, Friday, 15 December 1827

32. Rev. J.A. Bartlett in *The Chelmsfordian* of 1900, quoted by Tony Tuckwell in *"That Honourable and Gentlemanlike House"*, page 57 (Free Range Publishing, 2008)

33. Hilda Grieve, *The Sleepers and the Shadows*, Vol. 2, page 296 (ERO 1994)

34. Anon., *Alumni Oxoniensis, 1715–1886*, page 593

35. *Crockford's Clerical Directory*, 1883

36. *Essex Chronicle*, Friday, 15 January 1875

37. *Essex Weekly News*, 2 April 1875

38. *The London Gazette*, Issue 19654, pages 1968–1969 (11 September 1838)

CHAPTER 2 – CHRISTOPHER RALPH MUSTON

1. *Chelmsford Chronicle*, Friday, 12 August 1859

2. Details from www.lancasterfamilytree.com (accessed 31 October 2009)

3. Rev. Christopher Muston, *A funeral sermon, occasioned by the death of Miss March, daughter of Thomas March, Esq., of Borden; who departed this life 15 October 1792. aged 25 Years. Preached 28 October 1792 at the Independent Meeting Chapel, Milton, Kent.* Printed by J. Chalmers for Ash, Barnes, Sittingbourne and Flowers, Milton, Kent. (accessed on Google Books, 7 April 2011)

4. *The Surman Index* at the Centre for Dissenting Studies (accessed as www.surman.english.qmul.ac.uk on 27 April 2011)

5.   *The Evangelical Magazine*, Vol. 17, page 382 (1809) This relates that Christopher Muston preached a sermon at the funeral in Epping of the Rev. Archibald Bill, a well-known dissenting minister (accessed on Google Books 31 March 2011)

6.   Rev James Churchill, *An Essay on Unbelief, describing its nature and operations and showing its baneful influence in distressing awakened and renewed souls* (Oxford, 1811) (accessed on Google Books, 16 February 2011)

7.   *The New Monthly Magazine and Universal Register*, Vol. V, page 475 (January–June 1816) See Also *The Literary Panorama and National Register*, ed. Charles Taylor, Vol. 4, page 180 (July–December 1818) (both accessed on Google Books, 4 April 2011)

8.   *The New Monthly Magazine and Universal Register,* Vol. X, page 180 (July-December 1818) (accessed on Google Books, 19 April 2011)

9.   *The Critical Review (or, Annals of Literature)*, the Fourth Series, (ed. Tobias Smollet) Vol. IV, page 220 (1813) (accessed on Google Books, 3 May 2010)

10.   For a typical reference, see Owen Chadwick, *The Victorian Church*, Part I, page 81 (the Third Edition, A. & C. Black, London 1971)

11.   W. Innes Addison, *A Roll of Graduates of the University of Glasgow, from 31 December 1772 to 31 December 1897*, page 313 (Glasgow, 1910) (accessed on www.openlibrary.org on 20 April 2011)

12.   Anon., *Prize Lists of the University of Glasgow, from 31 December 1772 to 31 December 1883*, page 216 (Glasgow, 1911) (accessed on www.openlibrary.org on 9 April 2011)

13.   *ibid.*, page 224

14.   W. Innes Addison, *op. cit.,* page 465

15.   *The Christian Remembrancer (or the Churchman's Biblical, Ecclesiastical and Library Miscellany)*, Vol. 4, page 445 (January–December 1822) (accessed on Google Books 21 April 2011)

16.   *The London Christian Instructor or Congregational Magazine*, Vol. VII, pages 4456 (August 1824) (accessed on Google Books, 15 April 2011)

17.   *The Congregational Magazine, New Series*, Vol. III, page 686 (1827) (accessed on Google Books, 12 April 2011)

18.   J.H. Matthiason, *Bedford and it Environs; or an Historical and Topographical Sketch of the Town of Bedford*, pages 48–49, (Bedford, 1831) (accessed on Google Books, 17 November 2010)

19.   Anon., *The Baptist Magazine*, Vol. XXIII, page 31 (London, George Wightman, 1831) (accessed on Google Books, 21 April 2011)

20.   C.R. Muston, *Recognition in the World to Come, or, Christian Fellowship on Earth Perpetuated in Heaven*. First Edition, London, Holdsworth and Bell, 1830 (accessed on Google Books 21 April 2011)

21.   Anon., *The Eclectic Review*, Vol. IV, pages 178–179 (1830) (accessed on Google Books 29 September 2010)

22.   For a typical discussion, see *Chalmers and the Church Establishment Questions*, in *Fraser's Magazine for Town and Country*, Vol. XVII (January–June 1838), page 750 and Rev R.S. Maitland, *The Voluntary System*, second edition, (Rivingtons, London, 1837)

23.   Anon, *The Gentleman's Magazine*, Vol. 161, pages 392–393 (1837), which contains a review of Christopher Ralph Muston's book

24.   Rev William Steven, *The History of the Scottish Church, Rotterdam*, page 335 (Waugh and Innes: Whittaker and Co, London, 1833 (accessed on Google Books 3 May 2011)

25.   C.R. Muston, *Sermons preached at the British Episcopal Church, Rotterdam*, (Hatchard, 1837) Reviewed in the *Evangelical Magazine and Missionary Chronicle*, Vol. 15 pages 124–125 (January 1837) (accessed on Google Books, 25 December 2009)

26.   CCEd (www.clergydatabase.org.uk) Record ID 117896. (accessed 11 May 2011)

27.   Rev Dr J. Bosworth, *A Dictionary of the Anglo-Saxon Language* (Longman, London 1838)

28.   Dabney A. Bankert, The Dictionary Society of North America, Laurence Urdang Award Lecture, 2007 (see www.dictionarysociety. com) (accessed 11 May 2011)

29.   Anon, *The Catalogue of the Albany Institute Library*, page 249 (ed. George Wood, 1855) (accessed on Google Books 5 May 2011)

30. J. Anderson, jnr., *Testimonials on behalf of George Combe as candidate for the Chair of Logic in the University of Edinburgh,* page 158 (1836)

31. Anon, *The Church of England Magazine, February Review Section,* Vol. II, page 8 (January–June 1837) (accessed on Google Books 30 September 2010)

32. Rev William Steven, *op. cit.,* page 370

33. *St Mary's, Chelmsford, Baptism Register* (ERO D/P 94/1/13)

34. Malcolm Johnson, *op. cit.,* pages 104–105

35. *The Incorporated Church Building Society,* Folios 31ff., at Lambeth Palace Library

36. C.R. Muston, *Recognition in the World to Come,* fourth edition, (Hatchard, 1837) The passage from the forward is quoted in the *Chelmsford Chronicle,* Friday 27 March 1840

37. Anon, *The Church of England Magazine, the Register of Ecclesiastical Intelligence,* Vol. XXII, page 8 (January 1847)

38. A transcription of the marriage details is to be found in the *Gemeentearchief Rotterdam.* A digital image of the original register is available at www.rotterdam.digitalstamboom.nl

39. *Chelmsford Chronicle,* Friday, 13 April 1849

40. *The Church of England Magazine,* Vol. XXII (January 1847) *The register of Ecclesiastical Intelligence,* page 9

41. ICBS 04287 at Lambeth Palace Library

42. ERO, A9978

43. From the *Civil Engineer and Architects' Journal, incorporated with The Architect,* Vol. XIV, page 312 (3 May 1851)

44. *Chelmsford Chronicle,* Friday, 28 April 1851

45. *Chelmsford Chronicle,* Friday, 26 September 1851

46. *Chelmsford Chronicle,* Friday, 24 October 1851

47. *St Mary's, Chelmsford Baptism Register,* (ERO D/P 94/1/9)

48. Hilda Grieve, *op. cit.,* page 224

49. *ibid.,* page 259

50. *Essex Standard,* Friday, 11 January 1834

51. *Chelmsford Chronicle,* Friday, 28 October 1859

52. *The Christian Magazine and Universal Review,* Vol. I, page 125 (January–June 1844)

53. Anon, *Alumni Oxonienses,* 1715–1886, page 630

54. *Crockford's Clerical Directory*, 1883

55. Much of the information on Henry Hawkins is derived from the website of 'together' at www.together-uk.org

56. *Annals of some of the British Norman Isles*, part 2, page 184

57. *Punch, or the London Charivari*, Vol. XXVX (*sic*), 15 September 1855, page 103 (accessed on Google Books, 29 September 2010)

58. *Chelmsford Chronicle*, Friday, 30 September 1859

59. *Chelmsford Chronicle*, Friday, 23 December 1859

60. For details of the incumbents of Stoke Gifford, see www.stokegifford.org.uk

61. Charles James Blomfield, *Letters, FP 43f 108* (at Lambeth Palace Library)

62. *Chelmsford Chronicle*, Friday, 15 December 1843

63. *The English Journal of Education*, Vol. VI, No. XI, pages 417–421 (1848)

64. General Record Office (GRO) September 1859 (Dover, 2a 478)

65. *The Legal observer, Digest and Journal of Jurisprudence*, Vol. XXXVI, page 366 (May–October 1848)

CHAPTER 3 – ALFRED WILLIAM MASON

1. *Essex Weekly News*, Friday, 4 May 1877, page 3

2. From Docklands Ancestors, at www.findmypast.com (accessed 25 July 2009)

3. Rev C.A. Jones, *A History of Dedham* (privately published, Colchester, 1907) pages 124–126 (Copy accessed in ERO)

4. J.A. Venn, *Alumni Cantabrignenses*, Part II (1752–1900), Vol. IV, page 349

5. ERO D/P 94/1/14

6. *Chelmsford Chronicle*, Friday, 14 August 1859

7. *Chelmsford Chronicle*, Friday, 21 August 1859

8. GRO West Ham, 4a13, April/June 1857

9. *Essex Weekly News*, Friday, 4 May 1877, page 2

10. ERO E/P 23/1

11. *Church and State Review*, 1 October 1862, pages 211–212 (accessed on Google Books 23 May 2010)

12. *Chelmsford Chronicle*, Friday, 26 July 1861

13. *St John's School Logbook*, Vol. I (1863-1892), ERO E/ML 58/1

14. *Chelmsford Chronicle*, Friday, 28 October 1859
15. *Essex Weekly News*, Saturday, 11 April 1863
16. *The Essex Almanac*, 1864 (copy accessed at the ERO)
17. *Chelmsford Chronicle*, Friday, 1 April 1864
18. *St John's School Logbook*, Vol. I, (1863–92), ERO E/ML 58/1, entry for 18 September 1863
19. *The Ecclesiastical Gazette*, 11 July 1865, page 17 (accessed on Google Books 23 May 2010)
20. *Chelmsford Chronicle*, Friday, 26 August 1859
21. Hilda Grieve, *The Sleepers and the Shadows*, Vol. 2, pages 324 *et seq.*, (ERO 1994)
22. J. Erle, *Reports of Cases Argued and Determined in the Court of Queen's Bench*, London, H. Sweet, 3, Chancery Lane, Fleet Street, 1860 XXI and XXII Vict.
23. John Coke Fowler, *Church Pews, their Origins and Legal Incidents, with some observations on the Propriety of Abolishing them.* London, Francis and John Rivington, 1844. (accessed at www.anglicanhistory.org 21 August 2011)
24. ERO, A9978, File 1, section L
25. ERO D/F 8/530A
26. *Bury and Norwich Post*, 30 September 1862 (accessed at www.foxearth.org.uk 21 August 2011)
27. *Home News*, 20 January 1865 (accessed at www.newhamstory.com 20 September 2011)
28. *Chelmsford Chronicle*, Friday, 27 January 1865
29. *Chelmsford Chronicle*, Friday, 17 February 1872
30. *Chelmsford Chronicle*, Friday, 21 June 1872
31. *The London Gazette*, 20 October 1874, pages 4765–4767
32. ERO A9978, Box 7
33. *Essex Weekly News*, Friday, 22 May 1874
34. *Chelmsford Chronicle*, Friday, 29 May 1874
35. *Chelmsford Chronicle*, Friday, 25 September 1874
36. *Chelmsford Chronicle*, Friday, 2 April 1875
37. ERO T/Z 133/2
38. *The Mechanic's Magazine, Museum, Register, Journal and Gazette*, Vol. 45, page 161 (1864) (accessed on Google Books, 2 October 2011)

39. John Booker, *Essex and the Industrial Revolution*, page 189 (Essex County Council, 1874) (accessed at the ERO)
40. *Transactions of the Incorporated Gas Institute*, Vol. 33, pages 32, 252 (1896) (accessed on Google Books, 26 September 2011)
41. *Chelmsford Chronicle*, Friday, 28 May 1875
42. See information on the de Veley family of Yverdon, Switzerland, at www.gen-gen.ch
43. *Essex Weekly News*, Friday, 2 April 1875
44. *Essex Weekly News*, Friday, 21 April 1876
45. *Essex Weekly News*, Friday, 6 April 1877
46. *Chelmsford Chronicle*, Friday, 6 April 1877
47. See information on Mobberley parish at www.thornber.net
48. Joseph Foster, *Alumni Oxonensis*, Vol. III page 906 (1715–1886)
49. *ibid.*, Vol. II, page 760
50. *Crockford's Clerical Directory*, 1883, page 405
51. *ibid.*, page 91
52. J.A. Venn, *Alumni Cantabrignenses*, Part II, Vol. II, page 537
53. *Crockford's Clerical Directory*, 1883, page 405
54. *ibid.*, page 173
55. *ibid.*, page 1288
56. J.A. Venn, *Alumni Cantabrignenses*, Part II, Vol. VI, page 575
57. *Crockford's Clerical Directory*, 1883, page 105
58. J.A. Venn, *Alumni Cantabrignenses*, Part II, Vol. I, page 279
59. ERO, A9978, Box 1, section W
60. *Crockford's Clerical Directory*, 1883, page 500
61. J.A. Venn, *Alumni Cantabrignenses*, Part II, Vol. V, page 453
62. *Crockford's Clerical Directory*, 1883, page 730
63. *The Register and Magazine of Biography*, Vol. 1, page 238 (Nicholls and Son, Westminster, 1869) (accessed on Google Books, 2 October 2011)
64. *Chelmsford Chronicle*, Friday, 12 June 1877
65. *Fulton's Book of Pigeons, with Standards for Judging*, ed. Lewis Wright. Revised, Supplemented and Enlarged by Rev William Faithfull Lumley, Author, 1893
66. J.A. Venn, *Alumni Cantabrignenses*, Part II, Vol. II, page 69
67. *Chelmsford Chronicle*, Friday, 9 October 1874
68. *Essex Weekly News*, Friday, 4 May 1877

69. *Essex Chronicle*, Friday, 5 December 1890
70. *Essex Weekly News*, Saturday, 13 December 1890
71. *Essex Chronicle*, Friday, 12 December 1890
72. ERO, A12859
73. Will Index, Principal Probate Registry Office, London

CHAPTER 4 – THOMAS HENRY WILKINSON

1. *The Gospeller*, September 1879, quoted in the *Essex Weekly News*, Friday, 5 September 1879
2. *The International Genealogical Index* (IGI), Film C047932
3. Joseph Foster, *Alumni Oxoniensis*, Vol. III, page 630 (1715–1886)
4. *Crockford's Clerical Directory,* 1883, page 1029
5. *ibid,* 1868, page26
6. *Chelmsford Chronicle*, Friday, 20 April 1877
7. *Chelmsford Chronicle*, Friday, 15 June 1877
8. *Essex Weekly News*, Friday, 6 July 1877
9. *Essex Weekly News*, Friday, 7 September 1877
10. *Chelmsford Chronicle*, Friday, 4 January 1878
11. *Essex Weekly News*, Friday, 11 January 1878
12. *Chelmsford Chronicle*, Friday, 11 January 1878
13. *Essex Weekly News*, Friday, 4 January 1878
14. *Essex Weekly News*, Friday, 26 April 1878
15. *Chelmsford Chronicle*, Friday, 26 April 1878
16. *Chelmsford Chronicle*, Friday, 19 July 1878
17. CCEd (www.theclergydatabase.org.uk) Record ID 82364. (accessed 11 May 2011)
18. *The Royal Lady's Magazine and Archives of the Court of St James',* Vol. I, page 62 (1831) (accessed on Google Books, 2 October 2011)
19. *Chelmsford Chronicle*, Friday, 26 July 1878
20. *Punch, or The London Charivari,* 19 September 1857, page 115 (accessed on Google Books, 16 February 2011)
21. *Chelmsford Chronicle*, Friday, 18 October 1878
22. *Burke's Peerage, Baronetage and Knightage*, 107th edition (ed. Charles Morley) Vol. 2, page 1834 (2003)
23. *Essex Weekly News*, Friday, 18 April 1879

24.   *Essex Weekly News*, Friday, 20 June 1879
25.   *Chelmsford Chronicle*, Friday, 20 June 1879
26.   *Essex Weekly News*, Friday, 5 September 1879
27.   *Essex Weekly News*, Friday, 12 September 1879
28.   *Chelmsford Chronicle*, Friday, 6 June 1879
29.   *Chelmsford Chronicle*, Friday, 5 September 1879
30.   *Chelmsford Chronicle*, Friday, 3 October 1879
31.   *The London Gazette*, 2 May 1879, Copy in ERO, A9978, Box 1, final section

CHAPTER 5 – GEORGE St ALBAN GODSON

1.   William Gibbens, *The Essex Review*, Vol. X, page 111 (1901) (accessed at ERO)
2.   J.A. Venn, *Alumni Cantabrignensis*, Part II, Vol. III, page 72 (1715–1900)
3.   For information on the Episcopal Church of St Peter, Barnet Road, Arkley, see www.hertfordshire-genealogy.co.uk. See also *Kelly's Directory for Hertfordshire*, 1912
4.   *Essex Weekly News*, Friday, 11 July 1879
5.   *Chelmsford Chronicle*, Friday, 17 October 1879
6.   *Chelmsford Chronicle*, Friday, 24 October 1879
7.   *Essex Weekly News*, Friday, 2 April 1880
8.   *Chelmsford Chronicle*, Friday, 9 June 1882
9.   *Essex Weekly News*, Friday, 22 April 1881
10. *Chelmsford Chronicle*, Friday, 31 March 1882
11. *Chelmsford Chronicle*, Friday, 10 March 1882
12. *Chelmsford Chronicle*, Friday, 6 January 1882
13. *Essex Weekly News*, Friday, 14 April 1882
14. ERO, D/CF 21/6 (entries for 24 February and 25 March 1883)
15. *Chelmsford Chronicle*, Friday, 6 October 1882
16. *Chelmsford Chronicle*, Friday, 5 January 1883
17. *Chelmsford Chronicle*, Friday, 30 March 1883
18. *Essex Weekly News*, Friday, 6 April 1883
19. *Essex Weekly News*, Friday, 13 April 1883
20. *Essex Weekly News*, Friday, 27 April 1883
21. *The Moulsham Parish Magazine*, as quoted in the *Essex Weekly News*, Friday, 25 March 1883

22. *Essex Weekly News*, Friday, 1 June 1883
23. *Essex Weekly News*, Friday, 8 June 1883
24. *Essex Weekly News*, Friday, 29 June 1883
25. *The Moulsham Parish Magazine*, as quoted in the *Essex Weekly News*, Friday, 6 July 1883
26. *Essex Weekly News*, Friday, 20 July 1883
27. A report form the Council for the Care of Churches, 83, London Wall, EC2M 5NA (reference PM 1480, 1988)
28. *Essex Standard*, Saturday, 27 October 1883
29. *Essex Newsman*, Saturday, 23 July 1883
30. *Essex Newsman*, Saturday, 4 August 1883
31. *Essex Newsman*, Saturday, 18 August 1883
32. ERO D/DU 826/1
33. *Essex Newsman*, Saturday, 24 March 1883
34. *Essex Weekly News*, Friday, 30 March 1883
35. *Essex Newsman*, Saturday, 31 March 1883
36. *Essex Weekly News*, Friday, 13 April 1883
37. *Essex Newsman*, Saturday, 15 September 1883
38. *Essex Newsman*, Saturday, 22 September 1883
39. *Essex Standard*, Saturday, 13 August 1883
40. ERO D/CF 21/6 (entry for 16 June 1884)
41. *Essex Newsman*, Saturday, 17 November 1883
42. *Essex Newsman*, Saturday, 19 January 1884
43. *Essex Weekly News*, Friday, 18 April 1884
44. *Essex Newsman*, Saturday, 19 January 1884
45. *Essex Newsman*, Saturday, 9 February 1884
46. *Essex Newsman*, Saturday, 12 January 1884
47. *Essex Newsman*, Saturday, 5 April 1884 (page 2)
48. *Essex Newsman*, Saturday, 5 April 1884 (page 3)
49. *Essex Newsman*, Saturday, 2 August 1884
50. *Essex Standard*, Saturday, 20 September 1884
51. *Essex Weekly News*, Friday, 3 October 1884
52. *Essex County Chronicle*, Friday, 10 October 1884
53. *Essex Standard*, Saturday, 1 November 1884
54. *Essex Standard*, Saturday, 22 November 1884
55. *Essex Weekly News*, Friday, 10 April 1885
56. *Essex Newsman*, Saturday, 27 June 1885

57. *Essex Newsman*, Saturday, 7 August 1885

58. *Essex Newsman*, Saturday, 12 December 1885

59. *Essex Newsman*, Saturday, 19 December 1885

60. *Essex Newsman*, Saturday, 6 March 1886

61. *Essex Newsman*, Saturday, 1 May 1886

62. *Essex Newsman*. Saturday, 22 May 1886

63. ERO, A8136, Box 2, *St John's Register of Services* (1885–96)

64. *Essex Standard*, Saturday, 7 August 1886

65. *Essex Newsman*, Saturday, 9 October 1886

66. *Essex Newsman*, Saturday, 16 October 1886

67. *Essex Weekly News*, Friday, 15 April 1887

68. *Essex Newsman*, Saturday, 11 February 1888

69. *Essex Newsman*, Saturday, 18 February 1888

70. *Essex Newsman*, Saturday, 5 May 1888

71. *Essex Newsman*, Saturday, 9 June 1888

72. ERO A9978, Box 1, section 1

73. *Essex Standard*, Saturday 29 June 1889

74. *Essex County Chronicle*, Friday, 11 April 1890

75. *Essex County Chronicle*, Friday, 25 July 1890

76. *Essex Newsman*, Saturday, 9 August 1890

77. *Essex Newsman*, Saturday, 16 August 1890

78. *Essex County Chronicle*, Friday, 15 August 1890

79. *Essex County Chronicle*, Friday, 12 September 1890

80. *Essex County Chronicle*, Friday, 3 October 1890

81. *Essex Newsman*, Saturday, 25 October 1890

82. *Essex County Chronicle*, Friday, 12 December 1890

83. *Essex County Chronicle*, Friday, 9 January 1891

84. *Essex Newsman*, Saturday, 15 November 1884

85. *Essex Newsman*, Saturday, 14 February 1891

86. *Essex County Chronicle*, Friday, 13 March 1891

87. *Essex County Chronicle*, Friday, 1 May 1891

88. *Essex Newsman*, Saturday, 6 June 1891

89. *Essex County Chronicle*, Friday, 3 April 1891

90. *Essex County Chronicle*, Friday, 14 August 1891

91. *Essex County Chronicle*, Friday, 16 October 1891

92. *Essex Newsman*, Saturday, 12 March 1892

93. *Essex Newsman*, Saturday, 26 March 1892

94. *Essex Weekly News*, Friday, 22 April 1892
95. *Essex Weekly News*, Friday, 29 April 1892
96. Information on the de Veley family history from www.gen-gen.ch, (accessed on 21 September 2010)
97. *Essex Weekly News*, Friday 9 September 1892
98. *Essex Newsman*, Saturday, 3 December 1892
99. *Essex Newsman*, Saturday, 3 September 1892
100. ERO A9978, Box 1, lever-arch file, section L
101. *Essex County Chronicle*, Friday, 30 June 1893
102. *Essex County Chronicle*, Friday, 7 July 1893
103. *Essex Newsman*, Saturday, 8 July 1893
104. Information from www.books.google.com accessed 14 February 2012 (note that no details of the publication itself are available, only the title)
105. *Essex County Chronicle*, Frida,y 17 November 1893
106. *Essex Newsman*, Saturday, 30 June 1894
107. *Essex County Standard (sic)*, Saturday, 29 December 1894
108. *Essex Independent and Farmers' Gazette*, Monday, 22 April 1895
109. *Essex Weekly News*, Friday, 19 April 1895
110. *Essex County Chronicle*, Friday, 10 April 1896
111. *Essex Newsman*, Saturday, 15 August 1896
112. *Essex Newsman*, Saturday, 18 July 1896
113. *Essex Newsman*, Saturday, 7 November 1896
114. *Essex Newsman*, Saturday, 5 September 1896
115. *Essex Newsman*, Saturday, 26 December 1896
116. *Essex County Chronicle*, Friday, 23 April 1897
117. *Essex County Chronicle*, Friday, 7 April 1899
118. *Essex Newsman*, Saturday, 10 February 1900
119. *Essex Weekly News*, Friday, 20 April 1900
120. *Essex Standard*, Saturday, 22 November 1879
121. *Essex Standard*, Saturday, 21 December 1879
122. *Events and People: events in Russian Mennonite History and the people that made them happen*, ed., Helmut T. Heubert, Springfield Publishers, Canada (1999)
123. *Essex County Chronicle*, Friday, 29 September 1882
124. *Essex County Chronicle*, Friday, 22 December 1882

125. *Crockford's Clerical Directory*, 1896, page 1246
126. *Manchester Courier and Lancashire General Advertiser*, 14 July 1866
127. *Worcester Journal*, Saturday, 22 December 1877
128. *The London Gazette*, issue 24545, 22 January 1878
129. *Essex Newsman*, Saturday, 3 March 1883
130. *Worcester Chronicle*, Saturday, 14 April 1883
131. *Yorkshire Gazette*, 12 January 1884
132. *Essex Newsman*, Saturday, 1 September 1883
133. *Essex County Chronicle*, Friday, 7 September 1883
134. *Crockford's Clerical Directory*, 1896, page 1243
135. GRO Scotland, Statutory Marriages 110/010005 (1885) (accessed at www.scotlandspeople.gov.uk 19 April 2012)
136. *Essex Standard*, Saturday, 26 December 1885
137. *Crockford's Clerical Directory*, 1896, page 914
138. *Essex County Chronicle*, Friday, 14 October 1887
139. *Essex County Chronicle*, Friday, 4 November 1887
140. *Essex County Chronicle*, Friday, 29 April 1887
141. *Essex Herald,* Tuesday, 9 August 1887
142. *Crockford's Clerical Directory*, 1896, page 1332
143. J.A. Venn, *Alumni Cantabrignenses*, Part II, Vol. VI, page 161 (1715–1900)
144. *Essex Standard*, Saturday 24, December 1881
145. *Essex County Chronicle*, Friday, 30 September 1887
146. ERO A8136, *St John's Register of Services, 1885–96*
147. J.A. Venn, *Alumni Cantabrignenses*, Part II, Vol. VI, page 84 (1715–1900)
148. *Essex Standard*, Saturday, 24 December 1887
149. *Essex Standard*, Saturday, 29 December 1888
150. *Essex Standard*, Saturday, 9 March 1889
151. J.A. Venn, *Alumni Cantabrignenses*, Part II, Vol. VI, page 377 (1715–1900)
152. J.A. Venn, *Alumni Cantabrignenses*, Part II, Vol, VI, page 167 (1715–1900)
153. *Essex Newsman*, Saturday, 21 June 1890
154. *Essex Newsman*, Saturday, 8 July 1890
155. *Essex County Chronicle*, Friday, 26 December 1890

156. GRO Scotland, Statutory Births, (accessed at www.scotlands people.gov.uk on 24 April 2012)

157. *Essex Standard*, Saturday, 22 June 1889

158. *Essex County Chronicle*, Friday, 20 June 1890

159. *Essex County Chronicle*, Friday, 8 February 1901

160. *Essex County Chronicle*, Friday, 19 April 1901

161. *Essex Standard*, Saturday, 27 December 1879

162. *Crockford's Clerical Directory*, 1896, page 1025

163. *Essex Standard*, Saturday, 24 August 1889

164. *Essex County Chronicle*, Friday, 17 June 1892

165. *Essex Newsman*, Saturday, 25 February 1893

166. *Essex Standard*, Saturday, 17 June 1893

167. J.A Venn, *Alumni Cantabrignenses,* Part II, Vol. I, page 238 (1715–1900)

168. *Essex Standard*, Saturday, 26 December 1891

169. *Essex Standard*, Saturday, 24 December 1892

170. *Essex Standard*, Saturday, 23 June 1894

171. *Essex Newsman*, Saturday, 28 April 1900

172. *Essex County Chronicle*, Friday, 4 January 1901

173. *Essex County Chronicle*, Friday, 7 December 1900

174. *Essex County Chronicle*, Friday, 14 December 1900

175. *Essex County Chronicle*, Friday, 18 January 1901

176. *Essex Weekly News*, Friday, 21 December 1900

177. *Essex Review*, Vol. XII, page 172 (1902)

178. *Essex Newsman*, Saturday, 15 March1902

179. *Essex County Chronicle*, Friday, 22 February 1901

CHAPTER 6 – ROBERT TRAVERS SAULEZ

1. *Essex County Chronicle*, Friday, 15 March 1901

2. Information from www.pendleyusa.com (accessed 21 September 2011)

3. *Cheshire Observer*, Saturday, 7 March 1874

4. *Cheshire Observer*, Saturday, 27 February 1875

5. *Lincolnshire Chronicle*, Friday, 3 November 1876

6. *Nottinghamshire Guardian*, Friday, 3 August 1877

7. *Liverpool Mercury*, Saturday, 14 January 1882

8. *Bath Chronicle and Weekly Gazette*, Thursday, 28 June 1883

9. *Manchester Courier and Lancashire General Advertiser*, Friday, 19 June 1885
10. *Manchester Courier and Lancashire General Advertiser*, Monday, 11 October 1886
11. *York Herald*, Friday, 23 August 1889
12. *Essex Standard*, Saturday, 8 November 1890
13. *Essex Newsman*, Saturday, 19 November 1892
14. *Essex Newsman*, Saturday, 5 February 1892
15. *Essex Newsman*, Saturday, 10 February 1894
16. *Essex Standard*, Saturday, 27 October 1894
17. *Liverpool Mercury*, Friday, 5 May 1899
18. *Essex Newsman*, Saturday, 12 January 1901
19. *Essex Newsman*, Saturday, 30 March 1901
20. *Essex Newsman*, Saturday, 9 March 1901
21. *Essex Newsman*, Saturday, 13 April 1901
22. *Essex Newsman*, Saturday, 5 October 1901
23. *Essex Newsman*, Saturday, 7 December 1901
24. *Essex County Chronicle*, Friday, 27 December 1901
25. *Essex Newsman*, Saturday, 25 January 1902
26. *Essex Newsman*, Saturday, 15 February 1902
27. *Essex Weekly News*, Friday, 4 April 1902
28. *Essex Newsman*, Saturday, 24 May 1902
29. *Essex Newsman*, Saturday, 11 October 1902
30. *Essex Newsman*, Saturday, 22 November 1902
31. *Essex Weekly News*, Friday, 17 April 1903
32. *Essex Newsman*, Saturday, 16 May 1903
33. *Essex Newsman*, Saturday, 22 August 1903
34. *Essex Newsman*, Saturday, 7 November 1903
35. *Essex County Chronicle*, Friday, 15 January 1904
36. *Essex County Chronicle*, Friday, 22 April 1903
37. *Essex County Chronicle*, Friday, 6 May 1904
38. *Essex County Chronicle*, Friday, 29 April 1904
39. *Essex County Chronicle*, Friday, 20 May 1904
40. *Essex County Chronicle*, Friday, 8 July 1904
41. *Essex County Chronicle*, Friday, 28 October 1904
42. *Tourists Church guide,* (1902) quoted in Owen Chadwick, *The Victorian Church*, Part II, pages 318–319 (A. & C. Black, London, 1970)

43. *Essex County Chronicle*, Friday, 11 November 1904
44. *Essex Newsman*, Sunday, (*sic*) 29 October 1904
45. *Essex County Chronicle*, Friday, 4 November 1904
46. *Essex County Chronicle*, Friday, 18 November 1904
47. *Essex Newsman*, Saturday, 28 January 1905
48. *Essex County Chronicle*, Friday, 3 February 1905
49. *Essex County Chronicle*, Friday, 24 February 1905
50. *Essex Weekly News*, Friday, 28 April 1905
51. *Essex Weekly News*, Friday, 5 May 1905
52. *Essex Newsman*, Saturday, 6 May 1905
53. *Essex Weekly News*, Friday, 19 May 1905
54. *Essex Newsman*, Saturday, 5 August 1905
55. *Essex Newsman*, Saturday, 26 August 1905
56. *Essex Newsman*, Saturday, 11 November 1905
57. *Essex Newsman*, Saturday, 18 November 1905
58. *Essex Weekly News*, Friday, 1 December 1905
59. *Essex Newsman*, Saturday, 13 January 1906
60. *Essex Newsman*, Saturday, 10 February 1906
61. *Essex Weekly News*, Friday, 27 April 1906
62. *Essex Weekly News*, Friday, 29 June 1906
63. Information from www.willingale.org (accessed 8 July 2012)
64. *Essex Newsman*, Saturday, 2 June 1906
65. *Essex Newsman*, Saturday, 20 June 1906
66. *Essex Newsman*, Saturday, 7 July 1906
67. *Essex Newsman*, Saturday, 4 August 1906
68. *Essex Newsman*, Saturday, 11 August 1906
69. *Essex Newsman*, Saturday, 22 September 1906
70. *Essex Newsman*, Saturday, 6 July 1901
71. *Essex Newsman*, Saturday, 5 October 1901
72. *Essex County Chronicle*, Friday, 27 December 1901
73. J.A. Venn, *Alumni Cantabrignenses*, Part II, Vol. I, page 174 (1715–1900)
74. *Essex Newsman*, Saturday, 27 December 1902
75. *Essex Newsman*, Saturday, 25 January 1903
76. *Essex Newsman*, Saturday, 7 November 1903
77. *Essex County Chronicle*, Friday, 8 January 1904
78. *Essex Newsman*, Saturday, 24 November 1904

79. *Crockford's Clerical Directory*, 1904, page 416

80. J.A. Venn, *Alumni Cantabrignenses*, Part II, Vol. II, page 364 (1715–1900)

81. *Essex County Chronicle*, Friday, 29 April 1904

82. *Essex Newsman*, Saturday, 8 October 1904

83. *Essex Newsman*, Saturday, 26 August 1905

84. *Crockford's Clerical Directory*, 1918–19, page 1132

85. *Whitstable Times and Herne Bay Herald*, Saturday, 14 June 1902

86. *Essex Newsman*, Saturday, 18 November 1905

87. *Essex County Chronicle*, Friday, 20 June 1919

88. *Essex County Chronicle*, Friday, 24 October 1919

89. *Essex County Chronicle*, Friday, 25 December 1925

90. *Essex County Chronicle*, Friday, 26 January 1926

91. ERO D/CN 3/1

92. *Essex County Chronicle*, Friday, 23 February 1917

93. Information from www.cwgc.org/search (accessed on 15 July 2009 – this reference contains a photograph of the cemetery at Bailleul, St Laurent-Blagny, where he is buried)

94. Information from www.willingale.org (accessed 15 July 2009)

95. *Essex County Chronicle*, Friday, 15 July 1921

96. Information from www.cwgc.org (accessed 15 July 2009)

97. *Essex County Chronicle*, Friday, 22 January 1926

98. *Essex Newsman*, Saturday, 20 April 1929

99. *Essex County Chronicle*, Friday, 3 February 1933

100. *Essex County Chronicle*, Friday, 15 November 1946

CHAPTER 7 – WILLIAM JAMES PRESSEY

1. *Essex County Chronicle*, Friday, 8 June 1906

2. *Essex County Chronicle*, Friday, 10 August 1906

3. *Reading Mercury*, Saturday, 6 June 1885

4. *Reading Mercury*, Saturday, 10 July 1885

5. *Morning Post*, Saturday, 18 June 1887

6. *London Daily News*, Monday, 21 April 1890

7. *Essex Newsman*, Saturday, 26 March 1892

8. *Suffolk and Essex Free Press*, 17 August 1892

9. *The Graphic*, Saturday, 3 February 1894

10. *Hastings and St Leonard's Observer*, Saturday, 3 March 1894

11. *Essex County Chronicle*, Friday, 8 June 1906
12. *Western Times*, Thursday, 9 August 1906
13. *Essex Newsman*, Saturday, 18 August 1906
14. *Essex Newsman*, Saturday, 8 September 1906
15. *Essex County Chronicle*, Friday, 8 June 1906
16. *Suffolk and Essex Free Press*, 7 October 1885
17. For photographs of the interior of SS. Peter and Paul, Foxearth, see www.foxearth.org.uk/Foxearth Pictures (accessed 20 April 2011)
18. *Essex Weekly News*, Friday, 5 April 1907
19. *Essex Weekly News,* Friday, 12 April 1907
20. *Essex Newsman*, Saturday, 12 October 1907
21. *Essex Newsman*, Saturday, 1 February 1908
22. *Essex Newsman*, Saturday, 4 January 1908
23. *Essex Newsman*, Saturday, 14 March 1908
24. ERO A9978, Box 1, Box File, section H1
25. F.L. Cross and E.A. Livingstone, *The Oxford Dictionary of the Christian Church,* page 97 (Oxford University Press, 1997)
26. *St John's Vestry Minutes*, 1895–1921, ERO 8136 Box 1 (accessed June 2010)
27. *Essex Newsman*, Saturday, 4 July 1908
28. *St John's Vestry Minutes,* 1895–1921, ERO 8136 Box 1 (accessed July 2010)
29. *Essex Newsman*, Saturday, 31 October 1908
30. *Essex County Chronicle*, Friday, 19 February 1909
31. *St John's Vestry Minutes,* 1895–1921, ERO 8136 Box 1 (accessed August 2010)
32. *Essex Newsman*, Saturday, 24 April 1909
33. *Essex Newsman*, Saturday, 8 January 1910
34. *Essex County Chronicle*, Friday, 8 April 1910
35. *Essex Newsman*, Saturday, 25 June 1910
36. *Essex Newsman*, Saturday, 16 July 1910
37. *Essex Newsman*, Saturday, 6 August 1910
38. *Essex Newsman*, Saturday, 23 July 1910
39. *Essex County Chronicle*, Friday, 28 April 1911
40. *Essex County Chronicle*, Friday, 30 June 1911
41. *Essex Newsman*, Saturday, 20 January 1912

42. *Essex Newsman*, Saturday, 23 March 1912
43. *Essex Newsman*, Saturday, 25 May 1912
44. *Essex Newsman*, Saturday, 9 March 1912
45. *Essex Newsman*, Saturday, 28 September 1912
46. *Essex Newsman*, Saturday, 5 October 1912
47. *Essex Newsman*, Saturday, 28 December 1912
48. *Essex Newsman*, Saturday, 11 January 1913
49. *Essex Weekly News*, Friday, 4 April 1913
50. *Essex County Chronicle*, Friday, 4 April 1913
51. *Essex Newsman*, Saturday, 5 April 1913
52. *Essex Newsman*, Saturday, 7 June 1913
53. *Essex Newsman*, Saturday, 6 December 1913
54. *Essex Newsman*, Saturday, 29 November 1913
55. Gordon Hewitt, *A History of the Diocese of Chelmsford*, page 59 (Chelmsford Diocesan Board of Finance, 1984)
56. *Essex Newsman*, Saturday, 21 February 1914
57. *Essex Newsman*, Saturday, 3 January 1914
58. *Essex Newsman*, Saturday, 10 January 1914
59. *Essex Weekly News*, Friday, 23 January 1914
60. *Essex Newsman*, Saturday, 17 January 1914
61. *Essex Newsman*, Saturday, 7 February 1914
62. Gordon Hewitt, *op. cit.*, page 60
63. *Essex Newsman*, Saturday, 6 June 1914
64. *Essex Newsman*, Saturday, 27 June 1914
65. *Essex Newsman*, Saturday, 11 July 1914
66. *Essex Newsman*, Saturday, 8 August 1914
67. *Essex Newsman*, Saturday, 15 August 1914
68. *Essex Newsman*, Saturday, 17 October1914
69. *Essex Newsman*, Saturday, 5 December 1914
70. *Essex Newsman*, Saturday, 27 February 1915
71. *Essex Newsman*, Saturday, 6 March 1915
72. *Essex Newsman*, Saturday, 24 April 1915
73. *St John's Vestry Minutes*, 1895-1921, ERO 8136 Box 1 (accessed March 2011)
74. *Essex Newsman*, Saturday, 1 May 1915
75. *Essex Newsman*, Saturday, 15 May 1915
76. *Essex Newsman*, Saturday, 21 August 1915

77. *Essex County Chronicle*, Friday, 23 March 1916
78. *Essex Newsman*, Saturday, 7 April 1916
79. *St John's Vestry Minutes*, 1895-1921, ERO 8136 Box 1 (accessed April 2011)
80. *Essex County Chronicle*, Friday, 18 August 1916
81. *Essex Weekly News*, Saturday, 19 August 1916
82. *Essex County Chronicle*, Friday, 5 January 1917
83. *Essex County Chronicle*, Friday, 20 April 1917
84. *Essex County Chronicle*, Friday, 10 August 1917
85. *Essex County Chronicle*, Friday, 12 October 1917
86. *Essex County Chronicle*, Friday, 25 January 1918
87. *Essex County Chronicle*, Friday, 12 April 1918
88. *Essex County Chronicle*, Friday, 19 April 1918
89. *Essex Newsman*, Saturday 31 August 1918
90. *Essex County Chronicle*, Friday 4 October 1918
91. *Essex Newsman*, Saturday, 26 October 1918
92. *Essex County Chronicle*, Friday, 22 November 1918
93. *Essex County Chronicle*, Friday, 8 November 1918
94. *Essex County Chronicle*, Friday, 15 November 1918
95. *The Morning Post*, Friday, 9 October 1896
96. *The Morning Post*, Monday, 20 December 1897
97. *Crockford's Clerical Directory*, 1926, page 751
98. *Essex Newsman*, Saturday, 18 August 1906
99. *Essex County Chronicle*, Friday, 5 December 1919
100. *Essex Weekly News*, Friday, 23 January 1914
101. *Essex Newsman*, Saturday, 10 January 1914
102. *Essex Standard,* Saturday, 6 October 1900
103. *Essex County Chronicle*, Friday, 4 October 1901
104. *Crockford's Clerical Directory*, 1918–19, page 175
105. *Essex Newsman*, Saturday, 10 January 1914
106. *Essex Newsman*, Saturday, 27 June 1914
107. *Essex County Chronicle*, Friday, 27 December 1912
108. *Essex County Chronicle,* Friday, 26 December 1913
109. *Essex Newsman,* Saturday, 20 July 1907
110. *Essex Newsman*, Saturday, 9 May 1914
111. *Essex County Chronicle*, Friday, 9 May 1941
112. *Essex County Chronicle*, Friday, 29 December 1905

113. *Essex County Chronicle*, Friday, 16 February 1917
114. *Crockford's Clerical Directory*, 1932, page 806
115. *The Archive of St John the Evangelist, Moulsham*. Miscellaneous papers
116. *Essex County Chronicle*, Friday, 13 December 1911
117. *Essex County Chronicle*, Friday, 19 April 1940
118. *Essex Newsman*, Saturday, 28 August 1943
119. *Essex Newsman*, Tuesday, 6 February 1945
120. *Essex County Chronicle*, 5 November 1943

CHAPTER 8 – ROBERT FREDERICK BURNETT

1.   *Essex Newsman*, Saturday, 22 November 1930
2.   *Crockford's Clerical Directory*, 1932, page 182
3.   *Northampton Mercury*, Friday, 30 September 1904
4.   *Stamford Mercury*, Friday, 4 January 1907
5.   *Essex County Chronicle*, Friday, 28 February 1919
6.   *Essex County Chronicle*, Friday, 2 May 1919
7.   *Essex County Chronicle*, Friday, 16 May 1919
8.   *Essex Newsman*, Saturday, 19 July 1919
9.   *Essex Newsman*, Saturday, 26 July 1919
10. *Essex County Chronicle*, Friday, 19 March 1920
11. *Essex County Chronicle*, Friday, 12 November 1920
12. *Essex Newsman*, Saturday, 13 November 1920
13. *Essex County Chronicle*, Friday, 18 February 1921
14. *Essex County Chronicle*, Friday, 24 June 1921
15. *Essex County Chronicle*, Friday, 29 April 1921
16. *Essex Newsman*, Saturday, 16 August 1919
17. *Essex Newsman*, Saturday, 19 July 1919
18. *Essex County Chronicle*, Friday, 25 July 1919
19. *Essex County Chronicle*, Friday, 9 April 1920
20. *Essex County Chronicle*, Friday, 17 May 1918
21. *Essex Newsman*, Saturday, 23 August 1919
22. *Essex Newsman*, Saturday, 14 May 1921
23. *Essex County Chronicle*, Friday, 1 April 1921
24. *Essex County Chronicle*, Friday, 22 July 1921
25. *Chelmsford Diocesan Chronicle*, October 1931
26. *Essex County Chronicle*, Friday, 21 August 1921

27. *Essex County Chronicle*, Friday, 16 December 1921
28. *Essex County Chronicle*, Friday, 21 April 1922
29. *Essex County Chronicle*, Friday, 28 July 1922
30. *Essex County Chronicle*, Friday, 4 August 1922
31. *The Gloucester Journal*, Saturday, 30 September 1922
32. *Essex County Chronicle*, Friday, 22 September 1922
33. *Essex County Chronicle,* Friday, 8 December 1922
34. *Essex County Chronicle,* Friday, 10 November 1922
35. *Essex County Chronicle*, Friday, 17 November 1922
36. *Essex Newsman*, Saturday, 31 March 1923
37. *Essex County Chronicle*, Friday, 6 April 1923
38. *Essex County Chronicle*, Friday, 18 May 1023
39. *Essex County Chronicle*, Friday, 22 June 1923
40. *Essex County Chronicle*, Friday, 6 July 1923
41. *Essex County Chronicle*, Friday, 19 October 1923
42. *Essex County Chronicle*, Friday, 2 November 1923
43. *Essex County Chronicle*, Friday, 1 February 1924
44. *Essex County Chronicle*, Friday, 25 April 1924
45. *Essex Newsman*, Saturday, 3 May 1924
46. *Essex Newsman*, Saturday, 5 July 1924
47. *Essex County Chronicle*, Friday, 20 June 1924
48. *Essex County Chronicle*, Friday, 26 September 1924
49. *Essex County Chronicle*, Friday, 24 April 1925
50. *Essex County Chronicle*, Friday, 2 June 1925
51. *Essex County Chronicle*, Friday, 2 October 1925
52. *Essex County Chronicle*, Friday, 30 October 1925
53. *Essex County Chronicle*, Friday, 9 October 1925
54. *Essex County Chronicle*, Friday, 6 November 1925
55. *Essex County Chronicle*, Friday, 22 January 1926
56. *Essex Newsman*, Saturday, 10 April 1926
57. *Essex County Chronicle*, Friday, 9 April 1926
58. *Essex County Chronicle*, Friday, 9 July 1926
59. *Essex County Chronicle*, Friday, 5 November 1926
60. *Essex Newsman*, Saturday, 25 December 1926
61. *Essex Newsman*, Saturday, 19 February 1927
62. *Essex Newsman*, Saturday, 23 April 1927
63. *Essex County Chronicle*, Friday, 29 July 1927

64. *Essex Newsman*, Saturday, 12 November 1927
65. *Essex Newsman*, Saturday, 19 November 1927
66. *Essex Newsman*, Saturday, 7 January 1928
67. *Essex County Chronicle*, Friday, 20 January 1928
68. *Essex County Chronicle*, Friday, 30 March 1928
69. *Essex County Chronicle*, Friday, 11 May 1928
70. *Essex County Chronicle*, Friday, 1 June 1928
71. *Essex County Chronicle*, Friday, 15 June 1928
72. *Essex County Chronicle*, Friday, 13 July 1928
73. *Essex County Chronicle*, Friday, 20 July 1928
74. *Essex County Chronicle*, Friday, 3 August 1928
75. *Essex County Chronicle*, Friday, 23 January 1929
76. *Essex Newsman*, Saturday, 16 March 1929
77. *Essex Newsman*, Saturday, 27 April 1929
78. *Essex County Chronicle*, Friday 19 July 1929
79. *Essex Newsman*, Saturday 13 July 1929
80. *Essex County Chronicle*, Friday, 11 October 1929
81. *Essex County Chronicle*, Friday, 8 November 1929
82. *Essex County Chronicle*, Friday, 31 January 1930
83. *Essex County Chronicle*, Friday, 21 February 1930
84. *Essex County Chronicle*, Friday, 14 February 1930
85. *Essex County Chronicle*, Friday, 30 March 1930
86. *Essex County Chronicle*, Friday, 23 May 1930
87. *Essex County Chronicle*, Friday, 22 August 1930
88. *Essex County Chronicle*, Friday, 12 September 1930
89. *Essex County Chronicle*, Friday, 26 September 1930
90. *Crockford's Clerical Directory*, 1926, page 703
91. *Crockford's Clerical Directory*, 1926, page 538
92. *Essex County Chronicle*, Friday, 23 September 1913
93. *Essex County Chronicle*, Friday, 9 October 1914
94. *Supplement to the London Gazette,* 6 October 1915, page 9851. On www.london-gazette.co.uk (accessed 11 September 2014)
95. *Essex County Chronicle*, Friday, 2 January 1920
96. *Essex County Chronicle*, Friday, 15 October 1920
97. *Essex County Chronicle*, Friday, 29 April 1921
98. *Essex County Chronicle*, Friday, 23 June 1922

99. *Lancashire Online Parish Clerk project,* St James' Register of Baptisms 1849–1902 page 108, entry 836
100. *Essex County Chronicle,* Friday, 23 December 1892
101. *Essex Newsman,* Saturday, 24 December 1892
102. *Essex County Chronicle,* Friday, 29 December 1893
103. *Essex County Chronicle,* Friday, 5 August 1898
104. *Essex County Chronicle,* Friday, 10 November 1911
105. *Essex County Chronicle,* Friday, 17 May 1918
106. *Essex County Chronicle,* Friday, 8 August 1918
107. *The Gloucester Journal,* Saturday, 30 September 1922
108. *The Gloucester Journal,* Saturday, 23 December 1922
109. *Essex County Chronicle,* Friday, 20 February 1925
110. *Sussex Agricultural Express,* Friday, 28 June 1918
111. *Essex County Chronicle,* Friday, 23 May 1923
112. *Sussex Agricultural Express,* Friday, 8 June 1923
113. *Kent and Sussex Courier,* Friday, 22 August 1930
114. *Essex County Chronicle,* Friday, 30 September 1910
115. *Essex County Chronicle,* Friday, 29 September 1911
116. *Essex County Chronicle,* Friday, 9 January 1920
117. *Essex County Chronicle,* Friday, 27 April 1927
118. *Essex County Chronicle,* Friday, 30 December 1927
119. *Biggleswade Chronicle,* Friday, 25 August 1951
120. *Essex County Chronicle,* Friday, 6 November 1925
121. *The Gloucester Journal,* Saturday, 7 April 1928
122. *Biggleswade Chronicle,* Frida,y 6 November 1942
123. *Lichfield Mercury,* Friday, 16 June 1922
124. *Lichfield Mercury,* Friday, 1 June 1923
125. *Essex County Chronicle,* Friday, 13 November 1925
126. *Essex County Chronicle,* Friday, 3 April 1931
127. *Essex Newsman,* Saturday 25 April 1931
128. *Essex County Chronicle,* Friday 29 January 1932
129. *Essex Newsman,* Saturday, 10 March 1932
130. *Essex County Chronicle,* Friday, 19 October 1930
131. *Essex County Chronicle,* Friday, 21 October 1931
132. *Moulsham Parish Magazine,* November 1930, as quoted in the *Essex County Chronicle,* Friday, 7 November 1930
133. *Essex Newsman,* Saturday, 22 November 1930

134. *Essex Newsman*, Saturday, 29 November 1930
135. *Essex County Chronicle*, Friday, 5 December 1930
136. *Essex Newsman*, Saturday, 29 January 1938
137. *Essex County Chronicle*, Friday, 22 April 1938

CHAPTER 9 – WILLIAM STANLEY BROWNLESS

1. *Essex Newsman Herald*, Tuesday, 5 September 1950
2. *Hastings and St Leonard's Observer,* Saturday, 24 June 1905
3. *East Sussex Record Office*, PAR 369/5/1/3
4. *Hastings and St Leonard's Observer*, Saturday, 29 December 1906
5. *Hastings and St Leonard's Observer*, Saturday, 3 August 1910
6. *Hastings and St Leonard's Observer*, Friday, 27 February 1931
7. *Hastings and St Leonard's Observer*, Saturday, 19 February 1918
8. *Liverpool Echo*, Friday, 16 August 1918
9. *Derby Daily Telegraph*, Friday, 13 February 1931
10. *Essex Newsman*, Saturday, 28 February 1931
11. *Essex County Chronicle*, Friday, 23 January 1931
12. *Essex Newsman*, Saturday, 28 February 1931
13. *Essex County Chronicle*, Friday, 8 May 1931
14. *Essex County Chronicle*, Friday, 6 November 1931
15. *Essex Newsman*, Saturday, 30 May 1931
16. *Essex County Chronicle*, Friday, 2 October 1931
17. *Essex County Chronicle*, Friday, 29 January 1932
18. *Essex County Chronicle*, Friday, 29 July 1932
19. *Essex Newsman*, Saturday, 10 December 1932
20. *Essex County Chronicle*, Friday, 17 February 1933
21. *Essex County Chronicle*, Friday, 16 February 1934
22. *Essex County Chronicle*, Friday, 23 March 1934
23. *Essex Newsman*, Saturday, 23 September 1934
24. *Essex County Chronicle*, Friday, 15 February 1935
25. *Essex County Chronicle*, Friday, 19 July 1935
26. *Essex County Chronicle*, Friday, 4 October 1935
27. *Essex County Chronicle*, Friday, 27 September 1935
28. *Essex County Chronicle*, Friday, 11 October 1935
29. *Essex Newsman*, Saturday, 19 October 1935
30. *Essex County Chronicle*, Friday, 6 March 1936

31. *Essex County Chronicle*, Friday, 10 July 1936
32. *Moulsham Parish Magazine*, July 1936, as quoted in the *Essex Newsman*, Saturday, 18 July 1936
33. ERO, A9978 Box 1, section W9
34. *Essex County Chronicle*, Friday, 22 January 1937
35. *Essex County Chronicle*, Friday, 29 January 1937
36. *Essex County Chronicle*, Friday, 2 April 1937
37. *Essex County Chronicle*, Friday, 23 July 1937
38. *Essex County Chronicle*, Friday, 28 May 1937
39. *Essex Newsman*, Saturday, 29 May 1937
40. *Essex County Chronicle*, Friday, 23 September 1932
41. *Essex County Chronicle*, Friday, 27 September 1935
42. Details from www.tiltyhistoryprojects.co.uk (accessed 14 January 2015)
43. Probate Record Office, London, 1964, 1968
44. *Essex County Chronicle*, Friday, 25 September 1936
45. *Essex Newsman*, Saturday, 4 April 1939
46. *Moulsham Parish Magazine,* September 1950, as quoted in the *Essex Newsman Herald,* Tuesday, 19 September 1950
47. Probate Record Office, London, 1965

APPENDIX 2

THE CURATES OF ST JOHN THE EVANGELIST, MOULSHAM

1837 – 1937

1849–52	Henry HAWKINS
1853–54	Peter Rivers de JERSEY
1855–57	William Osborne Pocock WILSON
1856–58	Walter James SOWERBY
1858–59	Lewis Theodore PENNINGTON
1858–60	Newman TIBBITTS
1860–61	George MALLORY
1861–63	William Boys JOHNSTON
1862–64	Frederick Charles Howard BENT
1864–65	Thomas Guest FORREST
1865–69	John Charles BURNSIDE
1866–73	John Peckham Skirrow WOODWARD
1870–71	William Black
1872–73	William Patrick Leonard HAND
1873–77	William Faithfull LUMLEY
1874–79	Edward CLIVE
1879–82	Harry Percy GRUBB
1882–85	Sydney William Wentworth WILKIN
1883	Tom Beverley ATHORNE
1883	Walter Edward SMITH
1883–87	John Francis SMITH
1885–87	Andrew MELLIS
1886–87	George Alfred THOMPSON
1887–89	William North ANDREWS
1887–89	Arthur William Benjamin Walmesley WATTS
1889–90	Arthur Baynes Merriman LEY

1889–1901	George Victor COLLIER
1889–93	Edward PARKINSON
1894–98	William Louis BENTHALL
1898–1901	Francis Charles SEAR
1901–04	Edward Morton BARTLETT
1904–05	John Lansbury DUTTON
1905–06	William Watson King ORMSBY
1906–14	Edward Arthur HORT
1914	Alfred Augustine BRAUND
1914–16	Leonard Wilcher WRIGHT
1916–17	John Alexander LIVINGSTONE
1919–20	Alec Percy DANIELS
1919–22	George Cecil TWIST
1921–23	Sidney Gelder FARRAR
1923–24	Alexander COLVIN
1924–25	Henry Thomas PIMM
1925–31	Frederick Arthur STROUD
1931–35	Sidney John BURLING
1935–36	William Atherstone GETLIFFE
1936–39	James Dudley JOHNS

INDEX

Note: *italicised* page references indicate illustrations

A

accounts of St John the Evangelist, Moulsham
  under Alfred Mason 81–2
  under Thomas Wilkinson 99, 108
  under George St Alban Godson 118–19, 122–3, 125–6, 139, 143, 144, 150, 155, 162–3
  under Robert Saulez 188, 192–3, 195, 197–8, 204–6, 209–11, 212–13
  under Frederick Stroud 303–4
  under William Pressey 228, 229, 230–1, *231*, 237–8, 239–40, 242–3, 248, 250, 251, 252
  under Robert Burnett 263, 271, 272, 276, 278, 280, 281, 282–3, 284, 285, 286, 289
  under William Stanley Brownless 308–9, 310, 313
additional curates' fund 204, 215
Additional Curates Society 193
Adelaide, Queen 5, 39
almshouses 140, 272, 276, 289–90
altar 40, 77, 234–5, 312–13
  lights 199, 200, 242, 243, 304
  linen 229, 234
  wine 210

Anchor Street 128, 143, 191
Andrews, William North 172–3
Arc works, Anchor Street 128, 149, 150, 191
Arnold, Rev W.C. 56
Asquith, Herbert 244
Assistant Clergy fund 196, 252, 263, 271, 272, 274, 290
Assistant Curates' Society 237
asylums 43, 45
Athorne, Rev Tom Beverly (1883) 126, 138, 168–9

B

Back Street 41
Baedel and Sons 54–5, *55*
Bailey, Henry 236
Band of Hope 234, 238, 243, 244–5, 289
Barker, Miss 229
Barker, Mr J. 212, 228, 230, 232, 234, 248, 250, 252, 253, 258, 263, 271
Barker, Mrs J. 243–4
Barking 43, 44
Barking, Bishop of 175, 187, 233, 252–3, 258–9, 273, 295
Barnard, Aleck (organist) 82, 83, 140, 143–4, 145, 151, 152, 153

Ecclesiastical Commissioners for
England 114–15
Ecclesiastical Gazette 64–5
Eclectic Review 29–30
Edinburgh, University of 31–2
Edmunds, Rev Vaughan 317
Edwards, John 70
Egypt 168, 252, 263, 297
Elm Road 252
Emery, Ven W. 78
English Church Union 189–90
Epping 26, 27
Essex Church Building Society 13
Essex Church Schoolmasters'
Association 54
Essex (County) Chronicle 153,
154, 160, 181–2, 184, 187,
199, 203, 223, 249–50, 252,
253–4, 281, 291, 293, 297,
299, 300, 305, 314
*Essex Independent and Farmers'
Gazette* 163
Essex Industrial school 142
Essex Newsman 130–1, 147, 152,
154–5, 187, 189–90, 194,
215, 217, 229, 243, 246–7,
250, 253, 255, 256, 267,
270, 271–2, 278–9, 305
Essex Weekly News 83, 117,
125–6, 127–8
evening classes 89, 160–1

F

Farrar, Sydney Gelder (1921-23)
273, 274, 277, 294–5
Fenton, James 11–12, 63–4, 134
Festing, Rt Rev Dr (Bishop of St
Albans) 93

Finch, W.J. 289, 290
First World War *see* Great War
Fisher, Mr 134
Flower, Major and Mrs C.J. 290
font 69, 73, 78, 107–8
Forrest, Rev Thomas Guest
(1864-1865) 85
Foster, Evelyne Margaret 217
Foster, Rev John 224
Foster, Laura Agnes 295
foundation stone 10, 98
Foxearth, Essex 69, 208, 223,
224–5, 226–7, 231, *231*,
236, 247
Foxwell, Mr (church secretary)
308, 309, 313
Franklin, Miss 229
Franklin, Mr 212–13, 228, 232,
234, 235, 237, 239–40, 241,
248–9, 254–5
Free Will Offering fund 237, 238,
251, 263, 271, 272, 284
French, F.J. 267
frescoes 226, 227, 230–1
Frye, F.R. 247
Fulcher, Mr 249
Furhop, Theodore 69–70

G

Galleywood district 72, 133, 140
gas 142
    gas explosion 74–6
    gas lighting 73, 74, 79, 140,
    232
    gas works 80, 262
George IV, King 41
George Street 149, 164, 182, 217,
230, 261

Hawkins, Rev Henry (1849-1852)
40, 43–6, *44*, *56*
Hawkins, Rev Sir John Caesar
107, 118
Hawkins, Mary 44–5, 128
Hearn, Rev 78
heating system 73, 74, 77, 108,
123, 139, 144, 162, 164, 308
Hemmings, E.O. 227, 230, *231*,
238
Henderson, Mr (artist) 21
Henley, Rev Robert 185
Herbert, Rev Edward 263, 270, 292
High Street, Chelmsford 7, 41–2,
90, 142, 247
Highes, Miss 274
Hillyard, Samuel 29
Hoffman, Dr 136–7
Holmes, Mary 41
Holy Communion 74, 76, 107,
118, 201, 202, 306
Home Office 135–7, 141
Hort, Rev Edward Arthur (1906-14)
234, 239, 241, 244–5, 251,
254–5, 287
Howes, W. 242
Howley, Archbishop 58–9
Hunt, Margaret Schofield 185
Hutchinson, Rev James 3, 16, 19,
20, 21–3, *22*, 43, 154
Hylands House 128, 162, 204

I

Incorporated Gas Institute 80
Incorporated Society for
Promoting the Enlargement,
Building and Repairing of
Churches and Chapels 13,
18–19, 38

India 86, 87, 155, 184–5
infant mortality 133, 184–5
influenza 156, 166, 178–9, 186,
197, 247–8
Irvine, Rev J.W. 93
Isle of Wight 85, 106

J

Jacobsen, William (Bishop of
Chester) 86
Jersey, Rev Peter Rivers de (1853-
1854) 46
Johns, Rev James Dudley (1936-
39) 310, 311, 314, 316–17
Johnston, Rev William Boys
(1861-1863) 62, 84
Jones, Archdeacon 59–60
Journal of Medical Science 45

K

Keble, John 214
Kempe, Charles Eamer 182–3
Kempthorne, Sampson 23
Kershaw, Rev John Albert 110,
112–13, 114, 117, 118, 154,
159, 166
Kindersley, Vice-Chancellor 61
King's College, London 85, 87,
168, 178, 254, 256, 295,
305, 315
Kohl, Karl 69–70

L

Lake, Rev Canon H.A. 179, 187,
189, 192, 225–6, 247, 252,
253, 254, 258, 262, 266,
267–8, 269

organs 16, 40, 64, 68, 69, 72, 76,
77, 139, 147, 162, 164, 188,
196–7, 226, 232, 233, 234,
236, 237–8, 251, 269–70, 276
Ormsby, Robert George 220–1
Ormsby, Rev William Watson
King (1905-06) 209, 211,
213, 214, 218–21, 225–6,
228
Osborn, George 136, 252
Osborn, Hedley 200
Osborne Place, New London
Road 169, 271, 294
Our Lady Immaculate 63–4
Oxford University 20, 24, 27, 43,
46, 47, 65, 84, 95, 102, 107,
169, 170, 223–4, 293

P

Pace, Mr 238
parish hall 149–50, 280
Parker, Herbert A. 226, 236, 251,
285
Parker, Oxley 109, 275
Parkhurst, Henry 164
Parkinson, Rev Edward (1889-93)
175, 176–7, 346a
Parmiter, Rev John 98, 104–5
Parochial Boards 120
Parochial Church Council (PCC)
188–9, 273, 274, 276,
278–80, 281, 285, 290
parochial fund 274, 276, 278,
284, 308–9
parochial hall 261, 267–9, 276,
277, 278, 280–3, 284, 287,
290, 306, 307
Parry, Major Gambier 275
Parry, Sir Hubert 275

parsonage house 30, 53, 54–5, 55,
176
Passmore, C.R. 287
Pattison, Miss 82–3
Paynter, Rev F.B. 262, 267–8
Pearson, Rev Arthur 56, 90
Pearson, Mary 86
Pennington, Beatrice Ernestine
Florence 52
Pennington, Rev Lewis Theodore
(1858-1859) 49–52, 56, 59,
64, 345a
Pepys, Henry (Bishop of
Winchester) 85
Pertwee, Mr Charles (surveyor)
109, 125–6, 232–3, 240, 267
Peterborough, Bishop of 87, 95–6,
217, 262
pews 66–9, 68, 140, 311, 312
pew appropriations 67, 69,
100–1
pew rents 1–2, 33, 35–6, 42,
66–7
Phillips, Miss 126
Philpotts, Bishop Henry 218
Phoenix House 125
Pigot, H.C. 238
Pimm, Rev Thomas Henry
(1924-25) 279, 281, 296
Pitts, J.A.R. 283, 284
Plumpton 85, 86
Pomeroy, Phyllis 293
Poor Law Amendment Act (1834)
11
Poor Law Commissionaires 23
poor, the 11, 42, 43–4, 49, 51,
53–4, 60, 63, 122–3, 124,
160, 162, 232, 270
religious provision for 6–7,
33–4, 35, 36, 38, 66–7, 121

U

Unwin, Mr 162
Usborne, Mary Elizabeth 176

V

van Holmrigh, Miss *231*, 234
Vaughan, Margaret Rose 169
Veley Chapel 158–9, 232
Veley family vault 81, 136, 158
Veley, Frederick 56, 59, 61, 63,
    64, 73, 81, 92, 123, 131,
    133, 136, 137, 149, 155,
    158, 228
Veley, Frederick Arthur 81
Veley, Frederick Thomas 47, 56
Veley, Gertrude 154, 159
Veley, Juliana 123, 270, 271, 292
Veley, Louisa (née Curtis) 81,
    158
vestry meetings
    under Christopher Muston 36
    under Alfred Mason 64, 67–8,
        79, 81–2
    under Thomas Wilkinson
        99–101, 108–9
    under George St Alban Godson
        118–21, 122–4, 125–6,
        132–3, 139–40, 143, 144–5,
        148, 149–51, 155–6, 161,
        162–3, 165, 166
    under Robert Saulez 188–90,
        192–3, 195, 197–8, 204–8,
        209–11, 212–13
    under Frederick Stroud 303–4
    under William Pressey 228,
        232, 235, 237–8, 239–41,
        242–3, 248, 250, 251, 252–3

under Robert Burnett 262–3,
    271, 272–4, 275–6, 278,
    279–80, 283–4, 285–6,
    288–9, 291
under William Stanley
    Brownless 308–10, 313
Vicarage Road 54–5, *55*, 62, 109,
    289, 290
Victoria, Queen 122, 146–7
Villiers, Henry 84

W

Wace, Gerald 272
Wackrill, Miss 74, 227, 228, 230,
    231
Wackrill, R.E. 228
Wackrill, Samuel 64
Wackrill, Thomas 59
Waddington, Elizabeth Mary 96
Wallis, C.H. 242, 250, 251
war memorial 264–7
Ward, D. 236
Warman, Rt Rev Guy 277–8
Warrick, Mr 100
Warwick, James 157
Watchem, PC 146
Watts, Arthur William Benjamin
    Walmesley (1887-89) 173,
    345a
Watts-Ditchfield, Rt Rev John
    Edwin 219, 244, 267, 277–8
Webb, Stephen 7, 10
Welch, Rev Neville 317
Wells, Frederick 125, 258
Wells, Georgina 49–50
west end of St John's 6, *16*, *17*, 75,
    76–7, 121, *121*, 131, 132,
    144, 163

West Essex Militia 47–8, 62, 66, 75
Western Gallery 68
Wheeler, H. 283
Whetton, Mr H. Davan 233
Whiffen, Thomas 140
Whistance, Mr and Mrs 276
Whitcombe, Robert Henry 234
Widford 25, 155, 156–7, 175, 176–7, 253
Wild, J. W. 5, 7
Wilkin, Frederick 300
Wilkin, Rev Sydney William Wentworth (1882-1885) 129, 130, 136, 167–8
Wilkinson, Rev George 133–4, 135, 167
Wilkinson, Octavia Rebecca 46
Wilkinson, Thomas Henry (1877-79) 89, 95–115, *115*, 133, 134–5, 154
Willingale Doe 213–14, 221, 222, 225, 254, 287, 295–6
Wilson, Dr Henry 300, 302
Wilson, Rev William Osborne Pocock (1855-1857) 47–8, 56

Winchester, Bishop of 85, 102
windows 40, 75–7, 113, 131, 182–3, 192, 312
Winterflood, H. 228
Wolverson, Matilda Agatha 294–5
Wood, Mr 230, 237
Wood Street 12, 19, 23, 141, 153, 315
Woodbury Villas 252
Woodward, Rev John Peckham Skirrow (1866-1873) 85
workhouses 11–12, 23, 24, 70, 133, 153, 171, 173, 295
Wortley, Stamp 271, 273, 274, 275–6
Wray, George 7–8
Wright, Leonard Wilcher (1914-16) 247, 249, 251, 255–7
Writtle Road cemetery 141, 145, 146, 180–1, 198, 229, 252

Y

York, Archbishop of 13, 96
Yverdon House 81, 123, 149, 158

Milton Keynes UK
Ingram Content Group UK Ltd.
UKHW040610030823
426260UK00001B/47